FINANCIAL ACCOUNTING AND REPORTING
Text and Cases

PAUL R. BERNEY
Professor of Accounting

WILLIAM P. LYONS
Associate Professor (Adjunct)
  of Financial Accounting

STANLEY J. GARSTKA
Associate Professor of Accounting

All at the School of Organization and Management
Yale University

FINANCIAL ACCOUNTING AND REPORTING
Text and Cases

1981

BUSINESS PUBLICATIONS, INC.   Dallas, Texas   75243
Irwin-Dorsey Limited   Georgetown, Ontario   L7G 4B3

ISBN 0-256-02418-9
Library of Congress Catalog Card No. 80–67668
Printed in the United States of America

1 2 3 4 5 6 7 8 9 0 MP 8 7 6 5 4 3 2 1

To

Joyce Bailey Berney
William, John, Michael, and Deanna Lyons
Janet and Jennifer Garstka

PREFACE

We have written a text with cases and problems which is specifically designed to meet what we consider to be the basic objectives of a core course in financial accounting.

1. Users of financial statements should be generally familiar with business practices, the technical language of accounting, and the nature of the information reported in the financial statements. One of the basic objectives of the core course is to make sure students are intelligent users of financial statements within the context of this definition.

2. Financial statements are prepared by management, not independent public accountants. Management's decisions about which generally accepted accounting procedure to use can have a major impact on reported net income, cash flow, and financial position of the enterprise. Analysis of these managerial decisions can be a useful tool in evaluating the quality of management. Our objective is to make the student aware of the implications of accounting decisions.

3. Accounting as a discipline does not exist in a vacuum. Our objective is to point out the relationship of accounting to economics, finance, politics, law, and other disciplines.

We feel the mass of detail, the repetition, and the lack of clarity of most accounting texts are the reasons many students find accounting intellectually stifling and educationally unexciting.

In our text this mass of accounting detail is synthesized into important techniques and concepts which can be used in analyzing the problems related to the preparation and understanding of financial statements. We do not use repetition as a means of learning, nor do we attempt to cover the analysis of every possible type of transaction. Rather, techniques of analysis and measurement are explained, and the student learns by applying these techniques to the cases.

The first part of this text (Chapters 1 to 4) is different from most texts in that it takes the student from a simple problem case in balance sheet construction to a more complex problem case in the preparation of an income statement and balance sheet without in-depth coverage of specialized areas such as fixed assets, depreciation, or inventory valuation. This approach makes it possible for students to understand the entire accounting framework before they have to deal with more intricate accounting problems.

The second part of the text covers the more specialized areas of financial accounting and reporting that we feel should be studied in greater depth. Many cases in this part of the text are based on excerpts from actual financial statements. The attempt in these cases is to make the material real but not so complex that it cannot be taught in a simple fashion.

An unusual feature of this text is a chapter on manufacturing-costing issues which covers absorption costing, direct costing, and the cost-volume-profit model. We have included this material, which is usually included in a managerial accounting course, because we feel that the student of financial accounting should understand how costs are allocated to products and also get an insight into the type of financial information that is useful for decision making and how it differs from the information generated for financial statements.

This text is appropriate for the first and/or second course in accounting for both nonaccounting and accounting majors. The teacher's guide contains a number of different course configurations as well as detailed solutions and notes prepared by the authors.

ACKNOWLEDGMENTS

All of the cases were written by the authors except for those which were generously contributed by our colleagues, Ralph C. Jones, Professor Emeritus, Yale University; Arthur N. Haut, Lecturer in Accounting, School of Organization and Management, Yale University; and C. David Goldman, Lecturer in Accounting, Yale University; and our students, Raymond L. M. Wong, John H. Friedman, Douglas Karp, and Thomas Metzloff.

The authors are indebted to Arthur N. Haut for his review of the manuscript.

Paul R. Berney gratefully acknowledges the influence of Ralph C. Jones, Professor Emeritus of Economics at Yale University, who has been his teacher and colleague for the past 25 years.

The authors benefited from the contributions made by their students and the following reviewers: Jerry L. Arnold, University of Southern California; James Don Edwards, University of Georgia; Martin L. Gosman, Boston University; Eric W. Noreen, University of Washington; and Ray G. Stephens, Ohio State University.

We are also grateful to Linda Rodman, who was responsible for the production of this manuscript, and Dale Dreyfus, who contributed his editorial skills.

Paul R. Berney
William P. Lyons
Stanley J. Garstka

CONTENTS

5. **Inventories** 111

Classification of Inventories. Inventory Valuation. Deducing Cost of Goods Sold in a Merchandising Company (periodic inventory method). Inventories in Manufacturing Companies. Manufacturing Flow of Costs. Factory Overhead. The Cost of Goods Sold. Statement of Cost of Goods Sold. Significance of the Process.

6. **Inventory Cost Flow Methods** 125

Illustrative Data. First-In, First-Out (Fifo) Method. Last-In, First-Out (Lifo) Method. Weighted Average. Specific (identification) Lot. Lower-of-Cost-or-Market Rule (LCM). The Argument for Fifo. The Argument for Lifo. Evaluation of Lifo. Financial Statement Disclosure. Summary.

7. **Focus on Manufacturing Costing Issues** 149

Absorption Costing. Direct Costing. Cost-Volume-Profit Model (break-even analysis).

8. **Long-Lived Assets** 177

The Cost of Plant and Equipment. Depreciation of Plant and Equipment—The Allocation Process. Methods of Depreciation. Comparison of Depreciation Methods. Depreciation and Repairs. Disposal of Plant and Equipment. Depreciation, Federal Income Tax, and

Net Income. Depreciation Policy Decisions. The Investment Credit. Natural Resources and Intangible Assets.

9. Long-Term Equities 197

Long-Term Notes Payable (interest bearing). Long-Term Notes Payable (noninterest bearing). Bonds. Bond Issue Cost. Straight-Line Amortization of Bond Discount and Bond Premium. Compound (effective) Interest Rate Method of Amortization of Bond Discount and Premium. Bond Redemption. Bond Conversion. Leases. Stockholders' Equity. Treasury Stock. Preferred Stock. Cash Dividends. Stock Splits. Stock Dividends. Retained Earnings. Book Value of Common Stock. Summary.

10. The All-Inclusive Income Statement: A Closer Look 241

All-Inclusive Income Statement. Prior Period Adjustments. Extraordinary Items. Accounting Changes. Changes in Accounting Estimates. Discontinued Operations. Accounting for Income Taxes. Disclosure.

11. Intercorporate Investments and Business Combinations .. 281

Short-Term Investments. Long-Term Investments. Preparation of Consolidated Statements. Consolidated Balance Sheet. Fair Value of Fixed Assets and Excess of Purchase Price over Fair Value of Net Assets (goodwill). Minority Interest in Consolidated Subsidiary. Complete Consolidation Process. Balance Sheet Adjustments and Eliminations. Income Statement Adjustments and Eliminations. Disclosure of Principles of Consolidation. Summary. Business Combinations. Disclosure on the Financial Statements of Purchase and Pooling of Interests Methods. Summary.

12. Statement of Changes in Financial Position 373

Major Sources of Funds. Major Uses of Funds. Schedule of Working Capital Accounts. All Resources Concept of Statement of Changes in Financial Position. Method of Preparing a Statement of Changes in Financial Position. Cash Defined as Funds. Uses of the Statement of Changes in Financial Position.

13. Changing Prices and Foreign Currency Translations 399

Financial Reporting and Changing Prices. General Price Level Accounting (constant dollar accounting). Balance Sheet Accounts. Income Statement. An Example—General Price Level Adjustment. Specific Price Level Adjustments. Balance Sheet. Income Statement. Financial Reporting and Changing Prices. Foreign Currency Translations.

14. Special Topics 467

Segment Reporting. Interim Reporting. Forecasts. Pensions.

15. Introduction to Financial Statement Analysis 497

Comparative Financial Statement Analysis. Ratio Analysis. Ratios Indicating Profitability. Ratios Indicating Current Position. Uses of Ratio Analysis. Financial Reporting and Analysis in Practice.

FINANCIAL ACCOUNTING AND REPORTING
Text and Cases

1

Preparing and Understanding Financial Statements

A n analysis of the financial transactions of an enterprise is necessary in order to prepare financial statements that will indicate the financial condition of the enterprise at a moment in time (balance sheet) and the results of the operations of the enterprise over a period of time (statement of income).

The balance sheet consists of two main categories, *assets* and *equities*. Assets are resources owned by the company which can be expressed in monetary terms. Equities are monetary claims against those resources. There are two major types of equities or claims: those of outsiders (nonowners), which are called *liabilities*, and those of the owners, which are called *owners' equity*.

Every financial transaction of an enterprise can be recorded in terms of its effect on the balance sheet.

For example, assume that on July 15, 1979, a corporation (one form of a business enterprise) called Joyce Markets, Inc., was organized to sell groceries. The owners of this corporation made an initial investment (the purchase of the corporation's common stock) of $30,000 on this date. Joyce Markets, Inc., would record this transaction by increasing the asset, cash, $30,000, and the owners' equity category, common stock, $30,000.

Common stock is the account title for the ownership investment in a corporation. It is evidenced by a written agreement (stock certificate) between the owner and the corporation. The ownership interest in a partnership would be called *partners' capital*, and in an individual's business it would be called *proprietorship*, *net worth*, or *owners' equity*. The balance sheet will appear as in Illustration 1–1.

On July 16, 1979, the company purchased display equipment in the amount of $10,000: $6,000 was paid in cash and $4,000 in a 12 percent per annum, 90-day note. The asset, *equipment*, was increased by $10,000; the asset, *cash*, was decreased by $6,000; and the liability, *notes payable*, was increased by $4,000. The total assets of $34,000 are equal to the claims against these assets of $34,000 (see Illustration 1–2).

ILLUSTRATION 1–1

JOYCE MARKETS, INC.
Balance Sheet
July 15, 1979

Assets		Equities	
Cash	$30,000	Common stock	$30,000

ILLUSTRATION 1–2

JOYCE MARKETS, INC.
Balance Sheet
July 16, 1979

Assets		Equities	
Current assets:		Current liabilities:	
Cash	$24,000	Notes payable	$ 4,000
Fixed assets:		Stockholders' equity:	
Equipment	10,000	Common stock	30,000
	$34,000		$34,000

All resources (assets) are equal to the claims against these resources (equities). Another way to state this equation is to say that the owners' claim is equal to the total assets of the enterprise, minus claims owed to outsiders.

$$\text{Assets} - \text{Liabilities} = \text{Owners' equity}$$

In accounting it is customary to classify assets and liabilities into different categories. Assets which will be converted into cash within one year are generally classified as *current*. Physical assets, with a life exceeding a year, are generally classified as *fixed*.[1] Assets such as long-term investments and intangibles that do not fit into the current or fixed categories are classified as *other assets*. Liabilities are also classified as *current* (to be paid within one year) and *long-term* (to be paid after one year). The relationship of the current assets to current liabilities is a very important one because it indicates the firm's ability to pay its obligations on a current basis.

On July 16 the company paid rent of $750—$250 for July, and $500 for a security deposit to be returned at the end of the two-year lease.

---

[1] This category is often classified as *property, plant,* and *equipment.*

On July 16 the rent for July is a current asset (prepaid rent) that will be used up on a daily basis as the month progresses. The $500 security deposit will exist until the end of the two-year lease; it is classified as an *other asset.*

The increase in these assets (prepaid rent of $250 and security deposit of $500) is offset by a decrease in the asset, cash, of $750. Total assets and the claims against them (equities) remain at $34,000 (see Illustration 1–3).

ILLUSTRATION 1–3 _____

JOYCE MARKETS, INC.
Balance Sheet
July 16, 1979

Assets		*Equities*	
Current assets:		Current liabilities:	
Cash	$23,250	Notes payable	$ 4,000
Prepaid rent	250		
	$23,500		
Fixed assets:			
Equipment	10,000		
Other assets:		Stockholders' equity:	
Security deposit	500	Common stock	30,000
	$34,000		$34,000

On July 17 Joyce Markets purchased $15,000 worth of fruits and vegetables for cash.

The fruits and vegetables are the merchandise that Joyce Markets is going to sell in the normal operations of its business. This merchandise is called *merchandise inventory* (inventory) and is classified as a current asset because the intention is to sell it and convert it into cash in a current (no longer than one year) operating cycle. The increase in inventory is offset by a decrease in cash (see Illustration 1–4).

During the month of July the company sold $10,000 of the merchandise inventory for $13,500. The customers paid $8,000 and charged $5,500.

On the sale of the merchandise inventory, the current asset, cash, increased $8,000; the current asset, accounts receivable (amounts due from customers) increased $5,500; and the current asset, inventory, decreased $10,000. The net increase in assets of $3,500

ILLUSTRATION 1–4 ─────────────────────────────────────

JOYCE MARKETS, INC.
Balance Sheet
July 17, 1979

Assets		Equities	
Current assets:		Current liabilities:	
Cash	$ 8,250	Notes payable	$ 4,000
Inventory	15,000		
Prepaid rent	250		
	$23,500		
Fixed assets:			
Equipment	10,000		
Other assets:		Stockholders' equity:	
Security deposit	500	Common stock	30,000
	$34,000		$34,000

($8,000 + $5,500 − $10,000) represents the income (profit) on the sale of the merchandise.

The income from this transaction is recognized in the period in which the sale is made rather than when the cash is collected because it enables Joyce Markets to match the cost of the merchandise

ILLUSTRATION 1–5 ─────────────────────────────────────

JOYCE MARKETS, INC.
Balance Sheet
July 31, 1979*

Assets		Equities		
Current assets:		Current liabilities:		
Cash	$16,250	Notes payable		$ 4,000
Accounts receivable	5,500			
Inventory	5,000			
Prepaid rent	250			
	$27,000			
Fixed assets:		Stockholders' equity:		
Equipment	10,000	Common stock	$30,000	
Other assets:		Retained		
Security deposit	500	earnings	3,500	33,500
	$37,500			$37,500

* For purposes of this balance sheet only, we are assuming that the sales occurred on July 31, the date this statement was prepared. Normally these sales would be made throughout the month.

sold ($10,000) against the sale ($13,500). This system of matching is more accurate in measuring an enterprise's performance for a period of time than is a system based on cash receipts (collections) and cash disbursements (payments), which could result in the cost of the sale and the sale being in different periods.

Since income belongs to the owners (stockholders), their claim on the assets is increased by $3,500. The $3,500 is reflected in the stockholders' equity account, *retained earnings* (see Illustration 1–5). If the company had suffered losses, the owners' claim •would have decreased. Retained earnings is not a resource that may be expended. It is only a claim of the owners. All the resources owned by Joyce Markets, Inc., are reported on the asset side of the balance sheet.

During the month of July, the customers paid the $5,500 they owed Joyce Markets. The current asset, cash, was increased $5,500, and the current asset, accounts receivable, was decreased by $5,500 (see Illustration 1–6).

ILLUSTRATION 1–6

JOYCE MARKETS, INC.
Balance Sheet
July 31, 1979

Assets		Equities		
Current assets:		Current liabilities:		
Cash	$21,750	Notes payable		$ 4,000
Inventory	5,000			
Prepaid rent	250			
	$27,000			
Fixed assets:		Stockholders' equity:		
Equipment	10,000	Common stock	$30,000	
Other assets:		Retained		
Security deposit	500	earnings	3,500	33,500
	$37,500			$37,500

During the month of July the company purchased $9,000 of fruits and vegetables on account.

The current asset, inventory, was increased by $9,000, and the current liability, accounts payable, was increased by $9,000 (see Illustration 1–7).

Accounts payable is the account title used for purchases of merchandise on credit. The vendor (seller) will usually indicate the terms of payment, that is, the full amount within 30 days, or a 2

ILLUSTRATION 1–7

JOYCE MARKETS, INC.
Balance Sheet
July 31, 1979*

Assets		Equities		
Current assets:		Current liabilities:		
Cash	$21,750	Accounts payable	$ 9,000	
Inventory	14,000	Notes payable	4,000	
Prepaid rent	250		$13,000	
	$36,000			
Fixed assets:		Stockholders' Equity:		
Equipment	10,000	Common stock	$30,000	
Other assets:		Retained		
Security deposit	500	earnings	3,500	33,500
	$46,500			$46,500

* For purposes of this balance sheet only, we are assuming that the purchases occurred on July 31, the date this statement was prepared, rather than during the month.

percent cash discount if paid in 10 days (usually written as 2/10, n/30).

During the period from July 15, 1979, to July 31, 1979, Joyce Markets paid its employees wages of $1,500 for work performed during this period.

The asset, cash, decreased by $1,500 and retained earnings decreased by $1,500. Wages for services performed reduce the owners' income and are therefore reflected as a decrease in retained earnings (see Illustration 1–8).

In order to prepare a correct balance sheet (statement of financial condition) on July 31, 1979, the company will have to recognize and record other accounting phenomena which occurred during the month of July.

The rent we prepaid for the period July 15 to July 31 has expired, and it is necessary to recognize that Joyce Markets, Inc., no longer has an asset in the amount of $250. Joyce Markets, Inc., would reflect this by decreasing the prepaid rent to zero and by decreasing retained earnings by $250. The $250 rent for July 15 to July 31, 1979, is a reduction in the amount of the owners' income and reduces retained earnings where all the components of net income are reflected on the balance sheet.

The cost of the equipment has to be allocated over its useful life. This equipment cost is allocated to the period benefited in the same

ILLUSTRATION 1–8 _____

JOYCE MARKETS, INC.
Balance Sheet
July 31, 1979

Assets		Equities		
Current assets:		Current liabilities:		
Cash	$20,250	Accounts payable		$ 9,000
Inventory	14,000	Notes payable		4,000
Prepaid rent	250			$13,000
	$34,500			
Fixed assets:		Stockholders' equity:		
Equipment	10,000	Common stock	$30,000	
Other assets:		Retained		
Security deposit	500	earnings	2,000	32,000
	$45,000			$45,000

manner as is the prepaid rent. It has been determined that the useful life of the equipment is 40 months. The allocated cost that we have to consider is for the period of July 16 (the date the equipment was purchased) until July 31, 1979 (the date of our balance sheet).

The equipment was used for one half of the month of July, so Joyce Markets, Inc., would reduce the owners' income and retained earnings by $125 ($10,000 ÷ 40 months = $250 per month or $125 for one half of a month). This allocation of the cost of a fixed asset to an accounting period is called *depreciation*. The other part of this transaction is a reduction in the asset, equipment. The equipment would now be recorded at $10,000 less $125, or $9,875. It has been a convention in accounting to show this allocation of cost in a separate category called *accumulated depreciation* (allowance for depreciation). The balance in accumulated depreciation is the total amount of depreciation accumulated from the date the equipment was purchased to the date of the particular balance sheet being prepared.

As of July 31, one-half month's interest on the 12 percent note payable has accrued with time. This amounts to $20 ($4,000 × 0.5% = $20) for the one-half month period from July 16 to July 31. Joyce Markets, Inc., would reduce retained earnings (owners' income) by this amount. The other part of this transaction would be to recognize that we have an additional liability called *accrued interest payable* in the amount of $20 on July 31, 1979.

The completed balance sheet on July 31, 1979 (see Illustration 1–9),

ILLUSTRATION 1–9 ────────────────────────────────────

JOYCE MARKETS, INC.
Balance Sheet
July 31, 1979

Assets			*Equities*		
Current assets:			Current liabilities:		
Cash	$20,250		Accounts payable		$ 9,000
Inventory	14,000	$34,250	Notes payable		4,000
			Accrued interest		
Fixed assets:			payable		20
Equipment	10,000				$13,020
Less: Accumu-					
lated depreci-					
ation	125	9,875	Stockholders' equity:		
			Common		
Other assets:			stock	$30,000	
Security			Retained		
deposit		500	earnings	1,605	31,605
		$44,625			$44,625

reflects the entries for the expiration of prepaid rent, the depreciation of the equipment, and the accrual of interest.

The balance sheet (statement of financial condition) indicates that Joyce Markets has $44,625 of assets and that they owe liabilities of $13,020. This leaves stockholders' equity of $31,605. The stockholders' original investment was $30,000, so the increase in their claim attributable to net income is $1,605.

The balance sheet shows only the financial condition of Joyce Markets at a particular moment in time—July 31, 1979. It indicates that retained earnings and stockholders' equity has increased by the amount of the net income, but it does not give us the details of how the net income was earned.

In order to better evaluate the financial accomplishment of the enterprise, we would like to know not only the net income but the composition of all the items which increased net income and of all the items that decreased net income.

The statement that presents all the items that increase and decrease net income is called a *statement of income* (statement of profit and loss). It measures the results of operations of an enterprise for a period of time. It is a dynamic statement. It differs from the balance sheet, which is a static statement that measures the financial condition of the enterprise at a moment in time. The statement of income measures the results of operations between two balance sheet dates. In the Joyce Markets problem, it would measure the results of operations from the inception of the corporation on July 15, 1979, to July 31, 1979, the date when we prepared our last balance sheet.

In order to prepare a statement of income as well as a balance sheet on a current basis, it is necessary to expand the entries made directly to retained earnings into separate categories called *revenues* (increase net income) and *expenses* (decrease net income). During the period, we record revenues and expenses separately, rather than directly adding them to or deducting them from the retained earnings account. Net income (revenues minus expenses) is the periodic increase in retained earnings.

Each financial transaction will have to be analyzed in terms of assets, liabilities, owners' equity, and the new categories of revenues and expenses. The revenues and expenses are temporary (nominal) categories, and they exist only to aid us in preparing a statement of income. At the end of each accounting period the balances in the revenue and expense accounts will be transferred to retained earnings.

In the Joyce Markets example, sales is a *revenue* (it increases net income), and cost of merchandise sold, wages expense, rent expense, depreciation expense, and interest expense are *expenses* (they all decrease net income).

To prepare an income statement for Joyce Markets for the period July 15, 1979, to July 31, 1979, we have to analyze the transactions that affect net income differently than when we prepared only a balance sheet and put all revenue and expense items directly into retained earnings.

1. **Sale to customers of $10,000 of fruits and vegetables for $13,500:**

    In terms of balance sheet only:
    Increase cash $13,500
    Decrease inventory 10,000
    Increase retained earnings 3,500
    In a complete accounting system resulting in a balance sheet and a statement of income:
    Increase cash 13,500
    Increase sales (increases income) 13,500
    Increase cost of merchandise sold (decreases income) 10,000
    Decrease inventory 10,000

Sales of $13,500 minus cost of merchandise sold of $10,000 is nothing more than expansion of the retained earnings increase of $3,500 for purposes of income statement preparation.

2. **The company paid wages of $1,500 for work performed:**

    In terms of balance sheet only:
    Decrease retained earnings $1,500
    Decrease cash 1,500

*In a complete accounting system resulting in a balance sheet and income state-
ment:*
    Increase wages expense 1,500
    Decrease cash 1,500

The increase in the expense account, wages expense, has the
same effect as a decrease in retained earnings.

3. Expiration of the prepaid rent of $250:

In terms of balance sheet only:
    Decrease retained earnings.. $250
    Decrease prepaid rent 250
*In a complete accounting system resulting in a balance sheet and income state-
ment:*
    Increase rent expense 250
    Decrease prepaid rent 250

An increase in the rent expense account (reduction of net income)
has the same effect as a decrease in retained earnings.

4. Depreciation of equipment in the amount of $125:

In terms of balance sheet only:
    Decrease retained earnings.. $125
    Increase accumulated depreciation (deduction from the fixed asset
        account, equipment)... 125
*In a complete accounting system resulting in a balance sheet and income state-
ment:*
    Increase depreciation expense 125
    Increase accumulated depreciation 125

The increase in depreciation expense has the same effect as a
decrease in retained earnings.

5. Accrual of interest expense of $20:

In terms of balance sheet only:
    Decrease retained earnings.. $20
    Increase accrued interest payable 20
*In a complete accounting system resulting in a balance sheet and income state-
ment*
    Increase interest expense... 20
    Increase accrued interest payable 20

The increase in interest expense has the same effect as a decrease
in retained earnings.

With this additional information we are now able to prepare a
statement of income (Illustration 1–10) for Joyce Markets for the period July 15, 1979, to July 31, 1979, as well as the balance sheet (Illustration 1–9) on July 31, 1979.

ILLUSTRATION 1–10 ─────────────────────

JOYCE MARKETS, INC.
Statement of Income
For the Period
July 15 to July 31, 1979

Sales		$13,500
Cost of merchandise sold		10,000
Gross profit*.....................		$ 3,500
Other expenses:		
Wages	$1,500	
Rent	250	
Depreciation	125	
Interest	20	1,895
Net income (profit)		$ 1,605

* Gross profit or gross margin is the difference between the sales price and the cost of the merchandise sold.

CASES FOR CHAPTER 1

Case 1–1

The SSC Corporation

All the balance sheet account balances of SSC Corporation on December 31, 1981, are listed below ($000 omitted):

Notes payable	$2,024
Cash	326
Accounts receivable	3,458
Land and land improvements	263
Machinery and equipment	1,223
Accounts payable	1,245
Inventories	3,524
Allowance for uncollectible accounts receivable	81
Buildings	1,369
Accumulated depreciation	747
Common stock	3,462
Accrued liabilities	1,363
Excess of purchase price over net assets of companies acquired	1,731
Retained earnings	3,060
Prepaid expenses	88

Required:
Prepare a balance sheet as of December 31, 1981.

Case 1–2

Robert's Discount Store

The balance sheet of Robert's Discount Store on November 30, 1981, was as follows:

12

ROBERT'S DISCOUNT STORE
Balance Sheet
November 30, 1981

Assets

Cash	$22,500
Accounts receivable	7,500
Inventory	30,000
	$60,000

Equities

Accounts payable	$ 9,000
Notes payable—bank	6,000
Capital—Robert Kob	45,000
	$60,000

Required:

1. You are to record the effect of the following December occurrences, and prepare a balance sheet in good form on December 31, 1981. You may use any format you feel is appropriate to accumulate the information to prepare the balance sheet.
   a. Collected $4,500 of the amount owed by customers.
   b. Paid creditors $6,000 of the balance owed them.
   c. Sold merchandise inventory with a cost of $1,350 for $1,950. The customer paid $750 in cash and charged the balance.
   d. Ordered $2,250 of merchandise from the firm's supplier.
   e. Robert Kob withdrew $1,050 in cash from the store's bank account. He also took merchandise for his personal use. The merchandise cost $375 but had a retail value of $565.
   f. Paid December wages of $750 to the grocery clerk.
   g. The store paid off its $6,000 note (disregard interest).
   h. Paid $900 for three months rent (December, January, and February) on December 1. The rent is $300 a month.
   i. Received and paid for the $2,250 of merchandise ordered earlier in the month.
   j. Robert Kob was offered $52,500 for his equity in the store by a large discount chain. He rejected the offer but was pleased that the store had acquired goodwill.
   k. Incorporated Robert's Discount Store. Robert Kob received $43,125 in common stock for his equity in the store.
   l. Robert Kob sold one half of his stock to his brother-in-law, Sid Shap, for $26,250 (half of the $52,500 he was offered for the store).
2. Would you have invested $26,250 for a 50 percent ownership in the store?

Case 1-3

Henderson Brothers Service Station

For 23 years Pete King had owned a service station located off U.S. Highway 1, in Dedham, Massachusetts. On February 1, 1981, King celebrated his 60th birthday and announced his intention to retire and move to Florida as soon as a buyer for his service station could be found.

Two brothers, Ed and Richard Henderson, saw King's newspaper ad for the sale of the station and drove to Dedham on a Saturday to investigate. They liked what they saw. The station was easily visible and accessible from U.S. Highway 1 and also occupied a prime location on the town's main thoroughfare. It was obvious to them that King had taken great pride in the station; the grounds were immaculate, and the building and equipment appeared to be well-maintained and clean. The Henderson brothers also noted the steady flow of morning customers into the station.

The Hendersons arranged a meeting with King for the following Monday to discuss a possible purchase. At the meeting, King indicated that he expected $87,500 for his business. He showed the Hendersons his figures for the preceding five years. Net income from the station during that period ranged from a low of $14,375 in 1976, to a high of $25,375 in 1979. King said that this net income was derived mainly from gasoline sales and minor auto repairs. He expressed the belief that if major repairs were also performed, sales and income could probably be doubled. King had not done this because he had been satisfied with his return on the business and had wished to keep the operation small.

The Henderson brothers declared their desire to buy the station, but they indicated that they had only $37,500 in cash. By this time, King was rather eager to sell his station and retire. He proposed to settle for $37,500 in cash, and a 20-year loan on the remaining $50,000. The loan would be secured by the station and bear a 10 percent per annum interest rate. It was to be paid in 40 semiannual principal payments, plus interest on the unpaid balance.

Ed and Richard Henderson agreed to these terms, and on April 1, 1981, the sale papers were signed and the title transferred. King and his wife moved to Florida. The Henderson brothers took over the service station as equal partners, each having contributed half of the purchase price. The sale price included $18,750 for the land, $43,750 for the building and improvements, $12,500 for tools and equipment, and $12,500 for inventory (gasoline, oil, tires, and parts).

The brothers planned to expand the business by providing major repairs but soon discovered that in order to do so they would need a heavier duty hydraulic lift costing $2,250. Since the bank refused to lend this sum, Richard Henderson contributed $1,250 and Ed $1,000, and they purchased the hydraulic lift on July 1, 1981.

After six months of ownership, the Hendersons called Mr. Benson, a local accountant, to help them determine how they had done. Benson determined the following as of September 30, 1981:

1. There was $87 in the cash register and $2,250 in the checking account.
2. Customers owed the service station $875.
3. Unpaid bills due suppliers amounted to $500.
4. The physical inventory of gasoline, oil, tires, and parts amounted to $17,300.
5. The six-month payment of $3,750 for principal and interest on the loan was made on September 30, 1981.
6. The estimated useful life of the buildings and improvements is 35 years.
7. The estimated useful life of the tools and equipment is ten years.

Required:

1. Prepare a balance sheet for the Henderson Brothers Service Station as of April 1, 1981.
2. Prepare a balance sheet as of September 30, 1981.
3. What were the equities (capital accounts) of Ed and Richard Henderson on September 30, 1981? (In partnership law, the partners share equally in profits and losses unless there is a specific provision to the contrary.)
4. If the partnership was dissolved on September 30, 1981, do you suppose the partners would receive an amount equal to their capital account?

2

Mechanics of Accounting

The simple system which we used in the Joyce Markets, Inc., case to prepare a balance sheet and income statement was adequate because we had to analyze and classify only a few transactions. When there are many transactions, it is necessary to have a written analysis of each transaction and how it is recorded in the financial statements. We need a system that will analyze and record the transactions as they occur and transfer the increases and decreases to the correct category. In accounting, these categories are called *accounts*. Individual accounts are kept on separate sheets in a book (computer tape in automated systems) called a *general ledger*.[1]

Listed below are the general ledger accounts of Joyce Markets, Inc.

Cash	Accrued Interest Payable
Accounts Receivable	Common Stock
Inventory	Retained Earnings
Prepaid Rent	Sales
Equipment	Cost of Merchandise Sold
Accumulated Depreciation	Wages Expense
Security Deposit	Rent Expense
Accounts Payable	Depreciation Expense
Notes Payable	Interest Expense

Assets, current assets, fixed assets, other assets, equities, current liabilities, stockholders' equity, and revenues and expenses are not

---

[1] In practice, each general ledger account would have a number. The listing of all the accounts of the enterprise is called the *chart of accounts*. The number of accounts in the chart of accounts will depend on how much information management wishes to generate for the preparation of financial statements. The numerical range for a small company might be as follows:

Assets	1–200
Liabilities	201–400
Stockholders' equity	401–450
Revenues	451–550
Expenses..........................	551–750

accounts but headings for groups of accounts used in the balance sheet or income statement.

a. Cash is a current asset account.
b. Equipment is a fixed asset account.
c. Accumulated depreciation is a contra fixed asset account or deduction from a fixed asset account.
d. Accounts payable is a current liability account.
e. Retained earnings is a stockholders' (owners') equity account.
f. Sales is a revenue account.
g. Rent expense is an expense account.

The five major groupings of accounts are *assets, liabilities, owners' equities, revenues,* and *expenses.*

The number of accounts we have in the general ledger will be determined by the amount of detail the enterprise's management wishes to accumulate. For example, management could have one general ledger account called *miscellaneous expense* which includes bank charges, office supplies, and telephone expense or they could have three separate accounts called *bank charges, office supplies,* and *telephone expense.*

Generally, it is good practice to accumulate the information in as much detail (as many accounts) as is economically feasible in the general ledger. It is always possible to reclassify and combine accounts for purposes of preparing financial statements.

The general ledger account for cash for Joyce Markets would appear as in Illustration 2–1.

The Ref. (Reference) column indicates the book of original entry (CR = cash receipts book, CD = cash disbursements book) from which the transaction was posted. (Books of original entry and the process of posting are explained later in this chapter.)

ILLUSTRATION 2–1

CASH					
Date		Ref.	Increases	Decreases	Balance
7/15		CR	30,000		30,000
7/16		CD		6,000	24,000
7/16		CD		750	23,250
7/17		CD		15,000	8,250
7/31		CR	8,000		16,250
7/31		CR	5,500		21,750
7/31		CD		1,500	20,250

For purposes of solving classroom problems, only the center or increase-decrease portion of the formal general ledger account is used. This portion is called a *T-account*. (See Illustration 2–2).

The balance of $20,250 in the T (general ledger)-account, cash, is obtained by subtracting the total of the decrease side ($23,250) from the total of the increase side ($43,500).

ILLUSTRATION 2–2 _____

Cash	
Increases	Decreases

Cash	
30,000	6,000
8,000	750
5,500	15,000
	1,500

The accounting profession has decided that *assets should be on the left side of the balance sheet, and equities (liabilities and owners' equity) should be on the right side of the balance sheet.*[2] The basic accounting equation is assets (accounts with left-side balances) equals equities (accounts with right-side balances):

$$\text{Assets} = \text{Equities}$$

It was also decided by the accounting profession that *increases in asset accounts would be recorded on the left side, decreases on the right side.* To maintain the balance sheet equation (left-side account balances = right-side account balances) we would have to treat equity (liability and owners' equity) accounts in exactly the opposite fashion from asset accounts: increases on the right side, and decreases on the left side.

Asset Account		Equity Account	
Increases	Decreases	Decreases	Increases

---

[2] In some formal balance sheet presentations assets are listed at the top of the page and equities on the bottom.

The Joyce Markets transactions in general ledger (T-account) form would appear as follows:

1. Initial investment by stockholders of $30,000.

Asset Accounts	Equity Accounts
Cash	**Capital Stock**
(1) 30,000	(1) 30,000

The increase in the asset account, cash, is recorded as a left-side entry. It is equal to an increase in the stockholders' equity account, capital stock, which is recorded as a right-side entry.

2. The company purchases display equipment in the amount of $10,000; $6,000 was paid in cash and $4,000 in a 12 percent, 90-day note.

Asset Accounts	Equity Accounts
Cash	**Notes Payable**
(1) 30,000 (2) 6,000	(2) 4,000
Equipment	**Capital Stock**
(2) 10,000	(1) 30,000

The $10,000 increase in the asset, equipment, is a left-side entry. It is offset (balanced) by a decrease (right-side entry) in the asset, cash, in the amount of $6,000, and an increase (right-side entry) in the liability account, notes payable, in the amount of $4,000.

The balance in an account is the difference between the total of the increases minus the decreases. The cash balance is $24,000. It is a left-side balance because the left-side entry of $30,000 exceeds the right-side entry of $6,000.

Total assets, that is, left-side account balances (cash, $24,000; equipment, $10,000) of $34,000 are equal to total equities, that is, right-side account balances (notes payable, $4,000; capital stock, $30,000) of $34,000.

3. The company paid rent of $750 of which $250 was for July, and $500 was a security deposit.

Asset Accounts	Equity Accounts
Cash	**Notes Payable**
(1) 30,000 (2) 6,000 (3) 750	(2) 4,000

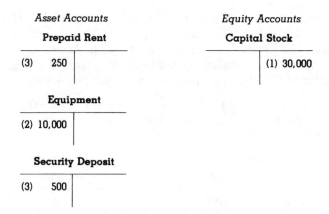

The increases in the asset accounts prepaid rent and security deposit are reflected by left-side entries which are offset by a decrease (right-side entry) in the asset account, cash.

4. On July 17, Joyce Markets purchased $15,000 worth of fruits and vegetables for cash.

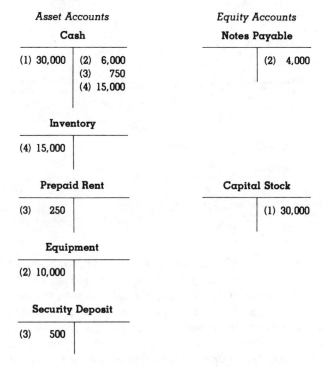

The increase (left-side entry) in the asset account, inventory, is balanced by the decrease (right-side entry) in the asset account, cash.

Accounts with left-side balances are: cash, $8,250 [$30,000 − ($6,000 + $750 + $15,000)]; inventory, $15,000; prepaid rent, $250; equipment, $10,000; and security deposit, $500. Accounts with right-side balances are: notes payable, $4,000, and capital stock, $30,000. Total assets of $34,000 are equal to total equities of $34,000.

5. During the month of July the company sold $10,000 of the merchandise inventory to customers for $13,500. The customers paid $8,000 and charged $5,500.

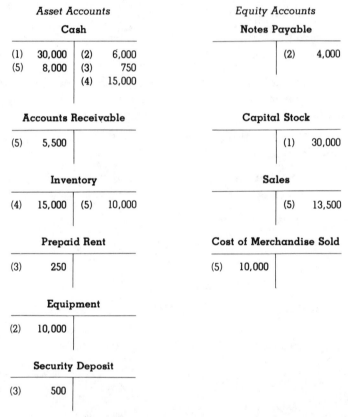

Asset Accounts

Cash

(1)	30,000	(2)	6,000
(5)	8,000	(3)	750
		(4)	15,000

Accounts Receivable

(5)	5,500		

Inventory

(4)	15,000	(5)	10,000

Prepaid Rent

(3)	250		

Equipment

(2)	10,000		

Security Deposit

(3)	500		

Equity Accounts

Notes Payable

		(2)	4,000

Capital Stock

		(1)	30,000

Sales

		(5)	13,500

Cost of Merchandise Sold

(5)	10,000		

The increases of $8,000 in the asset account, cash, and $5,500 in the asset account, accounts receivable (left-side entries), are balanced by an increase of $13,500 (right-side entry) in the revenue account, sales. *Increases in revenue accounts are recorded on the right-hand side because revenues increase net income and net income increases the owners' equity. Increases in owners' equity are right-side entries.* The increase (left-side entry) of $10,000 in the expense account, cost of merchandise sold, is balanced by a $10,000 decrease (right-side entry) in the asset account, inventory. *Increases in expense accounts are recorded on the left-hand side because expenses decrease net income. Decreases in net income (owners' equity) are left-side entries.*

6. During the month of July the customers paid the $5,500 they owed Joyce Markets, Inc.

Asset Accounts				*Equity Accounts*		

Cash   **Notes Payable**

(1)	30,000	(2)	6,000		(2)	4,000
(5)	8,000	(3)	750			
(6)	5,500	(4)	15,000			

Accounts Receivable   **Capital Stock**

(5)	5,500	(6)	5,500		(1)	30,000

Inventory   **Sales**

(4)	15,000	(5)	10,000		(5)	13,500

Prepaid Rent   **Cost of Merchandise Sold**

(3)	250			(5)	10,000	

Equipment

(2)	10,000		

Security Deposit

(3)	500		

The increase in the asset, cash (left-side entry), is balanced by the decrease in another asset, accounts receivable (right-side entry).

7. During the month of July the company purchased $9,000 of fruits and vegetables on account.

Asset Accounts				*Equity Accounts*		

Cash   **Accounts Payable**

(1)	30,000	(2)	6,000		(7)	9,000
(5)	8,000	(3)	750			
(6)	5,500	(4)	15,000			

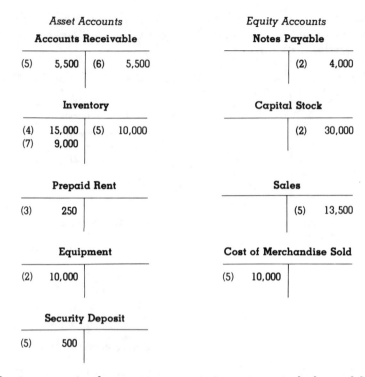

Asset Accounts

Accounts Receivable

(5)	5,500	(6)	5,500

Inventory

(4)	15,000	(5)	10,000
(7)	9,000		

Prepaid Rent

(3)	250

Equipment

(2)	10,000

Security Deposit

(5)	500

Equity Accounts

Notes Payable

(2)	4,000

Capital Stock

(2)	30,000

Sales

(5)	13,500

Cost of Merchandise Sold

(5)	10,000

The increase in the asset account, inventory, is balanced by an increase in the liability account, accounts payable.

Total assets of $46,500, that is, cash, $21,750; inventory, $14,000; prepaid rent, $250; equipment, $10,000; and security deposit, $500, are equal to total equities of $46,500 representing accounts payable, $9,000; notes payable, $4,000; capital stock, $30,000; and net income which increases retained earnings [Sales ($13,500) − Cost of merchandise sold ($10,000)] of $3,500.

8. Joyce Markets paid its employees wages of $1,500 for work performed from July 15, 1979, to July 31, 1979.

Asset Accounts

Cash

(1)	30,000	(2)	6,000
(5)	8,000	(3)	750
(6)	5,500	(4)	15,000
		(8)	1,500

Accounts Receivable

(5)	5,500	(6)	5,500

Equity Accounts

Accounts Payable

(7)	9,000

Notes Payable

(2)	4,000

Asset Accounts			*Equity Accounts*	

Inventory			Capital Stock	
(4)	15,000	(5) 10,000	(1) 30,000	
(7)	9,000			

Prepaid Rent		Sales	
(3)	250	(5) 13,500	

Equipment		Cost of Merchandise Sold	
(2)	10,000	(5) 10,000	

Security Deposit		Wages Expense	
(3)	500	(8) 1,500	

The increase in wages expense which is a reduction in net income is recorded by a left-side entry. It is balanced by a decrease in cash, a right-side entry.

Accountants call left-side entries *debits* and right-side entries *credits.*

In the recording of accounting transactions there is no meaning for debit (abbreviated Dr.) other than left, or for credit (abbreviated Cr.) other than right.

> Debits (left-side entries) increase assets and decrease liabilities and owners' equity.
>
> Credits (right-side entries) increase liabilities and owners' equity and decrease assets.

Revenues and expenses are owners' equity accounts because they are part of the computation of net income. Increases in revenue accounts which increase net income and therefore increase owners' equity are recorded as credits. Increases in expense accounts which decrease net income and therefore decrease owners' equity are recorded as debits.

9. The prepaid rent from July 15 to July 31 has expired.

Asset Accounts			*Equity Accounts*	

Cash			Accounts Payable	
(1)	30,000	(2) 6,000	(7) 9,000	
(5)	8,000	(3) 750		
(6)	5,500	(4) 15,000		
		(8) 1,500		

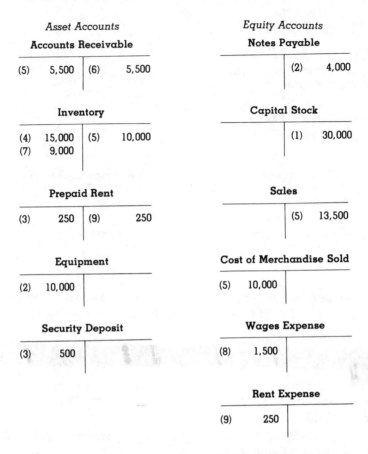

Asset Accounts

Accounts Receivable

(5)	5,500	(6)	5,500

Inventory

(4)	15,000	(5)	10,000
(7)	9,000		

Prepaid Rent

(3)	250	(9)	250

Equipment

(2)	10,000		

Security Deposit

(3)	500	

Equity Accounts

Notes Payable

	(2)	4,000

Capital Stock

	(1)	30,000

Sales

	(5)	13,500

Cost of Merchandise Sold

(5)	10,000	

Wages Expense

(8)	1,500	

Rent Expense

(9)	250	

Debit (left-side entry) rent expense to record the increase in this expense account (decrease in net income) and credit (right-side entry) prepaid rent to record the decrease in this asset account.

10. Depreciation (allocation of cost) of the equipment for the last half of July, $125.

Asset Accounts

Cash

(1)	30,000	(2)	6,000
(5)	8,000	(3)	750
(6)	5,500	(4)	15,000
		(8)	1,500

Accounts Receivable

(5)	5,500	(6)	5,500

Equity Accounts

Accounts Payable

	(7)	9,000

Notes Payable

	(2)	4,000

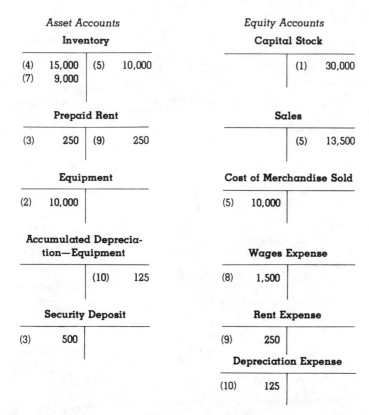

Debit (left-side entry) depreciation expense to record the increase in this expense account (decrease in net income) and credit accumulated depreciation—equipment, which results in a decrease in the asset, equipment.

It is the custom to accumulate the reductions in fixed-asset accounts due to depreciation in this special contra fixed asset (accumulated depreciation) account rather than directly deducting it from the fixed-asset account (equipment). This makes it possible to see both the original cost of the fixed asset and the total amount of cost allocated to operations since the purchase of the fixed asset.

11. Interest expense from July 16 to July 31 is accrued on the books.

Asset Accounts				Equity Accounts		
Cash				**Accounts Payable**		
(1)	30,000	(2)	6,000		(7)	9,000
(5)	8,000	(3)	750			
(6)	5,500	(4)	15,000			
		(8)	1,500			

Asset Accounts

Accounts Receivable

(5)	5,500	(6)	5,500

Inventory

(4)	15,000	(5)	10,000
(7)	9,000		

Prepaid Rent

(3)	250	(9)	250

Equipment

(2)	10,000		

Accumulated Depreciation—Equipment

		(10)	125

Security Deposit

(3)	500		

Accrued Interest Payable

		(11)	20

Notes Payable

		(2)	4,000

Capital Stock

		(1)	30,000

Sales

		(5)	13,500

Cost of Merchandise Sold

(5)	10,000		

Wages Expense

(8)	1,500		

Rent Expense

(9)	250		

Depreciation Expense

(10)	125		

Interest Expense

(11)	20		

Debit interest expense, and credit accrued interest payable. It is necessary to make this entry to reflect the interest expense for the period July 16 to July 31.

All the transactions and the adjustments for expired rent, depreciation of equipment, and accrual of interest have been recorded in the general ledger accounts.

It is good practice, prior to the preparation of the financial statements, to prove that all the accounts with debit balances are equal to all the accounts with credit balances. The unclassified listing of accounts in Illustration 2–3 is called a *trial balance* and proves only that the books are arithmetically correct.

ILLUSTRATION 2–3 _____

JOYCE MARKETS, INC.
Trial Balance
July 31, 1979

	Dr. (Debit)	Cr. (Credit)
Cash	$20,250.00	$
Inventory	14,000.00	
Equipment	10,000.00	
Accumulated depreciation		125.00
Security Deposit	500.00	
Accounts payable		9,000.00
Accrued interest payable		20.00
Notes payable		4,000.00
Capital stock		30,000.00
Sales		13,500.00
Cost of merchandise sold	10,000.00	
Wages expense	1,500.00	
Rent expense	250.00	
Depreciation expense	125.00	
Interest expense	20.00	
	$56,645.00	$56,645.00

The trial balance balances, and we can now prepare the balance sheet and income statement for Joyce Markets, Inc., from the general ledger accounts. (See Illustration 1–9—Balance Sheet and Illustration 1–10—Income Statement.)

BOOKS OF ORIGINAL ENTRY

In order to maintain a chronological history of the enterprise, each transaction is first recorded in a *book of original entry* and then transferred or posted to the general ledger accounts.

It is possible to enter all the transactions in one book of original entry called a *general journal*. The format to be followed in making an entry in the general journal (journal entry) is to place the exact title of the general ledger account to be debited on top and to the left-hand margin. The general ledger account to be credited is indented on the line below the account to be debited. Usually a simple

ILLUSTRATION 2-4

General Journal

Date	Accounts	Dr.	Cr.
1979 July 15	Cash	30,000	
	Capital Stock		30,000
	Sold $30,000 of common stock to R. Joyce.		
16	Equipment	10,000	
	Cash		6,000
	Notes Payable		4,000
	Purchased equipment from Heath Co., paid $4,000 cash and a 12%, 90-day note.		
16	Prepaid Rent	250	
	Security Deposit	500	
	Cash		750
	Rent for 7/16 to 7/31 plus a $500 security deposit.		
17	Inventory	15,000	
	Cash		15,000
	Purchased fruits and vegetables from Jones Market.		
31	Cash	8,000	
	Accounts Receivable	5,500	
	Sales		13,500
	Sales for 7/15–7/31.		
31	Cost of Merchandise Sold	10,000	
	Inventory		10,000
	Cost of the merchandise sold for 7/15–7/31.		
31	Cash	5,500	
	Accounts Receivable		5,500
	Collection of accounts receivable.		
31	Inventory	9,000	
	Accounts Payable		9,000
	Purchases from Jones Co. terms 30/n.		
31	Wages Expense	1,500	
	Cash		1,500
	Wages for 7/15–7/31.		
31	Rent Expense	250	
	Prepaid Rent		250
	To record the expiration of the prepaid rent.		
31	Depreciation Expense	125	
	Accumulated Depreciation		125
	To record depreciation for 15 days.		
31	Interest Expense	20	
	Accrued Interest Payable		20
	To accrue interest for 7/16 to 7/31.		

explanation of the journal entry is written under the accounts debited and credited.

All the *general journal entries* for Joyce Markets, Inc., which would have been made prior to their posting to the general ledger accounts, are shown in Illustration 2–4.

If a company had a large number of transactions each month, posting from the general journal to the general ledger would become very time-consuming and cumbersome. This would be particularly true for transactions which were repetitive in nature, such as sales, purchases, cash receipts, and cash disbursements. To solve this problem, separate books of original entry are used for each of these major types of transactions. For example, using a *cash receipts* book makes it possible to post the monthly *total* for cash receipts to the cash account in the general ledger instead of having to post each individual cash receipt, as would be necessary if we used only a general journal to record all transactions.

If the other books of original entry (sales, purchases, cash receipts, and cash disbursements) are used, the general journal will contain only adjustments and corrections to the general ledger accounts. Joyce Markets' entries for rent, depreciation, and interest are examples of *adjusting journal entries*.

A very special general journal entry which is only made once a year is called the *closing journal entry*. The purpose of this entry is to transfer the net income or net loss for the year to retained earnings.

Let us assume that the revenue and expense accounts for Joyce Markets at the end of the first year of operations were as follows:

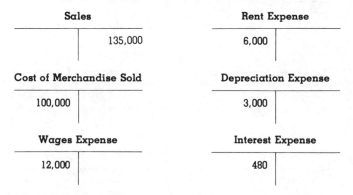

Sales	Rent Expense
	135,000	6,000	

Cost of Merchandise Sold	Depreciation Expense
100,000		3,000	

Wages Expense	Interest Expense
12,000		480	

The closing journal entry to close out the revenue and expense accounts and transfer the net income to retained earnings is shown in Illustration 2–5.

After the closing entry is posted, the revenue and expense (temporary, nominal) accounts will all have a zero balance, and the net

ILLUSTRATION 2–5

General Journal

Date	Accounts	Dr.	Cr.
1980 June 30	Sales	135,000	
	Cost of Merchandise Sold		100,000
	Wages Expense		12,000
	Rent Expense		6,000
	Depreciation Expense		3,000
	Interest Expense		480
	Retained Earnings		13,520
	To close the revenue and expense accounts for the fiscal year ended June 30, 1980, and transfer the profit to retained earnings.		

income of $13,520 will be transferred to the retained earnings account.

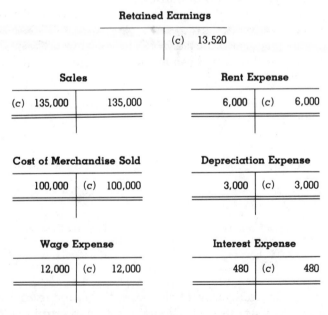

Retained Earnings

(c)   13,520

Sales

(c)   135,000 | 135,000

Rent Expense

6,000 | (c)   6,000

Cost of Merchandise Sold

100,000 | (c)   100,000

Depreciation Expense

3,000 | (c)   3,000

Wage Expense

12,000 | (c)   12,000

Interest Expense

480 | (c)   480

If we didn't make this closing entry each year, the revenue and expense accounts would accumulate totals of many years and make it difficult to isolate the current year's figures.

Asset, liability, and owners' equity accounts are not closed at the end of the year because they either represent an existing resource of the company or existing claims. The balance sheet account *retained earnings* will contain *all* of the net income earned from the inception of the enterprise less any distributions to the owners. If this account has a debit balance it is entitled *deficit* rather than retained earnings.

THE ACCOUNTING CYCLE

The accounting cycle may be represented graphically as follows:

Transactions
↓
Analyze transactions
↓
Record transactions in books of original entry
↓
Post books of original entry to the General Ledger
↓
Analyze General Ledger accounts and prepare
adjusting and correcting journal entries
↓
Post adjusting and correcting journal entries
to the General Ledger
↓
Prepare balance sheet and income statement
from the General Ledger
↓
Prepare closing journal entry and post
it to the General Ledger

The routine (recording transactions and posting them to the general ledger accounts) aspects of the accounting cycle are generally done by bookkeepers. Accountants focus on the more analytical (analyses of the transactions and general ledger accounts and preparation of financial statements) aspects of the accounting cycle.

CASES FOR CHAPTER 2

Case 2-1

Typo Company, Inc.

During January 1981, Al Jones and Donna Cestario were reviewing the results of operations of the Typo Company, Inc., a duplicating, typing, and bindery service. They formed the corporation on January 1, 1980, and commenced business as Typo Company, Inc., on that date. The corporation selected the calendar year (a year ending December 31) for reporting purposes.

A summary of the transactions that took place from January 1, 1980, to December 31, 1980, is given below:

1. On January 1, 1980, Al Jones paid $24,000 for 240 shares and Donna Cestario paid $12,000 for 120 shares of Typo Company, Inc., common stock.
2. Sales made to customers amounted to $84,282; $10,020 of these sales were made at the end of December 1980 and were not collected until January 1981.
3. Wages and salaries paid to employees (including $13,000 to Al Jones and $15,000 to Donna Cestario) for work performed through December 27, 1980, amounted to $40,480. Wages and salaries of $850 (including $300 for Al and $250 for Donna) for the last three days of December 1980 were paid on January 6, 1981.
4. Rent paid for the office was $3,900; $300 a month plus a security deposit of $300 which was paid on January 1, 1980.
5. Typo purchased $9,180 of paper during the year. It still owed for $1,040 of this paper on December 31, 1980. An inventory of paper on December 31, 1980, indicated there was still $3,200 of paper on hand.
6. Rental of the duplicating machines for 1980 was $34,517. Of this amount, $2,160 was unpaid on December 31, 1980.
7. Telephone expenses incurred and paid for the year were $322.

34

Required:

1. Prepare general journal entries for each of the transactions.
2. Post the journal entries to the general ledger (T-account form) accounts.
3. Prepare a statement of income for Typo Company, Inc., for the period January 1, 1980, to December 31, 1980.
4. Prepare a balance sheet as of December 31, 1980.
5. Was the Typo Company, Inc., successful in 1980?
6. Was it a good investment for the stockholders?

Case 2–2

The Total Toy Company

The Total Toy Company produced "Beautiful Baby," an incredible toy doll that the company claimed could do virtually everything a real infant could. It walked, talked, cried, and even soiled its diapers. The doll cost Total Toy $19.50, and they sold it for $26.00. (For purposes of this problem we assume that $19.50 is Total Toy's only cost.)

The company realized the importance of prompt shipments of its dolls and had a policy of always maintaining an inventory equal to 50 dolls more than the number of dolls sold during the previous 30 days. Because Total Toy was a new company, their suppliers required them to pay their bills promptly. Total Toy's customers paid them on a 30-day net basis.

On January 31, after one month's operations, their balance sheet was as follows:

TOTAL TOY COMPANY
Balance Sheet
January 31, 1981

Assets		*Equities*	
Cash	$2,925	Common stock	$7,800
Accounts receivable	2,600	Retained earnings	650
Inventory	2,925		
	$8,450		$8,450

Mr. Total, the president, was pleased that they had made a profit of $650 on the first month's (January) sales of 100 dolls. He predicted that sales would increase at a rate of 50 dolls a month for the next six months.

His predictions were correct for February. The company sold 150 dolls, collected their accounts receivable, and produced and paid for an inventory of 200 dolls in anticipation of March sales.

The predictions for March (sales of 200 dolls) and April (sales of 250 dolls) were also correct. Collections, payments to suppliers, and inventory purchases were made as expected.

Total was discussing the profits of $4,550 for the four months with his sales manager, when the bookkeeper told him that the company's bank balance was zero, and they needed funds in order to continue operating in May.

Required:

1. Make journal entries to record each transaction and post them to the general ledger accounts.
2. Prepare a balance sheet on April 30, 1981, and an income statement for the period January 1 to April 30, 1981.
3. How is it possible for a company that starts with $7,800 in capital and has profitable sales for a period of four months, to have a zero bank balance?
4. How much does the company need to borrow right away to sustain an increase in sales of 50 dolls a month for the remainder of the year?

3

Measuring and Adjusting

After the transactions for cash receipts, cash disbursements, sales, and purchases have been recorded and posted, it is necessary to analyze the general ledger accounts and make the appropriate adjusting journal entries. This is done to ensure that the balance sheet reflects all the assets and equities in existence on the balance sheet date and that the income statement includes all the revenue and expense accounts applicable to the time frame covered.

Typical adjusting journal entries preceding the preparation of the balance sheet and income statement are for:

1. Expenditures which affect more than one accounting period.
2. Receipts which affect more than one accounting period.
3. Revenues affecting the accounting period which have not been recorded.
4. Expenses affecting the accounting period which have not been recorded.

1. EXPENDITURES WHICH AFFECT MORE THAN ONE ACCOUNTING PERIOD

Joyce Markets purchases $10,000 of fire insurance coverage on its store for a 36-month period commencing April 1, 1980, by paying a premium (cost of the policy) of $360. Joyce Markets reports its income on a fiscal year ended June 30. A period of 12 consecutive months is called a fiscal year. If the fiscal year ends on December 31, it is called a calendar year.

On April 1, 1980, the transaction is recorded in the cash disbursement book as follows:

Unexpired (Prepaid) Insurance	360	
Cash..		360

The general ledger accounts after this transaction are:

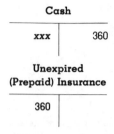

Cash

xxx	360

**Unexpired
(Prepaid) Insurance**

360	

An analysis (listing of policies, total and unexpired premium cost) of the unexpired insurance account as of June 30, 1980, indicates that the *coverage* for the months of April, May, and June has been used up (expired). The income statement should reflect the expense for these three months, and the balance sheet should reflect the fact that 33-months' insurance coverage is unexpired on June 30, 1980.

The appropriate adjusting journal entry is:

Insurance Expense.............................. 30
    Unexpired Insurance........................ 30
    To record expired insurance, April, May, June 1980.

After the posting of this entry the affected general ledger accounts correctly reflect the asset account of $330 (33 months at $10 per month) on June 30, 1980, and the expense of $30 (3 months at $10 per month) for the fiscal year ended June 30, 1980.

**Unexpired
(Prepaid) Insurance**

360	30

Insurance Expense

30	

General ledger accounts on *July 1, 1980,* the first day of the fiscal year ending *June 30, 1981* are:

Unexpired Insurance

360	30

Insurance Expense

30	30*

* Closed to retained earnings on 6/30/80.

The balance in the insurance expense account after the *June 30, 1980,* closing is zero ($30 − $30 = 0).

The appropriate adjusting journal entry for the fiscal year ended *June 30, 1981,* is:

Insurance Expense.............................. 120
    Unexpired Insurance........................ 120
    To record expired insurance FYE 6/30/81.

Unexpired Insurance		Insurance Expense	
360	30	30	30
	120		
		120	

The balance in the unexpired insurance account is $210 ($360 − $150). This is correct because it is the unexpired amount on the balance sheet date, June 30, 1981. (July 1, 1981, to March 31, 1983, is 21 months; 21 × $10 = $210.)

The expense account is correct because it represents expense for the months of July 1, 1980, to June 30, 1981 (12 months × $10 = $120).

On May 1, 1980, Joyce Markets purchases display equipment on credit for $12,000. It is estimated that the equipment will be used for ten years at which time it will have no salvage value.

On May 1, the transaction is recorded:

Equipment	12,000	
Accounts Payable............................		12,000
Purchase of equipment from Jones Brothers.		

The appropriate adjusting journal entry on June 30, 1980, to reflect the cost of the equipment allocated to May and June operations is:

Depreciation Expense...........................	200	
Accumulated Depreciation–Equipment		200
To record depreciation 5/1/80–6/30/80.		

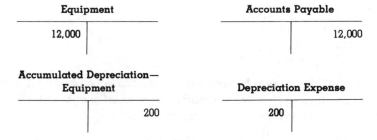

Equipment		Accounts Payable	
12,000			12,000

Accumulated Depreciation—Equipment		Depreciation Expense	
	200	200	

The depreciation expense of $200 correctly reflects the expense for the year ended June 30, 1980 ($12,000 ÷ 10 = $1,200 per year or $100 a month). The asset account, equipment ($12,000), minus the contra asset accumulated depreciation of $200, equals $11,800, the cost to be allocated to future periods.

The depreciation expense for the subsequent year ending June 30, 1981, would be $1,200 because the equipment would have been in service for the entire year.

On January 1, 1980, Joyce Markets purchases office supplies for $500. Although the bookkeeper knows that this is an asset on January 1, 1980, he expects that the supplies will be all used up on June 30, 1980, and therefore charges (debits) the $500 to office supplies expense rather than to the asset account, office supplies inventory.

On January 1, 1980, he makes the following entry to record the transaction:

Office Supplies Expense	500	
Cash.......................................		500
To record purchase of office supplies.		

The general ledger accounts, if there are no other entries, are:

Cash		Office Supplies Expense	
xxx	500	500	

On June 30, 1980, a physical inventory of the office supplies indicates that there are $150 of the office supplies on hand. If there had been no office supplies on hand, as the bookkeeper expected when he made the original entry, no adjusting journal entry would be necessary.

The appropriate adjusting journal entry will have to reflect an asset of $150 and an expense of $350 ($500 − $150).

Office Supplies Inventory	150	
Office Supplies Expense		150
To record the 6/30/80 office supplies inventory.		

Office Supplies Inventory		Office Supplies Expense	
150		500	150

If the bookkeeper had followed the procedure of charging the asset account on January 1, 1980, instead of the expense account, the general ledger account before adjustment would be:

Office Supplies Inventory	
500	

and the appropriate adjustment would be:

Office Supplies Expense	350	
Office Supplies Inventory		350
To record use of $350 of supplies.		

Office Supplies Inventory		Office Supplies Expense	
500	350	350	

In both cases we end up with the correct inventory, $150, and the correct office supplies expense of $350.

2. RECEIPTS WHICH AFFECT MORE THAN ONE ACCOUNTING PERIOD

Joyce Markets rents a portion of its store to a concessionaire who sells novelty items. The rent is $150 a month. On June 1, 1980, the date the lease was signed, the concessionaire paid Joyce Markets $450 rent for the months of June, July, and August 1980.

On June 1, 1980, the transaction is recorded:

Cash...	450	
Rent Received in Advance		450
To record the collection of three months' rent received in advance.		

On June 1, 1980, the rent received in advance account of $450 is a liability, as Joyce Markets has an obligation to provide three months' rental of space to the concessionaire.

Cash		Rent Received in Advance	
450			450

On June 30, 1980, the store has a liability of $300 for the months of July and August and has earned rental income of $150 for the month of June.

The appropriate journal entry on June 30, 1980 is:

Rent Received in Advance......................	150	
Rental (Revenue) Income		150
To record rent income for June.		

Rent Received in Advance	
150	450

Rental (Revenue) Income	
	150

The general ledger accounts reflect the correct liability on June 30, 1980 ($450 − $150 = $300) and the correct amount of rental income for the period ($150).

Rent Received in Advance is called a *deferred income account*. It is a liability account which will become income in the future. Two other examples of deferred income accounts are unearned magazine subscriptions (the entire subscription is paid for in advance and doesn't become earned income until the magazines are delivered), and advance payments made by customers (the advance payments become income when the merchandise is delivered or the services contracted for are performed).

3. REVENUES AFFECTING THE ACCOUNTING PERIOD WHICH HAVE NOT BEEN RECORDED

Procter and Gamble agrees to pay Joyce Markets a special commission of $5 a case for every case of new detergent they sell during a six-month promotion period commencing April 1, 1980. Payment is to be made at the end of the six-month period. From April 1, 1980, to June 30, 1980, Joyce Markets sells 1,000 cases of the new detergent.

No entry was made on April 1, 1980, the date of the agreement, as no monetary transaction had taken place.

The appropriate adjusting entry on June 30, 1980 is the one that reflects the fact that Joyce Markets has earned $5,000 in commissions for the period April 1, 1980, to June 30, 1980 for the 1,000 cases sold and has an asset, commissions receivable, of $5,000.

Commissions Receivable........................	5,000	
Commission Revenue (Income)		5,000
To record commissions earned (4/1/80–6/30/80).		

Commissions Receivable	Commission Revenue
5,000	5,000

Failure to make this entry would result in the $5,000 earned in the fiscal year ended June 30, 1980, becoming revenue in the fiscal year ended June 30, 1981. This would result in a mismatching of revenue and expense for both accounting periods. Revenue and net income would be understated by $5,000 in the fiscal year ended June 30, 1980, and overstated by $5,000 in the fiscal year ended June 30, 1981. Net income is an important measure of the economic performance of the enterprise for a particular period of time, and it is critical that it should be measured as accurately as possible.

On September 30, 1980, Procter and Gamble paid Joyce Markets

$12,500 for 2,500 cases sold during the six-month promotion period. The transaction is recorded:

```
Cash..........................................    12,500
    Commissions Receivable....................              5,000
    Commission Revenue .......................              7,500
```

To record cash received from Procter & Gamble as commission for 2,500 cases of special detergent sold.

Cash

12,500	

Commissions Receivable

5,000	5,000

Commission Revenue

5,000*	5,000
	7,500

* Closed to retained earnings on 6/30/80.

The adjustment to *accrue* (record on the books) the unrecorded commission revenue of $5,000 in the fiscal year ended June 30, 1980, results in commission revenue being recorded in the year in which it is earned: $5,000 in the fiscal year ended June 30, 1980, and $7,500 in the fiscal year ended June 30, 1981.

Another example of this type of adjustment is the accrual of interest revenue which is earned but not paid during the particular time period on notes receivable.

4. EXPENSES AFFECTING THE ACCOUNTING PERIOD WHICH HAVE NOT BEEN RECORDED

On May 16, 1980, Joyce Markets borrowed $10,000 from the bank. The note was for four months at 6 percent interest.

The transaction is recorded on May 16, 1980:

```
Cash..........................................    10,000
    Notes Payable ...............................              10,000
```

Cash

10,000	

Notes Payable

	10,000

On June 30, 1980, an adjusting journal entry has to be made to accrue on the books the interest expense for the period May 16, 1980 to June 30, 1980 (1 ½ months).

```
Interest Expense ................................          75
     Accrued Interest Payable ...................                          75
To accrue interest 5/16/80–6/30/80 on the 6%,
$10,000, four-month note.
```

Accrued Interest Payable

	75

Interest Expense

75	

The interest rate is customarily stated on an annual basis. It is 6 percent per year, or 0.5 percent per month, or 0.75 percent for the period May 16 to June 30, 1980 (.0075 × $10,000 = $75).

If we did not make this accrual (adjusting entry) for interest, net income for the fiscal year ended June 30, 1980, would be overstated by $75.

Accrued interest payable is a liability account on the June 30, 1980, balance sheet. It will be eliminated when the note and interest are paid on September 15, 1980.

```
Notes Payable ...................................      10,000
Accrued Interest Payable ........................          75
Interest Expense ................................         125
     Cash .......................................                      10,200
To record payment on 9/15/80 of $10,000, 6%, four-
month note.
```

General ledger accounts on September 15, 1980, after the above entry has been posted:

Cash

xxx	10,200

Notes Payable

10,000	10,000

Accrued Interest Payable

75	75

Interest Expense

75	75*
125	

* Closed to retained earnings on 6/30/80.

During the course of the fiscal year ended June 30, 1980, Joyce Markets paid wages of $12,000.

Wages Expense................................. 12,000
    Cash....................................... 12,000
    To record payment of wages earned in FYE 6/30/80.

The general ledger accounts are:

Cash		Wages Expense	
xxx	12,000	12,000	

Joyce Markets' weekly payroll is paid on Tuesday for the week ending the preceding Saturday. The payroll for the week ending Saturday, June 30, 1980, was $800.

The appropriate adjusting entry on June 30, 1980 is:

Wages Expense................................. 800
    Wages Payable 800
    To accrue wages for the week ending June 30, 1980.

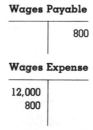

Wages Payable	
	800

Wages Expense	
12,000	
800	

Wages expense for the year ended June 30, 1980, is $12,800. It has to include wages earned but unpaid for the week ending June 30, 1980, if we are to match total expense for the fiscal year ended June 30, 1980, against the total revenues for the same time period.

On July 3, 1980, the wages of $800 are paid:

Wages Payable 800
    Cash....................................... 800

Cash		Wages Payable	
xxx	800	800	800

This entry eliminates the liability for wages payable which was accrued on June 30, 1980.

Federal corporate income tax for the year ended June 30, 1980, was $1,800. This tax has to be paid by September 15, 1980.

The appropriate adjusting entry on June 30, 1980 is:

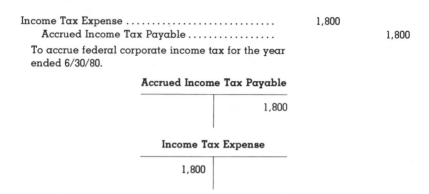

Income Tax Expense 1,800
    Accrued Income Tax Payable 1,800
To accrue federal corporate income tax for the year ended 6/30/80.

Accrued Income Tax Payable

| | 1,800 |

Income Tax Expense

| 1,800 | |

The income tax expense for the year ended June 30, 1980, has to be recorded and matched against the income for the year ended June 30, 1980.

When the income tax is paid on September 15, 1980, we would make the following entry:

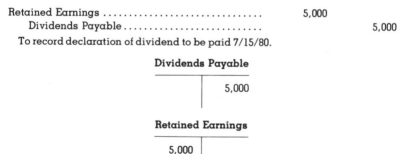

Accrued Income Tax Payable 1,800
    Cash 1,800

Cash

| xxx | 1,800 |

Accrued Income Tax Payable

| 1,800 | 1,800 |

This entry eliminates the June 30, 1980, liability.

On June 30, 1980, the Board of Directors declared dividends to stockholders in the amount of $5,000. The dividends were to be paid on July 15, 1980.

The appropriate adjusting journal entry on June 30, 1980, is:

Retained Earnings 5,000
    Dividends Payable 5,000
To record declaration of dividend to be paid 7/15/80.

Dividends Payable

| | 5,000 |

Retained Earnings

| 5,000 | |

The dividends are a *distribution of earnings* to the stockholders and become a legal liability when they are declared by the Board of Directors. Dividends are not a cost of operations (expense) and are not reflected on the income statement.

When the dividends are paid on July 15, 1980, we would make the following entry:

Dividends Payable.............................	5,000	
Cash.......................................		5,000

Cash		Dividends Payable	
xxx	5,000	5,000	5,000

This entry eliminates the June 30, 1980, liability.

Another area where an adjustment is required is in the measurement of sales that prove uncollectible.

For the fiscal year ended June 30, 1980, Joyce Markets sold $75,000 of fruits and vegetables. Of this amount $40,000 was received in cash and $35,000 was sold on credit. These fruits and vegetables cost Joyce Markets $63,000.

Cash...	40,000	
Accounts Receivable............................	35,000	
Sales		75,000

To record sales for the year (in practice the sales would be recorded on a daily basis and posted to the general ledger monthly).

Cost of Merchandise Sold	63,000	
Inventory....................................		63,000

To record cost of merchandise sold.

During the fiscal year, collections of accounts receivable amount to $14,000.

Cash...	14,000	
Accounts Receivable........................		14,000

To record collection of receivables.

The general ledger accounts would appear as follows:

Cash				Sales		
(a)	40,000				(a)	75,000
(c)	14,000					

Accounts Receivable				Cost of Merchandise Sold	
(a)	35,000	(c)	14,000	(b) 63,000	

Inventory		
xxx	(b)	63,000

Joyce Markets *estimates* that it will not collect approximately $1,000 of the charge sales made in the fiscal year ended June 30, 1980. They are unable to determine which of the charge customers will default on payment, but estimate based on a review of the customers that the amount will be approximately $1,000.

The appropriate adjusting entry is:

Bad Debt Expense (Sales Bad
    Debt Adjustment)   1,000
       Allowance for Uncollectible Accounts   1,000
To record estimated uncollectible accounts for the
FYE 6/30/80.

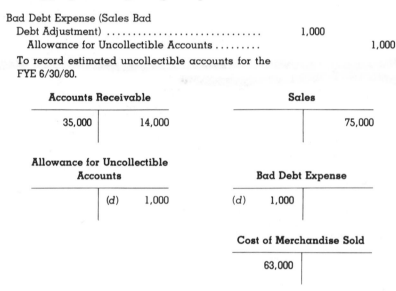

Accounts Receivable

| 35,000 | 14,000 |

Sales

| | 75,000 |

Allowance for Uncollectible Accounts

| | (d) | 1,000 |

Bad Debt Expense

| (d) | 1,000 | |

Cost of Merchandise Sold

| 63,000 | |

The debit to bad debt expense of $1,000 records the expense in the year the sales are made and results in the proper matching of revenue and expense.

Accounts receivable *cannot* be credited for the $1,000 because we do not know which of the store's customers will default. To solve this problem, an account called *allowance for uncollectible (doubtful) accounts* is created. This account is a contra asset account. It is deducted from the asset account, accounts receivable.

The formal balance sheet would show:

Accounts receivable... 21,000
    Less, allowance for uncollectible accounts   1,000   20,000

The balance sheet discloses to the reader that the store is owed $21,000 by customers, and that it expects to collect $20,000 of this amount.

Sometime in the future, when Joyce Markets finds out from their attorney that the $200 account of Mr. Rodgers cannot be collected, the following entry is made:

Allowance for Doubtful Accounts	200	
Accounts Receivable		200

To write off Mr. Rodgers' account as uncollectible.

Accounts Receivable

35,000			14,000
	(e)		200

Allowance for Uncollectible Accounts

(e)	200		1,000

This entry can be made now because the specific customer has been identified. In the subsidiary (individual accounts) ledger for accounts receivable, we would indicate on Rodgers's account that his balance was written off as uncollectible.

The balance sheet after the write-off would show:

Accounts receivable	20,800	
Less, allowance for uncollectible accounts	800	20,000

The store is now saying it is owed $20,800 and expects to collect $20,000. There is no effect from the write-off of an uncollectible account on the net amount ($20,000) expected to be collected.

Another possiblity in handling bad debts would be to record the expense in the year the accounts receivable became worthless. The problem with this direct write-off method is that it can result in the bad debt expense being recorded in a year other than the one in which the sale has occurred. In order to match revenue and expense properly, we should estimate the expense in the year the charge sale is made.

Sometimes, but not often, accounts which have been written off as uncollectible are collected at a later date. Assume that we collect $50 at a later date from Rodgers. The appropriate entry is to correct the write-off and treat the receipt as a collection of receivables. This entry should also be reflected on Rodgers's individual account receivable card in the subsidiary ledger.

Accounts Receivable	50	
Allowance for Uncollectible Accounts		50

To correct the write-off of $50 of Rodgers's account receivable.

Cash	50	
Accounts Receivable		50

To record the collection of $50 on Rodgers's account receivable.

BAD DEBT EXPENSE

It would be good disclosure to record the bad debt expense account as a deduction from sales on the formal income statement.

Sales	$75,000
Less, bad debt expense	1,000
Net sales	$74,000

In practice, the bad debt expense is usually listed with the other expenses rather than as a deduction from sales.

CORRECTING JOURNAL ENTRIES

An analysis of the general ledger accounts may reveal the need for a correcting journal entry due to an improper analysis or inaccurate posting of a transaction.

The bookkeeper charged (debited) repairs expense for the $12,000 cost of a new machine.

Cash		Repairs Expense	
xxx	12,000	12,000	

The journal entry to correct the error is:

Machinery	12,000	
Repairs Expense		12,000

To reclassify charge of $12,000 incorrectly made to Repairs Expense.

Machinery		Repairs Expense	
12,000		12,000	12,000

After this entry the repairs expense account has a zero balance ($12,000 − $12,000 = $0) and the asset account, machinery, is $12,000.

We will have to prepare adjusting entries whenever we prepare financial statements (monthly, quarterly, annually) if we are to measure accurately the amount of assets and equities on the balance sheet date and the revenue and expense amounts for the time frame covered by the income statement.

CASES FOR CHAPTER 3

Case 3–1 _____

Ye Olde Spirit Shoppe

For 15 years, Jack Crawford had worked as the manager of one of the 16 Tick Tock Liquor Stores in Jacksonville, Florida. In late 1979, Crawford decided to go into business for himself and began searching for a good location for his own retail liquor store. In October he found what he thought to be an ideal location: a 2,500-square-foot store in a newly opened shopping center on a busy intersection. Crawford asked the leasing agent to reserve the space for him while he applied for a city retail liquor license. The application was approved, and Crawford opened Ye Olde Spirit Shoppe on November 1, 1979.

Crawford realized that the first few months of business would be difficult, and therefore he planned to limit expenses to absolute essentials. He hoped to avoid the cost of an accountant by preparing his own financial statements and tax returns. On December 5, 1979, Crawford sat down at his desk to evaluate his first month of business. The following is a chronology of the store's November operations:

November 1 Jack Crawford opened a checking account at the Sunshine National Bank in the name of Ye Olde Spirit Shoppe, and deposited $15,000.

Signed a two-year lease calling for rent of $450 a month, to be paid in advance each month. Gave the leasing agent a check for the November rent.

Issued a $640 check to pay for a city retail liquor license for the remainder of the calendar year.

Arranged a $250,000 business liability insurance policy, and wrote a $391 check to pay for the first year's coverage.

Purchased and paid $890 for a new cash register. The salesman told Crawford that other store owners were getting ten years' use out of this type of register.

Accepted delivery of refrigerated display equipment costing $8,280. Made a $1,580 down payment, and signed a promissory note agreeing to pay the remainder on October 31, 1980, with interest at 12 percent per annum. Crawford expected the equipment to last at least 15 years.

Received $17,400 of wine, liquor, and beer from a local wholesaler who expected payment within 60 days. Crawford gave the delivery man a $150 check as a deposit on ten beer kegs.

November 8   Hired a salesclerk, agreeing to pay him at a rate of $130 a week. Payment was to be made once a month.

November 18   Ordered, but did not receive, another shipment of liquor and beer of $4,600 from his wholesaler. The terms of payment were the same as the previous order.

November 27   Took 22 bottles of table wine out of inventory and distributed them to his friends and relatives as a Thanksgiving gift. The wine's cost was $113, and its retail sales value was $143.

November 1–30   During November, Crawford had deposited a total of $7,744 in the Sunshine National Bank. This sum included $6,387 in cash sales and $1,357 in collections on credit sales. The amount owed by customers (accounts receivable) at the end of the month was $1,730.

November 30   Sent the liquor wholesaler a check for $9,500, and paid the December rent.

Received, but did not pay, $350 in utility and telephone bills for November.

✗   Crawford paid the salesclerk's salary for three weeks, deducting $25 from his check for the breakage of a case of wine the clerk had carelessly dropped.

Crawford wrote himself a $910 check on the business bank account for personal use, and cashed it at the bank.

Mr. Crawford and his clerk took a physical inventory by counting the unsold merchandise. After multiplying the quantities of wine, liquor, and beer by their unit wholesale cost, Crawford found that he had $10,850 in inventory.

Required:

1. Prepare general journal entries for all the transactions and make all necessary adjusting journal entries.

2. Post the journal entries to general ledger accounts.
3. Prepare financial statements (balance sheet and income statement) for November for Ye Old Spirit Shoppe.
4. Was Crawford successful?

Case 3–2
Severn Valley Publishing Company, Inc.

The Severn Valley Publishing Company, Inc., published the *Severn Chronicle*, a daily newspaper having a circulation of 75,000. The account balances in the general ledger for the fiscal year ending June 30, 1980, *before year-end adjusting entries*, are shown below:

Debit Balances

Cash	$ 112,660
Accounts receivable	451,860
Supplies inventory	75,720
Furniture, fixtures, and equipment	737,420
Prepaid insurance	7,800
Commission expense	45,600
Sales salaries	235,000
Printing expense	620,220
Production salaries	219,400
Administrative expense	474,640
Administrative salaries	169,800
Distribution expense	97,300
Payroll taxes	34,600
Interest expense	8,760
Miscellaneous general expense	119,400
	$3,410,180

Credit Balances

Allowance for bad debts	$ 18,600
Accumulated depreciation on furniture, fixtures, and equipment	186,460
Accounts payable	77,820
Notes payable	85,000
Common stock (20,000 shares, $10 par value)	200,000
Retained earnings	75,540
Current subscription income	1,143,060
Advertising income	1,463,020
Miscellaneous income	160,680
	$3,410,180

56

Adjusting entries are required for:

1. Depreciation on furniture, fixtures, and equipment .... $ 75,120
2. Estimated bad debts 37,660
3. Supplies consumed during the fiscal year 24,720
4. Accrued interest on notes payable 2,780
5. Production salaries earned but not paid 27,900
6. Current subscription income deferred to future
     periods 397,250
7. Expired insurance 2,600
8. Dividends declared on common stock, $5 per share
     payable to shareholders of record on June 30, 1980,
     payable July 15, 1981 100,000
9. Estimated federal income tax for the year 70,600

Required:

1. Set up T-accounts for the June 30, 1980, general ledger balances.
2. Journalize and post adjusting entries, adding other general ledger accounts as necessary.
3. Journalize and post the closing entry for the year.
4. Prepare an income statement and balance sheet.
5. Did the Severn Valley Company have a successful year?

Case 3–3

Venetian Publishing Company, Inc.

The Venetian Publishing Company published a monthly magazine which was only available by subscription. The subscription price for 12 issues was $12.

The trial balance (general ledger account balances) on December 31, 1980, after all transactions have been recorded but *before year-end adjusting entries*, is listed on the next page:

	Dr.	Cr.
Cash	$ 192,600	
Accounts receivable	592,000	
Allowance for bad debts		$ 4,500
Paper inventory	530,000	
Supplies inventory	76,000	
Unexpired insurance	34,800	
Furniture, fixtures, and equipment	1,066,000	
Accumulated depreciation—furniture, fixtures, and equipment		140,000
Accounts payable		95,600
Unearned (deferred) subscriptions		2,868,000
Notes payable		200,000
Common stock		70,000
Retained earnings		75,600
Advertising income		636,000
Production salaries	422,700	
Factory rent	180,000	
Light, heat, and power	74,600	
Maintenance and repairs	86,500	
Sales, salaries, and commissions	268,200	
Administrative salaries	337,600	
Interest expense	10,000	
Miscellaneous general and administrative expense	218,700	
	$4,089,700	$4,089,700

An analysis of these general ledger accounts by Venetian's accountant prior to the preparation of financial statements revealed the following:

Cash

Reconciliation of the bank statement and other analysis indicates that the cash balance reflected in the general ledger account is correct and doesn't need adjustment.

Accounts Receivable and Allowance for Doubtful Accounts

An adjusting entry is necessary to estimate bad debts for 1980. The company's bad debt policy is based on past experience and relates to the age of the accounts receivable on the balance sheet date.

Age of Receivables	Percent Estimated to Be Uncollectible
0– 30 days	.5
31– 60 days	1.0
61– 90 days	2.5
91–120 days	5.0
Over 120 days	10.0

For example, Venetian would expect 10 percent of all accounts receivable over 120 days old not to be collected.

An analysis of the general ledger accounts and the aging of the accounts receivable on 12/31/80 are shown below:

Accounts Receivable—Subscriptions

Balance 1/1/80	$ 152,000
Charge sales 1980	1,968,000
	$2,120,000
Collections 1980	1,520,000
Uncollectible accounts written off 1980	8,000
Balance 12/31/80	$ 592,000

Allowance for Doubtful Accounts

Balance 1/1/80	$ 12,500
Uncollectible accounts written off	8,000
Balance 12/31/80	$ 4,500

December 31, 1980, Aging of Accounts Receivable

0– 30 days	$ 300,000
31– 60 days	90,000
61– 90 days	80,000
91–120 days	70,000
Over 120 days	52,000
	$ 592,000

Paper Inventory

An adjusting entry is necessary to reflect the December 31, 1980, physical inventory of $156,000. The appropriate expense account for the paper used is printing materials consumed.

Supplies Inventory

An adjusting entry is necessary to reflect the December 31, 1980, inventory of $44,600. The appropriate expense account for supplies used is supplies expense.

Unexpired (Prepaid) Insurance

An adjusting entry is necessary to reflect the insurance coverage that has expired in 1980.

A schedule of all the insurance policies in force on 12/31/80:

Policy Dates	Types of Coverage	Premium
1-1-80 to 12-31-80	Workmen's compensation	$ 7,200
6-30-79 to 6-30-82	Liability $100,000/$1,000,000	18,000
1-1-80 to 12-31-82	Fire and extended coverage	12,600

The appropriate expense account for expired insurance is insurance expense.

Furniture, Fixtures, and Equipment and Accumulated Depreciation

An adjusting entry is necessary to record depreciation expense for 1980. A listing of the furniture, fixtures and equipment is shown below:

Date of Acquisition	Cost	Accumulated Depreciation 12-31-79	Depreciation Method	Estimated Life
1-1-76..............	$ 200,000	$ 80,000	Straight-line	10
6-30-78..............	400,000	60,000	Straight-line	10
6-30-80..............	350,000	—0—	Straight-line	10
12-31-80..............	116,000	—0—	Straight-line	10
	$1,066,000	$140,000		

Accounts Payable

The list of unpaid vendors' invoices is in agreement with the balance in the general ledger account and no adjusting entry is necessary.

Unearned Subscriptions (Deferred Income)

An adjusting entry is necessary to reflect magazines delivered in 1980.

The first issue of a subscription is delivered in the month following the receipt of the subscription. For example, if a subscription is received in February, the March issue will be the first one delivered to the subscriber.

An analysis of the unearned subscription account on December 31, 1980:

Balance 1-1-80 (subscriptions sold in 1979, magazines to be delivered in 1980)......................	$ 900,000
Subscriptions sold in 1980	1,968,000
Balance 12-31-80	$2,868,000

The appropriate income account for magazines delivered is subscription income.

Subscriptions (1980)

Date Sold	Number Sold	Amount
January....................	8,000	$ 96,000
February	10,000	120,000
March	10,000	120,000
April	8,000	96,000
May	10,000	120,000
June	11,000	132,000
July	12,000	144,000
August	15,000	180,000
September	15,000	180,000
October..................	20,000	240,000
November	20,000	240,000
December.................	25,000	300,000
	164,000	$1,968,000

Notes Payable

An adjustment is necessary to accrue the appropriate amount of interest expense on December 31, 1980.

Date Note Issued	Amount	Interest Rate	Interest Paid	Note Due
4-1-80.................	$200,000	10%	Quarterly	4-1-81

Income Tax Payable

An adjusting entry is necessary to accrue corporate income taxes using the following tax rates:

17 percent for the first $25,000 of taxable income.
20 percent for the next $25,000 of taxable income.
30 percent for the next $25,000 of taxable income.
40 percent for the next $25,000 of taxable income.
46 percent for all taxable income over $100,000.

Common Stock

No adjusting entry is necessary.

Retained Earnings

A closing entry is necessary to transfer net income for 1980 to retained earnings. An analysis of this account prior to this entry is:

Retained earnings 1-1-80	$175,600
Dividends declared and paid in 1980	100,000
	$ 75,600

Income and Expense Accounts

An analysis of the income (revenue) and expense accounts indicates that the only *additional* adjusting entry that needs to be made prior to the preparation of the financial statements is to accrue the payroll for the week ended December 31, 1980, which was paid on January 4, 1981.

Production salaries	$ 8,100
Sales salaries	4,000
Administrative salaries	6,500
Total	$18,600

Required:

1. Prepare a general ledger (T-account form) which includes all the accounts in the December 31, 1980, trial balance.
2. Prepare all the necessary adjusting journal entries and post these entries to the general ledger (T-accounts). Add any additional accounts you feel are necessary.
3. Prepare and post the closing journal entry.
4. Prepare an income statement for the year ended December 31, 1980, and a balance sheet as of December 31, 1980.

Case 3–4

Acton Racing, Inc.

"Bill, I have just reviewed the track's management contract with Management Group, Inc. (Exhibit 1), and the schedule of average daily handle (gross receipts) and racing days for the first six months of the year (Exhibit 2). I am having difficulty determining the correct

EXHIBIT 1 _____

Excerpts from a Contract between Acton Racing, Inc., and Management Group, Inc.

Acton Racing, Inc., agrees to compensate Management Group, Inc. for managerial services provided as follows:

> 1. In the event that racing is conducted at the Acton Track for 100 days or less, $150,000 per year.
> 2. For all racing days in excess of 100 days, 0.5 percent of the handle on each day that the handle is in excess of $225,000, provided, however, that the total amount paid to Management Group, Inc., shall not exceed $100,000, so that the total compensation to Management Group, Inc., shall not exceed $250,000 per year.
> 3. Compensation shall be paid to the Management Group, Inc., during the continuation of the racing meet or meets run during the year at the rate of $20,000 per month, with the balance, if any, to be paid within 30 days after the completion of the annual audit of Acton Racing, Inc., by its certified public accountant.

EXHIBIT 2 _____

1976	Average* Daily Handle	Racing Days
January	$380,000	25
February	420,000	24
March	475,000	26
April..................	460,000	26
May	410,000	26
June	325,000	25
		152

* For purposes of this problem, you may assume that the daily handle is equal to the average handle.

balance sheet and income statement figures for the management fee. My confusion is caused by the recent decision of the Racing Commission to allow the track (Acton Racing, Inc.) to operate for the entire year. The track will be open for 150 racing days for the period July 1, 1976, to December 31, 1976, in addition to the 152 racing days just completed for the first half of the year. I would really appreciate it if you could go over the possibilities with me."

This request was made by Sal Berns, staff accountant for Rogers and Rogers, a Massachusetts certified public accounting firm, to his supervisor, Bill Myers. The accounting firm was conducting an audit of Acton Racing, Inc., for the period January 1, 1976, to June 30, 1976. The Massachusetts Racing Commission required semiannual reports from Acton Racing. These reports were to include an unqualified opinion rendered by Acton Racing's auditors.

The books of Acton Racing, Inc., reflected an expense for management fees of $120,000 ($20,000 paid per month) for the period ended June 30, 1976. There was no liability for management fees payable recorded on June 30, 1976, balance sheet.

Required:

1. Assume you are Bill Myers. Explain to Sal Berns the amount you think should be recorded on the June 30, 1976, financial statements. Your explanation should include a computation of the June 30, 1976, liability and the expense for the six-month period ended June 30, 1976.
2. What journal entry would you suggest Acton Racing, Inc., make on their books, as of June 30, 1976?
3. The Management Group, Inc. is a corporation which provides complete management services to racetracks for a fee. They were required to prepare financial statements for the nine-month period ended September 30, 1976. Assume that the average handle at the Acton racetrack for the months of July through September were as follows: July, $200,000; August, $205,000; and September, $195,000.

   What should the Management Group, Inc. reflect as revenue earned from the Acton racetrack for the period January 1, 1976, to September 30, 1976?
4. Assume the monthly payments of $20,000 were made. How much should be reflected as Accounts Receivable—Acton Racing, Inc. on September 30, 1976?

Case 3–5

Medi Shoppe, Inc.

Medi Shoppe, Inc., a discount health and beauty aid store, incorporated in late 1979 and opened for business on January 2, 1980. The balance sheet as of that date is shown below:

MEDI SHOPPE, INC.
Balance Sheet
January 2, 1980

Assets

Current assets:

Cash	$ 2,240
Inventory	39,200
Total current assets	41,440

Fixed assets:

Building	98,000
Furniture and fixtures	24,360
Total assets	$163,800

Equities

Current liabilities:

Accounts payable	$ 16,800
Notes payable to bank	21,000
Total current liabilities	37,800
Mortgage on building	70,000
Capital stock	56,000
Total equities	$163,800

The capital stock was all owned by Theresa Weber. A checkbook was the only record that Weber kept to record Medi Shoppe, Inc.,'s business transactions.

At the end of the first year of operations, Weber asked Robert Anderson, a local CPA, to help prepare the annual financial statement required by the bank.

Anderson examined the Medi Shoppe checkbook and obtained the accompanying information:

MEDI SHOPPE, INC.
Record of Cash Receipts and Disbursements in 1980*

Cash receipts:

Cash sales	$377,720
Collections from customers—(these customers had received the merchandise but had not paid for it at the time of sale)	115,360
Total cash receipts	$493,080

Cash disbursements:

Advertising	$ 7,280
Insurance	2,800
Interest on bank loan	1,470
Maintenance and repairs	5,740
Merchandise purchases	302,400
Partial bank loan repayment on December 31, 1980	4,200
Payment of accounts payable	16,800
Property taxes	5,460
Selling expenses	19,880
Utilities	11,340
Wages and salaries	99,400
Total cash disbursements	$476,770

* Source: Medi Shoppe, Inc., Checkbook.

He also examined the file of unpaid bills to suppliers and unpaid customer accounts. While looking through the files, he also discovered other information he felt needed to be considered in preparing financial statements. This information is listed below:

1. Unpaid bills to suppliers (representing merchandise purchases)—$13,720.
2. Unpaid customer accounts—$9,940.
3. Interest at the rate of 8 percent on the mortgage was payable annually on January 1. No interest had been paid.
4. Wages and salaries were paid monthly on the third working day of the next month. Wages and salaries earned in December but not yet paid totaled $8,680.
5. Of the total insurance premium of $2,800 paid in 1980, $1,120 was for a health insurance policy expiring December 31, 1980, and $1,680 was for a fire insurance policy which was effective for three years, expiring December 31, 1982.
6. The estimated life of the store building was 35 years. The furniture and fixtures had an estimated life of ten years.
7. An inventory of merchandise on hand at the end of the year revealed goods in the store costing $58,800.
8. Interest at the annual rate of 7 percent on the bank loan was payable quarterly on the last day of each quarter. There were no delinquent interest charges in 1980.
9. Federal income tax rates for 1980 were:

   17 percent for the first $25,000 of taxable income.
   20 percent for the next $25,000 of taxable income.
   30 percent for the next $25,000 of taxable income.

40 percent for the next $25,000 of taxable income.

46 percent for all taxable income over $100,000.

Required:

1. Prepare a statement of income for 1980 and a balance sheet as of December 31, 1980.
2. Calculate the ratio of net income to sales and the ratio of net income to Weber's investment.
3. Was 1980 a successful year for Medi Shoppe, Inc.? For Weber?

Case 3–6

Associated Hardware

For the past ten years, two brothers, Frank and Roger Johnson, had operated a hardware store in a suburb of Boston. Although they kept only minimal accounting records, it seemed to them that they had been very successful. The store was always busy, and each partner had been able to draw a salary of $31,500.

In January 1981, Roger was offered a managerial position with a large chainstore operation on the West Coast. To help Roger make a decision, the two brothers decided to carefully evaluate the value of their business as of December 31, 1980. They hired a professional accountant, Roberta Franks, to prepare a balance sheet as of December 31, 1980, and an income statement for the past year.

Franks first prepared the accompanying trial balance as of January 1, 1980.

Trial Balance
January 1, 1980

	Dr.	Cr.
Cash	$ 29,925	
Accounts receivable	10,185	
Inventory	219,450	
Prepaid insurance	1,890	
Store fixtures and equipment	21,000	
Accumulated depreciation—equipment		$ 8,400
Accounts payable		7,795
Wages payable		235
Salaries payable		1,000
Capital—Roger Johnson		132,510
Capital—Frank Johnson		132,510
	$282,450	$282,450

She then examined the checkbook and bank statements for the year and prepared the accompanying list of *receipts and disbursements:*

Cash receipts
Cash sales	$210,000
Collections of charge sales...........................	
(accounts receivable)	7,875
Mortgage proceeds from Sunshine Bank	42,000
	$259,875

Cash disbursements
Payments to suppliers (accounts payable)..............	$ 96,000
Property taxes	420
Miscellaneous store expenses	3,675
Salaries—partners...................................	63,000
Wages—employees	15,750
Utilities	9,450
Shipping expenses	3,135
Payment—warehouse	51,870
Rent	3,780
	$247,080
Excess of receipts over disbursements	$ 12,795

Her examination also revealed the following additional information:

1. The prepaid insurance on the January 1, 1980, trial balance was for a fire contents policy that would provide coverage until June 30, 1981.
2. Associated Hardware pays rent for the hardware store at a rate of $315 per month.
3. The accounts receivable at the end of the year were $13,230. Included in this amount was $622, due from one customer, which had been owed for over one year. Further investigation revealed that the customer had moved out of town, and collection of this amount was considered unlikely.
4. Accounts payable on December 31, 1980, were $7,035.
5. Wages of $300 and partners' salaries of $1,200 for the week ended December 31, 1980, were not paid until January 4, 1981.
6. Because of the water damage that occurred during the winter and the need for additional space, the brothers purchased a building to be used as a warehouse on June 30, 1980.
   The closing statement for the purchase revealed the following:

Land	$ 8,190
Building	44,100
	$52,290
Less, property taxes, January 1, 1980	
to June 30, 1980	420
	$51,870

The 1980 property taxes are assessed based on a tax list date of January 1, 1980, with semiannual payments of the tax on July 1, 1980, and January 1, 1981. Associated Hardware made a payment of $420 representing one half of the year's tax on July 1, 1980.

7. They financed the building with partnership cash and a 10 percent mortgage for $42,000 taken out with the Sunshine Bank on June 30, 1980. The mortgage is payable in 40 equal semiannual principal payments with interest on the unpaid balance. Payments are to be made on January 1 and July 1 of each year.

8. Depreciation rates for the fixed assets were estimated as follows: Store fixtures and equipment, 10 percent and Warehouse, 2 percent.

9. The inventory on December 31, 1980, was counted and priced at $192,000. Included in the inventory figure were hardware tools that cost Associated $1,920, which had been ruined by water damage caused by flooding last January. Roger felt that this damaged inventory did not have any resale value. In the course of the discussion about the inventory, Frank remembered that they had made a donation of a Toro lawnmower, which cost them $521, to the high school. This lawnmower had a regular retail price of $837.

Required:

1. Prepare an income statement for the year ended December 31, 1980.
2. Prepare a balance sheet as of December 31, 1980.
3. Was the store successful in 1980?
4. What is the minimum salary Roger should request from the chainstore in order for him to consider leaving Associated Hardware?
5. If he leaves, how much should Frank pay him for his one-half interest in the partnership?

4

Accounting Principles

Accounting principles insure that financial statements are prepared within a consistent framework. The accounting principles used in the preparation of financial statements are called *generally accepted accounting principles* (GAAP).

Generally accepted accounting principles are established primarily by the Financial Accounting Standards Board (FASB) or the Securities and Exchange Commission (SEC).

The FASB promulgates new accounting principles and modifies existing principles in releases called Statements of Financial Accounting Standards (SFAS). These SFASs are based upon extensive research, preparation of exposure drafts, and responses to the exposure drafts by interested parties who are preparers and users of financial statements.

The SEC is the federal government agency charged with administering regulations relating to the disclosure of financial information by corporations whose stock is publicly traded. For the most part the SEC has delegated the rule-making authority to the FASB. The releases of the SEC are called Accounting Series Releases (ASR).

Prior to the establishment of the FASB in 1973 generally accepted accounting principles were formulated by the *Accounting Principles Board* (APB) of the *American Institute of Certified Public Accountants* (AICPA).

The 31 opinions previously issued by the APB were adopted by the FASB as being authoritative. The FASB has issued approximately 40 statements of financial accounting standards since its founding. These authoritative statements set standards for reporting particular financial transactions by firms.

Some general assumptions and concepts are accepted as underlying the construction of GAAP. These are:

1. The business entity.
2. The going concern.
3. The money measurement principle.
4. The cost principle.

5. Objective evidence.
6. Revenue realization.
7. The matching principle.
8. Conservatism.
9. Consistency.
10. Full disclosure.
11. Materiality.

1. THE BUSINESS ENTITY

In financial accounting, the entity is the specific business enterprise identified in the financial statements. The entity principle treats an enterprise as a separate unit, distinct from its owners and other suppliers of capital. The financial statements prepared for the enterprise present its operating performance and financial position and not those of stockholders, partners, proprietors, creditors, or other related parties.

2. THE GOING CONCERN

The going concern principle assumes an accounting entity operates indefinitely, in the absence of evidence to the contrary. Liquidation is not the usual expectation of business owners and managers, and it is not considered in conventional financial statements.

3. THE MONEY MEASUREMENT PRINCIPLE

Money is the common denominator of accounting. Accounting is concerned only with those events which can be measured in terms of dollars. The advantage this principle provides is that many heterogeneous facts about a business can be expressed in terms of numbers which can be added and subtracted. For example, although it may be true that a business firm owns $50,000 of cash, 10,000 pounds of raw material, eight machines, and 20,000 square feet of space, these items cannot be combined in any meaningful way for the readers of financial statements. By adhering to the money measurement principle (expressing these items in monetary terms, for example, $50,000 of cash, $30,000 of raw material, $80,000 of machines, $140,000 of building space) such addition is possible.

Two major difficulties are encountered when imposing the money measurement principle. First, accounting reports will never record important qualitative factors, such as the state of the president's health, the competence of management, the imminent possibility of a labor dispute, or the firm's competitive market situation.

The second difficulty is that the measurement unit, the dollar, changes in value over time due to inflation or deflation. A machine purchased for $10,000 in 1970, and a machine purchased for $10,000 in 1980, are both listed in the 1980 accounting records at their historical cost of $10,000, even though the purchasing power of $10,000 in 1980 is but a small percentage of what it was 10 years before.

4. THE COST PRINCIPLE

The cost principle requires assets to be recorded in the accounting records at their acquisition price (historical cost). All subsequent accounting for these assets is based on this initial cost.

For example, land purchased for $50,000 would be recorded at that amount (its acquisition cost). The fact that the market value of the land has appreciated over a period of time to $80,000 would not require any change in the accounting records. Uninformed readers of financial statements commonly believe that the amounts recorded for assets reflect their market value rather than their historical cost. As a general rule, the longer the asset has been owned by the company, the less likely it is that the amount at which it appears on the accounting records corresponds to its current market value.

In accordance with the cost principle, items which cannot be quantified in dollar terms will not appear on the records as assets; thus items such as a good reputation, a favorable location, organized distribution outlets, or an excellent management training program will never appear as assets on the balance sheet. Neither the death of a key executive nor a labor dispute will be recorded as a liability. All these events can change the real value of the company. These types of changes will typically be reflected in the market price of the company's common stock (which reflects investors' appraisal of value) but will not be recorded in the financial statements.

5. OBJECTIVE EVIDENCE

Accounting is based on verifiable, objective evidence. As used in an accounting sense, "objective" information refers to information that is free from personal bias or judgment. Objectivity connotes a high degree of reliability. Objectivity also implies verifiability, which means there is some feasible way of ascertaining the accuracy of the reported information.

Objective evidence can be illustrated using the cost principle. Some accountants argue that users of financial statements are more interested in the current cost of the company's assets than their original cost, and that the historical cost basis should therefore be discarded because it is not as meaningful a measure as current cost. Other members of the accounting profession would argue that the cost concept provides a relatively objective foundation for accounting and is certainly more objective than the alternative of attempting to estimate current cost. Essentially the developers of generally accepted accounting principles have suggested that the reader of financial statements must recognize that the statements are based on the cost principle, which is objective and verifiable. To obtain their own estimate of the current cost of assets, readers will have to supplement the financial information in the reports with other nonaccounting information.[1]

6. REVENUE REALIZATION

Revenue is any increase in owners' equity resulting from the operations of the business. Under generally accepted accounting principles, revenue results from three activities:

  a. selling products.
  b. rendering services and/or permitting others to use the firm's resources which results in revenue from interest, rent, royalties, and other sources.
  c. disposing of resources other than products (for example, selling a company truck).

Revenue is realized, and consequently recognized in the accounts, when a "critical event" occurs. The critical event in revenue realization is that point in the earnings process when the revenue has been *earned* and is capable of objective measurement. Revenue is "earned" when substantially all costs and efforts necessary to generate the revenue have been incurred and the amount to be received is nearly certain.

For most commercial enterprises the critical event occurs when ownership of the merchandise passes from the seller to the buyer. Service organizations recognize revenue at the time that they perform the services.

The revenue realization principle requires the use of the *accrual* method of accounting which records revenues when they are earned rather than when the cash is collected from the customer. The accrual method also requires the recording of expenses when they are incurred rather than when the cash for the expenditure is disbursed.

---

[1] Commencing October 1979, the largest corporations were required to disclose the current cost of many of their assets. *SFAS No. 33*, "Financial Reporting and Changing Prices," October 1979.

7. THE MATCHING PRINCIPLE

Closely related to the realization principle is the matching principle which states that expenses recognized in an accounting period are "matched" against the revenues recognized in that period. Expenses can be defined as any decrease in owners' equity resulting from the operation of a business. The excess of the revenues over expenses (the end result of the matching process) is called *net income*.[2]

The total cost of the product shipped to a customer (cost of goods sold) is recognized as an expense in the same period that the revenue from the sale of the product is recorded.

Expenses incurred in producing revenue are matched against the revenue produced. For example, if a salesperson received an advance commission for selling a product which is to be shipped and recognized as revenue next year, then the commission (although a cash outlay of this year will be recognized as an expense next year.

The word *cost* or *expenditure* is not synonymous with the word *expense*. Cost refers to the price paid for goods or services: It is a monetary sacrifice. An expense is an *expired cost*—it represents a decrease in owners' equity in the specific period in which it is matched against the appropriate revenues.

The first step of the "matching" process is to determine what revenues are to be recognized in a given accounting period; the second step is to determine the expenses (expired costs) associated with these revenues.

If certain costs or expenditures cannot be matched against specific items of revenue, they are charged to expenses in the period in which they are incurred. A salesperson's salary, received whether or not sales are made, as contrasted to a commission paid on a specific sale, is an example. The salesperson's salary is recorded as an expense in the period the salesperson earned it. The sales commission is recorded as an expense in the period in which the related sales revenue is recognized.

8. CONSERVATISM

The concept of conservatism suggests that when given a choice of two acceptable alternatives, the accountant should record transac-

---

[2] Accounting income differs from economic income. Economic income is generally defined as the amount that can be consumed or distributed by an entity, leaving itself as well off at the end of the period as it was at the beginning of the period.

The accountants, viewing income as the objectively determined residual of the matching process, recognize only realized changes and do not consider unrealized gains due to increases in the current value of assets, price level movements, or expected future business events.

tions so as not to overstate assets or income. The concept is often stated as: "Anticipate no profit, and provide for all possible losses."

The conservatism principle serves as a modifier to the cost concept. An illustration of this convention is its application to the asset, inventory. Inventory is recorded at either its acquisition cost or current replacement cost, whichever is *lower*. If inventory declines in value below acquisition cost, conservatism implies that the loss in value will be recognized immediately.

9. CONSISTENCY

The doctrine of consistency requires that once a business has adopted a particular accounting procedure or method, it will treat all subsequent events of the same basic nature in the same manner. The purpose of the consistency concept is to allow for comparability of performance and financial status over different accounting time periods.

The company's auditors, in summarizing their study of the firm's financial reports, annually state that the figures were prepared "in conformity with generally accepted accounting principles applied on a basis *consistent* with that of the preceding year." If there was a significant change in practice, it must be spelled out in the auditor's opinion. The auditor must also indicate the effect of the change on the financial statements and whether the changed practice is preferable to the prior one.

10. FULL DISCLOSURE

The standard of full and adequate disclosure holds that management should reveal all significant financial data so that an informed person will not be misled. Information should be presented in a way which facilitates understanding and avoids erroneous implications with emphasis on the information needs of existing and potential investors.

11. MATERIALITY

The concept of materiality refers to the accountants' concern with significant items. They are not concerned with items that have little impact on financial statements.

SUMMARY—THE OPINION OF THE INDEPENDENT CERTIFIED PUBLIC ACCOUNTANT

Upon completion of the audit, the CPA attests to the reasonableness of the statements by issuing an audit opinion. The opinion is published as an integral part of the company's annual report. Because of its importance, the wording of the audit opinion has been carefully scrutinized and a standard form developed. Considering the extensive investigation that precedes it, the audit opinion is uncommonly short. Generally it consists of two paragraphs: the first relates to the scope of the examination, and the second presents the CPA's opinion of the financial statements. A typical opinion might be:

> We have examined the balance sheet of the XYZ Company as of September 30, 19XX, and the related statements of income, retained earnings, and changes in financial position for the year then ended. Our examination was made in accordance with generally accepted auditing standards and accordingly included such tests of the accounting records, and such other auditing procedures as we considered necessary in the circumstances.
>
> In our opinion, the above financial statements present fairly the financial position of the XYZ Company at September 30, 19XX, and the results of its operations and the changes in its financial position for the year then ended, in conformity with generally accepted accounting principles applied on a basis consistent with that of the preceding year.

If the auditor is not satisfied that the financial statements are fairly presented in accordance with GAAP, the standard form is modified to denote the reasons for dissatisfaction.

Financial statements are issued by the management of the firm. The CPA does not guarantee the accuracy of the statements, but renders his opinion as to their *fairness*. The primary responsibility for the accuracy of the financial reports rests with management.

CASES FOR CHAPTER 4

Case 4-1

Crackerjohn Corporation

Crackerjohn Corporation
Comparative Balance Sheets
December 31, 1981 and 1980

	1981	1980
Assets		
Cash	$ 4,000	$ 8,000
Other current assets	22,000	24,000
Property, plant, and equipment (net of depreciation)	24,000	24,000
	$50,000	$56,000
Equities		
Current liabilities	$12,000	$20,000
Common stock	24,000	24,000
Retained earnings	14,000	12,000
	$50,000	$56,000

Crackerjohn Corporation
Statement of Income and Increase in Retained Earnings
For the Year Ended December 31, 1981

Sales	$60,000
Cost of goods sold	35,000
Gross profit	25,000
Selling, general, and administrative expense	20,000
Net income (before income taxes)	5,000
Income taxes	2,000
Net income	3,000
Dividends	1,000
Increase in retained earnings	$ 2,000

In reviewing the above statements the sales manager of Crackerjohn Corporation made the following observations. You are to comment on each of these observations.

1. The balance sheet of December 31, 1981, must be incorrect because it shows assets of only $50,000. The inventories alone could be sold for $24,000, and we had an offer of $40,000 for the plant last week.
2. We really don't have to be too concerned about the company's cash position. If an emergency arises, we can always use the retained earnings.
3. Sales for the year must be understated. A tabulation of all the sales orders obtained by the salespeople for 1981 amounted to $65,000, and there were no sales returns, allowances, or discounts.
4. These statements are all fouled up. The income statement shows net income of $3,000 for the year, and yet the assets of the company are less now than they were at the beginning of the year.
5. Included in selling, general, and administrative expenses on the income statement is an item of $1,400 for property taxes. I don't understand why this should be included, as these property taxes don't have to be paid until next month.

Case 4–2
The Pepper Manufacturing Company

The Pepper Manufacturing Company was incorporated and began business on January 1, 1981. It has been successful and now requires a bank loan for additional working capital (current assets − current liabilities) to finance expansion. The bank has requested an income statement for the year 1981. Pepper's accountant has provided the president with the accompanying income statement to submit to the bank:

Sales		$832,100
Dividends		12,300
Gain on condemnation of land (extraordinary)		28,400
		872,800
Less:		
Selling expenses	$101,100	
Cost of goods sold	532,200	
Advertising expense	13,700	
Loss on obsolescence of inventories	34,000	
Loss on discontinued operations	48,600	
Administrative expense	73,400	803,000
Income before income taxes		69,800
Income taxes		31,400
Net income		$ 38,400

Required:

1. Are certain revenues of higher quality than others? Explain.
2. Are certain expenses more likely to recur? What is their significance?
3. How would you recast this income statement to make it more useful to the reader?

Case 4–3

Alcolac, Inc. (A)

The comparative consolidated balance sheet of Alcolac, Inc., as of June 30, 1975, and June 30, 1974, is shown below:

ALCOLAC, INC.
Consolidated Balance Sheets
June 30, 1975 and June 30, 1974

	1975	1974
Assets		
Current assets:		
Cash	$ 1,098,487	$ 317,842
Accounts receivable, trade, net of allowance for doubtful accounts of $94,982 in 1975 and $108,221 in 1974	3,111,754	3,623,757
Inventories:		
Finished goods	1,584,154	1,285,843
Raw materials and supplies	1,572,124	1,538,931
Prepaid expenses	223,394	109,414
Total current assets	$ 7,589,913	$ 6,875,787
Fixed assets:		
Land	$ 202,794	$ 302,794
Buildings and equipment, at cost	$ 7,992,327	$ 7,421,071
Less: Accumulated depreciation	4,175,097	3,776,850
	$ 3,817,230	$ 3,644,221
Total fixed assets	$ 4,020,024	$ 3,947,015
Other assets:		
Investments	$ 226,757	$ 220,235
Other assets and investments, at cost	555,933	244,466
Total assets	$12,392,627	$11,287,503

Liabilities and Stockholders' Equity

Current liabilities:

Accounts payable, trade	$ 1,442,401	$ 1,619,808
Notes payable to banks	253,000	48,644
Accrued liabilities	286,822	545,302
Income taxes payable......................	846,897	886,157
Current portion of long-term debt	150,000	190,000
Total current liabilities	$ 2,979,120	$ 3,289,911
Long-term debt	988,408	1,259,038

Stockholders' equity:

Preferred stock, 5 percent cumulative, convertible, $100 par value, 250,000 shares authorized..............................	—	—
Common stock, par value 10¢, authorized 3,000,000 shares, issued 1,437,673 shares in 1975 and 1,473,171 shares in 1974	143,767	147,317
Additional paid-in capital.................	4,249,913	4,322,992
Retained earnings	4,037,627	2,279,694
	$ 8,431,307	$ 6,750,003
Less: Treasury stock, common, at cost: 1,356 shares in 1975; 2,162 shares in 1974.................................	6,208	11,449
Total stockholders' equity	$ 8,425,099	$ 6,738,554
Total liabilities and stockholders' equity.......................	$12,392,627	$11,287,503

Required:

Study the Alcolac, Inc., financial statement and answer the following questions.

1. What inferences can you draw from the data about:
   a. Type of business? Manufacturing or service?
   b. Profitability?
   c. Methods of financing the assets?
2. Is Alcolac, Inc., in danger of bankruptcy? List supporting reasons for your conclusion.
3. Identify the new asset, liability and stockholder equity accounts. Deduce a working definition of each new account from the terminology and location on the balance sheet.

Case 4–4

Alcolac, Inc. (B)

Following is the comparative income statement for Alcolac, Inc., for the fiscal years ending June 30, 1975, and June 30, 1974. The complementing balance sheets are provided in the Alcolac, Inc. (A) case. What inferences can you draw about the type(s) of business, profitability, operating efficiency, and dividend paying capacity of Alcolac, Inc.?

ALCOLAC, INC.
Statement of Income and Retained Earnings
For the Year Ended June 30, 1975, and 1974

	1975	1974
Sales	$23,691,850	$20,953,732
Sub-contracting revenue	2,881,251	1,841,423
	$26,573,101	$22,795,155
Cost of goods sold	17,190,836	14,804,762
Gross profit	$ 9,382,265	$ 7,990,393
Other costs and expenses:		
Selling, general, and administrative	4,564,554	4,161,908
Research and development expenses	559,048	562,334
Other charges, including interest expense of $107,392 in 1975 and $138,809 in 1974	278,171	203,157
	$ 5,401,773	$ 4,927,399
Income from continuing operations	$ 3,980,492	$ 3,062,994
Miscellaneous other income	62,469	21,005
Net income before taxes	$ 4,042,961	$ 3,083,999
Provision for income taxes	2,056,673	1,629,892
Net income	$ 1,986,288	$ 1,454,107
Earnings per common and common equivalent share—based on 1,453,717 and 1,471,727 average shares outstanding in 1975 and 1974:		
Earnings per share	$1.37	$.99
Retained earnings:		
Balance, June 30, 1974		$2,279,694
Add: Net income		1,986,288
		$4,265,982
Less: Cash dividends—$.155 per share		228,355
Balance, June 30, 1975		$4,037,627

Case 4–5

Stirling Homex

Refer to the financial statements and answer the following questions:

1. When does Stirling Homex recognize revenue? What is the critical event? Why do you suppose management uses a different revenue recognition method for the Manufacturing Division (sales of modules) than they use for the Installation Division (installation work)?

2. The staff of the Securities and Exchange Commission in reviewing Stirling Homex's 1971 registration statement questioned the validity of recognizing revenue in advance of the date the customer was invoiced and asked Stirling Homex to revise its financial statements to defer recognition ot income to the point at which the amount recorded was validly billable to customers.[1]

Recast Stirling Homex's income statement for the fiscal year ended July 31, 1971, and its balance sheet as of July 31, 1971, in accordance with the SEC request. Assume the increase in 1971 unbilled current receivables relates to 1971 sales and that unbilled current receivables are approximately 80 percent from the Manufacturing Division and 20 percent from the Installation Division.

3. During a meeting with the SEC attended by its auditor,[2] and in a written statement submitted shortly after the meeting, Stirling Homex set forth its rationale for the allocation of the total contract price between the module manufacturing phase and the installation phase and represented that no sales were recognized with respect to module manufacturing unless the following five conditions were met:

a. The company must be designated by the LHA (Local Housing Authority) nonprofit sponsor or other agencies as the contractor for the project. This designation is supported by a formal commitment from the customer to the company.

b. The customer must have obtained and submitted evidence to the company that a commitment of monies to fund the project has been obtained from the appropriate governmental agency under which the project has sponsorship.

c. The numbers and types of modules and the general site plan

---

[1] Accounting Series Release 173, July 2, 1975.
[2] Ibid.

and improvements must be identified and be the subject of the agreement between the company and its customers.

d. The company must assign the manufactured module to a specific project and physically identify the module as being assigned to and reserved exclusively for the specific project and customer. (This identification was to be physically attached at the earliest stage of the manufacture of the module.)

e. The module must be completed and be ready for shipment to the customer.

4. Should the SEC have *required* Stirling Homex to change their revenue recognition method? Should the auditors have rendered an opinion on Stirling Homex's financial statements for the year ended July 31, 1971?

STIRLING HOMEX CORPORATION AND CONSOLIDATED SUBSIDIARIES
Consolidated Balance Sheets July 31, 1971
With Comparative Figures for 1970

	1971	1970
Assets		
Current assets:		
Cash (Note 11)	$ 3,196,457	$ 2,778,077
Preferred stock proceeds receivable (Note 2)..........	19,000,000	—
Receivables (Notes 1 and 3)	37,845,572	15,486,119
Inventories (Note 5):		
Raw materials, work in process and salable merchandise at lower of cost (first-in, first-out) or replacement market	2,614,200	2,167,603
Land held for development or sale, at cost	1,878,343	1,583,621
Prepaid expenses and other current assets	226,530	124,765
Total current assets	$64,761,102	$22,140,185
Investment in unconsolidated subsidiary (Note 1)......	$ 1,134,579	—
Long-term receivables (Note 4)......................	4,225,349	$ 541,124
Property, plant, and equipment at cost, less accumulated depreciation and amortization: 1971— $733,705; 1970—$230,921 (Notes 6 and 8)	9,426,941	5,245,745
Deferred charges, less accumulated amortization: 1971—$586,011; 1970—$153,894 (Note 7)	2,558,792	944,109
	$82,106,763	$28,871,163

	1971	1970
Liabilities and Stockholders' Equity		
Current liabilities:		
Current portion of long-term debt (Note 8)	$ 295,630	$ 333,036
Notes payable to banks—unsecured (1971—6 to 6½ percent; 1970—8 to 8½ percent) (Note 11)	37,700,000	11,700,000
Accounts payable.................................	4,025,254	2,480,834
Due to unconsolidated subsidiary (Note 1)............	76,894	—
Accrued expenses and other liabilities...............	577,377	232,819
Current and deferred income taxes (Note 9)	3,528,125	1,387,338
Total current liabilities	$46,203,280	$16,134,027
Long-term debt (Note 8)	$ 236,588	$ 496,489
Deferred income taxes (Note 9)	2,098,767	587,265
Option deposit on land contract (Note 5)	235,000	—
Stockholders' equity:		
$2.40 cumulative convertible preferred stock (Note 2): Authorized 500,000 shares, $1 par value; shares subscribed: 1971—500,000 (aggregate involuntary liquidation value—$20 million); 1970—none	500,000	—
Common stock (Notes 2 and 10): Authorized 15 million shares, $.01 par value; shares issued: 1971—8,909,200; 1970—8,897,400	89,092	88,974
Additional paid-in capital (Note 2)..................	26,554,453	8,446,738
Retained earnings	6,370,333	3,117,670
	$33,513,878	$11,653,382
Less treasury stock at cost (60,000 shares)	180,750	—
Total stockholders' equity	$33,333,128	$11,653,382
Commitments and contingencies (Note 11)		
	$82,106,763	$28,871,163

STERLING HOMEX CORPORATION AND CONSOLIDATED SUBSIDIARIES
Consolidated Statement of Income
Year Ended July 31, 1971, with Comparative Figures for 1970

	1971	1970
Revenues:		
Manufacturing division—trade (Note 3)	$29,482,271	$16,492,770
Installation division (Note 3):		
Trade	7,230,878	5,601,357
Affiliate	—	459,941
Equity in undistributed net income of subsidiary (Note 1)......................................	134,579	—
Total revenues	$36,847,728	$22,554,068

	1971	1970
Costs and expenses:		
Cost of sales:		
Manufacturing division	$17,729,078	$ 9,919,327
Installation division	6,601,413	5,240,388
Administrative and selling expenses	4,048,113	2,390,604
Interest expense	1,838,461	648,181
Total costs and expenses	$30,217,065	$18,198,500
Income before federal and state income taxes	$ 6,630,663	$ 4,355,568
Federal and state income taxes (Note 9):		
Current	$ 368,000	$ 1,965,982
Deferred	3,010,000	354,397
	$ 3,378,000	$ 2,320,379
Net income	$ 3,252,663	$ 2,035,189
Average common shares outstanding (Note 12)	8,881,938	8,649,483
Earnings per common share (Note 12)	$ .37	.24

STIRLING HOMEX CORPORATION AND CONSOLIDATED SUBSIDIARIES
Consolidated Statement of Changes in Financial Position
Year Ended July 31, 1971, with Comparative Figures for 1970

	1971	1970
Source of working capital:		
Net income	$ 3,252,663	$ 2,035,189
Expenses not requiring outlay of working capital:		
Depreciation and amortization	529,116	220,227
Amortization of deferred charges	432,117	133,288
Deferred income taxes (noncurrent)	1,511,502	184,776
Undistributed net income of finance subsidiary	(134,579)	—
Working capital provided from operations	$ 5,590,819	$ 2,573,480
Net proceeds from sales of stock:		
Public offering of common stock	—	5,985,715
Private sale of common stock	—	516,500
Common stock issued under qualified stock option plan	37,200	—
Public offering of preferred stock	18,570,633	—
Long-term borrowings	51,402	124,677
Decrease in long-term receivables	10,000	43,421
Option deposit received on land contract	235,000	—
Total source of working capital	$24,495,054	$ 9,243,793

	1971	*1970*
Application of working capital:		
Purchase of treasury stock	$ 180,750	—
Additions to property, plant, and equipment	4,710,312	$ 4,422,506
Additions to deferred charges	2,046,800	735,093
Reduction in long-term debt	311,303	3,052,140
Increase in noncurrent portion of long-term receivables	3,694,225	—
Investment in unconsolidated subsidiary	1,000,000	—
Total application of working capital	$11,943,390	$ 8,209,739
Increase in working capital	$12,551,664	$ 1,034,054

	1971	*1970*
Changes in working capital:		
Increase in current assets:		
Cash	$ 418,380	$ 1,357,917
Preferred stock proceeds receivable	19,000,000	—
Receivables*	22,359,453	12,286,631
Inventories	741,319	1,236,215
Prepaid expenses and other current assets	101,765	34,973
	$42,620,917	$14,915,736

	1971	*1970*
Increase in current liabilities:		
Current portion of long-term debt and notes payable to banks	$25,962,594	$10,721,700
Accounts payable and accrued expenses	1,888,978	2,155,635
Due to unconsolidated subsidiary	76,894	—
Current and deferred income taxes	2,140,787	1,004,347
	$30,069,253	$13,881,682
Increase in working capital	$12,551,664	$ 1,034,054

* During the year ended July 31, 1971, the Company assigned $4,650,000 of its accounts receivable, without recourse, to an unconsolidated subsidiary for which that subsidiary paid $4,650,000 to the Company. See Note 1.

STIRLING HOMEX CORPORATION AND CONSOLIDATED SUBSIDIARIES
Consolidated Statements of Additional Paid-in Capital and Retained Earnings
Year Ended July 31, 1971, with Comparative Figures for 1970

	1971	1970
Additional Paid-in Capital		
Balance at beginning of period	$ 8,446,738	$1,949,813
Excess of proceeds over par value of 400,000 shares of common stock issued in public offering (less expenses of $118,285)	—	5,981,715
Excess of proceeds over par value of 129,000 shares of common stock issued in private sales (less applicable expenses)	—	515,210
Excess of proceeds over par value of 500,000 shares of preferred stock issued in public offering (less expenses of $429,367) (Note 2)	18,070,633	—
Excess of proceeds over par value of 11,800 common shares issued under stock options (Note 10)	37,082	—
Balance at end of period	$26,554,453	$8,446,738
Retained Earnings		
Balance at beginning of period	$ 3,117,670	$1,082,481
Net income	3,252,663	2,035,189
Balance at end of period	$ 6,370,333	$3,117,670

NOTES TO CONSOLIDATED FINANCIAL STATEMENTS JULY 31, 1971

Note 1. Principles of Consolidation.—The consolidated financial statements include the accounts of the company and its subsidiaries except for U.S. Shelter Corporation, its financing subsidiary (all of which are wholly owned). The company carries its investment in all subsidiaries at equity in the underlying net assets. On consolidation all significant accounts and transactions with consolidated subsidiaries have been eliminated.

The following are condensed financial statements of the unconsolidated financing subsidiary:

Balance Sheet
July 31, 1971

Assets

Cash	$ 5,171
Accounts receivable—unbilled*	4,950,000
Other assets	24,593
Due from parent company	76,894
	$5,056,658

Liabilities and Stockholder's Equity

Notes payable—bank (7 percent)†	$3,750,000
Payables, accruals, and other liabilities	172,079
Stockholder's equity	1,134,579
	$5,056,658

Statement of Income
From Date of Incorporation
September 25, 1970 to July 31, 1971

Finance income	$ 544,946
General and administrative expenses (including interest expense of $54,917)	263,367
	$ 281,579
Federal and state income taxes—current	147,000
Net income	$ 134,579

* Accounts receivable includes $4,650,000 relating to accounts assigned to U.S. Shelter by the company for which U.S. Shelter remitted cash.

† The subsidiary has obtained an unsecured $15,000,000 line of credit from a bank. These funds are being used in financing transactions involving customers of the company. The company has not guaranteed this line of credit.

Note 2. Preferred Stock Offering.—On July 29, 1971, the company, through its underwriters, offered 500,000 shares of $2.40 cumulative convertible preferred stock to the public at $40 per share. Net proceeds of $19 million, after deducting an underwriting discount, were received by the Company on August 5, 1971. Additional paid-in capital has been credited with the net proceeds received less the par value of the stock issued ($500,000) and expenses related to the offering ($429,367).

The preferred stock is nonvoting except for certain defined events which would significantly affect the preferred stockholders' equity interests. The preferred shares are convertible into 1,379,310 common shares subject to adjustment in certain events, including stock split-ups and stock dividends. At its option, the company may redeem the preferred stock at an initial price of $50 per share, as of August 1, 1971, ranging downward annually to $40 per share as of August 1, 1981, and thereafter.

Note 3. Receivables.—The company enters into various modular housing sales contracts which contain an allocation of the sales price between modules (based upon published price lists) and installation work. Sales of modules (Manufacturing Division) are recognized when units are manufactured and assigned to specific contracts. Installation work (Installation Division) is recorded on the percentage of completion method. The contracts generally provide for payment upon completion and receipt of all approvals necessary for occupancy, or for payment upon completion of each respective phase. "Unbilled" receivables represent recorded sales on contracts in process for which billings will be rendered in the future in accordance with the contracts.

	July 31, 1971	July 31, 1970
Contract receivables:		
Billed..................................	$10,382,626	$10,559,145
Unbilled	24,633,799	4,626,370
Total	$35,016,425	$15,185,515
Income tax refund receivable (Note 9)	2,498,672	—
Current portion of long-term receivables (Note 4)	12,500	17,500
Other receivables	317,975	283,104
	$37,845,572	$15,486,119

Substantially all sales are to local housing authorities and sponsors who qualify for financial assistance from federal agencies of the U.S. government or who have made arrangements for long-term financing. In light of this, no provision for doubtful accounts is considered necessary.

See the condensed financial statements of U.S. Shelter Corporation in Note 1 for information with respect to receivables assigned by the company to U.S. Shelter Corporation.

Note 4. Long-Term Receivables.—Long-term receivables consist of:

	July 31, 1971	July 31, 1970
Mortgages receivable:		
Mortgage due June 1, 1974—payments of $2,500 due quarterly with interest at the prime commercial rate in effect on the interest payment date	$ 241,624	$256,624
Mortgage due June 30, 1975—payments of $25,000 due June 30, 1973, and June 30, 1974, and the balance due June 30, 1975. Interest payable annually at the prime commercial rate in effect on the interest payment date	302,000	302,000
	$ 543,624	$558,624
Less installments due within one year (Note 3)	12,500	17,500
	$ 531,124	$541,124
Long-term portion of contract receivables—unbilled..	3,694,225	—
	$4,225,349	$541,124

The mortgage notes are secured by mortgages on the property sold.

Note 5. Inventories.—Inventories of the company consist of the following:

	July 31, 1971	July 31, 1970
Raw materials	$1,439,960	$ 963,664
Work in process	1,001,632	139,531
Salable merchandise	172,608	1,064,408
	$2,614,200	$2,167,603

Land held for development or sale is recorded at cost plus real estate taxes, mortgage interest, and other related carrying costs. The company has entered into a contract to sell a parcel of the land with costs of $673,017 for a sale price of $2.1 million. The company has received nonrefundable payments of $235,000 which have been accounted for as an option deposit.

Note 6. Property, Plant, and Equipment.—Property, plant, and equipment consist of the following:

	Useful Life	July 31, 1971	July 31, 1970
Land and land improvements	20	$ 1,136,499	$1,002,067
Buildings	10 and 45	4,822,055	1,702,924
Machinery, equipment, and tools	2–10	1,735,396	1,071,515
Furniture, fixtures, and office equipment	5–10	942,131	500,951
Other	1–15	135,952	27,998
Construction in progress		1,388,613	1,171,211
		$10,160,646	$5,476,666
Less accumulated depreciation and amortization		733,705	230,921
		$ 9,426,941	$5,245,745

The straight-line method of depreciation is used for all depreciable assets. Depreciation expense for the years ended July 31, 1971, and 1970, is $529,116 and $220,227; respectively.

Note 7. Deferred Charges.—The unamortized balance of deferred charges consist of:

	Amortization Period	Unamortized Balance	
		July 31, 1971	July 31, 1970
Patents pending and trademarks	Legal life	$ 171,680	$ 88,660
Training and professional development	3 years	491,641	148,636
Research and development	5 years	671,897	84,496
Project and production start-up costs	2 to 5 years	844,028	503,539
Property acquisition costs	*	379,546	118,778
		$2,558,792	$944,109

* Expenditures in connection with property acquisition will be added to the cost of property subsequently acquired.

In the event of project abandonment or other circumstances causing a loss of value to deferred items, the related unamortized costs are charged to current operations.

Note 8. Long-Term Debt.—Long-term debt consists of the following:

	July 31, 1971	July 31, 1970
Mortgages maturing at various dates through December 31, 1976, and bearing interest at rates ranging from 4¾ percent to 6 percent	$443,176	$704,615
Installment contracts and lease purchase agreements maturing at various dates through August 1974	89,042	124,910
	$532,218	$829,525
Less payments due within one year	295,630	333,036
	$236,588	$496,489

Land, buildings, and equipment with a net book value of $2,223,803 and $2,232,091 as of July 31, 1971, and July 31, 1970, respectively, are encumbered under the above agreements.

Note 9. Income Taxes.—Deferred taxes relate principally to manufacturing division and installation division sales, depreciation, deferred costs, and capitalized costs. None of the company's tax returns have been examined by the Internal Revenue Service. The tax refund included in Note 3 relates to refundable advance tax payments and the planned amendment of the prior year's tax returns.

Note 10. Stock Options.—The company has a qualified stock option plan in effect whereby options to purchase shares of common stock may be granted to officers and key employees at not less than the fair market value on the date of grant. During February 1971, authorized shares under the plan were increased from 400,000 to 900,000 shares. Options expire five years after the date of grant and are exercisable in cumulative installments of 20 percent after one year. A summary of activity for the year ended July 31, 1971, follows:

	Option price per share		Shares
	From	To	
Options outstanding at July 31, 1970.....	$ 3.00	$16.50	399,300
New options granted	15.13	22.00	275,500
Less: Options exercised	3.00	12.00	(11,800)
Cancellations	3.00	19.25	(61,900)
Options outstanding at July 31, 1971.....	3.00	22.00	601.100
Options outstanding at July 31, 1971 which are currently exercisable	3.00	16.50	58,360

No entries are recorded with respect to options until exercised at which time the excess of the option price over the par value of common stock issued is credited to additional paid-in capital.

Note 11. *Commitments and Contingencies.*—An action has been brought to enjoin the use of the word "Homex" by the company. In the opinion of legal counsel, the plaintiff will be unsuccessful in obtaining the relief which it seeks.

A former shareholder of restricted shares of company common stock has brought an action against the company and another party, a broker. It is claimed that the company refused, in concert with the other defendant, to permit the transfer of plaintiff's stock except at a price substantially below its alleged market price. Compensatory damages in the amount of $1,575,000 and treble damages are alleged. In the opinion of management, the suit can be successfully defended. In the opinion of counsel, the claim for treble damages is without merit.

The company is engaged in other disputes involving claims which, in the aggregate, are insignificant compared to the company's net worth.

Construction of a manufacturing plant in Mississippi is expected to be commenced in the latter part of 1971 at an approximate cost of $4.9 million. In a contract with the company, Harrison County (where the plant site is located) has agreed to take the steps necessary to authorize the issuance and sale of tax-exempt industrial revenue bonds in an amount necessary to meet the cost of constructing and equipping the plant. The contract also provides for a 30-year lease to the company of the completed facility and the related land. Semiannual payments in respect of the bonds will be based on principal and interest requirements: An additional $36,325 is due annually for the land. Options to purchase the plant and the land are provided for during and at the end of the lease term. If the bond offering is not consummated, the company will arrange to finance the cost of the facility itself.

At July 31, 1971, the company had leases on various equipment and office facilities with terms ranging from two to six years. Minimum annual rentals under such leases amount to approximately $404,000.

Notes payable consist of 90-day unsecured notes to 11 banks bearing interest at a rate ½ percent above the respective bank's best rate on the date of issue. The company is required to maintain average annual compensating cash balances at each of these banks equal to approximately 15 percent to 20 percent of the outstanding indebtedness to such bank.

Note 12. *Earnings per Share.*—Earnings per common share are based upon the weighted average number of common shares outstanding during the periods presented after giving retroactive effect to the four for one stock split effected in February 1970. The preferred stock is not considered a common stock equivalent in accordance with *Opinion No. 15* of the Accounting Principles Board of the American Institute of Certified Public Accountants. In addition, the effect of the preferred stock offering, for the fiscal year ended July 31, 1971, on a fully diluted earnings per share calculation is insignificant. Stock options outstanding have not been included in these computations since the effect of their inclusion would be insignificant.

ACCOUNTANTS' REPORT

The Board of Directors and Stockholders
Stirling Homex Corporation:

We have examined the consolidated balance sheet of Stirling Homex Corporation and consolidated subsidiaries as of July 31, 1971, and the related statements of income, additional paid-in capital, and retained earnings and changes in financial position for the year then ended. Our examination was made in accordance with generally accepted auditing standards, and accordingly included such tests of the accounting records and such other auditing procedures as we considered necessary in the circumstances. The financial statements for the year ended July 31, 1970, included for comparative purposes, were examined by other accountants.

In our opinion, such financial statements present fairly the consolidated financial position of Stirling Homex Corporation and consolidated subsidiaries at July 31, 1971, and the results of their operations and changes in their financial position for the year then ended, in conformity with generally accepted accounting principles applied on a basis consistent with that of the preceding year.

Rochester, New York
September 15, 1971   Peat, Marwick, Mitchell & Co.

Case 4–6

The General Electric Company (A)

Refer to the excerpts taken from GE's 1978 annual report and answer the following questions:

1. What is General Electric's concept of corporate governance?
2. Should GE's approach to corporate governance be used as a standard for other corporations to emulate?
3. What additional issues/disclosures/responsibilities might fall under the rubric of corporate governance?
4. Should responsibility for setting corporate governance standards lie in the public or private sector? Discuss.

REPORT OF MANAGEMENT

To the Share Owners of General Electric Company

We have prepared the accompanying statement of financial position of General Electric Company and consolidated affiliates as of December 31, 1978, and 1977, and the related statements of earnings, changes in financial position, and changes in share owners' equity for the years then ended, including the notes and industry and geographic segment information. The statements have been prepared in conformity with generally accepted accounting principles appropriate in the circumstances, and include amounts that are based on our best estimates and judgments. Financial information elsewhere in this Annual Report is consistent with that in the financial statements.

Your company maintains a strong system of internal financial controls and procedures, supported by a corporate staff of traveling auditors and supplemented by resident auditors located around the world. This system is designed to provide reasonable assurance, at appropriate cost, that assets are safeguarded and that transactions are executed in accordance with management's authorization and recorded and reported properly. The system is time-tested, innovative, and responsive to change. Perhaps the most important safeguard in this system for share owners is the fact that the company has long emphasized the selection, training, and development of professional financial managers to implement and oversee the proper application of its internal controls and the reporting of management's stewardship of corporate assets and maintenance of accounts in conformity with generally accepted accounting principles.

The independent public accountants provide an objective, independent review as to management's discharge of its responsibilities insofar as they relate to the fairness of reported operating results and financial condition. They obtain and maintain an understanding of GE's accounting and financial controls, and conduct such tests and related procedures as they deem necessary to arrive at an opinion on the fairness of financial statements.

The Audit Committee of the Board of Directors, composed solely of directors from outside the company, meets with the independent public accountants, management, and internal auditors periodically to review the work of each and ensure that each is properly discharging its responsibilities. The independent public accountants have free access to this committee, without management present, to discuss the results of their audit work and their opinions on the adequacy of internal financial controls and the quality of financial reporting.

Your management has long recognized its responsibility for conducting the company's affairs in a manner which is responsive to the ever-increasing complexity of society. This responsibility is reflected in key company policy statements regarding, among other things, potentially conflicting outside business interests of company employees, proper conduct of domestic and international business activities, and compliance with antitrust laws. Educational, communication, and review programs are designed to ensure that these policies are clearly understood and that there is awareness that deviation from them will not be tolerated.

Chairman of the Board
and Chief Executive Office

Senior Vice President, Finance
February 16, 1979

REPORT OF INDEPENDENT CERTIFIED PUBLIC ACCOUNTANTS

To the Share Owners and Board of Directors of General Electric Company

We have examined the statement of financial position of General Electric Company and consolidated affiliates as of December 31, 1978, and 1977, and the related statements of earnings, changes in financial position, and changes in share owners' equity for the years then ended. Our examinations were made in accordance with generally accepted auditing standards, and accordingly included such tests of the accounting records and such other auditing procedures as we considered necessary in the circumstances.

In our opinion, the aforementioned financial statements present fairly the financial position of General Electric Company and consolidated affiliates at December 31, 1978, and 1977, and the results of their operations and the changes in their financial position for the years then ended, in conformity with generally accepted accounting principles applied on a consistent basis.

Peat, Marwick, Mitchell & Co.
345 Park Avenue, New York, N.Y. 10022
February 16, 1979

THE CHAIRMAN COMMENTS

General Electric's Centennial year was one in which your company's sales and earnings reached new highs. Sales rose by 12 percent to $19.7 billion, while earnings of $1.2 billion, or $5.39 per share, were up 13 percent.

Several significant aspects of your company's performance deserve to be singled out:

1. Confident of the company's results and prospects, your Board of Directors increased the quarterly dividend for the third year in a row. The increase to 65 cents a share with the July 1978, payment represented an 18 percent increase, and together with the earlier increases amounts to more than a 62 percent climb in dividends since July 1976. These increases are in line with our objective of paying about 50 percent of current earnings in dividends, retaining the rest to grow the business in the share owners' interest.

2. General Electric's earnings are outperforming growth in the U.S. Gross National Product—an achievement that reflects management's long-term objective to outpace the growth of the economy. Through strategic planning and differentiated resource allocation, we have diversified our sources of earnings into a variety of expanding markets, international as well as domestic.

3. General Electric has outgrown its traditional role as an equipment manufacturer whose fortunes are governed by the U.S. electrical load growth curve—the rise in the demands for electricity. The Sector reviews that follow in this annual report show that our businesses are responding to a broad range of forces and trends as they tap new sources of growth, including new types of products, a wide array of man-made materials and natural resources, and varied services businesses.

The Outlook

The U.S. economy appears to be making a strong start in 1979—thanks to the tax cut, good housing starts in late 1978, and industry's high backlogs of orders for capital goods. Our GE economists do expect a slowdown in the second half as tight money and high consumer debt will probably dampen consumer and housing expenditures.

However, business investment—stimulated by tax reductions from the Revenue Act of 1978—should help to offset the slower growth of consumer markets. In addition, faster expansion in industrialized countries and some recovery in the developing nations should strengthen export markets and trim back this country's serious trade deficit.

The most serious long-term U.S. economic problem continues to be inflation. Its cure will depend primarily on strong government fiscal and monetary policies, and regulatory restraint. If the government's anti-inflationary efforts succeed in moderating the rate of inflation later in 1979, then our economists believe we should see a quarter-by-quarter improvement in 1980, leading to continued solid expansion based mainly on strong capital outlays, revived consumer spending, and a growing world economy.

For General Electric, the major area of uncertainty is near-term consumer spending—but plans have been developed, and are being implemented, to maintain good profit margins despite a possible slowing in consumer demand.

We face the future with ample financial strengths, including a solid cash position backed by a favorable 22.5 percent debt-to-capital ratio and a triple A credit rating.

Thus we feel that General Electric is well positioned to ride through any slowing in the economy's growth rate and to enter an upturn with strong, well-directed momentum.

We continue to invest strongly in the future. We maintained our vigorous commitment to research and development in 1978 with expenditures totaling $1,270 million for company-funded projects and R&D work performed under contract. Also, we made record plant and equipment investments of $1,055 million.

Most importantly, we have seasoned management, in depth—men and women who know how to make the most of the company's considerable assets.

Your managers are optimistic with regard to the successful negotiation of new contracts with labor unions to replace those that expire in June 1979. While inflation is a continuing problem, the wage increases granted under the 1976–79 contract, including cost-of-living adjustments have enabled GE employees' earnings to keep ahead of inflation, so that we do not anticipate the necessity for a substantial "catch-up" adjustment.

Corporate Governance

Your managers consider it one of our basic responsibilities to make our views known on public issues affecting business and to strive for changes that will improve the economic, political, and social environment in which business operates.

One issue that has been coming into increasing prominence directly concerns the relationships among share owners, their boards of directors, and business managers. The shorthand term for this issue is *corporate governance*. For *governance*, one might well substitute *responsibility* or *accountability*, since the focal point for this issue is whether sufficiently strong control mechanisms are in place to make sure that managers perform responsibly in the best interests of share owners, customers, employees, and the other constituencies of business.

Business critics, citing a few well-publicized lapses and failures in business performance, argue that present controls over corporate authority and power are inadequate, even though the cited cases are exceptions to the standards maintained by the overwhelming majority of enterprises. While some opponents try to make corporate governance a catchall for their varied grievances against business, the most substantive issue at present centers on the role and composition of corporate boards of directors. The critics claim that corporate boards, as presently constituted and organized, provide only a "rubber stamp" function, automatically giving managers the approvals they need. Proposals for change cover a wide spectrum, from severe limitations on who can qualify as directors to the idea of more stringent federal, as distinct from state, chartering.

This criticism does not seem to apply to General Electric. From the company's beginnings, GE share owners have been represented by a Board made up predominantly of directors from outside the company. Your managers through the years can verify that the GE Board has been vigorous and highly independent in its vigilance on behalf of the interests of share owners and the public generally.

Sales (billions)

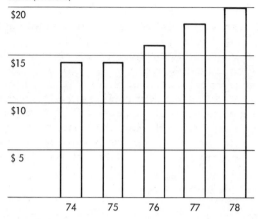

| | 74 | 75 | 76 | 77 | 78 |

Earnings per share

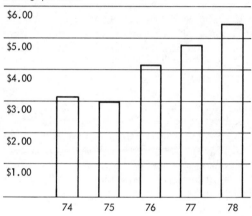

| | 74 | 75 | 76 | 77 | 78 |

Dividends declared per share

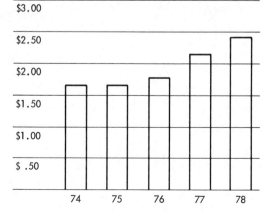

| | 74 | 75 | 76 | 77 | 78 |

Nevertheless, your board has accepted corporate governance as a valid issue. Your directors' early sensitivity has led to a structure of the General Electric Board that meets the objectives both of enlarging its role and of facilitating its work.

The front cover of this annual report depicts the board's organization into seven committees, with each assigned to concentrate on monitoring a major aspect of the business. Reports by the chairmen of these committees, included show that today's committee structure, which began to evolve in 1972, has been effective in enabling your directors to be more penetrating in their involvement in the business, as well as more informed and challenging in the appraisals of management's performance.

The governance of General Electric is we believe, illustrative of what responsible business enterprises are doing to maintain tight controls and disciplines. In business as in any large organization from governments to churches, there obviously can be no absolute safeguards against unethical or antisocial acts by individuals. But evolutionary business-initiated measures such as the more effective structure of boards of directors will help guard against substantial corporate misconduct or serious legal, social, or ethical lapses.

The great danger, as we see it, is that business critics will succeed in their effort to swell the ripple of concern represented by corporate governance into still another wave of government regulation and restriction. U.S. industry's efforts to provide good values for its customers, and to compete against international producers, are already hampered by the effects of excessive regulation in reducing managers flexibility and increasing costs. Rather than add new regulatory burdens, the wiser response to the issue of corporate governance is, in our view, to continue strengthening the systems of checks and balances and the lines of accountability that are already in place.

We ask the share owners of General Electric to enlarge their own understanding of corporate governance, believing that the great majority of those who do so will support the efforts of corporate managers both to make the system work better and to withstand the impractical and counterproductive measures that some critics propose.

Reginald H. Jones

Chairman of the Board
and Chief Executive Officer
February 16, 1979

BOARD OF DIRECTORS

In addition to its ten regular meetings and the numerous meetings of its Committees during 1978, the Board of Directors conducted a business review which included reports on GE operations in the United Kingdom, Western Europe, Eastern Europe, the Middle East and Africa.

The Directors also participated in GE Centennial activities, including a customer dinner and the 1978 Information Meeting in October in New York City.

The regular quarterly dividend was increased by the Board in May of 1978 by 18 percent, from 55 to 65 cents per share.

The Board is made up primarily of Directors from outside the Company. Only four are members of GE management; the other 16 Directors have earned positions of leadership in such fields as business, law, education, finance and public service. The listing of Directors below is in order of their Board seniority, with the year in which they were first elected shown in parentheses.

Frederick L. Hovde, President Emeritus, Purdue University, Lafayette, Ind. (1956)

John E. Lawrence, President, James Lawrence & Co., Inc., cotton merchants, Boston, Mass. (1957)

Walter B. Wriston, Chairman of the Board and Director, Citicorp and Citibank, N.A., New York, N.Y. (1962)

Ralph Lazarus, Chairman of the Board and Director, Federated Department Stores, Inc., Cincinnati, Ohio. (1962)

Gilbert H. Scribner, Jr., Chairman of the Board and Director, Scribner & Co., real estate and insurance, Chicago, Ill. (1962)

Edmund W. Littlefield, Chairman of the Board and Director, Utah International Inc., San Francisco, Calif. (1964)

J. Paul Austin, Chairman of the Board and Director, The Coca-Cola Company, Atlanta, Ga. (1964)

Jack S. Parker, Vice Chairman of the Board, Executive Officer and Director, General Electric Company, Fairfield, Conn. (1968)

Reginald H. Jones, Chairman of the Board, Chief Executive Officer and Director, General Electric Company, Fairfield, Conn. (1971)

Walter D. Dance, Vice Chairman of the Board, Executive Officer and Director, General Electric Company, Fairfield, Conn. (1971)

James G. Boswell II, President and Director, J. G. Boswell Company, farming and related businesses, Los Angeles, Calif. (1971)

Charles D. Dickey, Jr., Chairman of the Board, President and Director, Scott Paper Company, Philadelphia, Pa. (1972)

Henry L. Hillman, President and Director, The Hillman Company, diversified operations and investments, Pittsburgh, Pa. (1972)

Henry H. Henley, Jr., President and Director, Cluett, Peabody & Co., Inc., manufacturing and retailing of apparel, New York, N.Y. (1972)

Silas S. Cathcart, Chairman of the Board and Director, Illinois Tool Works Inc., diversified products, Chicago, Ill. (1972)

Samuel R. Pierce, Jr., Partner, Battle, Fowler, Jaffin, Pierce & Kheel, law firm, New York, N.Y. (1974)

Gertrude G. Michelson, Senior Vice President, Employee and Consumer Relations, Macy's-New York, retailers, New York, N.Y. (1976)

Lewis T. Preston, President and Director, J. P. Morgan & Co. Incorporated and Morgan Guaranty Trust Company, New York, N.Y. (1976)

George M. Low, President, Rensselaer Polytechnic Institute, Troy, N.Y. (1977)

Richart T. Baker, Consultant to Ernst & Ernst, public accountants, Cleveland, Ohio. (1977)

Board Committees: New Nominating Committee Assesses Director Candidates, Committee Memberships

The Committee structure of the Board was strengthened further in 1978 by the formation of a Nomating Committee, which will concentrate specifically on Board succession and organization.

The Nominating Committee, supplementing the work of the six other Committees of the Board summarized on pages 24 and 25, is composed of the Chairmen of these other Board Committees.

The new Committee's responsibilities include the selection of potential candidates for Directorships and the recommendation of Director candidates to the full Board of Directors. The Nominating Committee also makes recommendations to the full Board concerning the structure and membership of each of the other six Board Committees for the ensuing year.

Henry H. Henley, Jr., Chairman

Operations Committee: The Board's Monitor of GE Operating Performance

The members of this Committee see it as our function to extend the Board's reach by giving special attention to General Electric's operations. Our concern is to make sure that operating matters posing particular challenges and opportunities are brought before the full Board in a timely manner.

In view of the Company's growth in international markets, we continued in 1978 to give special emphasis to overseas businesses. We reviewed with the appropriate managers the Company's offshore sourcing operations. Our review included the strategic planning for these operations, the production resources allocated to them, and the planning for control and management of the financial risks involved.

In line with our interests, the full Board in April conducted a business review of the Company's activities in Europe, Africa and the Middle East.

Joint meetings with other Committees during the year gave us the opportunity to review the implementation of the Corporate Technology

Study and to study drafts of the Company's Annual Report and proxy materials.

The members of this Committee come from widely varied business backgrounds. We see this diversity as an advantage allowing us to apply an independent and broadly experienced perspective to operating matters, helping to assure that General Electric performs responsibly in the interests of the share owners and the public as a whole.

J. Paul Austin, Chairman

Technology and Science Committee: Seeking the Greatest Potential from GE Research and Development

With the strong approval of this Committee, General Electric has, in its Corporate Technology Study, made an exhaustive effort to appraise the present status of its technology and to anticipate future directions, needs and opportunities.

Having reviewed the final phases of this Study at the end of 1977, the Committee followed up in 1978 by examining the Study's implementation. We satisfied ourselves that the many "action recommendations" are already having impact in building technological strengths that will make GE businesses more competitive, and in shaping manpower programs that offer greater incentives and opportunities for technical creativity.

Our ongoing work included conducting our own independent assessments of the vitality and quality of GE research and development activities. We continued to use the Board's reviews with Sector Executives as opportunities to inquire into specific technologies we consider essential to each Sector's progress.

We remain mindful, as the share owners' representatives, that General Electric is a company based on technological innovation and product leadership. The reviews we conducted in 1978 assured us that GE is maintaining vigorous development programs in the areas of greatest potential to the Company and to society and that, by carrying through its Corporate Technology Study, management has taken responsible action aimed at further strengthening General Electric's technological thrust in the future.

James G. Boswell II, Chairman

Management Development and Compensation Committee: Maintaining the Quality of GE Managerial Leadership

Only nonemployee Directors serve on this Committee, which has two principal responsibilities entrusted to it by the Board: to monitor and evaluate officer-level appointments and succession planning; and to review changes in executive compensation and in the plans by which GE seeks to attract, retain and motivate key employees.

During 1978, we met with the Chairman of the Board to review his appraisals of key executives' performance. Independently and separately, we conducted an assessment both of his appraisals and of his own performance. The Board's business reviews, customer relations activities and other events enabled us to develop firsthand knowledge of GE executives and their potentials for increased responsibility. We reviewed the status and depth of the Company's executive resources with the Chairman and with the Vice President—Executive Manpower.

We acted in support of the Board's long-standing position that nonemployee Directors should determine the compensation and benefit plans appropriate to the executive group. As an example, the Stock Option/Performance Unit Plan was developed through several working sessions of the Committee, and our modifications were incorporated by the Board in the final plan which was submitted to, and approved by, the share owners in 1978. Again, we met regularly with the Chairman to review and decide such matters as executive salaries, option grants, compensation plan awards and executive pensions.

Ralph Lazarus, Chairman

Public Issues Committee: Assuring a Thoughtful GE Voice on Key Issues

News headlines have made clear the powerful negative effects that societal, regulatory, economic and political issues can have on business. Yet other news stories have underscored the benefits that can accrue when business leaders speak out effectively on key public issues such as capital formation, tax legislation, regulatory excesses and overseas investments.

In this climate, the members of the Board's Public Issues Committee see our role as two-fold: to provide an independent checkpoint on the issues—present or potential—that affect General Electric; and to appraise the effectiveness of management's response.

On the basis of our assessments in 1978, we are assured that the Company has in place the procedures essential for issue identification, analysis and strategy development, and for implementation of coordinated internal and external communications programs. These procedures are working, and GE's voice on key issues is being heard.

For the past several years, we have stayed particularly alert to changes in Governmental regulations that affect business. Our reviews have covered the Company's compliance with regulations in the areas of occupational safety and health, product safety, and equal opportunity. On this last issue, we welcomed the 1978 conciliation agreement reached with the U.S. Equal Employment Opportunity Commission. We agree that this settlement can be implemented as a fresh opportunity for affirmative actions in support of the Company's equal opportunity goals.

Henry H. Henley, Jr., Chairman

Finance Committee, Appraisal of GE Financial Planning

A typical agenda for the Finance Committee begins with a report on the Company's financial position, moves to reviews of GE's investments in foreign companies and its exposure in terms of foreign currency, and includes reports on the operations of the General Electric Credit Corporation, on purchases of debentures for sinking fund purposes, and on GE Pension Trust operations. The agenda also includes discussion of new business ventures or other matters involving large-scale utilization of Company funds.

There is a good reason why we on the Finance Committee give close attention to matters such as these: they represent financial situations that, if not properly managed, could have a disproportionate "swing" effect on the Company's financial results. The Board expects us to monitor these situations, using the strong financial and business experience of our members to anticipate potential problems and see that appropriate strategies are developed early enough to deal with them.

Joint meetings with other Committees broaden our opportunities to examine the financial aspects of the Company's programs and plans. In February, as an example, we shared in the review of the Company's Annual Report and proxy materials.

General Electric's financial strengths are a great resource. We see it as our special province to help assure that this resource is used widely, prudently and responsibly in the interests of share owners and of society generally.

Edmund W. Littlefield, Chairman

Audit Committee: Independent Assessments of Audits of GE

The Audit Committee, which includes only Directors from outside the Company, maintains an ongoing appraisal of the effectiveness of audits and the independence of the public accountants. It recommends, for approval by the full Board and the share owners, the appointment of the independent public accountants. It also reviews accounting principles and internal accounting controls, and the Annual Report and proxy materials.

In February, May and September, 1978, the Committee met with partners of Peat, Marwick Mitchell & Co. At the February meeting, we reviewed the firm's audit for 1977, and inquired into the degree of cooperation received from General Electric in carrying out the audit. In May, we reviewed the organization and makeup of the firm's audit team assigned to GE, its plan for conducting the 1978 audit, and other services to be provided.

At our May and September meetings, we also met with the manager of GE's corporate audit staff to review the organization and scope of the Company's own internal audits.

On the basis of these reviews, we were able to report with confidence to the full Board that the resources allocated to the audit function both by the independent auditors and by General Electric itself are adequate to provide the assurances required by the Board.

We conducted a number of other reviews, including a meeting with the Senior Vice President—Finance and the Senior Vice President General Counsel and Secretary to examine the results of reviews and audits covering the compliance of employees with key GE policies.

Charles D. Dickey, Jr., Chairman

FINANCIAL ISSUES

Corporate governance covers many activities which encompass financial accounting and reporting. Debate continues over such issues as independence of public accountants, adequacy of financial reporting, and responsibility for establishing accounting standards.

The fundamental question is whether continued business-initiated efforts will do the job, or whether additional government regulation is required.

A current financial issue is whether some services provided by public accountants are incompatible with the primary audit function and thus compromise audit firm independence.

The AICPA's independent Commission on Auditors' Responsibilities concluded, based on its research, that the facts did not justify a restriction of such services but that management should report on their nature in general response to questions raised by those concerned. Subsequently, the Securities and Exchange Commission issued regulations requiring such disclosure in 1979 proxy statements.

As discussed elsewhere in this report, the Audit Committee of the GE Board of Directors reviews with the independent public accountants the scope of regular audit work as well as the type and extent of their "nonaudit" services performed for General Electric. In 1978, these services consisted of such items as tax return preparation and consultation, reviews and development of computer systems, audits of employee benefit plan trusts, and acquisition reviews. The Audit Committee determined that performance of these services could not reasonably have affected the independence of Peat, Marwick, Mitchell & Co's regular audit work for GE.

In our view, concern about the impact of "nonaudit" services on auditor independence is exaggerated. However, since the credibility of auditors is vital to investor confidence, we hope the information now being provided by public companies, coupled with board of director review, will work to lay this issue to rest.

With respect to financial reporting by public companies, we believe that considerable progress is being made. At General Electric, we continue to stress a strong system of internal financial controls, as discussed in the Report of Management, and timely reporting of financial results and information essential to informed decision making by investors. Responsible financial reporting is a shared interest among those having a stake in the progress of your company. We intend to remain at the forefront of high-quality financial reporting.

We also believe that the responsibility for establishing standards of financial accounting and reporting should be kept in the private sector. GE management vigorously supports the Financial Accounting Standards Board and its procedures, which we feel contribute significantly to even-handed accounting and reporting standards.

Regulation of the private sector by government in the United States has been accelerating at an alarming pace. Conservative estimates by the Center for the Study of American Business at Washington University put private sector costs to comply with federal regulations at about $98 billion for fiscal 1979. Added to that is another $4.8 billion to operate the regulatory agencies themselves. These combined costs increased 58 percent since 1976.

There are serious questions about the ability of U.S. business to underwrite, as rapidly as is being required, the increasing levels of resources committed to complying with government regulations. The pressure of these expenditures on a pervasive inflation rate, combined with their negative impact on badly needed productivity improvements, are legitimate concerns.

General Electric management will continue to represent these concerns while participating the regulatory rule-making process.

Capital formation and the related impacts of inflation and tax policy have been commented on in the company's previous annual reports. The issues are worth repeating.

For the individual taxpayer, inflation boosts earnings into higher tax brackets, reduces or eats into savings, and increases the costs of most goods and services. For the corporation, the impact is much the same. As a result, real earnings are often much lower than reported by conventional accounting procedures, and the real return on investment falls below levels needed to provide adequate capital for business growth and jobs.

Accounting procedures are being developed to help measure the impact of inflation. However, existing tax policy on depreciation of plant and equipment does not adequately address the economic consequences of inflation on capital formation.

In General Electric's case, the hidden impact of inflation is reduced by use of Lifo accounting for approximately 80 percent of inventories. For plant and equipment no similar tax allowable practice is permitted. Using the Securities and Exchange Commission's replacement cost approach, depreciation expense for your company in 1978 would have been about $310 million greater than amounts reflected in reported financial results, compared with $290 million for 1977. In general, funds necessary to replace these shortfalls must come entirely from aftertax profits or from the infusion of capital. General Electric spent $1,055 million for plant and equipment additions in 1978, some 28 percent more than a year earlier. The company's resource allocation procedures take into account the need to maximize the real return on these expenditures.

The tax burden of your company, including affiliates, amounted in 1978 to over $1.4 billion, consisting of payments and accruals for federal, state, local, and foreign income taxes; Social Security taxes: other taxes such as those on property; and certain export duties. In the aggregate, this tax cost equaled 7.3 percent of net sales billed, somewhat higher than company aftertax earnings of 6.3 percent.

Taxes are also paid by our employees on salaries and wages, share owners on dividends, suppliers of materials and services utilized in company operations, and, in many cases, by customers on their purchase and use of company products. The magnitude of the total of these taxes shows the significant contribution the company and its principal constituencies make to the funding of government.

Taxes today do far more than pay for the cost of government. They affect the whole base of the economy. Because of this critical impact, all citizens should remain informed about taxation and the expenditure programs of government and make their views known.

5

Inventories

Inventory is an asset held by the business firm for the purpose of future sale or for utilization in the manufacture of goods for sale. This definition is further amplified in *Accounting Research Bulletin No. 43.*[1] Chapter 4 states:

> The term *inventory* embraces goods awaiting sale (the merchandise of a retail company or the finished goods of a manufacturer), goods in the course of production for such sale (commonly termed, work in process inventory), and goods to be consumed directly or indirectly in the production of goods to be available for sale (raw materials and supplies).

For most manufacturing and merchandising companies, inventory is a major asset and often the single largest current asset. The cost of goods sold account, which represents the inventory sold, frequently is the largest expense in the income statement. At the date of acquisition, inventory items are recorded in accordance with the cost principle. Subsequently, when sold, their cost is matched with revenue in accordance with the matching principle.

CLASSIFICATION OF INVENTORIES

Inventories are commonly classified as follows:

1. Merchandise Inventory: goods on hand purchased by a mercantile company for resale. Typically the trading concern purchases merchandise inventory from a wholesaler at wholesale prices and sells it to its customers at retail prices. The difference between the retail price at which the merchandise inventory is sold (sales) and the cost of the merchandise sold is called the *gross margin* (gross profit).

2. Manufacturing Inventories consist of:

   a. Raw materials inventory: Physical goods purchased for conversion through the manufacturing process into finished goods.

---

[1] Issued in 1953 by the Committee on Accounting Procedure and Terminology of the AICPA. It is basically a revision and restatement of the first 42 accounting research bulletins.

b. Work in process inventory. Goods partly processed (or converted) and requiring further processing before sale.

c. Finished goods inventory. Fully manufactured or converted goods held for sale.

d. Supplies inventory. Those factory supplies on hand such as oil, paint, and packaging materials, which comprise an insignificant part of the finished product. A common example in the apparel industry is the thread used to sew buttons on a coat.

INVENTORY VALUATION

Inventory value is determined by multiplying the quantity of inventory items on hand by their unit prices. The unit prices are determined by using one of the inventory cost flow methods.[2]

The *periodic inventory method* determines the ending inventory quantity by an actual physical count of the goods on hand on the balance sheet date. Cost of goods sold is calculated by subtracting the ending inventory from the cost of goods available for sale (beginning inventory plus purchases during the period). The assumption is that all goods not in the ending inventory have been sold. In actual practice this will result in losses due to pilferage and evaporation being treated as cost of goods sold.

Under a *perpetual inventory method* each purchase and sale is identified and recorded. The cost of goods sold can be determined at any point. It is the actual number of units sold multiplied by their unit cost. The perpetual inventory method requires more elaborate and expensive recordkeeping, but it maintains updated information on quantities sold and on hand. This information is particularly useful for determining the number of units that need to be produced or purchased for inventory. Periodic physical counts are taken from time to time to ascertain the accuracy of the perpetual inventory method.

DEDUCING COST OF GOODS SOLD IN A MERCHANDISING COMPANY (PERIODIC INVENTORY METHOD)

Merchandising companies generally determine cost of goods sold by subtracting the ending inventory from the cost of the goods available for sale. A physical count is taken at the end of the accounting period to determine the quantity of ending inventory, which is then priced using one of the cost flow methods. (See the accompanying table.)

---

[2] Inventory cost flow methods are the subject matter of the following chapter.

Beginning inventory		$ 450,000
Add: Purchases (gross invoice price)	$2,125,000	
Freight-in	42,500	
	$2,167,500	
Deduct: Purchase returns and discounts	54,000	
Net purchases		2,113,500
Goods available for sale		$2,563,500
Less: ending inventory		822,300
Cost of goods sold		$1,741,200

The cost of inventory purchases includes the invoice cost of the merchandise plus all freight or related costs to get it to the company. To obtain net purchases for the period, purchase discounts and purchase returns should be subtracted. Purchase discounts are cash discounts for paying within a specific period of time. It is common in some industries to give a two percent discount if a bill is paid within ten days. Purchase returns are merchandise returned for credit.

At the end of the accounting period, the merchandise inventory general ledger account had a balance of $2,563,500 and would appear as follows:

Merchandise Inventory

Beginning balance	450,000	54,000	........Purchase
Gross purchases	2,125,000		returns and
Freight-in	42,500		discounts

The periodic inventory taken at the end of the year showed merchandise on hand costing $822,300. A journal entry is necessary to adjust the inventory account to $822,300 and to reflect that the cost of goods sold during the period was $1,741,200 ($2,563,500 − $822,300).

Using our illustrative data, we see that the entry would be:

Cost of Goods Sold	1,741,200	
Merchandise Inventory		1,741,200
To record cost of goods sold		

The relevant general ledger accounts would appear as follows:

Merchandise Inventory				**Cost of Goods Sold**	
Beginning balance	450,000	54,000	.....Purchase		
Gross			returns and		
purchases	2,125,000		discounts		
Freight-in........	42,500	1,741,200	.....Cost of.....	1,741,200	
			goods		
			sold		

INVENTORIES IN MANUFACTURING COMPANIES

The measurement of cost of goods sold in a manufacturing company is more complex than in a trading concern because the manufacturer has, as a major function, the conversion of raw materials into finished goods. The manufacturing company is required by GAAP to include in cost of goods sold the cost of raw materials used, the cost of direct labor applied, and all other factory costs (factory overhead).

In the manufacturing firm, the product often is manufactured in one period for delivery to customers in a later period. Manufacturing processes are designed to add value to purchased materials by using labor and machinery to convert them to finished goods. All manufacturing costs during the production process are charged to the asset account, inventory, and are expensed through the cost of goods sold account only when the sale is made.

MANUFACTURING FLOW OF COSTS

The flow of costs in the manufacturing concern is described below:

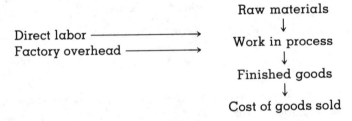

Raw materials cost includes all the costs necessary to put the material into production. Only the materials that become part of the product are included in raw materials.

Direct labor is the labor used to convert the raw material into the finished product. Direct labor cost includes only the wages of the people working directly on the product, for example, production workers on the assembly line.

Factory overhead, the third element of cost of manufacturing, encompasses *all manufacturing costs* other than raw materials and direct labor. Included is the cost of indirect labor, which represents the wages and benefits earned by employees such as factory supervisors, forklift operators, and the plant manager, who do not work directly on the product but whose services are closely related to the production process.

Factory overhead also includes depreciation on the production machinery and factory building, factory utilities and supplies, factory rent, if applicable, and insurance and taxes on the assets used in the manufacturing operation.

The production and sales cycle of a manufacturing company may be illustrated by means of a line graph:

Raw materials   Work in   Finished   Accounts
   purchased $\longrightarrow$ process $\longrightarrow$ goods $\longrightarrow$ Sales $\longrightarrow$ receivable $\longrightarrow$ Cash

It begins when raw materials are purchased and ends when cash is collected from the sale of the goods which have been manufactured.

A diagram of the manufacturing flow in a hacksaw blade factory is shown in Illustration 5–1.

ILLUSTRATION 5–1
Manufacturing Facility of the Hood Hacksaw Company

The raw material inventory is composed of large rolls of steel banding material in varying thicknesses. On command from the Production Control Office, a roll is sent to Station 1. The entire continuous roll of steel banding material is machine serrated, giving the band its sawtooth edge. The serrated roll is then sent to the cutting department where it is machine cut in varying lengths, generally 9 to 12 inches. After Station 2, the cut material is sanded, cleaned, and glazed with a chemical compound in the Glazing Department. On completion, the finished hacksaw blades are sent to Station 4 for special packing instructions. From packaging, the blades are sent to the Finished Goods area where, if there is an open order, they are immediately shipped; otherwise, inventory is placed on the shelf and is available for sale.

The accounting for the cost of the hacksaw blade follows the flow of the product through the factory. For example, let us assume a beginning raw materials inventory of $22,000. During the period, $49,000 of steel banding material was purchased. The entry recording the purchase would be:

```
Raw Materials Inventory ........................    49,000
    Accounts Payable............................               49,000
        To record raw materials purchased.
```

During the period, $65,000 of the raw materials inventory was put into production (that is, sent to Station 1). The entry reflecting this is:

```
Work in Process Inventory .......................    65,000
    Raw Materials Inventory .....................               65,000
        To record raw materials transferred to production.
```

The raw materials inventory general ledger account, after the above transactions, would appear as follows:

**Raw Materials
Inventory**

Beginning balance	22,000	65,000	.....To work in process inventory
Purchases	49,000		

The next item to consider is the wages of the production workers (direct labor). These wages are charged to the asset account, work in process inventory. Factory labor is being used to create an *asset* (in this case hacksaw blades), and the cost of such labor does not become an *expense* until the hacksaw blades are sold. This differs from the wages of the office employees, which are not a part of the inventory cost and are expenses in the period incurred.

During the period, the production direct labor cost was $34,000. The appropriate entry would be:

```
Work in Process Inventory .......................    34,000
    Wages Payable ..............................               34,000
        To record direct labor earned.
```

FACTORY OVERHEAD

The third item of manufacturing cost is factory overhead. Factory overhead represents all those costs associated with the manufacturing process other than raw materials and direct labor. During the period under review, indirect labor wages totaled $18,000, the factory rent bill was $4,000, and depreciation on the machinery was $3,500 (depreciation on factory machinery is a part of the cost of making the product and will be charged to an inventory account). Other miscellaneous manufacturing costs for light, heat, power, and manufacturing supplies totaled $13,000.[3]

The entries reflecting these transactions would be:

Work in Process Inventory	18,000	
Wages Payable		18,000
To record indirect factory labor earned.		
Work in Process Inventory	4,000	
Rent Payable		4,000
To record factory rent.		
Work in Process Inventory	3,500	
Accumulated Depreciation—Factory		3,500
To record depreciation on factory machinery.		
Work in Process Inventory	13,000	
Accounts Payable		13,000
To record miscellaneous manufacturing costs.		

Completed goods during the period are moved to the finished goods area in the factory. The accounting entry is:

Finished Goods Inventory	93,500	
Work in Process Inventory		93,500
To transfer cost of goods finished.		

This transfer of costs indicates that some partially manufactured goods (work in process) have been converted into finished goods.

Partially manufactured goods will be located throughout the factory on the last day of the period. The balance in the work in process account ($44,000 in our illustration) represents the cost of unfinished hacksaw blades in various stages of production at that time.

The general ledger account for work in process inventory after posting the above entries is:

Work in Process Inventory

Beginning balance	0	93,500	.........Transferred to finished
Raw materials	65,000		goods inventory
Direct labor	34,000		
Factory overhead:			
Indirect labor	18,000		
Rent	4,000		
Depreciation	3,500		
Miscellaneous	13,000		

---

[3] See Chapter 7, "Focus on Manufacturing Costing Issues," for a discussion of the allocation of factory overhead to units manufactured.

THE COST OF GOODS SOLD

The finished goods inventory account represents the total manufacturing cost of the goods available for sale. To complete our example, assume hacksaw blades sold during the period cost $87,000. The entry to record this is:

Cost of Goods Sold 87,000
    Finished Goods Inventory 87,000
      To transfer finished goods sold.

The balance of $6,500 in the finished goods inventory account represents the cost of the finished goods.

**Finished Goods
Inventory**

Beginning balance	0	87,000	..Transferred to cost of goods sold
From work in process..	93,500		

STATEMENT OF COST OF GOODS SOLD

The operating cycle of this manufacturing company is now completed. The cycle consists of purchasing materials, processing them into finished goods, and selling them to customers (Illustration 5–2). The flow of manufacturing costs through the accounts can be summarized in the statement of cost of goods sold.

SIGNIFICANCE OF THE PROCESS

Merchandising companies purchase their product (inventory) in the finished form. Manufacturing companies produce their product by adding direct labor and other factory costs to raw materials. All costs of manufacturing are *product costs* and become expenses in the accounting period in which the product is sold.

ILLUSTRATION 5-2 ——————————————————————————————

THE HOOD HACKSAW COMPANY
Statement of Cost of Goods Sold
For *X* Months Ended December 31, 19*XX*

Raw materials:
Beginning raw material inventory	$ 22,000
Raw material purchases	49,000
	$ 71,000
Less: Ending raw materials	6,000
Cost of materials used	$ 65,000
Direct labor	34,000

Factory overhead:
Indirect labor	18,000
Rent	4,000
Depreciation	3,500
Other	13,000
Total manufacturing cost	$137,500
Plus: Beginning work in process inventory	—0—
Less: Ending work in process inventory	44,000
Cost of goods finished	$ 93,500
Plus: Beginning finished goods inventory	—0—
Less: Ending finished goods inventory	6,500
Cost of goods sold	$ 87,000

CASES FOR CHAPTER 5

Case 5–1

General Electric Company (B)

Why is the increase in inventories during the year included in the computation of operating costs in GE's statement of earnings?

GENERAL ELECTRIC COMPANY AND CONSOLIDATED AFFILIATES
Statement of Earnings
For the Years Ended December 31
(in millions)

	1977	1976
Sales of products and services to customers	$17,518.6	$15,697.3
Operating costs:		
Employee compensation, including benefits	6,555.5	5,849.9
Materials, supplies, services, and other costs.............................	8,753.9	7,726.0
Depreciation, depletion, and amortization	522.1	486.2
Taxes, except those on income	239.0	258.8
Increase in inventories during the year...................................	(249.9)	(151.5)
	$15,820.6	$14,169.4
Operating margin.........................	$ 1,698.0	$ 1,527.9
Other income	390.3	274.3
Interest and other financial charges	(199.5)	(174.7)
Earnings before income taxes and minority interest	$ 1,888.8	$ 1,627.5
Provision for income taxes	(773.1)	(668.6)
Minority interest in earnings of consolidated affiliates	(27.5)	(28.3)
Net earnings applicable to common stock	$ 1,088.2	$ 930.6

	1977	1976
Earnings per common share (in dollars)	$4.79	$4.12
Dividends declared per General Electric common share (in dollars)	$2.10	$1.70
Operating margin as a percentage of sales	9.7%	9.7%
Net earnings as a percentage of sales	6.2%	5.9%

Case 5–2

The Rasholm Chemical Corporation

The Rasholm Chemical Corporation is a marginal producer of molding-powder pellets, a basic raw material used in the manufacture of Plexiglas sheets. On January 1, 1981, the accounts of the Rasholm Corporation were as follows:

	Dr.	Cr.
Cash	$ 55,500	
Accounts Receivable	72,000	
Raw Materials	25,500	
Work in Process	9,750	
Finished Goods	31,500	
Land	18,000	
Buildings	90,000	
Accumulated Depreciation—Buildings		$ 9,000
Equipment	120,000	
Accumulated Depreciation—Equipment		48,000
Accounts Payable		19,500
Notes Payable		30,000
Accrued Interest Payable (On Notes)		1,800
Wages Payable		1,500
Capital Stock		225,000
Retained Earnings		87,450
	$422,250	$422,250

A summary of business operations for the *ensuing quarter* follows:

1. Raw materials purchased on account, $180,000.
2. Direct labor cost accrued, $147,000.
3. Indirect labor cost accrued, $91,500.
4. General manufacturing costs paid by check, $58,500.
5. Depreciation on equipment is 20 percent a year and is all chargeable to factory overhead.
6. Depreciation on the building is 5 percent a year (80 percent of the

building space is used for manufacturing operations, 10 percent for general administration, and 10 percent for the sales staff).

7. General and administrative expenses, paid in cash, $58,500. Selling expenses, paid in cash, $48,000.
8. Notes payable bear interest at the rate of 12 percent.
9. Raw materials put into production during the quarter, $163,500.
10. Fully manufactured goods transferred to finished goods, $414,000.
11. Sales on account, $540,000. Cost of goods shipped to customers totaled $363,000.
12. Collection of accounts receivable, $480,000.
13. Cash disbursements made:
    a. Accounts payable—$136,500.
    b. Wages payable —$231,000.
14. The federal income tax rate is 50 percent.

Required:

1. Prepare a statement of cost of goods sold and an income statement for the period January 1 to March 31, 1981.
2. Prepare a balance sheet as of March 31, 1981.

Case 5–3

Yeastall Pharmaceutical Company

The Yeastall Pharmaceutical Company manufactures vitamin pills containing brewer's yeast extract. On the first of March the company had on hand raw materials which had cost $324,000, finished pills and containers costing $600,000, and partially processed pills embodying a total of $448,000 worth of raw materials, direct labor, and manufacturing overhead.

During March, receipts of additional materials totaled $680,000, and $948,000 worth of material was put into production. Direct labor applying to March production was $500,000, and manufacturing overhead totaled $292,000. At the end of March partially processed pills on hand represented $36,000 in materials, $24,000 in direct labor, and $16,000 of manufacturing overhead. Pills costing $1,930,000 were shipped to customers during March.

Required:

1. What was the total manufacturing cost for March?
2. What was the cost of goods finished?
3. What was the cost of goods sold?
4. What was the finished goods inventory on March 31?

6

Inventory Cost
Flow Methods

The value of the inventory on the balance sheet is determined by multiplying the quantities on hand by their unit cost. The periodic and perpetual methods of ascertaining inventory quantities were described in the preceding chapter. The pricing of these inventories is discussed in this chapter.

Accounting Research Bulletin No. 43, Chapter 4, states:

> Cost for inventory purposes may be determined under any one of several assumptions as to the flow of cost factors (such as first-in, first-out, average, and last-in, first-out) the major objective in selecting a method should be to choose the one which, under the circumstances, most clearly reflects periodic income.
>
> The cost to be matched against revenue from a sale may not be the identified cost of the specific item which is sold, especially in cases in which similar goods are purchased at different times and at different prices. . . . Ordinarily the identity of goods is lost between the time of acquisition and the time of sale. This fact has resulted in the development of general acceptance of several assumptions with respect to the flow of cost factors to provide practical bases for the measurement of periodic income.

During any given period, items may be manufactured or purchased at different unit costs. When these units are sold, the business firm is faced with the problem of selecting the appropriate unit cost for the item sold. Selection of an appropriate unit cost necessitates the establishment of an inventory cost flow policy by the management of the firm.

There are four major inventory cost flow methods: (*a*) first-in, first-out (Fifo), (*b*) last-in, first-out (Lifo), (*c*) weighted average, and (*d*) specific (identification) lot.

ARB Opinion No. 43 indicates you should choose the inventory cost flow method which most clearly reflects periodic income. Thus the basis for selection of a particular method is not the actual physical flow of the goods but *the one that best matches cost with revenue* (*matching principle*).

ILLUSTRATIVE DATA

To illustrate the inventory cost flow methods, let us use the data in Illustration 6–1.

The inventory equation is Beginning inventory + Materials purchased − Ending inventory = Cost of goods sold. In our example

ILLUSTRATION 6–1

		Units	Received Unit Cost	Units Sold	Units on Hand
December 1	Inventory.........	100	$100		100
4	Purchase	80	120		180
10	Sale			110	70
16	Purchase	150	140		220
19	Sale			160	60
26	Purchase	90	150		150

(periodic inventory method) we have to value the 150 units in the December 31 inventory.

Including the beginning inventory, purchases have been made at four different unit prices. A good way to view the inventory buildup process is in terms of cost layers: As new units are acquired at different prices, new cost layers are added to the inventory. In our illustration there are four cost layers.

FIRST-IN, FIRST-OUT (FIFO) METHOD

The Fifo cost flow method assumes that goods flow out in the same order as they flow in. The oldest goods are the first ones sold. The goods sold are costed at the oldest unit prices, and the remaining inventory is costed at the most recent unit prices. Using the illustrative data, we see that the Fifo ending inventory and cost of goods sold computation would be:

Cost of beginning inventory (100 units at $100)		$10,000
Plus purchases:		
December 4— 80 units at $120		9,600
December 16—150 units at $140		21,000
December 26— 90 units at $150		13,500
Total cost of goods available for sale		$54,100
Deduct ending inventory (150 units)		
90 units at $150	$13,500	
60 units at $140	8,400	21,900
Cost of goods sold		$32,200

LAST-IN, FIRST-OUT (LIFO) METHOD

The last-in, first-out inventory cost flow method assumes the reverse of the Fifo method, namely, the latest goods purchased are the goods sold and the ending inventory is made up of the oldest units. The underlying hypothesis is that current purchases are largely incurred to meet current sales.

Using the illustrative data, we see that the Lifo calculation would appear as follows:

Total cost of goods available for sale (from the preceding example)		$54,100
Deduct ending inventory		
100 units at $100	$10,000	
50 units at $120	6,000	16,000
Cost of goods sold		$38,100

During periods of rising prices and assuming constant or increasing inventory levels, Lifo cost of goods sold will always be higher than Fifo cost of goods sold.

WEIGHTED AVERAGE

The weighted average cost flow method assumes that an average unit cost is a *representative* cost of all items available for sale during the period.

Total cost of goods available for sale (from the preceding example)		$54,100
Total units available for sale (beginning inventory plus total purchases)	420	
Average unit cost ($54,100 ÷ 420) = $128.81		
Ending inventory = Number of units × Average unit cost = 150 × $128.81		19,321
Cost of goods sold = Number of units × Average unit cost = 270 × $128.81		$34,779

The weighted average method generally produces cost of goods sold and inventory values which are in between those produced by the Fifo and Lifo methods.

SPECIFIC (IDENTIFICATION) LOT

The specific lot cost flow method is generally employed when the goods involved are relatively large in size, easily identifiable, and few in number. For example, automobiles are often costed using this method. The specific lot cost flow method identifies a specific cost with each item. If a dealer sold ten automobiles that had a unit cost of $2,500, and six vehicles that had a cost of $3,000, his cost of goods sold would be $43,000 [(10 × $2,500) + (6 × $3,000)]. The auto dealer would probably identify which cars were sold based on the model, color, engine number, and other easily distinguishable characteristics. Because of the careful identification process required for each item, this cost flow method which requires a perpetual inventory is seldom used except where there are large and easily identifiable units.

LOWER-OF-COST-OR-MARKET RULE (LCM)

In all cost flow methods the principle of conservatism requires that year-end inventory be written down whenever the market price of the units in inventory is less than the historical cost of the units. As used here, market price means current replacement cost.

To illustrate how the rule works, let us assume that the market price of the inventory dropped to $130 per unit at the end of the accounting period on December 31. Using our sample data, and assuming that the company was using Fifo, we see that a year-end write-down must be made in accordance with the LCM rule.

Calculation:

Current ending inventory, Fifo		
90 units at $150	$13,500	
60 units at $140	8,400	$21,900
Current ending inventory, at market prices		
90 units at $130	11,700	
60 units at $130	7,800	19,500
Write-down		$ 2,400

The write-down would increase cost of goods sold for the period and would reduce the amount shown in inventory on the balance sheet by the same amount.

THE ARGUMENT FOR FIFO

As long as prices remain constant, both the Fifo method and Lifo method give the same results. When unit prices change, however, the two methods provide significant differences in inventory valuation, cost of goods sold, and net income.

In the post-World War II economic era, rising prices have been prevalent throughout the world. With rising prices, Fifo matches the lowest (oldest) costs against sales revenue and values inventory on the balance sheet at the most recent purchase prices.

Proponents of Fifo generally point to the fact that the balance sheet account, inventory, is more realistic under Fifo. Thus the important current ratio (current assets divided by current liabilities—a key measure of corporate short-term liquidity) and other measures related to current assets are not distorted. They also argue that Fifo more closely approximates the actual physical flow of goods.

Managements of some companies have chosen to use the Fifo inventory cost flow method during periods of rising prices because it results in higher net income and earnings per share than the other cost flow methods. This is particularly true in companies where management compensation is based on net income.

THE ARGUMENT FOR LIFO

Under Lifo, during a period of rising prices, the most recent (highest) costs are matched with sales revenue (most recent sales prices) and inventory is valued at the oldest (lowest) costs. The argument in favor of Lifo (apart from tax considerations) is that it states cost of goods sold in relatively current dollars and more correctly reports net income on a current dollar basis than the other inventory cost flow methods.

Proponents of Lifo suggest that in a period of rising prices, other methods of inventory valuation produce misleading and fictitious profits because a portion of such profits must be used to replace, at higher costs, the units sold from inventory.

EVALUATION OF LIFO

A number of factors, basically rooted in economics and in the quality of reported earnings, have contributed to a recent increase in the shift to Lifo costing. Historically, managements have shied away from Lifo because of its depressing effect on reported earnings. The Internal Revenue Service has permitted the use of Lifo but has required that the same method of inventory valuation be used on the company's books that is used for tax purposes. This eliminated the possibility of using Fifo for annual report purposes (with higher earnings and better inventory values) and Lifo for tax purposes (better income measurement and lower tax payments). During the 1974–75 recession, however, corporate management looked at the tax and other benefits of Lifo with renewed interest because of a need for increased cash flow and the belief that their published earnings reports were having little impact on the market prices of their securities. Companies using the Lifo method receive improved cash flows from the tax savings. Under Lifo, during periods of rising prices and assuming inventory levels don't decrease, cost of goods sold is higher and reported net income is lower than it would be under an alternative method of inventory costing; consequently federal and state income taxes will be lower, resulting in a cash savings.

Many financial analysts and accounting theoreticians have challenged the quality of non-Lifo earnings. They have raised the question of the validity of these earnings when the inventory units sold have to be replaced at higher prices. They also question the payment of higher federal income taxes by companies that don't use Lifo, since this results in the depletion of cash that would otherwise be available for capital expenditures and dividend distributions.

A disadvantage of using Lifo is the difficulty which readers of financial statements encounter in comparing relative performance to other companies in the same industry that do not use Lifo.

Some cash flow advantages from Lifo can be lost in subsequent years if inventory quantities are reduced so that the base inventory or other low-cost layers are liquidated. In this instance, low-cost inventory would flow into cost of goods sold to be matched with current sales revenue, resulting in a gross profit which includes a large holding gain on inventory.

When deciding whether to adopt Lifo, company managements must resolve the conflict between the desire for tax savings and improved cash flow on the one hand, and for higher reported earnings and a balance sheet that reflects more working capital on the other.

FINANCIAL STATEMENT DISCLOSURE

FASB *Statement No. 33*, "Financial Reporting and Changing Prices," October 1979, requires the largest corporations to make a supplementary disclosure in the footnotes to their financial statements of the current (replacement) cost of inventory. This disclosure will now make it possible to obtain current inventory values for companies who use the Lifo inventory cost flow methods.

SUMMARY

Without gains (or losses) attributable to holding inventory, all inventory cost flow methods would produce the same results. Such gains are common due to inflation and specific commodity price changes and are frequently substantial. The choice of inventory method will not change the inventory holding gain, but it will affect the amounts reported on the income statement and balance sheet.

Many financial analysts prefer Lifo-based companies because they like managements who seek to conserve real asset values. Also, conservatively determined earnings are considered higher in quality because they are less likely to prove overstated in the light of future developments.

CASES FOR CHAPTER 6

Case 6–1

Dayco Corporation

The Accounting Principles section of Dayco Corporation's annual report contains the following explanation of how the company accounts for inventories.

> Inventories: Substantially all domestic inventories are stated at the lower of last-in, first-out cost or market. If the first-in, first-out method of inventory accounting had been used by the corporation, inventories would have been approximately $21,690,000 and $17,480,000 higher than reported at October 31, 1977, and October 31, 1976, respectively.

The balance sheet showed that inventories at October 31, 1977, and October 31, 1976, were $70,077,182 and $69,265,402, respectively. Net earnings (after taxes) for 1977 were $13,623,409, and for 1976 were $12,414,168. Dayco's effective income tax rate was 48 percent.

Required:
1. If Dayco had used Fifo instead of Lifo as an inventory flow assumption, how much larger or smaller would 1977 aftertax net income have been?
2. If Dayco had used Fifo instead of Lifo for 1976 and 1977, how much larger or smaller would total assets have been on October 31, 1977? (Assume Dayco switched from Fifo to Lifo on November 1, 1975.)

Case 6–2

Devlin Corporation

The Devlin Corporation, a diversified distribution company, purchases cartons of canned tennis balls (three balls per can) from the Questor Company and markets the balls under the Devlin brand name.

Purchase and sales data for Devlin's first three years of business are shown in the accompanying table.

1978

Sales		19,200 cartons at $54/carton
Purchases.................	February	6,500 cartons at $27
	July	10,000 cartons at $29
	September	8,000 cartons at $35

1979

Sales		24,000 cartons at $64/carton
Purchases.................	January	9,000 cartons at $37
	June	10,000 cartons at $39
	September	6,500 cartons at $42

1980

Sales		29,000 cartons at $70/carton
Purchases.................	June	11,000 cartons at $45
	August	7,500 cartons at $48
	September	8,000 cartons at $50

Required:

1. Calculate the year-end inventories and prepare income statements for each of the three years using:
   a. Fifo.
   b. Lifo.
2. Assuming an income tax rate of 50 percent, compute the tax savings associated with the Lifo method in each year.
3. Which method would you prefer, assuming you were:
   a. The general manager (being paid a bonus based on earnings).
   b. A bank creditor.
   c. A present shareholder.
   d. A prospective shareholder.
   e. A labor union official.
   f. An internal revenue agent.

Case 6–3

Asarco Incorporated and Consolidated Subsidiaries (A)

Below is Asarco's consolidated statement of earnings for the years ended December 31, 1978; 1977; 1976; 1975; and 1974, as well as a footnote about their inventory flow methods, and a speech made by Ralph L. Hennebach, president of Asarco on Lifo inventory valuation.

ASARCO, INC.
For the Years Ended December 31
(dollars in thousands, except per share amounts)

	1978	1977	1976	1975	1974
Sales of products and services	$ 1,174,911	$ 1,045,794	$ 1,103,737	$ 1,004,638	$ 1,344,050
Cost of products and services—exclusive of items deducted separately below	1,023,683	933,850	960,981	898,293	1,183,943
Income from products and services	$ 151,228	$ 111,944	$ 142,756	$ 106,345	$ 160,107
Equity in earnings of nonconsolidated associated companies (Note 2)	62,563	35,895	30,668	27,829	103,378
Other income:					
Dividends	51	60	53	171	1,091
Interest	5,127	5,763	4,712	3,051	7,318
Miscellaneous	2,985	3,017	3,911	2,460	4,441
Unusual items	(10,000)	(39,025)	—	(20,500)	(29,838)
Income before other deductions	$ 211,954	$ 117,654	$ 182,100	$ 119,356	$ 246,497
Other deductions:					
Research expense	$ 4,621	$ 4,885	$ 4,416	$ 5,282	$ 4,412
Exploration expense	8,020	12,308	7,185	7,104	6,637
Selling and administrative expenses	32,958	33,325	30,817	30,406	26,555
Corporate taxes	1,637	1,570	984	2,059	2,188
Depreciation and depletion	54,480	52,617	50,667	36,484	34,877
Interest on debt	37,786	36,316	33,106	21,943	11,362
Other interest	657	691	747	714	390
Total other deductions	$ 140,159	$ 141,712	$ 127,922	$ 103,992	$ 86,421
Earnings (loss) before taxes on income	$ 71,795	$ (24,058)	$ 54,178	$ 15,364	$ 160,076
Taxes on income	22,321	5,448	11,865	(10,074)	35,456
Net earnings (loss)	$ 49,474	$ (29,506)	$ 42,313	$ 25,438	$ 124,620
Net earnings (loss)—per share	$1.69	$(1.10)	$1.58	$0.95	$4.66
Average number of shares outstanding	29,352,895	26,739,781	26,743,987	26,791,453	26,731,976
Cash dividends per share	$0.40	$0.70	$0.70	$1.05	$1.43

Required:

1. Where is the $37.4 million which arose from the liquidation of excess metal inventories reported for on the Lifo basis reflected in the December 31, 1978, income statement?
2. Do you think Asarco had net earnings of $49,474,000 for the year ended December 31, 1978?
3. How would you have accounted for the $37.4 million?
4. Is it possible for a company like Asarco to "manage" its earnings?
5. Which inventory flow method do you think best reflects Asarco's earnings?

NOTES TO FINANCIAL STATEMENTS

Note 1. Summary of Significant Accounting Policies.—Principles of Consolidation: The consolidated financial statements include all subsidiaries 100 percent owned. Unconsolidated subsidiaries and significant investments of 20 percent or more in associated companies are accounted for by the equity method. Other investments are carried at cost or less.

Inventories: Metals at smelters, refineries, and recycling plants are valued at the lower of last-in, first-out cost (Lifo) or market. Metals at mines are valued at the lower of first-in, first-out cost (Fifo) or market.

Property: Assets are valued at cost or less. Betterments, renewals, costs of bringing new mineral properties into production, and the costs of major development programs at existing mines are capitalized.

Maintenance, repairs, development costs to maintain production at existing mines, and losses or gains on assets retired or sold are reflected in earnings as incurred.

Plant assets are depreciated over their estimated useful lives, generally by the straight-line method.

Mine asset depreciation and depletion are computed generally on the unit-of-production method using economic ore reserves.

Exploration: Tangible and intangible costs incurred in the search for mineral properties are charged generally against earnings when incurred. When a commercial ore body is discovered, the related exploration costs previously charged against earnings are credited to earnings and capitalized in "Property" and then depleted.

Taxes on Income: Certain items of income and expense are included in the financial statements in years different from those reported in the tax returns in accordance with applicable income tax laws. The resulting difference between the financial statement income tax provision and income taxes currently payable is included in the caption "Deferred Credits." Investment tax credits on qualified property reduce the provision for federal income taxes in the year utilized.

Retirement plans: Current service costs are funded and charged against earnings each year. Prior service costs generally are being funded and amortized over a period of 25 years.

Note 2.   Investments.—Dividends from companies accounted for by the equity method were (in millions): 1978—$17.0; 1977—$16.7; 1976—$10.0; 1975—$22.0; 1974—$43.3.

Taxes have not been provided on the undistributed earnings of associated companies more than 50 percent owned and corporate joint ventures, accounted for by the equity method, as such earnings have been reinvested indefinitely, and no remittance of such earnings to Asarco is foreseen. At December 31, 1978, the cumulative amount of equity in such undistributed earnings on which income taxes have not been provided is $237.4 million. (See accompanying table.)

Major Investments Accounted for by the Equity Method[a]
($000)

	SPCC December 31, 1978	MIM June 30, 1978	Revere December 31, 1978	IMM and Subsidiaries December 31, 1978
Financial Position		[b]		[c]
Current assets................	$208,380	$235,456	$254,810	$107,685
Current liabilities	(149,124)	(143,079)	(95,770)	(53,423)
Working capital	$ 59,256	$ 92,377	$159,040	$ 54,262
Property—net.................	704,658	442,182	171,889	76,688
Other assets..................	2,605	53,134	48,401	4,850
Deferred income taxes	(62,108)	(120,989)	(16,317)	(3,664)
Long-term debt	(301,838)	(130,609)	(228,036)	(9,282)
Other liabilities	(36,038)	(5,245)	—	(3,012)
Billiton B.V. joint venture participation in Cuajone Project.............	(30,704)	—	—	—
Net assets................	$335,831	$330,850	$134,977	$119,842
At December 31, 1978				
Asarco's interest..............	52.3%	48.9%	33.1%	34.0%
Asarco's investment	$175,639	$184,701	$ 61,888[d]	$ 51,332
Market value[e]	n.a.	$394,500	$ 24,900	n.a.

For the Years Ended December 31

		f		f
Net sales				
1978	$309,430	$467,456	$680,767	$276,615
1977	268,170	442,283	597,604	240,422
1976	124,438	396,379	498,418	258,554
1975	96,558	383,890	382,059	229,562
1974	190,526	481,855	517,458	293,065
Net income (loss)		f		f
1978	$ 29,861	$ 51,968	$(19,043)^h	$ 26,360
1977	4,174	41,385	14,877^g	24,746
1976	8,354^g	40,084	2,211^g	19,334
1975	(9,597)	49,978	(31,278)^h	19,866
1974	29,325	133,214	17,151	37,116
Equity earnings (loss)				
1978	$ 15,617	$ 32,774	$ 7,074^f	$ 6,774
1977	3,046	20,253	5,031^g	5,558
1976	4,369^g	19,642	801^g	4,194
1975	(4,942)	24,489	(1,417)^i	7,800
1974	15,102	65,275	5,836	12,513
Dividends to Asarco				
1978	$ —	$ 14,264	$ —	$ 2,090
1977	—	14,105	—	1,510
1976	—	6,867	—	2,613
1975	—	18,037	469	2,286
1974	—	34,985	235	5,982

^{a} Asarco's investments in "Nonconsolidated associated companies" carried on the equity method include, in addition to those shown above, a total of $9,762,000 for Neptune Mining Company (52.2 percent owned) and some other minor companies. Equity in earnings of such companies, included in the consolidated statement of earnings, was (in thousands): 1978—$324; 1977—$2,007; 1976—$1,662; 1975—$1,899; 1974—$4,652.

^{b} Translated into U.S. dollars at rate in effect at December 31, 1978, of Australian $1 = US$1.1417 (rate at June 30, 1978, was A$1 = US$1.1415).

^{c} Translated into U.S. dollars at rate in effect at December 31, 1978, of Mexican MN$1 = US$0.0438.

^{d} Includes investment of $22,839,000 in 5½ percent convertible subordinated debentures due 1992.

^{e} Represents value for common stock investments only, based upon quoted market prices where available. Values are not necessarily indicative of amounts realizable in the event of a sale.

^{f} Translated at monthly average rate.

^{g} Includes extraordinary income resulting from tax benefit of net operating loss carry-forward.

^{h} Includes aftertax writedown of Jamaican alumina plant of $40.2 and $23.8 million in 1978 and 1975, respectively.

^{i} Does not include Asarco's equity in the write-down of Jamaican alumina plant.

LIFO INVENTORY LIQUIDATION

Ralph L. Hennebach
President

In 1978 Asarco recorded a nonrecurring pretax profit of $37.4 million which arose from the liquidation of excess metal inventories which we account for on a Lifo basis. This liquidation of metal inventories continued through the first quarter of this year, and we may, depending on our experience over the remainder of the year, have a similar kind of profit in 1979. We thought, therefore, that you might like an explanation of how the excess metal inventory came into being, why it is deemed excess, and how we were able prudently to liquidate much of it last year and so far this year.

Asarco's Pipeline of Metals

As you know we are in part a custom smelter and refiner of nonferrous metals, and therefore, we buy the metal content of lead, copper, and zinc ores and concentrates and process these materials through our smelters and refineries into refined metals for the market. This processing step from time of receipt of the crude concentrate at a smelter to availability of refined metal at a refinery requires, depending on the metal, two to three months. We therefore must always have locked up in process a physical quantity of metal equivalent to two to three months' production. This required base quantity of pipeline of metals was established in our early years and is part of our working capital.

Under our Lifo system of accounting, which we have been using since 1935, metal is carried in our inventory at the average cost of the year in which it was accumulated and, therefore, at any time our respective gold, silver, lead, copper, and zinc inventories are composed of layers of metals, each layer carrying the average cost of the year in which it was accumulated. These layers are added to our inventory chronologically and, if and when they are liquidated, the disposal is done in reverse chronological order. The last annual layer in is the first annual layer out, that is, Lifo.

LIFO INVENTORY LIQUIDATION (continued)

How Excess Inventory Accumulates

When operating the *custom* smelting and refining portion of our business, in order to minimize market risk, we try to sell each month the amount of metal that we purchase each month, and we try to buy and sell on the same quotation. We do this to provide an effective hedge and to protect our smelting and refining margins. However, at times when markets are weak, we may not be wholly successful in selling our purchased intake, and we may accumulate metal.

Using copper as an example, since the Second World War we have had two periods of significant metal accumulation—a period of chronic small annual accumulations that existed from 1965 through 1970, and an explosive one in 1974 and 1975, which was the aftermath of the OPEC oil embargo, price controls, and the turbulent international markets created by them.

As the result of these two periods of metal accumulation, we began the year 1976 with significantly increased inventories of metals. These were primarily of copper, although to a lesser degree silver and lead were also involved. The extent to which these inventories were deemed excess depended upon both the quantity on hand and the amount of company-owned metal that was needed to maintain our pipeline of physical metal.

Since 1970 we have been consciously reducing the portion of the required physical metal pipeline owned by the company by two actions: deliberately switching a larger portion of our business from custom—that is purchased—to toll, where the customer, not Asarco, carries the pipeline inventory; and wherever possible, extending the pricing periods in our ore purchase contracts so as not to price, that is, purchase, metals until they are available for sale. In the case of copper, for example, we try to purchase copper contained in concentrates at the market price for the third calendar month following date of receipt at one of our smelters. To the extent we are successful in doing this, the mine or shipper carries the pipeline.

Getting back to 1976, in that year we maintained a balance between intake and sales. We modestly reduced our excess metal inventory in 1977. Then in 1978, because of the surging demand for metals and the resulting rising markets, we made

LIFO INVENTORY LIQUIDATION (*concluded*)

substantial sales in excess of our purchases which resulted in the nonrecurring profits which are the subject of this presentation. The oversales have continued through the first four months of this year.

To sum up, our excess inventory was created by buying more metal than we could sell—mainly during the 1965–70 period and in the years 1974 and 1975—and by taking actions which reduced the quantity of company-owned pipeline inventory required to run our business. However, our opportunity to sell this excess inventory wisely and profitably required improved demand and rising prices. These conditions emerged halfway through 1978 and are still with us today.

Timing of Inventory Sales and Profits

The questions we now have to consider are the amount of oversales that it is prudent for us to make and the appropriate time to reflect inventory profits in our earnings. We don't want to overliquidate and sell into historically old low-cost layers of metals so as to generate a book profit which would attract an income tax, and then due to an increased volume of business or future weak markets have to reaccumulate the same quantity of metal at a higher price. The same considerations bear upon the timing of including inventory profits in our earnings. Since additions to new Lifo inventory layers, or the elimination of old layers, are made only on results for the full accounting year, it is the company's policy not to recognize any Lifo profits in an interim period until it has a high level of confidence that metals will not in fact be reaccumulated before year-end. Accordingly, we did not think it appropriate to recognize any Lifo profits in our first quarter 1979 results. We will review these questions again at the end of each quarterly period to determine it if is then appropriate to include any part of these apparent profits in our interim results.

Case 6–4

The Wolohan Lumber Company (A)

The Wolohan Lumber Company merchandises building materials. It was founded in 1964 when three supply centers were opened, and by 1974 had grown into a six state chain of 26 one-stop retail centers.

Each of these centers distributes more than 3,500 different products, including nearly every item used in constructing, remodeling, or maintaining a home. Sales are divided evenly between professional contractors and retail customers.

Exhibits 1 through 7 are reproduced from the 1974 Wolohan Lumber Company annual report.

Required:

Read the following exhibits and answer the following questions:

1. Comment on the president's letter. Do you think the president is more concerned with corporate liquidity and cash flow, or reported profits? Which is more important?
2. Comment on the company's explanation (Exhibit 3) of the impact of Lifo versus Fifo. Have any significant ramifications been ignored?
3. Compare Wolohan's performance in 1974 to its 1973 performance. In which year was the company more successful? Why?
4. Comment on the auditor's opinion (Exhibit 6). Do you agree that the financial statements of Wolohan Lumber are fairly presented?

EXHIBIT 1 _____

THE WOLOHAN LUMBER COMPANY
Financial Highlights
Years Ended December 31,

	*1974**	*1973*
Sales	$72,349,076	$66,924,517
Gross profit	15,785,869	13,516,983
Income before income taxes	2,008,859	2,432,329
Net income	1,007,859	1,200,329
Per share:†		
Net income	$ .49	$ .59
Shareowners' equity	6.39	6.00
Dividend	.10	.05
Financial position at year-end		
Working capital	9,191,316	7,012,855
Total assets	22,974,635	24,010,080
Long-term debt	5,400,517	3,426,699
Total liabilities	9,936,409	11,775,713
Shareowners' equity	13,038,226	12,234,367
Key ratios and percentages		
Current ratio	3.2:1	1.9:1
Gross profit margin	21.8%	20.2%
Operating margin	3.9%	4.3%
Pretax profit margin	2.8%	3.6%
Return on sales.....................	1.4%	1.8%
Return on shareowners' equity	8.2%	10.8%

* In 1974, the company changed its method of accounting for substantially all of its inventories from the first-in, first-out (Fifo) method to the last-in, first-out (Lifo) method. This was done because the adoption of the Lifo method during a period of rising costs provides a better matching of current costs with current sales, and at the same time permits a substantial reduction in the cash outlay for income taxes. The effect on reported earnings for the year was a decrease of $514,000, or $.25 per share.

† Calculated on 2,040,000 shares outstanding both years.

EXHIBIT 2

Excerpts from the President's Letter

To Our Shareowners:

The year that ended December 31, 1974, presented an operating environment marked by more numerous and serious problems than our industry has faced for many years. A persisting inflation that increased operating costs . . . high interest rates that discouraged home buying . . . a continuing decline in home building . . . rising energy costs . . . continued shortages of some materials . . . an erosion of consumer confidence . . . many industry layoffs and other difficulties . . . all of which resulted in seriously slowing our economy.

Despite this environment—as a result of the steps taken to increase sales, to more effectively control profit margins on those sales, and to better manage assets and expenses so as to improve our return—we feel that our performance was satisfactory.

Sales of Wolohan Lumber Co. were $72.3 million, the ninth consecutive year they climbed to record highs, and an 8.1 percent increase from 1973's $66.9 million.

Net income was $1 million, equivalent to 49 cents a share, 16 percent less than 1973's $1.2 million, equivalent to 59 cents a share. It should be noted, however, that in 1974, the company changed its method of accounting for substantially all of its inventories from the first-in, first-out (Fifo) method to the last-in, first-out (Lifo) method. This was done because the adoption of the Lifo method during a period of rising costs provides a better matching of current costs with current sales, and at the same time permits a substantial reduction in the cash outlay for income taxes. The effect on reported earnings for the year was a decrease of $514,000, or 25 cents a share. The two methods are described later in the report.

Shareowners' equity rose 6.6 percent to $13 million ($6.39 per share), from $12.2 million ($6 per share) the year before.

We opened two building materials retail centers—one in Terre Haute, Indiana; the other in Saginaw, Michigan—a central warehouse operation in Madison, Wisconsin, and a second roof-truss manufacturing facility in Clarks Hill, Indiana.

Many of our operating ratios were lower, 1974 versus 1973, as a result of the inventory accounting change. Our return on sales went from 1.8 percent to 1.4 percent; our return on assets from 5.4 percent to 4.0 percent; our return on shareowners' equity from 10.8 percent to 8.2 percent; our operating profit margin from 4.3 percent to 3.9 percent; and our net profit margin before taxes from 3.6 percent to 2.8 percent. But here, too, it should be noted that without that accounting change, these ratios would have shown improvement.

Therefore, in October, the Board of Directors felt it appropriate to declare a 10-cent dividend, payable November 29, 1974, up from 5 cents a share the year before.

Richard V. Wolohan
President

EXHIBIT 3
Lifo versus Fifo

Shareowners of hundreds of corporations have been made conscious lately of two strange-sounding words—new to many of them—Lifo and Fifo. What do they mean? Why are companies switching from one to the other? What is the impact of each on reported earnings and cash available to the company?

Both refer to methods of inventory accounting. Fifo stands for first-in, first-out; Lifo, for last-in, first-out.

To illustrate how the two methods work, assume a merchant buys five cases of nails over a period of time with progressive costs of $1, $2, $3, $4, and $5. Their total cost to him, then, and the value of the five cases if one assumes no sales have been made yet from the inventory, under each accounting method is $15 ($1 + $2 + $3 + $4 + $5).

If three cases were sold at $10 each, this would be the impact:

	Fifo		*Lifo*	
Sales	$30	($10 × 3)	$30	($10 × 3)
Cost of sales	6	($1 + $2 + $3)	12	($5 + $4 + $3)
Pre-tax earnings	24		18	
Taxes	12	($24 × 50%)	9	(18 × 50%)
Net earnings	$12		$ 9	

Although gross sales stay the same under each method, taxes on earnings in this simplified example would be 25 percent less using Lifo.

Note the value of the inventory left on hand under each method:

	Fifo	*Lifo*
Cost value	$9 ($15 − $6, cost of sales, or cases costing $4 and $5)	$3 ($15 − $12, cost of sales, or cases costing $1 and $2)

The value of inventory on hand, which is also subject to taxes, is 66.7 percent less under Lifo.

Note, too, the cash available to the company under each method:

	Fifo	*Lifo*
Sales	$30	$30
Addition to inventories....................	15	15
	15	15
Taxes	12	9
Cash available to the company	$ 3	$ 6

The cash available to the company, in this example, is 100 percent greater under Lifo.

To sum up, these are the major effects of switching from traditional Fifo inventory accounting to Lifo:

EXHIBIT 3 (continued) ────────────────────────────────

1. Most visibly: Reported earnings are lower. This means that Comparisons with previous years when earnings were based on Fifo are less favorable. This may affect the price of the shares—though less than normally in today's depressed market.
2. The cost of sales now reflects more accurately the rising cost of replacement.
3. Taxes are reduced.
4. Cash available to the company for growth is now greater—at a time when money is not only costly but difficult to obtain.

(This is a much-simplified explanation, of course. In practice, there are other important factors involved, with advantages and disadvantages not always so obvious, and legal complexities involved in the change.)

EXHIBIT 4 ────────────────────────────────

THE WOLOHAN LUMBER COMPANY
Statement of Income and Retained Earnings
Years Ended December 31, 1974 and 1973

	1974	1973
Net sales	$72,349,076	$66,924,517
Other income	118,749	109,919
	$72,467,825	$67,034,436
Costs and expenses:		
Cost of sales	56,653,207	53,407,534
Selling and administrative expenses	13,084,690	10,747,210
Interest on long-term debt	447,457	171,950
Other interest	363,612	275,413
	$70,458,966	$64,602,107
Income before income taxes	$ 2,008,859	$ 2,432,329
Income Taxes:		
Current:		
Federal	747,000	904,000
State	154,000	178,000
Deferred federal and state	100,000	150,000
	$ 1,001,000	$ 1,232,000
Net income:		
(per share, based on 2,040,000 shares:		
1974—$.49; 1973—$.59)	$ 1,007,859	$ 1,200,329
Retained earnings at beginning of year	6,023,959	4,925,630
	$ 7,031,818	$ 6,125,959
Cash dividends paid		
(per share: 1974—$.10; 1973—$.05)	204,000	102,000
Retained earnings at end of year	$ 6,827,818	$ 6,023,959

EXHIBIT 5

THE WOLOHAN LUMBER COMPANY
Balance Sheet
December 31, 1974 and 1973
Assets

	1974	1973
Current assets:		
Cash	$ 1,205,227	$ 970,195
Trade receivables, less allowance for doubtful accounts: (1974—$111,000; 1973—$93,100)	3,732,412	3,594,613
Inventories (less adjustment to last-in, first-out cost of $1,069,000 in 1974) (Note B)	8,335,392	10,404,921
Prepaid expenses and other current accounts	11,125	49,088
Total current assets	$13,284,156	$15,018,817
Other assets	77,387	56,405
Properties:		
Land	1,542,050	1,507,850
Land improvements	1,921,907	1,622,593
Buildings	6,209,750	5,559,119
Equipment	2,342,317	1,901,833
Construction in progress	—0—	123,644
Allowances for depreciation (deduction)	(2,402,932)	(1,780,181)
	$ 9,613,092	$ 8,934,858
	$22,974,635	$24,010,080

Liabilities and Stockholders' Equity

	1974	1973
Current liabilities:		
Notes payable to banks	$ —0—	$ 3,000,000
Trade accounts payable	2,228,880	3,248,788
Employee compensation	868,857	615,971
Accrued expenses	467,776	449,861
Federal and state income taxes	1,146	139,348
Current portion of long-term debt	526,181	551,994
Total current liabilities	$ 4,092,840	$ 8,005,962
Long-term debt (Less portion classified as current liability)..............................	5,400,517	3,426,699
Deferred income taxes...........................	443,052	343,052
Stockholders' equity:		
Common stock, par value $1 a share:		
Authorized—3,000,000 shares	2,040,000	2,040,000
Outstanding—2,040,000 shares		
Additional paid-in capital	4,170,408	4,170,408
Retained Earnings	6,827,818	6,023,959
	$13,038,226	$12,234,367
	$22,974,635	$24,010,080

EXHIBIT 6

Notes to Financial Statements

Note B. Change in Accounting Method. Effective January 1, 1974, the company changed its method of determining the cost of substantially all inventories from the first-in, first-out (Fifo method to the last-in, first-out (Lifo) method. The change reduced net income for 1974 by $514,400 ($.25 a share). Prior years' earnings are not affected since the ending inventories under the Fifo method at December 31, 1973, represent the beginning inventories for 1974 under the Lifo method.

The company believes that the adoption of Lifo during a period of rising costs provides a better matching of current costs with current sales, and at the same time permits a substantial reduction in the cash outlay for income taxes.

EXHIBIT 7

The Auditor's Report

Board of Directors
Wolohan Lumber Co.
Saginaw, Michigan

We have examined the balance sheet of Wolohan Lumber Co. as of December 31, 1974, and 1973, and the related statements of income and retained earnings and changes in financial position for the years then ended. Our examinations were made in accordance with generally accepted auditing standards and, accordingly, included such tests of the accounting records and such other auditing procedures as we considered necessary in the circumstances.

In our opinion, the financial statements referred to above present fairly the financial position of Wolohan Lumber Co. at December 31, 1974, and 1973, and the results of its operations and changes in financial position for the years then ended, in conformity with generally accepted accounting principles consistently applied during the period except for the change, with which we concur, in the method of determining inventory cost as described in Note B to the financial statements.

Ernst & Ernst

7

Focus on Manufacturing Costing Issues

Generally accepted accounting principles require that the absorption (full) costing method be used to assign manufacturing costs to inventory. The absorption costing method assigns *all* manufacturing costs to each unit of output.

Manufacturing costs include both direct product costs and factory overhead costs. Raw material and direct labor are direct product costs which can be specifically traced to the manufacture of an individual product. Factory (manufacturing) overhead costs include all costs incurred in the manufacturing process which cannot be assigned directly to an individual product. *Fixed factory overhead costs* do not change as the output level of the factory varies over reasonable levels. Depreciation on manufacturing equipment, property taxes on the factory building, and the plant manager's salary are examples of fixed factory overhead costs. *Variable factory overhead costs* vary with changes in the output level of the factory. The amount and cost of oil consumed in a machine shop increases roughly proportionate to the total output of the shop. The cost of oil is a factory overhead cost rather than a direct product cost because of the difficulty (or impossibility) of assigning the oil consumed to a particular unit of output.

Assigning fixed factory overhead costs to individual units of production is a subjective and mechanically complicated accounting process. To avoid this allocation of fixed factory overhead costs some manufacturers use a method called direct (variable) costing which treats fixed factory overhead cost as a period expense rather than a cost of product.

ABSORPTION COSTING

To illustrate the valuation of inventory and calculation of net income using the absorption costing method we can use the data in Illustration 7–1 for the SOM Manufacturing Co. SOM Manufacturing began operations in 1981 and manufactures a single product. Direct

ILLUSTRATION 7–1
Data for SOM Manufacturing Company*

Actual direct manufacturing costs (per unit of output):	
Raw materials	$1.50
Labor (1 direct labor hour at $3.25)	$3.25
Estimated (and actual) factory overhead costs	
Fixed factory overhead cost per year	$3,000.00
Variable factory overhead per unit of output	
(1 direct labor hour at $.75)	$.75
Actual selling costs	
Fixed selling cost per year	$1,000.00
Variable selling cost per unit of output	$1.00
Sales price per unit of output	$11.50

* SOM Manufacturing uses the Lifo inventory flow assumption. There are no work in process inventories at the end of 1981 or 1982.

product costs are $4.75 ($3.25 direct labor + $1.50 raw materials) per unit. Usually such costs are listed on an individual job ticket which accompanies the job through the manufacturing process. Upon completion of one unit this information is the basis for the following journal entry:

Work in Process Inventory........................	4.75	
Raw Material Inventory		1.50
Wages Payable		3.25

In addition to the cost of direct labor and raw material, each unit produced is assigned its fair share of factory overhead under the absorption costing method.

Fixed factory overhead is assigned to individual products using the following process:

1. Estimate fixed factory overhead costs for the year. SOM estimates these costs to be $3,000.

2. Choose a basis for allocating fixed factory overhead to individual products. Selection of a basis is subjective. Are particular products worth more than others? If so, should more factory overhead be assigned to them? Is there more time spent making one product than another? Most companies use either direct labor hours, direct machine hours, or direct labor costs as a basis for allocating fixed factory overhead costs. SOM Co. uses direct labor hours as a means of assigning fixed factory overhead to finished product.

3. Estimate the normal or anticipated level of the activity base selected in (2). SOM estimates that production will average 1,500

units per year for the immediate future. Since one unit of production requires one direct labor hour, the normal or anticipated level of direct labor hours is 1,500.

4. Compute an overhead allocation rate (OAR = Estimated fixed factory overhead costs/Estimated normal activity level). Factory overhead allocation is based on the ratio of *estimated* fixed factory overhead costs for the year to *estimated* direct labor hours for the year because assignment of overhead to individual products takes place throughout the year *before actual* factory overhead and direct labor hours worked are known. The OAR for SOM Manufacturing is $2 per direct labor hour ($3,000/1,500 direct labor hours).

5. Record fixed factory overhead costs as incurred during the period. For instance, SOM's payment of the annual fire insurance bill on the factory for $500 is recorded as:

Fixed Factory Overhead	500	
Cash...		500

The fixed factory overhead account is an asset account which temporarily collects overhead costs before their assignment to the inventory account, work in process.

SOM uses a similar method to allocate variable factory overhead cost to units of production. The variable factory overhead cost per direct labor hour (and per unit of production since there is one direct labor hour in each unit of finished product) is $.75. Since every unit produced by SOM Manufacturing contains one direct labor hour, the following journal entry allocates a portion of total factory overhead to an individual unit:

Work in Process Inventory	2.75	
Fixed Factory Overhead		2.00
Variable Factory Overhead...................		.75

Transfer of a completed item to finished goods can now be made.

Finished Goods Inventory	7.50	
Work in Process Inventory		7.50

Under absorption costing one unit of finished goods inventory is valued at $7.50 (direct material cost of $1.50, direct labor cost of $3.25, variable factory overhead cost of $.75, and fixed factory overhead cost of $2.00). Each unit produced absorbs its fair (reasonable) share of fixed factory overhead.

Assume manufacturing costs incurred during the first two years of operation equaled estimated costs and actual production and sales levels were as follows:

	1981	*1982*
Production (units)	1,000	2,000
Sales (units)	900	900

Fixed factory overhead cost incurred during 1981 was $3,000. Because actual production was less than estimated normal or anticipated production, only $2,000 (1,000 units at $2) of the $3,000 fixed factory overhead cost was absorbed by (applied to) finished products. At the end of 1981 the fixed factory overhead account appeared as follows:

Fixed Factory Overhead

(actual) $3,000	$2,000*

* Transferred to Work in Process Inventory.

This $1,000 balance is called a fixed factory overhead *volume* variance. It represents the amount of actual fixed factory overhead that was not applied to units produced and is called unabsorbed (underapplied) overhead. Absorption costing requires that all manufacturing costs of the period be associated with production during the period, whether the units are currently in work in process inventory, finished goods inventory, or were sold during the period and are included in cost of goods sold. In practice, the total volume variance is usually charged as an adjustment to cost of goods sold unless the amount is material in the calculation of net income. In 1981 the entry to adjust cost of goods sold for the $1,000 unabsorbed (unapplied) fixed factory overhead is

Cost of Goods Sold—Adjustment for Fixed Factory Overhead Volume Variance	1,000	
Fixed Factory Overhead		1,000

This reduces the end of period balance in the Fixed Factory Overhead account to zero and *increases* expense for the period by $1,000.

At the end of 1982 the Fixed Factory Overhead account before adjustment appeared as follows:

Fixed Factory Overhead

(actual) 3,000	4,000*

* Transferred to Work in Process Inventory.

In 1982 actual production of 2,000 units exceeded estimated or normal production of 1,500 units and the fixed factory overhead volume variance was a credit of $1,000 (500 units at $2). The journal entry to record the volume variance (overabsorbed fixed factory overhead) on the income statement was:

Fixed Factory Overhead 1,000
Cost of Goods Sold—Adjustment for Fixed
  Overhead Volume Variance 1,000

This reduces the balance in Fixed Factory Overhead to zero and decreases 1982 cost of goods sold by $1,000.

Since actual variable factory overhead equaled estimated variable factory overhead, there was no variance associated with variable factory overhead.

Absorption (full) costing income statements with overhead volume variances as adjustments to cost of goods sold are presented in Illustration 7–2. Although sales levels remained constant at 900 units, net

ILLUSTRATION 7–2

SOM MANUFACTURING CO.
Absorption Costing Income Statements
(variance charged to cost of goods sold)

	1981	1982
Sales revenue (900 at $11.50)	$10,350	$10,350
Cost of goods sold (900 at $7.50)	6,750	6,750
Gross margin..	$ 3,600	$ 3,600
Adjustment for over (under) applied overhead—		
volume variance...............................	(1,000)	1,000
Adjusted gross margin	$ 2,600	$ 4,600
Variable selling expenses (900 at $1)................	$ 900	$ 900
Fixed selling expenses............................	1,000	1,000
	$ 1,900	$ 1,900
Net income..	$ 700	$ 2,700
Ending inventory	$ 750*	$ 9,000†

* 100 units left in inventory at a cost per unit of $7.50.
† The inventory consists of two Lifo layers. The original $750 layer added in 1981 and the 1,100 units valued at $8,250 (1,100 at $7.50) added in 1982.

income increased from $700 in 1981 to $2,700 in 1982. The $2,000 difference is explained in terms of the adjustments to cost of goods sold for the volume variance. Lower than estimated normal production in 1981 resulted in unabsorbed fixed factory overhead of $1,000 which reduced net income. Higher than estimated normal production in 1982 resulted in overabsorption of fixed factory overhead which increased income by $1,000. The size of the volume variance and the adjustment to cost of goods sold is dependent on the level of production. If actual production levels exceed estimated normal production levels, fixed factory overhead will be overabsorbed and net income will be increased by the amount of the overabsorption. The opposite is true for production levels below normal production levels. Production level changes affect the allocation of fixed factory overhead, the fixed factory overhead volume variance, and ultimately the assignment of fixed overhead costs to inventory and to the income statement. *Absorption costing net income is dependent on production as well as sales levels.*

If production and sales levels are significantly different in any period, charging cost of goods sold with the entire volume variance could lead to a material distortion in reported net income. Generally accepted accounting principles would require allocation of the volume variance to work in process inventory, finished goods inventory, and cost of goods sold in proportion to the amount of the activity level allocation base (direct labor hours for SOM) in each. Illustration 7–3 contains the absorption costing statements with adjust-

ILLUSTRATION 7–3

SOM MANUFACTURING CO.
Absorption Costing Income Statements
(variance apportioned to inventory and cost of goods sold)

	1981	1982
Sales revenue (900 at $11.50)	$10,350	$10,350
Cost of goods sold (900 at $7.50)	6,750	6,750
Gross margin	$ 3,600	$ 3,600
Adjustment for over (under) applied overhead— volume variance	(900)*	450†
Adjusted gross margin	$ 2,700	$ 4,050
Variable selling expenses (900 at $1)	$ 900	$ 900
Fixed selling expense	1,000	1,000
	$ 1,900	$ 1,900
Net income	$ 800	$ 2,150
Ending inventory	$ 850*	$ 8,550†

* Total production is 1,000 units of which 900 were sold. Therefore 9/10 of the volume variance ($900) is attributed to cost of goods sold. 1/10 of the volume variance ($100) is absorbed into inventory which will be valued at $850 (100 at $7.50 plus $100 of the volume variance).

† Total production is 2,000 units of which 900 were sold. Therefore 9/20 of the volume variance ($450) is attributed to cost of goods sold. 11/20 of the variance ($550) is an adjustment to the value of inventory. Inventory will be valued at $8,550 (original layer at $850 plus the value of the new layer—1,100 at $7.50 minus $550).

ments to inventories and cost of goods sold. Although the difference between 1981 and 1982 net income is smaller than when the variance was absorbed entirely by cost of goods sold it is still material. The main point made earlier is still valid. Absorption costing incomes depend upon production levels and not just sales levels.

Many short-run operating decisions are concerned primarily with variable costs of production. Suppose a machine with idle capacity can be used to produce either one unit of Product A or one unit of Product B. Product A and Product B both have the same selling price. Since fixed costs do not change if either Product A or Product B is made, the product with the lowest variable cost of production and selling should be produced. A cost accumulation and measurement system which distinguishes between variable costs which change with the level of production and fixed costs which do not change with the level of production is a useful aid to management. Direct costing is such an accounting system.

DIRECT COSTING[1]

The treatment of fixed factory overhead distinguishes direct costing from absorption costing. In direct costing there is no allocation of fixed factory overhead to product. Fixed factory overhead is treated as an expense in the accounting period it is incurred rather than a cost of units produced as in the absorption costing method. Units produced are valued at the variable cost to produce them. The direct costing income statement format (Illustration 7–4) is illustrated using the SOM Manufacturing company data.

Since fixed production costs are not averaged over differential numbers of units produced in each period, direct costing income is independent of fluctuations in the production level. The fixed factory overhead cost for SOM Manufacturing in 1981 and 1982 will be $3,000 and the direct costing net income is $500 each year.

The difference in net income computed using full and direct costing is due only to the fixed factory overhead costs reflected in the income statement.[2] Illustration 7–5 illustrates the process of reconciling absorption costing net income with direct costing net income.

Direct costing presents a clear picture of a firm's ability to generate profits in the *short run*. Direct costing income depends on the

---

[1] The direct costing method is not allowable for the preparation of financial statements or the calculation of net income for federal income taxes.

[2] If sales equal production, net income for full and direct costing should be the same. The fixed factory overhead in the units sold plus the volume variance which is charged on the full costing income statement will be equal to actual fixed cost which is charged on the direct costing income statement.

ILLUSTRATION 7–4 _____

SOM MANUFACTURING CO.
Direct Costing Income Statements

	1981		1982	
Sales revenue (900 at $11.50)		$10,350		$10,350
Less variable costs:				
Direct materials (900 at $1.50).....	$1,350		$1,350	
Direct labor (900 at $3.25).........	2,925		2,925	
Factory overhead (900 at $.75)	675		675	
Variable cost of goods sold.....	$4,950		$4,950	
Selling expense (900 at $1.00).....	900		900	
Total variable costs...........		5,850		5,850
Contribution margin		$ 4,500		$ 4,500
Less fixed costs:				
Production	$3,000		$3,000	
Selling	1,000		1,000	
Total fixed costs		4,000		4,000
Net income		$ 500		$ 500
Ending inventory		$ 550*		$ 6,600*

* Inventory is valued at the variable cost to produce it. 100 units at $5.50 in 1981 and 1,200 units at $5.50 in 1982.

sales level but is independent of the production level for the period.

Direct costing undervalues inventory in the balance sheet. It fails to include in inventory the fixed costs of production which certainly must be incurred if goods are to be manufactured and which must be covered by selling prices in the *long run* if the firm is to remain in business.

COST-VOLUME-PROFIT MODEL (BREAK-EVEN ANALYSIS)

The difference between sales revenue and all variable expenses (including variable selling expense and variable factory overhead) is called the contribution margin. For a single product firm the *unit contribution margin* is the contribution margin divided by the number of units sold. The unit contribution margin for SOM Manufacturing's single product is $5 ($11.50 selling price less $1.50 direct material cost, $3.25 direct labor cost, $.75 variable factory overhead, and $1 variable selling cost). The total contribution margin is $4,500 for the 900 units sold in 1981 and 1982. This focus on variable costs

ILLUSTRATION 7–5

Reconciliation of Absorption Costing Net Income with Direct Costing
Net Income

	1981	1982
Absorption costing		
Fixed factory overhead:		
In cost of goods sold (900 units sold at $2)	$1,800	$1,800
Volume variance	1,000	(1,000)
Total fixed factory overhead in income statement	$2,800	$ 800
Direct costing		
Fixed factory overhead in income statement	3,000	3,000
Difference	($200)	(2,200)
Absorption costing net income (Illustration 7–2)	700	2,700
Direct costing net income	$ 500	$ 500
Ending Inventories		
Ending inventory values:		
Absorption costing (Illustration 7–2)	$ 750	$9,000
Less: Fixed costs allocated to absorption costing inventory	200*	2,400†
Ending inventory values:		
Direct costing	$ 550	$6,600

* 100 at $2 fixed factory overhead allocation.
† 1,200 at $2 fixed factory overhead allocation.

versus fixed costs is a useful distinction in many decision situations
and is highlighted by the direct costing statements.[3] For example, if
SOM were to sell one more unit in 1981 without incurring additional
fixed costs (entirely reasonable), then direct costing income would
increase by $5, the amount of the unit contribution margin, and

---

[3] Modern financial theories suggest that the valuation of a firm in an equity (stock)
market depends on the firm's future prospects of paying cash dividends to investors.
Managers therefore should choose among alternatives on the basis of their effects on
future cash flows, not on their effects on future reported accounting net incomes.
Direct costing income statements make it easier for managers to focus on the cash
flow effects of alternatives when making several common short-run decisions.

Since the focus should be on cash flows in decision making, adjustments must
usually be made to direct costing income statements so that net income corresponds
to net cash inflow. For instance, depreciation on the factory, as will be illustrated in a
later chapter, requires such an adjustment. In this chapter we *assume that all items
listed on the direct costing income statement correspond to cash flows of the period.*

SOM would have $5 more in cash ($11.50 from the sale less the $6.50 of variable costs to produce and sell the additional unit).

Most firms are interested in how many units they must sell in a period in order to cover all their fixed costs of the period and break even. The *break-even point* (BEP) is the level of sales which generates neither a profit nor a loss. The unit contribution margin is the key to computing the BEP.

Let p = Selling price per unit ($11.50).

   v = *Total* variable cost per unit ($6.50).

   F = *Total* fixed costs per period ($4,000).

   x = Number of units sold in a period.

The break-even point is expressed algebraically as

$$(p - v)x = F \text{ (Contribution margin equals fixed costs)}$$

$$\text{BEP} = x = \frac{F}{(p - v)}.$$

The break-even point for SOM Manufacturing is 800 units. It is equal to fixed costs of $4,000 divided by the unit contribution margin of $5. The break-even point can also be expressed in terms of dollars of sales required to break even, $\text{BEP}_\$$.

$$\text{BEP}_\$ = (\text{BEP})p = \frac{Fp}{(p - v)} = \frac{F}{\dfrac{(p - v)}{p}}.$$

$(p - v)/p$ is called the contribution margin ratio, the portion of every sales dollar which goes to covering fixed costs. SOM Co.'s contribution margin ratio is $5/11.5 \simeq .435$. If every sales dollar contributes 43.5 cents toward covering overhead, it will take $4,000/.435 \simeq $9,200 total sales dollars (800 units at $11.50) to cover $4,000 in fixed costs in addition to all variable costs and just break even.

Let π denote direct costing income. The contribution margin, the break-even point, and direct costing income are related according to the following equation:

$$\begin{aligned} \pi = px - vx - F &= (p - v)x - F \\ &= \$11.50x - \$6.50x - \$4,000 \\ &= \$5x - \$4,000. \end{aligned}$$

The above profit equation is called a cost-volume-profit (CVP) model since it relates sales volume and costs to profits. $p - v$ is the unit contribution margin and $(p - v)x$ is the total contribution margin. Profits will be positive as long as the total contribution "covers" (at least as large or exceeds) fixed costs. When $\pi = 0$, $(p - v)x$ equals F, and the break-even point is generated.

ILLUSTRATION 7–6

Break-Even Chart (cost-volume-profit graph)

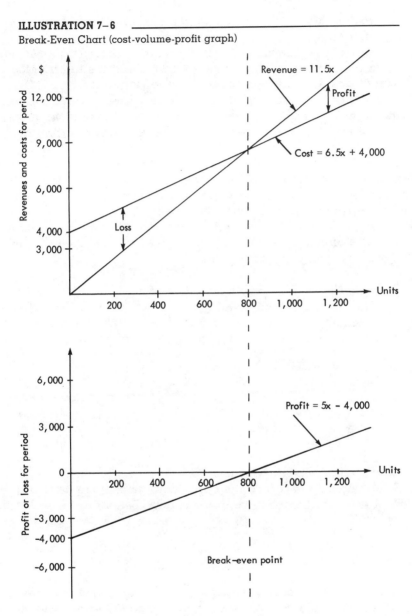

Illustration 7–6 is a graphical representation of the CVP model. In the upper portion SOM Manufacturing Co.'s costs and revenues are plotted individually. Profit at any particular level is measured as the vertical distance (parallel to the $ axis) between the revenue line and the cost line. At a sales level of 1,000 units revenues are $11,500, total

costs are $10,500 ($4,000 + $6,500) and profits are $1,000. At any sales level where the cost curve is above the revenue curve SOM would experience a loss. The BEP is the intersection of the revenue and cost lines in the upper portion of Illustration 7–6 and the intersection of the profit line with the sales axis in the lower portion.

Frequently the profit equation is plotted directly (revenues and costs are not shown separately) making it easier to read what profit levels will be for given sales levels. See the lower portion of the chart.

The CVP model is a compact expression which generates abbreviated direct costing income statements for any sales level assuming total fixed costs and variable costs per unit do not change. The CVP model direct costing statements are not actual income statements. *They represent expectations about income if everything occurs as planned.* The following examples illustrate the usefulness of the CVP model as a managerial tool.

Example (Sales Necessary for a Given Profit Level).

At what sales level will SOM generate profits of $2,500? Illustration 7–6 can be used to find that a sales level of 1,300 units generates $2,500 profit. Algebraically the basic CVP equation can be used.

$$\$2,500 = \$5x - \$4,000$$
$$x = \frac{\$2,500 + \$4,000}{\$5 \text{ per Unit}} = 1,300 \text{ Units}$$
$$\left(\text{In general:} \quad x = \frac{F + \text{Desired profit}}{(p - v)} \right)$$

Example (Incremental Business).

SOM Manufacturing has the opportunity to sell one more unit in 1982 at a reduced sales price of $8. Is SOM better off if it sells this 901st unit?

Cost of producing 900 units = $6.50(900) + $4,000 = $9,850
Cost of producing 901 units = $6.50(901) + $4,000 = $9,856.50

The incremental cost of producing and selling one more unit is $6.50 (the variable cost of production). Since SOM receives $8 for selling the unit it will be better off. An alternative approach is to note that the unit contribution margin for the additional unit is $8.00 − $6.50 = $1.50, which is positive. SOM will be better off producing and selling the unit since it contributes $1.50 to covering fixed costs (which haven't changed) and generating profits.

Example (Cost Changes).

Suppose SOM Manufacturing's fixed costs per period increase from \$4,000 to \$4,900 due to an increase in property taxes. Market conditions will not permit the selling price to be raised above the current \$11.50 per unit. What will SOM's variable cost have to decrease to in order to maintain a profit level of \$500? From the basic equation: Profit $= (p - v)x - F$.

Therefore,

$$\$500 = (\$11.50 - v)(900) - \$4,900$$

$$\frac{\$5,400}{900} = \$11.50 - v$$

$$v = \$5.50.$$

SOM must introduce cost cutting measures which reduce variable costs by \$1 per unit from their current \$6.50 per unit level in order to maintain profit levels at \$500 per year.

If used intelligently the CVP model can be a very useful descriptive model of the profit behavior of a firm. Its usefulness is usually limited to analyzing small changes in p, v, x, or F. Large assumed changes in model parameters (particularly the sales level, x) are likely to invalidate the model's assumptions. For instance, output probably cannot be tripled without incurring additional fixed costs. The basic CVP model has been extended to multiple product settings and to allow for uncertainty in the variable or fixed cost components of the model. These extensions are beyond the scope of this chapter.

The CVP model, although useful, cannot be used to address many extremely important decisions a manager faces. It is concerned primarily with cash flows in the very short run. It approximates the true changes in costs and revenues which result when the current level of production is either slightly increased or slightly decreased.

CASES FOR CHAPTER 7

Case 7–1

Samuel Breese Corporation

When Mr. Lewis, sales manager of Samuel Breese Corporation, returned from a sales convention early in April, he told the controller, Mr. Morse, about a talk in which a financial officer of a competing company strongly recommended the break-even chart as a device for indicating the approximate profit to be expected at various levels of output. Morse said that such a chart could be prepared for the Samuel Breese Corporation without much difficulty and within a few days gave Lewis the chart reproduced in Exhibit 1. In its cost accounts, the corporation treats 10,000 units a month as normal (standard) production.

On June 1, as soon as he learned that 6,200 units had been sold in May, Lewis erected the line at 6.2 on the chart and from it estimated that the net profit (before income tax) for May would be between $1,400 and $1,500. He was pleasantly surprised therefore when he got the May income statement on June 8 and saw that the book profit was $2,500. While he could not complain about the reported profit, he did want to know why it was some 70 percent higher than he had expected.

SAMUEL BREESE CORPORATION
Income Statement for May 1975

Sales (6,200 units).........................		$12,300
Expenses:		
Standard cost of goods sold	$6,820	
Manufacturing variances:		
Volume (debit).........................	400	
All other (debit).......................	280	
Selling and general.....................	2,300	9,800
Net profit before income tax		$ 2,500

EXHIBIT 1

Samuel Breese Corporation Break-Even Chart

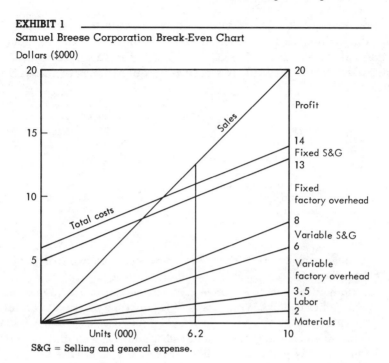

S&G = Selling and general expense.

Required:

1. Compute the break-even point for the Samuel Breese Corporation.
2. Compute the exact profit indicated by the break-even chart for sales of 6,200 units.
3. Determine the number of units produced in May.
4. Reconcile the profit just computed with the book profit of $2,500.

Case 7–2

Big Time Manufacturing

The Big Time Manufacturing Company recently hired (January 1, 1980) a new chief executive to assume startup responsibility (marketing strategy, advertising, production levels, and so forth) for its new operations. In addition to a generous salary, the new executive officer is to be given a bonus amounting to 20 percent of net income from operations (before income taxes or the bonus) computed using GAAP.

Big Time sells its single product for $6 per unit. The normal production level of 50,000 units is used to allocate the estimated fixed manufacturing overhead cost ($150,000) to units of final product (allocation rate is equal to $3 ($150,000/50,000) per unit produced).

On December 31, 1980, the results of operations for the year are collected:

Sales	40,000 units
Production	60,000 units
Fixed costs:	
Manufacturing overhead	$150,000
Selling	$ 70,000
Variable costs (per unit)	
Manufacturing	$1.00
Selling	$ .70

Required:

1. What is the amount of the bonus the new officer earned in 1980? (Ignore income taxes.)

2. Calculate income before bonus and income taxes for 1980 using the direct costing method. Why does it differ from the absorption costing income figure computed in (1) above? Did the officer "deserve" the bonus?

3. Assume sales continue at a level of 40,000 units a year and costs do not change. What is your assessment of the success of Big Time's operations? Which of the two income statements (direct costing or absorption costing) presents an income figure consistent with your assessment?

4. Would your evaluation of the executive's performance change if you knew that sales would increase to 80,000 units next year? Why?

Case 7–3

Blow Out, Inc.

Blow Out, Inc., has the capacity to produce 200,000 steel-belted radial tires per year. It currently produces 150,000 tires per year and sells them for $15 per tire; 150,000 units per year is also Blow Out's normal production level used to allocate fixed factory overhead costs. At this level of output the *average* cost to produce and sell a tire is $11. The average cost consists of:

Variable manufacturing cost	
(raw materials, direct labor,	
variable factory overhead)	$ 2
Fixed factory overhead........................	5
Variable selling cost	1
Fixed selling cost............................	3
	$11

Required:

1. Construct a cost-volume-profit graph for Blow Out. What is the break-even sales level?

2. A major discount department store has indicated a desire to purchase 30,000 tires (this would be in addition to Blow Out's current 150,000 sales level) of varying sizes for $8 per tire. No sales commission would have to be paid on this order.

   On the basis of the following analysis, the management of Blow Out concluded not to accept the order.

Selling price per tire	$8
Variable manufacturing cost	2
Fixed manufacturing cost	5
Fixed selling cost	3
Loss per tire	($2)

   Should Blow Out have accepted the order?

3. Suppose the order was for 70,000 tires at $8 per tire. In order to produce the additional 20,000 units if it accepts the order, it can do either one of two things: rent capacity for 1 year to produce the additional 20,000 tires (this would cost $60,000), or not supply some of the regular customers (supply them with 130,000 tires instead of 150,000 tires this year).

   What should Blow Out do? Reject the order for 70,000 additional tires, accept the order and rent additional capacity, or accept the order and supply its regular customers with 20,000 fewer tires this year?

Case 7–4

The Exorcist: Blatty v. Warner Bros.

Fixed costs of production are allocated to manufactured products, operating costs not directly associated with the generation of a revenue are allocated to quarters in constructing quarterly income statements, and general corporate expenses are sometimes allocated to segments of a business to determine segment income.

Whenever costs are assigned to products, periods, or segments using a "reasonable" allocation scheme, the "reasonableness" of the scheme is likely to be questioned.

You are an accounting expert asked to comment on *The Exorcist* suit described in the following articles from *The Wall Street Journal* (10/16/78). Defend the accounting in either Blatty's or Warner Bros.' position.

FEUD IN FILMDOM*

**Movie Studios' System of Splitting Profits Divides Hollywood
Author Wages a Court Battle over *Exorcist* Earnings
Auditing Business Booms
Michael Caine Makes a Deal**

By Earl C. Gottschalk Jr.
Staff Reporter of The Wall Street Journal

Hollywood—William Peter Blatty made about $17 million from the hit movie version of his best selling novel, *The Exorcist*. All very well, says Mr. Blatty—but it's not enough, not nearly enough.

The author has already spent about $200,000 in bringing a civil suit against Warner Bros., a unit of Warner Communications Inc., and the studio that bankrolled and released the movie. Mr. Blatty alleges that Warner Bros. cheated him out of his full profit share on the film through accounting flimflam, including the padding of expenses charged to the picture. He wants $1.5 million in compensatory damages and $10 million more for punitive damages.

Warner Bros. President Frank Wells vehemently denies that the studio cheated anybody. In fact, he says, Mr. Blatty got a "highly advantageous" deal. Neither the studio nor the author seems inclined to compromise, and a rare court airing of key Hollywood business practices seems likely.

The court battle will be closely watched in the entertainment industry because its outcome could have an important impact on the way studios treat their profit participants—the writers, producers, directors, and stars who bring the studios ideas and develop them into movies with studio backing in exchange for a cut of the profits. If Mr. Blatty wins his case, Hollywood's creative people could increase their slice of the pie at studio expense.

Hopping Mad

It's a big pie. Over the past three years the seven major studios have paid out $831 million in profit participations and TV residual fees to producers, writers, directors, and actors. The recipients claim that that is a lot less than they were really entitled to, however.

Hollywood's creative guilds are hopping mad about alleged creative accounting by the studios. Leonard Chasman, executive director of the Writers Guild West, says there is "general disillusionment and cynicism among screenwriters" about profit participation deals because the writer's profit proves illusory. Michael Franklin, executive director of the Directors Guild, complains of "widespread" studio finagling with the figures and says his members are "seriously concerned."

Disputes between Hollywood's creative people and its studios have become so common, in fact, that a mini-industry has established itself in Beverly Hills and New York to deal with them. It comprises accounting firms that specialize in auditing studio books on behalf of profit participants in hopes of finding errors in favor of their clients.

"Every successful movie is audited these days," declares David J. Bloom, a partner with the accounting firm of Berlfein & Co. of Beverly Hills. "There's a good reason: Almost every audit finds significant errors by the studios and more than pays for itself." Nathan Cohen, a Hollywood business manager and accountant, adds, "It's the only industry I know where they use two sets of books—one to show the stockholders how well they're doing and the other to show the profit participants how bad things are."

Warner Bros.' Reply

Studio executives take violent exception to charges of rigged bookkeeping. Ralph Peterson, vice president and treasurer of Warner Bros., says, "We state unequivocally that Warner Bros.—and we believe this to be true of all major studios—applies the highest standards of integrity and fair dealing in making its computations of net profits."

That doesn't mean there are never any mistakes, the studios concede. In the accounting for *The Exorcist*, for example, well over 100,000 different transactions had to be entered on the books—in short, 100,000 possibilities for error. Indeed, a review of this film's books by Mr. Blatty's accountants and the studio disclosed many mistakes. Warner Bros. says it has already corrected $1,140,861 worth of errors and adjustments on the total accounting for the picture.

Though it isn't unusual for lawsuits to be filed by profit participants seeking what they consider their fair share, few of the suits ever reach a courtroom. A quiet out-of-court settlement, with neither party discussing the terms, is the usual outcome. Such settlements cut short recent suits by actors Sean Connery and Michael Caine against Allied Artists Industries Inc., over *The Man Who Would Be King* and by Robert Redford and director Sydney Pollack against Columbia Pictures Industries Inc., over *The Way We Were*.

Waiting until Doomsday

The studios point to the relative infrequency of lawsuits as an indication that squabbles over profit participation aren't as common or as serious as critics say they are. But creative people, along with their accountants, attorneys, and guilds, say the real reason is that actors, writers, directors, and producers fear they won't get more work if they make too much trouble. And they add, an individual usually doesn't have the financial resources to take on a big company that can "string out a lawsuit until doomsday with delays, appeals, and other devices," as an official of one guild puts it.

Mr. Blatty, however, has plenty of money and determination. "I am not going to settle on the courthouse steps," he vows. "I would love to catch a reform-minded judge who agreed with my position and who would punish them severely. Not to be too cynical about it, this would probably have the refreshing effect of stopping this thievery for about three to five years. After that, they'll start all over again."

Like so many other filmdom squabbles, Mr. Blatty's suit centers on the movie industry definition of what comprises net profit on a movie; Warner Bros. definition covers eight pages of opaque legalese. But generally speaking, until a picture recovers its production, promotion, distribution, and overhead costs and fees, for accounting purposes, it is a loser and the "profit participants" don't get a nickel.

Mr. Blatty's original agreement with Warner Bros. gave him an initial payment of $500,000, made him the producer of the film as well as the screenwriter, and assigned him 39 percent of the net profit. (He later yielded a 4 percent interest to his director, William Friedkin.) Net profit, the contract said, would occur for participants when the following conditions were met:

Gross receipts to the studio covered the production cost of the film plus a 15 percent surcharge for general support of the studio's production facilities.

Warner Bros.' advertising and promotion costs for the picture were paid, plus a 10 percent overhead fee for general support of the studio ad and promotion department.

The studio took out its fee distributing the movie, amounting to 30 percent of the gross receipts in the United States and more elsewhere.

Under such a contract, which is fairly typical, it is to the studio's advantage to charge as many expense items to the picture as it can. Mr. Blatty claims Warner Bros. went overboard in doing just that.

For one thing, *The Exorcist* was charged with $161,000 for payments to attorneys in civil antitrust cases involving two other movie companies and the Motion Picture Association of America, the industry trade group. Warner Bros. claims the contract includes allowable expenses for "dues and assessments of the MPAA and other associations." Mr. Blatty contends that the payments, besides being totally unrelated to his film, weren't dues and assessments because not all members of the MPAA contributed to them.

Nonexistent Taxes

The studio also charged the film with $81,957 in Italian taxes on gross receipts, but Italy doesn't have such a tax. Warner replies that Italy is currently involved in a dispute with American movie concerns and could impose such a tax at any time, leading movie companies here to create reserves for that contingency.

Mr. Blatty is particularly incensed by another reserve, this for $133,366. It's for attorney's fees incurred in any lawsuits that are brought against the studio in connection with *The Exorcist*—including his own. "How can they withhold money from me to fight my own lawsuit?" demands the author. Mr. Peterson of Warner Bros. says that the reserve will be eliminated when legal action is concluded and that Mr. Blatty won't wind up paying the studio freight for his own suit.

The author also wonders why his picture should be billed $16,000 for what he calls "sending Warner Bros. executives and their wives or sweethearts to resorts." The item was for expenses for trips to two conventions of theater owners, and Warner Bros. said that according to the contract such expenses are chargeable to the pictures being promoted at such meetings.

The Exorcist was also charged with another $26,000 for travel and entertainment expenses of studio ad executives, a cost Mr. Blatty claims should have been included in the 10 percent ad overhead fee. Not so, says Warner Bros., claiming these were out-of-pocket expenses to stimulate press and exhibitor interest in the film. The contract, the studio claims, allows these items to be billed as direct costs.

Warner Bros. has agreed to adjust some items previously billed to the movie. These include a $452 tab run up by a studio executive at the swank Mauna Kea Hotel in Hawaii, a $446 contribution to the 92d St. Young Men's Hebrew Association in New York to "support an educational series on film making," and a $556 party tab for a post Academy Award bash at Chasen's, a Los Angeles restaurant.

The studio is hanging tough, however, on an alleged overcharge of $81,171 for cost of workman's compensation insurance for employees on *The Exorcist*. Complaints about overcharges on fringe benefits appear in most movie audits. In this case, Mr. Peterson of Warner Bros. says the formula used by the studio was "fair and equitable and based on actual payroll cost."

Warner Bros. also is resisting adjustment to a claimed overcharge of $37,987 on items purchased for the movie—including a huge refrigeration unit, a $6,000 oil painting, an antique rug, and chandeliers.

Since Warner still has these in its possession, Mr. Blatty argues, they shouldn't be charged to the movie. Mr. Peterson says that the author will get his share when the items are sold and adds disgustedly, "We can't sell or rent that huge refrigeration unit or even give it away. All it does is take up space and collects dust." Mr. Blatty can have the unit, he says, or sell it himself if he can.

The author and his accountants are also protesting other alleged abuses, including improper calculation of interest charges, inaccurate calculation of foreign-exchange rates, unfair allocation of excess shipping and handling charges, and misclassification of certain expenses to production costs instead of distribution costs. Warner Bros. replies that these and other allegations are based on erroneous information and assumptions or represent the opinions of Mr. Blatty's accountants who were, after all, hired to find errors on their client's behalf.

The Principal Disagreement

The biggest bone of contention, however, lies in an unusual special agreement that Mr. Blatty arrived at with Warner Bros. when production problems on *The Exorcist* began to push the production cost to an eventual $10.4 million from the $4 million originally budgeted.

Not knowing that the movie would be a smash—it has yielded $125 million in film rentals and is the biggest grosser in the studio's history—the author began to fear that the swollen production costs would erase his chances of getting into profit at all. So he negotiated a new way of computing his profit participation.

He says he was able to get the revised agreements because he threatened a lawsuit against the studio alleging that he was producer in name only, had no real control over the rising costs, and would be penalized unfairly. Mr. Wells, the Warner Bros. president, says the studio acceded to the new agreements because Mr. Blatty threatened to bring out a Broadway stage version of *The Exorcist* at around the same time the movie would be released.

Whatever the reason, a deal was made ostensibly protecting Mr. Blatty. It stipulated that if the movie didn't reach a break-even point before gross receipts to the studio totaled $19,250,000 that figure would be considered an "artificial break-even" and Mr. Blatty would begin to share in profits and be protected against the impact of production and advertising costs beyond that point. If the film did cover its costs before $19,250,000 was taken in, however, the original agreement would be in force.

According to Mr. Blatty's accountant, Bennett L. Newman of Solomon & Finger, Warner Bros. made sure that the movie would break even before $19,250,000 by reversing its usual accounting procedures. It accelerated income by logging it on the books when billings were made instead of waiting, as it ordinarily did, for the cash to actually come in. And it minimized immediate expense by charging as costs only those distribution expenses actually paid out instead of all those incurred, as it usually did. The result: At one point the studio could claim, using these accounting measures, that the picture had indeed broken even—although some of the "income" on the books hadn't come in and all expenses actually incurred hadn't been listed as charges.

This, Mr. Blatty charges, prevented him from participating in the revised agreement, where he would have been spared his share of about $3 million in additional advertising costs the studio would have had to absorb. Under the old agreement, he had to pay a proportionate share of them equaling about $1 million. He wants it back.

Mr. Wells, the Warner Bros. president, said that the agreement on an artificial break-even was the first and only time Warner has ever negotiated such a clause and he adds: "It necessarily requires a different method of determining costs up to that point. The method we used followed what logically would have to apply, given that definition of net profits."

Mr. Blatty's suit is one of three actions that have been brought against Warner Bros. over participation in *The Exorcist*. Director Friedkin sued, but the studio settled with him out of court. Writer-producer Paul Monash, who received $2.1 million from a 5 percent share of profit for screen rights, says he is entitled to more; his case is pending.

Mr. Monash is challenging a typical studio condition in profit participations, the "double add-on penalty clause." If a movie runs over its production budget, as *The Exorcist* did, studios commonly reserve the right to assess a cost item to it amounting to double the difference between the budgeted and actual cost, thus penalizing profit participants. The idea is to encourage the producers, directors, and others to keep cost in bounds. Mr. Monash claims that since he had nothing to do with making the movie he shouldn't be so penalized. Mr. Peterson of Warners says Mr. Monash is merely complaining that "he shouldn't have made the agreement that he did in fact make." Mr. Blatty didn't have such a penalty clause in his contract.

Case 7–5
Jensen Company

The Jensen Company operates under a full cost system. Manufacturing variances are never deferred but are reported each month as gains or losses on the income statement. Selling and administrative expenses are treated as period costs.

The company's budgeted monthly sales volume, production, and costs for a normal month are shown in the accompanying table.

Sales (400,000 units at $3).................................		$1,200,000
Costs:		
Raw material	$200,000	
Direct labor..	400,000	
Factory overhead: Variable	100,000	
Nonvariable	200,000	
Total factory cost	$900,000	
Selling expense ($40,000 + $.20 per unit sold)..............	$120,000	
General and administrative expense		
($30,000 + $.10 per unit sold)..........................	70,000	
Total selling and administrative expense	$190,000	
Total costs.....................................		1,090,000
Net income		$ 110,000

In May, sales soared to 500,000 units while production fell to only 200,000 units. The president of the company, a Mr. Watts who had risen to his present position through the sales department, was expecting a nice fat profit for May, due to the exceptionally high volume of sales. On June 6, the controller presented the May income statement, and Watts went practically into a state of shock when he saw that the net income was only $55,000, which was less than half the amount budgeted for a normal month.

Required:

In order to explain to Mr. Watts what happened, make the following calculations:

1. Calculate the net income Watts expected (based on the budget) for the month of May.
2. An explanation of the difference between the net income Watts expected and actual net income.
3. The net income that would have been reported if the Jensen Company used the direct costing system in May.

Case 7–6

The Profit in Blood[1]

MANY HOSPITALS ARE MAKING MONEY ON EVERY PINT

Many American hospitals charge patients more for blood than it costs the hospitals to obtain it and administer transfusions.

The hospital charge to patients ranges from $30 to $110 a pint, and usually is between $35 and $75 a pint, according to American Red Cross headquarters in Washington and the Blue Cross Association in Chicago. In most cases, the blood the hospitals use has been donated voluntarily to blood banks which charge the hospitals only the collection cost—usually $18 to $25 a pint, the Red Cross says.

The American Hospital Association says the "profit" on blood is justified to cover the rising cost of hospital care and thus keep hospitals in business. Critics say the money to run the hospitals should come from other sources.

"There are all two few places where blood is available to the entire population at no charge for the blood itself," says David W. Stewart, managing director of the Blue Cross organization in Rochester, N.Y., where the nation's first free blood program was established. In Rochester, Blue Cross covers all the charge for blood, and

[1] Article by Brian Sullivan and Judy Moore. Reprinted with permission from *The Chicago Sun-Times*, May 10, 1975.

the hospitals charge Blue Cross only the actual cost—normally less than $30.

A recent conversation at a hospital near New York City exemplifies the much more common practice of adding an "excess amount over the cost" of blood when the patient is billed for a transfusion.

"Hospitals have a right to make a fair profit on all their services, including blood," said a doctor at the hospital to an official from a blood donor program.

"No," replied the official, "you should make it on something else and not on part of the human body."

That approach is echoed by other blood-program experts.

In New York City, the 282 hospitals in the Greater New York Blood Donor Program charge patients who are not in the program from $35 to $110 for a pint of blood, with the average running about $55 to $65. Those in the program get blood transfusions free under an arrangement with Blue Cross similar to the free program in Rochester.

The charge to the New York hospitals by the Blood Donor Program—the processing fee—is $29 for a unit of whole blood. The hospitals charge Blue Cross only the $29 for patients in the free blood program. But what of the difference between the $29 and the charges listed on the bills of patients not covered by the free blood plan?

Lee Epstein, a financial expert at the American Hospital Association office in Chicago, says blood should not be provided to a patient at cost. "That's not reasonable. There are a lot more things involved in delivering that blood. And it's only good business."

To cite just one other factor involved, Epstein mentioned the administration of the laboratory where the blood is cross-matched with a sample of the patient's own blood to avoid any incompatibility that might cause an adverse reaction.

"It's shortsighted to say, "Your're building in other costs," Epstein argued. "Of course we are, but we're doing it on everything. That's an accepted business practice. If we didn't do it, we'd be out of business.

"We build into our charge structure what in business would be called profit, but in our world is called risk factor—the excess amount over cost for maintaining reserves, expansion, modernizing, or just keeping up with inflation."

At the University of Chicago hospitals, for example, the blood-processing fee billed to the patient is $38 a pint. In addition, there is a $13 fee for cross-matching, a $10 fee for the hospital's administrative services, and a $14 "responsible fee," which is refunded if someone replaces the unit of blood used. So the cost is $75 a pint if the blood isn't replaced, $61 if it is.

Many hospitals argue that these additional fees are simply the cost of handling the blood in the hospital and getting it into a patient's veins. But Epstein maintains that it is not reasonable to say that such fees are 100 percent related to just handling blood.

"There is usually a certain allocation for overhead," he said. "They shouldn't be afraid to say there's a 5 to 6 percent fudge factor in there to cover hospital administration."

In the pioneering blood program in Rochester, established with Blue Cross, Stewart said, "No blood is ever paid for. It all comes from donations of the people in the area and it works. There is very strong grassroots support for it among Rochester business, industry, and labor. Employers give employees paid time off to donate.

"Blue Cross pays the full cost of processing in the regular contract," he continued. "No one is paid for blood itself, but the administrative machinery costs money. A processing fee is set by the Red Cross, charged to the hospital, which bills Blue Cross and Medicare."

Required:

Using data from the article, answer the following question: What is the cost of a pint of blood?

8

Long-Lived Assets

L and, buildings, building improvements, machinery, trucks, furniture, fixtures, tools, and office equipment are long-lived assets which are classified on the balance sheet as *fixed assets* or more descriptively as *property, plant, and equipment.*

Fixed assets are purchased because they are expected to produce benefits (earn revenue) for the enterprise in future accounting periods. Unlike inventory, they are not held for resale in the normal course of business.

The acquisition of fixed assets represents a major commitment of the economic resources of the firm. Accounting for fixed assets is concerned with problems related to:

a. The cost of acquiring the assets.
b. The allocation of the acquisition cost to expense over the estimated useful life of the asset in a systematic and rational manner. (The allocation process for tangible physical assets is termed *depreciation.*)
c. The disposal of the asset by sale, discard, or exchange.

THE COST OF PLANT AND EQUIPMENT

The cost of plant and equipment includes all reasonable expenditures necessary to put it into operating use. For example, assume that a company purchases a machine for $50,000 at terms of 1/10, n/60, freight to be paid by the buyer. The machine requires specialized electrical wiring and must be mounted on a concrete support.

The cost of the machine would be:

Purchase price	$50,000
Less: 1 percent cash discount	500
Net purchase price	$49,500
Freight	300
Electrical wiring	1,250
Concrete support construction	825
Total asset cost	$51,875

The journal entries would be:

Machinery......................................	49,500	
Cash..		49,500
To record the net cash paid on purchase.		
Machinery......................................	300	
Cash..		300
To record freight payment.		
Machinery......................................	2,075	
Cash..		2,075
To record machinery installation costs.		

DEPRECIATION OF PLANT AND EQUIPMENT—
THE ALLOCATION PROCESS

An important characteristic of fixed assets, other than land, is that although they can be kept in usable operating condition for some time, eventually they are no longer productive and are retired from service. The purpose of depreciation is to recognize that the fixed assets have a limited useful life and to allocate the expired cost of these assets to the accounting periods which they benefit.

The journal entry to allocate the cost of a fixed asset not used in manufacturing (sales, administration) to the period benefited is:

Depreciation Expense...........................	*XXX*	
Accumulated Depreciation		*XXX*

The journal entry to allocate the cost of a fixed asset used in manufacturing is:

Work in Process (Depreciation)	*XXX*	
Accumulated Depreciation		*XXX*

Depreciation cost on nonmanufacturing assets appears in the income statement as a period expense. The depreciation cost on manufacturing assets becomes part of the product (inventory) cost and becomes an expense when the product is sold.

The accumulated depreciation account is a contra-asset account; it is deducted from the related asset account. The preferred balance sheet presentation is:

Equipment......................................	$1,200,000	
Less: Accumulated depreciation	500,000	$700,000

METHODS OF DEPRECIATION

To calculate the periodic depreciation charge, three items must be considered:

1. The depreciable base: generally the acquisition cost of the asset, including all costs incurred to get the asset ready for operation.

2. The salvage value of the asset: the amount expected to be recovered when the asset is ultimately scrapped, sold, or traded in. Frequently zero salvage value is assumed on the theory that the salvage value will equal the cost to remove the asset.

3. The estimated useful life of the asset: generally determined by past experience with similar assets, corrected for differences in planned usage and/or maintenance policy changes. In 1967 the Internal Revenue Service published guidelines for suggested useful lives of broad categories of assets. For example:

Warehouses	60 years
Buildings and plant	45 years
Land improvements	20 years
Office furniture	10 years
Machinery and equipment	10 years
Heavy trucks	6 years
Automobiles	3 years

In the early 1970s, the IRS modified their guidelines and suggested that taxpayers could use a life estimate anywhere in the range from 80 percent to 120 percent of the guideline life. Such ranges are called *asset depreciation ranges.*

There are several methods available for computing the asset cost to be allocated to each period. The most common ones are:

1. The straight-line depreciation method.
2. The units-of-production method.
3. The double-declining balance method.
4. The sum-of-the-years'-digits method.

Straight-Line Depreciation

The straight-line-depreciation method assumes that the cost of the asset expires as a steady (straight-line) function of time. The formula is:

$$\text{Depreciation/year} = \frac{\text{Cost} - \text{Salvage value}}{\text{Estimated useful life in years}}$$

For example, if a machine costing $20,000 has an estimated life expectancy of six years and a salvage value of $2,000, the annual depreciation charge would be ($20,000 − $2,000)/6 = $3,000.

The straight-line method owes its popularity primarily to its simplicity. It assumes level operating efficiency and level maintenance procedures.

The Units-of-Production Method

This method assumes the useful life is best estimated by the number of units produced by the asset. Under this method, a depreciation rate per unit is calculated:

$$\text{Rate of depreciation/unit} = \frac{\text{Cost} - \text{Salvage value}}{\text{Estimated units of production during service life}}$$

For example, a machine costing $1,200 is purchased and is expected to produce 1,000 widgets during its service life. Its salvage value is $300. The amount of depreciation in 1981, if 300 widgets were produced is:

$$\frac{\$1,200 - 300}{1,000} = \$.90 \text{ per widget produced}$$

$$300 \times \$.90 = \$270, \text{ depreciation expense in 1981}$$

The Double-Declining Balance Method

The double-declining balance method assumes that as assets grow older they become less efficient and their earning power declines. A new car functions more efficiently than a used car; rentals in an old office building are lower than those of its shining new neighbor. These examples illustrate a common tendency of some assets to provide more service in early years and to require more maintenance in later years. In such instances the double-declining balance depreciation method may be justified, as it results in larger depreciation charges during the early years of asset life with gradually decreasing charges in later years.

Under the double-declining balance method, a uniform rate, computed at twice the straight-line rate, is applied in each period to the *net book value* or *carrying value* (cost less accumulated depreciation) of the asset. Salvage value is not taken into account in making the computation for double-declining balance depreciation.

To illustrate, assume that a machine was purchased on January 1, 1979, for $5,000, and that it had an estimated life of five years. The depreciation rate under the double-declining balance method would be 40 percent (1/5 years × 2), and this rate would be applied each year to the net book value of the asset. The annual depreciation charges would be calculated as shown in Illustration 8–1.

The double-declining balance method is allowable for federal income tax purposes on most new assets except buildings and land improvements, where the maximum allowable rate is 150 percent, or 1.5 times the straight-line rate.

ILLUSTRATION 8–1

Year	Original Cost	Accumulated Depreciation as of January 1	Net Book (carrying) Value as of January 1	Depreciation Rate	Depreciation Charge for the Year
1979	$5,000	$ 0	$5,000	.40	$2,000
1980	5,000	2,000	3,000	.40	1,200
1981	5,000	3,200	1,800	.40	720
1982	5,000	3,920	1,080	.40	432
1983	5,000	4,352	648	.40	259

The Sum-of-the-Years'-Digits Method

The sum-of-the-years'-digits method, another accelerated (fast write-off) method, allocates the cost of the fixed assets as follows:

1. Determine the sum of the digits. If the useful life of the asset is five years, the sum of the digits is: $1 + 2 + 3 + 4 + 5 = 15$. The formula for the sum of the digits is $(n/2)(n + 1)$, where n equals the useful life of the asset.

$$\frac{5}{2} \times (5 + 1) = 15$$

2. Determine the depreciation rate. It is expressed by a fraction whose numerator is the years in reverse order (5, 4, 3, 2, 1), and whose denominator is the sum of the digits as computed in (1) above. Thus depreciation rates for a five-year asset are 5/15, 4/15, 3/15, 2/15, and 1/15, a total of 15/15.

3. Compute the depreciation expense for the period—depreciation rate times cost minus salvage value.

To illustrate, consider an asset costing $5,000 purchased January 1, 1979, which has an estimated life of five years and an estimated salvage value of $200. The sum-of-the-years'-digits calculation is shown in Illustration 8–2.

COMPARISON OF DEPRECIATION METHODS

The annual depreciation charges for an asset with a cost of $5,000, an estimated useful life of five years, and a salvage value of $200 is shown in Illustration 8–3.

Some enterprises switch from double-declining balance to straight-line depreciation for tax purposes at the point that straight-

ILLUSTRATION 8-2 ─────────────────────────────────

Year	Cost Minus Salvage Value	Remaining Life in Years	Depreciation Rate Fraction	Annual Depreciation Charge
1979	$4,800	5	5/15	$1,600
1980	4,800	4	4/15	1,280
1981	4,800	3	3/15	960
1982	4,800	2	2/15	640
1983	4,800	1	1/15	320
				$4,800

ILLUSTRATION 8-3 ─────────────────────────────────

Year	Straight Line	Double- Declining Balance	Sum-of-the- Years' Digits
1979.........	$ 960	$2,000	$1,600
1980.........	960	1,200	1,280
1981.........	960	720	960
1982.........	960	432	640
1983.........	960	259	320
	$4,800	$4,611	$4,800

line depreciation (calculated using the remaining depreciable amount over the remaining useful life) is larger than double-declining balance depreciation. In our example a switch would be made in the fourth year and would result in depreciation of $440 for the next two years. Net book value of $1,080 ($5,000 − $3,920) less salvage of $200 (required under the straight-line method) divided by the two remaining years of life equals $440.

DEPRECIATION AND REPAIRS

Maintenance and repair costs influence the length of life of assets and, together with the depreciation charges, constitute the full cost of using a depreciable asset. A distinction should be made between expenditures which do not increase the original expected productive capacity (service life and/or output) of the fixed asset and those that do. Normal repairs and maintenance do not increase the original expected productive capacity of the fixed asset and are charged to expense in the period incurred. Expenditures which do increase the productive capacity of the fixed asset are called *betterments* and are capitalized (recorded as a fixed asset). Betterments are allocated to future periods as part of the depreciation charge. In practice it is often hard to make an exact judgment as to whether an expenditure is a repair or betterment.

DISPOSAL OF PLANT AND EQUIPMENT

An asset may be disposed of by sale, by being traded in as part of the purchase price of a replacement, or simply by being discarded or scrapped. The accounting treatment to reflect the retirement or disposal of an asset involves a three-step process:

1. The asset must be depreciated to the date of disposal.

2. The cost of the disposed asset must be removed from the asset account, and the accumulated depreciation associated with the asset must be removed from the accumulated depreciation account. An asset may still be kept in service after it is fully depreciated. In that event, the asset remains on the books and no further depreciation is taken. Only at the time of disposition is it necessary to remove the asset and its associated accumulated depreciation from the accounts.

3. Any gain or loss relating to the disposal must be recorded.[1]

To illustrate the technique, assume the machinery account includes $4,000 as the original cost of a machine bought July 1, 1979, with a four-year useful life and no salvage value. Depreciation on a straight-line basis through December 31, 1981 (2.5 years) totals $2,500.[2] If the machine is to be sold on July 1, 1982, for $800, then the following entries must be made on July 1:

Depreciation	500	
Accumulated Depreciation		500
To record depreciation on machine (January 1 to June 30, 1982).		

Cash...	800	
Accumulated Depreciation	3,000	
Loss on Sale of Fixed Asset	200	
Machinery....................................		4,000
To record disposal of equipment at a loss.		

Because the company received $800 for an asset with a net book value of $1,000 ($4,000 − $3,000), the company will recognize a loss on sale of $200. The loss may be attributable to early termination,

[1] Gains on trade-ins of similar assets result in an adjustment to the cost basis of the new asset rather than a gain on disposal.

[2] Depreciation is usually calculated on a monthly basis. More than 15 days are considered a month for purposes of this calculation.

184

unexpected obsolescence, or simply because of errors in estimating the salvage value or estimated life. This type of loss is apt to occur frequently and should be thought of as a nonoperating expense on the income statement.

If the asset had been sold for more than its book value, a gain on the sale would be recognized.

DEPRECIATION, FEDERAL INCOME TAX, AND NET INCOME

The method management chooses to depreciate its assets will affect the federal income taxes it pays and the amount of net income it reports.[3] The accelerated depreciation methods (double-declining balance, sum-of-the-years'-digits) charge more depreciation expense in the early years of an asset's life than the straight-line method and result in lower income taxes and net income in those years. In subsequent years, the effect will be reversed.

Assume that a company paying federal income tax at the rate of 50 percent has purchased a truck for $1,000, with an estimated life of five years and salvage value of $100. Since 50 percent of each dollar of income must be paid as income taxes, each dollar of expense that is deductible from taxable revenue will save $.50 in income taxes. A *depreciation tax savings* can be calculated in each year of the useful life of the asset by multiplying $.50 times the depreciation that is reported for tax purposes. A comparison of the straight-line method to the sum-of-the-years'-digits method is shown in Illustration 8–4.

Over the five-year asset life, the total tax savings from both depreciation methods is $450. The savings occur sooner under the sum-of-

ILLUSTRATION 8–4

Year	Depreciation Tax Savings Straight-Line Method	Sum-of-Years' Digits	Difference
1979	.50 × $180 = $ 90	.50 × $300 = $150	$ 60
1980	.50 × 180 = 90	.50 × 240 = 120	30
1981	.50 × 180 = 90	.50 × 180 = 90	0
1982	.50 × 180 = 90	.50 × 120 = 60	(30)
1983	.50 × 180 = 90	.50 × 60 = 30	(60)
	$450	$450	$–0–

[3] Unlike Lifo, management may use a different depreciation method on its tax returns than it uses for its financial statements.

the-years'-digits method, and this time factor is the incentive for the firm to use the accelerated method for tax purposes. The availability to the company of the tax savings at an earlier date amounts to an interest free loan from the government. Many companies use an accelerated depreciation method for tax purposes while using the straight-line method for their financial statements.[4]

Assume that income before depreciation and taxes in 1979 was $1,000 and that the straight-line method is used to prepare the financial statements while the sum-of-the-years'-digits method is used on the tax return.

	Books	Tax Return
Income before depreciation	$1,000	$1,000
Depreciation expense	180	300
	$ 820	$ 700
Income tax	410	350
Net income	$ 410	$ 350

The journal entry on the *books* to record the income tax expense for the year is

Income Tax Expense	410	
Deferred Income Tax.........................		60
Income Tax Payable		350

The difference between the income tax expense (straight-line method) shown on the books (financial statements) and the actual tax liability (accelerated depreciation method) on the tax return is reported on the balance sheet as *deferred income taxes*.

The deferred income tax account which reconciles the income tax expense recorded on the books with the income tax payable to the federal government is treated as a liability by the corporation. This account represents that amount of tax savings that should become payable in later years, when depreciation expense under the accelerated method is less than depreciation expense under the straight-line method.

Assume the company in the example on the preceding page has annual income before depreciation and taxes of $1,000 for 1979 through 1983. Illustration 8–5 presents the effect of depreciation timing differences on tax payments and deferrals.

Many accountants disagree with the classification of deferred taxes as a liability. They argue that the deferred tax is not an *actual*

---

[4] Accelerated depreciation and the resulting deferral of income taxes are used by the U.S. government as an instrument of economic policy to encourage investment in fixed assets.

ILLUSTRATION 8–5

Year	Income before Depreciation	Book Depreciation	Book Income Pre-Tax	Tax Depreciation	Taxable Income Pre-Tax	Book Tax Expense	Taxes Payable	Deferred Tax Liability
1979	$1,000	$180	$ 820	$300	$ 700	$ 410	$ 350	$60
1980	1,000	180	820	240	760	410	380	30
1981	1,000	180	820	180	820	410	410	0
1982	1,000	180	820	120	880	410	440	(30)
1983	1,000	180	820	60	940	410	470	(60)
Total	$5,000	$900	$4,100	$900	$4,100	$2,050	$2,050	$—0—

obligation to pay the government and that in all likelihood the deferred portion of the tax will never be paid because of continued timing differences, that is, new deferrals created by the acquisition of new assets.

DEPRECIATION POLICY DECISIONS

For tax purposes *management* should select the depreciation method which results in the lowest income tax. This will generally be an accelerated method as long as the enterprise is earning income and investing in fixed assets.

For financial reporting purposes *management* will select a depreciation method that reflects their financial objectives.[5] Management's financial reporting strategy will also be reflected in their choice of the estimated useful life of assets and decisions about capitalizing or expensing all gray area repairs.

Accelerated depreciation methods, short estimated useful lives of assets, and expensing all gray area repairs will result in lower net income in the earlier years than straight-line depreciation, longer estimated useful lives and capitalizing all gray area repairs. For example, if management wishes to report lower earnings to avoid requests for wage and salary increases or dividend distributions, an accelerated depreciation method, and a short useful life will be selected. In times of depressed profitability, some companies have switched to straight-line depreciation to increase reported earnings.

The informed reader of financial statements should be aware of management's flexibility in this area. Evaluation of the choices made by management assists in evaluating the quality of that management.

THE INVESTMENT CREDIT

Since the Revenue Act of 1962 the investment tax credit has been used by the U.S. government as an instrument of economic policy to encourage investment in fixed assets, particularly productive facilities. The credit, which is calculated as a percentage of the cost of depreciable assets placed in service, is deducted directly from the business firm's income tax liability. It encourages investment because it reduces the cost of the investment by the amount of the tax credit. Currently a 10 percent credit is allowed, subject to specified conditions.

---

[5] All the different methods are allowable under generally accepted accounting principles.

There are two generally accepted methods for reporting the investment tax credit in the financial reports. It can be treated as a reduction in the federal income tax expense in the year the asset is placed in service (*flow-through method*), or it can be spread over the life of the asset on which the credit is granted.

The flow-through method results in an increase in net income (decrease in income tax expense on the books) in the year the asset is placed in service and raises the question of whether a business firm can earn income by purchasing an asset.

The method which spreads the credit over the life of the asset more closely matches revenues and expenses. This method will result in a different income tax expense on the income tax return (entire investment credit used) than on the financial reports (investment credit spread over the life of the asset) and will require the establishment of a *deferred investment tax credit account* which is similar to the deferred income tax account.

Management's choice of which investment tax credit method to use for financial reporting purposes is another indication of their overall financial strategy.

NATURAL RESOURCES AND INTANGIBLE ASSETS

In addition to tangible fixed assets, there are two other types of long-lived assets: natural resources and intangible assets.

Natural resources include assets such as oil properties and timberlands. This type of asset is classified separately from plant and equipment and is generally termed a *wasting asset* because the object in acquiring the natural resource is to convert the resource into inventory, process it, and then sell the output.

In general, natural resources are recorded at cost when acquired. The conversion of the resource into inventory (barrels of oil, tons of coal, or feet of lumber) exhausts the cost of the wasting asset. The process of writing off the original cost of the resource to expense over the life of the asset is called *depletion*. The depletion method most commonly used is the *units-of-production* method. For example, if an oil company purchases an oil well for $750,000 and it estimates the well contains 1.5 million barrels of oil, then the cost ($750,000) would be written off at the rate of $.50 for each barrel of oil removed from the well.

Intangible assets represent nonphysical assets which provide future benefits. Examples are patents, trademarks, franchises, copyrights, goodwill, and organization costs. The difficulty with such intangible assets is to decide whether the expenditures have future benefits and should be "capitalized" and amortized over a period of time, or whether they have no future benefits and thus are expenses of the period.

Most intangibles have a limited term of existence, fixed by law or regulations, or by their very nature. The cost of the intangible is amortized to expense over its useful (economic) life. If a patent right had a remaining legal life of 12 years but was expected to be useful to the business for only 7 years, the acquisition cost should be amortized over the 7 years.

There are some intangibles, such as goodwill, trade names, subscription lists, which may have no determinable term of existence. *Opinion No. 17* of the Accounting Principles Board requires that these intangibles be amortized over a period not to exceed 40 years.

A special intangible asset is goodwill. Goodwill may be defined as the excess earning power of a business beyond the earning power that would be expected for a firm in a similar business and with a similar amount of assets. Goodwill can be attributed to such things as a good location, good customer and employee relations, a solid reputation, strong marketing distribution outlets, and so on. The accounting for goodwill is in accordance with the objectivity principle. Goodwill is recorded in the accounts *only if it is purchased*. Goodwill arises from the purchase of one company by another. It is the difference between the fair value of an acquired company's assets and the price another company is willing to pay to purchase the business. Many companies now use the account, excess of purchase price over fair value of assets acquired, instead of goodwill.

CASES FOR CHAPTER 8

Case 8–1 _____

Vantyke Printing Company

The Vantyke Printing Company was founded in 1936 by Charles Vantyke. The company printed scholarly books and journals and had a reputation as a high quality printer.

In late 1981 John Draykin, the sales manager of a local printing company that specialized in color offset work, purchased Vantyke Printing from its founder. Draykin's strategy was to establish the company as a full line printer. This would enable him to use the sales volume in scholarly books and journals as a base on which to develop future sales in the more profitable color offset area.

In order to implement this strategy he had to make substantial capital expenditures.

Listed below are the transactions that arose from the implementation of Draykin's strategy. Prepare a journal entry for each of these transactions.

1. Sold two old Heidelberg presses which he no longer needed for $11,000. These presses had cost $15,000 each when they were purchased and were fully depreciated on the books and tax returns on the date of sale.

2. Purchased land and building in an adjacent town for $450,000. Borrowed $315,000 on a 9 percent, 25-year, first mortgage and $110,000 on a 12 percent, 5-year second mortgage. The balance of $25,000 was taken from the company's cash account. The town assessed the property for $270,000 (land, $54,000; and building, $216,000) for property tax purposes.

3. The cost of transporting and installing all the old equipment in the new plant amounted to $18,320.

4. Purchased a new four-color press from Karris Intertype. The invoice price of this press was $125,000. Vantyke paid Karris $122,500 because they were able to take advantage of the 2 percent cash

discount that Karris offered. The Dijoa Trucking Company charged Vantyke $3,600 to deliver the press. Installation of the press was done by local tradespeople for $1,200.

5. Prior to using the four-color press on actual jobs the company made test runs to make sure the printing was on register. Approximately 40 hours were spent on these test runs. The work crew that operated this press and did the test runs was paid $17 ($8.00 for the lead printer and $4.50 for each of the two assistants) an hour. Draykin expected to charge his customers $40 an hour for all work done on this press.

6. Traded in the 1975 delivery truck on a new larger truck at the Westfield Ford Company. Paid $5,000 plus the old truck for the new truck which had a list (invoice) price of $9,000. The book value of the old truck on the date it was traded in was $3,200 (original cost of $6,000 less accumulated depreciation of $2,800). The Westfield Ford salesperson and Draykin agreed that the market value of the old truck on the date of the trade-in was $2,600.

7. Paid Jones Electrical Company $18,000 for replacing the wiring in the building with heavy duty wiring which was needed to operate the printing equipment.

8. Paid $8,500 to overhaul a two-color press which had been purchased ten years ago. The overhaul was done to increase the quality of the impressions, and it was not expected to change either the capacity or the useful life of the press. Prior to this time approximately $400 a year was spent on the maintenance of this press.

Case 8–2

The Depreciation Company

Trial Balance
December 31, 1979

	Debit Balances	Credit Balances
Cash	$ 14,000	
Accounts receivable	35,000	
Inventory	105,000	
Land	14,000	
Land improvements	7,000	
Accumulated depreciation—land improvements		$ 263
Building	280,000	
Accumulated depreciation—building		5,250
Furniture, fixtures, and equipment	42,000	
Accumulated depreciation—furniture, fixtures, and equipment		1,950
Accounts payable		28,000
Income tax payable		—
Mortgage loan payable		210,000
Deferred income tax		1,305
Capital stock		210,000
Retained earnings		5,232
Sales		350,000
Cost of sales (exclusive of depreciation)	245,000	
Selling and administrative expenses (exclusive of depreciation)	70,000	
	$812,000	$812,000

The above account balances reflect all required year-end adjusting journal entries except for the recording of depreciation and income taxes.

The fixed assets shown below were acquired by the Depreciation Company on April 1, 1978, the date the company commenced operations.

	Cost	Estimated Salvage	Estimated Useful Life
Land Improvements	$ 7,000	—0—	20 years
Building	280,000	*	40 years
Furniture, Fixtures, and Equipment	28,000	$2,000	10 years

* It is estimated that the cost of demolition will approximate salvage value.

On September 1, 1979, the Depreciation Company acquired a forklift truck for $14,000. It had an estimated useful life of eight years, and its salvage value is estimated to be $2,000.

The Depreciation Company uses accelerated (fast write-off) methods of depreciation on its federal income tax returns (150 percent declining balance method for land improvements and buildings and the sum-of-years'-digits method for furniture, fixtures, and equipment). For book (financial statement) purposes, the Depreciation Company uses the straight-line method of depreciation.

Under existing tax laws, the company is allowed a credit against their federal income tax liability equal to 10 percent of the cost of new equipment purchased during the year. This investment tax credit is accounted for as a reduction of tax expense (flow-through method) in the year the asset is acquired.

Federal income taxes for the Depreciation Company for 1979 were 30 percent of net income.

Required:

1. Prepare journal entries to record depreciation and income taxes for the year ended December 31, 1979.
2. Why would a company want to use accelerated depreciation methods?
3. When will the deferred income tax be paid?

Case 8–3

Cummins Engine Company

The following note is taken from the Cummins Engine Company annual report for 1977:

> *Property, Plant, and Equipment:* Property, plant, and equipment are recorded at cost. Depreciation is charged to earnings on a straight-line basis over the estimated service life of an asset. The service lives used in computing depreciation range from 10 to 40 years for buildings and 3 to 15 years for machinery and equipment. Maintenance and repair costs are charged to earnings as they occur.

Required:

1. What is the annual depreciation expense for a $2.8 million plant addition that is estimated to have a service life of 40 years and a salvage value of $400,000?
2. For the plant addition described in (1), what would be the depreciation deduction on Cummins' income tax return in the 1st, 10th, and 40th years? Assume that Cummins uses the sum-of-the-years'-digits depreciation method on its tax return.
3. Record the journal entry for tax expense and taxes payable in the 1st, 10th, and 40th years. Let I = Income before depreciation and taxes. The

effective tax rate is 47.7 percent. What does a debit to deferred taxes signify?

The Cummins annual report states that for 1977, the excess of tax over book depreciation on all depreciable assets resulted in a credit to deferred taxes of $8.2 million.

4. How much larger or smaller was depreciation expense on the income statement than on the tax return? (The effective tax rate was 47.7 percent.)
5. Why doesn't Cummins use the same depreciation methods for their annual report (books) as they do on their tax return?

Case 8–4

Bentley Rug Company

Bentley Rug Company reported the following net income before taxes for financial statement purposes:

	1978	1979	1980
Net income before tax.............	$40,000	$50,000	$60,000

Included in expenses was depreciation on a $15,000 weaving machine with an estimated life of three years. The company used the straight-line method of depreciating for financial statement purposes and the sum-of-the-years'-digits method for tax purposes. The income tax rate for each of the three years was 30 percent. There were no other differences between net income for book purposes and net income for tax purposes.

Required:

1. Prepare the journal entry to record income tax expense for each of the three years.
2. Why do deferred income taxes arise? When are they payable?

9

Long-Term Equities

The major sources of long-term enterprise capital are funds borrowed from outsiders (long-term notes, bonds, leases) and funds invested by stockholders (capital stock). Long-term notes payable and bonds require repayment of the principal amount borrowed, plus specified interest payments for the use of the money. There is usually no promise to repay stockholders for the use of invested capital.

LONG-TERM NOTES PAYABLE (INTEREST BEARING)

A term loan (long-term note payable) is usually made by an institutional lender such as a bank or insurance company for long-term enterprise purposes. Long-term lenders often impose restrictive covenants on the borrower to ensure that these term loans, which are often unsecured, are repaid. Common restrictive covenants required by lenders are that working capital is maintained at a certain level and that officers' salaries cannot be increased, dividends paid, additional borrowings made, or equipment purchased without the consent of the lender. If the loan is secured by the specific pledge of assets, it is called a *mortgage loan* (mortgage note payable). In the case of default (failure to make payments or violation of restrictive covenants) on a mortgage loan payable, the lender can foreclose and sell the mortgaged assets and use the proceeds to retire the debt.

Assume that on January 1, 1979, the Santiago Corporation borrows $100,000 from the First National Bank of Texas. Loan terms require repayment of the principal (loan amount) in ten equal annual installments with interest of 10 percent on the unpaid balance. The interest rate of 10 percent was established as a result of negotiations between the bank vice president and Santiago's chief financial officer. Items considered by the parties in deciding on the interest rate were current market interest rates, the financial condition of Santiago, the quality of Santiago's management, Santiago's bank balance, the future growth of Santiago, the opportunity for Santiago to borrow these funds from another bank at a lower rate of interest, and the opportunity of the bank to loan these funds to other customers.

Entries made on Santiago's books for the first two years of the loan are:

January 1, 1979

| Cash | 100,000 | |
| Notes Payable | | 100,000 |

To record at face value, ten-year, 10 percent term loan from FNB of Texas.

December 31, 1979

Interest Expense (10 percent of $100,000)	10,000	
Note Payable	10,000	
Cash		20,000

To record payment of interest and principal, FNB of Texas loan.

December 31, 1980

Interest Expense (10 percent of $90,000)	9,000	
Note Payable	10,000	
Cash		19,000

To record payment of interest and principal. FNB of Texas loan.

The payment schedule for the entire ten-year period is listed in Illustration 9–1.

ILLUSTRATION 9–1

	Interest Payment	Principal Payment	Loan Balance
1- 1-79			$100,000
12-31-79	$10,000	$ 10,000	90,000
12-31-80	9,000	10,000	80,000
12-31-81	8,000	10,000	70,000
12-31-82	7,000	10,000	60,000
12-31-83	6,000	10,000	50,000
12-31-84	5,000	10,000	40,000
12-31-85	4,000	10,000	30,000
12-31-86	3,000	10,000	20,000
12-31-87	2,000	10,000	10,000
12-31-88	1,000	10,000	—0—
	$55,000	$100,000	

The portion of the note payable due within one year of the balance sheet date is classified as a *current liability* and the amount maturing beyond one year is classified as a *long-term liability.*

SANTIAGO CORPORATION
Balance Sheet—December 31, 1980

Current liabilities:
    Notes payable (due within one year) $10,000
Long-term liabilities:
    Notes payable 70,000

LONG-TERM NOTES PAYABLE (NONINTEREST BEARING)

Generally accepted accounting principles recognize that there is an interest charge for the use of money borrowed regardless of the terms stipulated in the loan agreement.[1] Where the loan agreement does not stipulate an interest rate or indicates a rate which is substantially below the fair rate, it will be necessary to recalculate the transaction using an imputed interest rate which is implicit in the transaction.

Assume the Santiago Company purchases a parcel of land from Texas Realtors on January 1, 1979, for $100,000. The agreement requires Santiago to make ten annual payments of $10,000 on December 31 of each year to retire the debt. The contract is silent as to any interest payments.

Would the appropriate entry be?

Land   100,000
    Notes Payable   100,000
        Purchase of land from Texas Realtors.

Compare the liability of $100,000 with the liability of $100,000 for the ten-year, 10 percent loan from the First National Bank of Texas. That loan required payments of $155,000 ($100,000 principal and $55,000 interest) over the ten-year period. If the amounts repaid on two loans are substantially different, how can the liability on January 1, 1979, the date of the loan, be the same?

Do you think $100,000 is the price Santiago would pay for the land if they could make a lump sum cash payment on January 1, 1979? If so, why would Texas Realtors allow them to make installment payments over a ten-year period? Certainly, Texas Realtors would rather receive $100,000 on January 1, 1979, than receive $10,000 at the

---

[1] *Accounting Principles Board Opinion No. 21*, "Interest on Receivables and Payables," August 1971.

end of each year for the next ten years. They would have the opportunity to earn interest on a larger sum for a longer period of time.

Given these facts, how can we determine the amount of the installment payments that should be allocated to the purchase price of the land and the amount that should be considered as interest?

APB No. 21 requires that we record the transaction at its equivalent *cash price* or if that is not determinable ". . . to approximate the rate which would have resulted if an independent borrower and an independent lender had negotiated a similar transaction under comparable terms and conditions with the option to pay the cash price upon purchase or to give a note for the amount of the purchase which bears the prevailing rate of interest to maturity."

Let us assume that we cannot determine the equivalent cash price and that the rate of interest implicit in the transaction is 10 percent. The purchase price of the land and the amount of the liability would be the value today (present value) of all the installment payments at a 10 percent interest rate.

What is the present value (January 1, 1979) of the $10,000 paid on December 31, 1979? It is the amount on January 1, 1979, which at 10 percent interest will accumulate to $10,000 on December 31, 1979. The present value of $1.00 to be received *one* period from now at 10 percent is $.909.[2]

$$\$.909 + .10\ (\$.909) = \$1.00$$

The present value of the $10,000 to be received on December 31, 1979, is $9,090 (.909 × $10,000). The $9,090 on January 1, 1979, will accumulate to $10,000 on December 31, 1979, if it is invested at 10 percent.

What is the present value (January 1, 1979) of the $10,000 to be received on December 31, 1980? The present value of $1.00 to be received *two* periods from now at 10 percent is $.826.

1/1/79	*12/31/79*	*12/31/80*

$$\$.826 + .10\ (\$.826) = \$.909$$
$$\$.909 + .10\ (\$.909) = \$1.00$$

The present value of the $10,000 to be received on December 31, 1980, is $8,260 (.826 × $10,000).

---

[2] The present value of $1 is readily available in printed tables as is the present value of $1 received *annually* for n periods. The formula for calculating the present value of $1 to be received in n periods at an interest rate of *i* is

$$\frac{1}{(1 + i)^n}$$

Illustration 9–2 lists the present value of $1 at 10 percent for ten years and calculates the present value of all the note payments for each of the ten years.

ILLUSTRATION 9–2

Period	Present Value of $1	Installment Payment	Present Value of Installment Payment
1	$ .909	$ 10,000	$ 9,090
2	.826	10,000	8,260
3	.751	10,000	7,510
4	.683	10,000	6,830
5	.621	10,000	6,210
6	.565	10,000	5,650
7	.513	10,000	5,130
8	.467	10,000	4,670
9	.424	10,000	4,240
10	.386	10,000	3,860
	$6.145	$100,000	$61,450

We can obtain the present value of all the installment payments using the present value of $1 table as we did in this calculation or we could have referred to a table which gives the present value of $1 received *annually* at the end of each period for *n* periods.[3] The present value of $1 received annually for ten years at 10 percent is $6.145, which is the sum of all the *time adjusted present values* over a ten-year period.

The present value (January 1, 1979) of all the installment payments is $61,450 (6.145 × $10,000). This is the equivalent cash price of the land purchased by Santiago (sales price of Texas Realtors).

APB No. 21 requires the following journal entry on January 1, 1979, by Santiago to record the purchase of the land.

Land	61,450	
Unamortized Discount on Notes Payable	38,550	
Notes Payable		100,000
To record purchase of land.		

Unamortized Discount on Notes Payable is a contra-liability account. It is equal (in notes on which interest is imputed) to the differ-

---

[3] The formula for calculating the present value of $1 received at the end of each period (in arrears) for *n* periods is

$$\frac{1 - \dfrac{1}{(1 + i)^n}}{i}$$

ence between the face amount of the note and the present value of the installment payments.

Disclosure of the note payable on the January 1, 1979, balance sheet would reflect the liability of $61,450 and appear as follows:

Note Payable (noninterest bearing)	$100,000
Less, Unamortized discount based on	
an imputed interest rate of 10 percent	38,550
	$ 61,450

The journal entries for the installment payment on December 31, 1979, would be:

Note Payable	10,000	
Cash		10,000
To record 1979 installment payment.		
Interest Expense (10 percent of $61,450)	6,145	
Unamortized Discount on Note Payable		6,145
To record 1979 interest based on imputed rate of 10 percent.		

The general ledger accounts on December 31, 1979, reflect a liability of $57,595 ($90,000 − $32,405).

Notes Payable

10,000	100,000

Unamortized Discount—Note Payable

38,550	6,145

The December 31, 1979, balance sheet disclosure is:

Notes Payable (noninterest bearing)	$90,000
Less, Unamortized discount based on	
an imputed interest rate of 10 percent	32,405
	$57,595

The journal entries and general ledger accounts for the year ended December 31, 1980, reflect a liability of $53,355 ($80,000 − $26,645).

Note Payable	10,000	
Cash		10,000
To record 1980 installment payment.		
Interest Expense (10 percent of $57,595)	5,760	
Unamortized Discount on Note Payable		5,760
To record 1980 interest based on imputed rate of 10 percent.		

Notes Payable

10,000	100,000
10,000	

Unamortized Discount—Note Payable

38,550	6,145
	5,760

The December 31, 1980, balance sheet disclosure is:

Notes Payable (noninterest bearing) $80,000
  Less, Unamortized discount based on
  an imputed interest rate of 10 percent 26,645
                                                        $53,355

At the end of the ten-year period both the note payable and the unamortized discount accounts will have a zero balance (see Illustration 9–3).

The method we have used to amortize the discount is called the effective interest rate method.

ILLUSTRATION 9–3

	Pay-ment	Interest Expense (10 Per-cent of Liability)	Notes Payable	Unamor-tized Discount	Balance Sheet Liability
1- 1-79			$100,000	$38,550	$61.450
12-31-79	$10,000	$6,145	(10,000)	(6,145)	57,595
12-31-80	10,000	5,760	(10,000)	(5,760)	53,355
12-31-81	10,000	5,335	(10,000)	(5,335)	48,690
12-31-82	10,000	4,869	(10,000)	(4,869)	43,559
12-31-83	10,000	4,356	(10,000)	(4,356)	37,915
12-31-84	10,000	3,792	(10,000)	(3,792)	31,707
12-31-85	10,000	3,171	(10,000)	(3,171)	24,878
12-31-86	10,000	2,488	(10,000)	(2,488)	17,366
12-31-87	10,000	1,737	(10,000)	(1,737)	9,103
12-31-88	10,000	897*	(10,000)	(897)*	—0—

* Adjusted for differences in rounding to the nearest dollar.

BONDS

A bond is a formal contract containing promises (legal obligations) made by the issuing company (borrower) to the lender of the funds (bondholders). The two most important promises are to repay the amount borrowed (principal) at a future (maturity) date and to make periodic payments (interest) for the use of the money. The borrower (issuing company) divides the total amount to be borrowed into denominations of $1,000 and sells them to the public through an investment bank. A trustee acts on behalf of the bondholders to make sure all covenants spelled out in the bond contract are fulfilled. The amount ($1,000) to be paid at maturity is called the face (par) value or face amount of the bond. The interest rate stipulated on the bond, which determines the amount of the periodic interest payments, is called the *coupon* rate. Although bonds are issued in denominations of $1,000, they are quoted in the bond market in percentages based on 100. A $1,000 bond quoted at 108 has a market price of $1,080.

Bonds secured only by the general credit of the issuing company are called debentures. Mortgage bonds are secured by a mortgage on specific assets. Serial bonds are retired in installments over the life of the bond issue by providing for retirement of specific bonds included in the issue at specific dates. Revenue bonds are secured by specific revenues set aside for the payment of the revenue bondholders. Convertible bonds are bonds that have the right to be converted into common stock at a specified price. The bond indenture (contract) specifies all the obligations and rights of the lender and the borrower.

Investors decide the prices at which bonds are sold by determining what they are willing to pay for the contractual cash flows (principal and coupon rate of interest) offered by the bond issuer. The major ingredients in this decision are current money market (interest) rates and the issuer's financial condition, an indication of its ability to repay the loan.

During the last quarter of 1978 Santiago determines that they will need to borrow approximately $100,000 at the beginning of 1979. They decide to sell a ten-year, $100,000 bond issue on January 1, 1979. The coupon interest is fixed in late 1978 at an annual rate of 10 percent with the expectation that this will also be the yield (market) rate that investors will expect for this type of bond issue on January 1, 1979.

On January 1, 1979, investors agree to buy Santiago's bonds for $100,000.[4] These bonds will yield the investor 10 percent because the

---

[4] For purposes of this example we assume that there are no costs to issue the bonds.

present value of the cash flows paid by Santiago (principal and coupon interest) is equal to 10 percent.

The present value of $10,000 a period (annual
coupon interest is 10 percent of $100,000) for
ten annual periods* ($10,000 × 6.145) .... $ 61,450
The present value of $100,000 to be paid in ten
years [principal (face value) amount paid at
maturity] at 10 percent ($100,000 × .3855) ...... <u>38,550</u>
$100,000

* We assume *annual* coupon interest payments in order to sim-
plify the computations. Most bonds pay coupon interest on a semiannual basis.

The entries on Santiago's books for these bonds are:

January 1, 1979

Cash...	100,000	
Bonds Payable		100,000
Issued ten-year, 10 percent bonds due 12/31/88		

Annually on December 31 of Each Year

Interest Expense...............................	10,000	
Cash..		10,000
To record annual interest expense		

December 31, 1988

Bonds Payable	100,000	
Cash..		100,000
To record retirement of the bonds		

Suppose that on January 1, 1979, when Santiago was ready to issue their $100,000, ten-year, *10 percent coupon* bonds, investors (bondbuyers) were demanding a 12 percent return on bonds of companies comparable to Santiago. The bondholders will pay (Santiago will receive) $88,700 because this is the present value of the cash flows at 12 percent.

The present value of $10,000 a period for ten
annual periods (annual coupon interest is
10 percent of $100,000) at 12 percent
($10,000 × 5.6502) $56,502
The present value of $100,000 to be paid in ten
years (principal amount paid at maturity) at
12 percent ($100,000 × .32198) .... <u>32,198</u>
$88,700

The $11,300 ($100,000 − $88,700) difference between the face amount of the bonds and the issue price is a *bond discount*. The bond discount represents the additional amount of interest that investors require to make this investment yield 12 percent. The investors will receive this $11,300 when the bonds mature in ten years.

The total amount of interest that Santiago will pay on these bonds is the difference between what they receive from the bondholders on the issue date and what they actually pay out over the life of the bonds.

Total payment:
Annual coupon interest of $10,000 ($100,000 ×
  10 percent) × ten years $100,000
Repayment of face amount at maturity........   100,000
                              $200,000
Issue price: (proceeds received by Santiago)   88,700
Interest expense for ten years $111,300

Whenever the market (effective, yield) rate of interest is higher than the coupon rate, the borrower will receive less than the face amount of the bonds.

If the market rate of interest is lower than the coupon rate, the borrower will receive more than the face amount and the difference will be a bond premium. If the Santiago bonds had been sold to yield 8 percent, the company would have received $113,420 on the issuance of the bonds resulting in a bond premium of $13,420.

The present value of $10,000 a period for ten
annual periods (annual coupon interest is
10 percent of $100,000) at 8 percent
($10,000 × 6.710) .... $ 67,100
The present value of $100,000 to be paid in ten
years (principal amount paid at maturity)
at 8 percent ($100,000 × .46320)   46,320
                        $113,420

The total amount of interest that Santiago will pay on these bonds is $86,580.

Total payment:
Annual coupon interest of $10,000 ($100,000 ×
  10 percent) × 10 years $100,000
Repayment of face amount at maturity........   100,000
                              $200,000
Issue price: (proceeds received by Santiago)   113,420
Interest expense for ten years .... $ 86,580

The cash received from the sale of the bonds is the borrower's liability on the issue date. On the formal balance sheet, bond discount (a contra long-term liability account) will be deducted from bonds payable at par value, and a bond premium (an adjunct long-term liability account) will be added to bonds payable at par value in order to reflect the correct liability.

Balance sheet disclosures on January 1, 1979:

Bonds payable (10 percent, due December 31, 1988)	$100,000
Less, unamortized bond discount	11,300
	$ 88,700

Bonds payable (10 percent, due December 31, 1988)	$100,000
Add, unamortized bond premium	13,420
	$113,420

BOND ISSUE COSTS

The costs to issue bonds (underwriters' fees, legal and accounting fees, printing costs, and so forth) are classified as an intangible asset on the balance sheet. They are charged to expense (amortized) on a straight-line basis over the life of the bond issue.

STRAIGHT-LINE AMORTIZATION OF BOND DISCOUNT AND BOND PREMIUM

The straight-line and the compound (effective) interest methods are the two methods most often used in amortizing bond discount and bond premium.

Entries using the straight-line amortization method, assuming the 10 percent bonds were issued at an effective interest rate (yield to investors) of 12 percent, are:

January 1, 1979

Cash	88,700	
Bond Discount	11,300	
Bonds Payable		100,000

To record issuance of ten year, 10 percent bonds due 12/31/88.

Each Year on December 31

Interest Expense	11,130	
Bond Discount		1,130
Cash		10,000

To record annual interest expense.

The amount of the additional interest (bond discount) to make the 10 percent coupon rate bonds yield 12 percent is amortized on a straight-line basis ($11,300 ÷ 10). The interest expense is $11,130 each year and the net liability (bonds payable − bond discount) increases $1,130 each year until at the end of ten years it is $100,000. The amortization of the bond discount for the ten-year period is calculated in Illustration 9–4.

ILLUSTRATION 9–4

	Interest Expense	Coupon Payment	Par Value	Bond Discount	Balance Sheet Liability
1- 1-79			$100,000	$11,300	$ 88,700
12-31-79	$11,130	$10,000		(1,130)	89,830
12-31-80	11,130	10,000		(1,130)	90,960
12-31-81	11,130	10,000		(1,130)	92,090
12-31-82	11,130	10,000		(1,130)	93,220
12-31-83	11,130	10,000		(1,130)	94,350
12-31-84	11,130	10,000		(1,130)	95,480
12-31-85	11,130	10,000		(1,130)	96,610
12-31-86	11,130	10,000		(1,130)	97,740
12-31-87	11,130	10,000		(1,130)	98,870
12-31-88	11,130	10,000		(1,130)	100,000

December 31, 1988

Bonds Payable	100,000	
Cash.......................................		100,000

To retire ten year, 10 percent bonds.

Entries using the straight-line amortization method assuming the 10 percent bonds were issued at an effective interest rate (yield to investors) of 8 percent are:

January 1, 1979

Cash..	113,420	
Bonds Payable		100,000
Bond Premium.............................		13,420

To record issuance of ten year, 10 percent bonds due 12/31/88.

Each Year on December 31

Interest Expense	8,658	
Bond Premium..................................	1,342	
Cash.......................................		10,000

To record annual interest expense.

The reduction of the interest (bond premium) to make the 10 percent coupon rate bonds yield 8 percent is amortized on a straight-line basis ($13,420 ÷ 10). The interest expense is $8,658 each year, and the liability decreases $1,320 each year until at the end of ten years it is $100,000 (see Illustration 9–5).

December 31, 1988

Bonds Payable	100,000	
Cash.......................................		100,000

To retire ten years, 10 percent bonds.

ILLUSTRATION 9–5

	Interest Expense	Coupon Payment	Par Value	Bond Premium	Balance Sheet Liability
1- 1-79			$100,000	$13,420	$113,420
12-31-79	$8,658	$10,000		(1,342)	112,078
12-31-80	8,658	10,000		(1,342)	110,736
12-31-81	8,658	10,000		(1,342)	109,394
12-31-82	8,658	10,000		(1,342)	108,052
12-31-83	8;658	10,000		(1,342)	106,710
12-31-84	8,658	10,000		(1,342)	105,368
12-31-85	8,658	10,000		(1,342)	104,026
12-31-86	8,658	10,000		(1,342)	102,684
12-31-87	8,658	10,000		(1,342)	101,342
12-31-88	8,658	10,000		(1,342)	100,000

Even though the straight-line method of amortization is often used in practice (primarily because it is computationally simple), it is not conceptually correct and cannot be used (*APB No. 21*) if the results are *materially* different from those which would be obtained using the compound (effective interest) method of bond amortization.

COMPOUND (EFFECTIVE) INTEREST RATE METHOD OF AMORTIZATION OF BOND DISCOUNT AND PREMIUM

Entries using the compound interest method of amortization, assuming the 10 percent bonds were issued at an effective interest rate of 12 percent, are:

January 1, 1979

Cash...	88,700	
Bond Discount	11,300	
Bonds Payable		100,000

To record issuance of ten year, 10 percent bonds due 12/31/88.

December 31, 1979

Interest Expense (12 percent of $88,700) 10,644
    Bond Discount 644
    Cash 10,000
    To record annual interest expense.

The interest expense for any period is the effective interest rate applied to the outstanding liability. On January 1, 1979, the liability is $88,700 and the interest expense for 1979 is $10,644 (12 percent of $88,700). The amortization of bond discount of $644 ($10,644 − $10,000) increases the bond liability on December 31, 1979, to $89,344 ($88,700 + $644).

The interest expense for the year ended December 31, 1980, is $10,721 (12 percent of $89,344). The entry on December 31, 1980 is:

Interest Expense 10,721
    Bond Discount 721
    Cash 10,000
    To record annual interest expense.

The general ledger liability accounts on December 31, 1980, are:

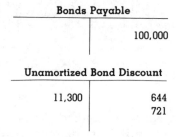

Bonds Payable

| | 100,000 |

Unamortized Bond Discount

| 11,300 | 644 |
| | 721 |

The balance sheet disclosure on December 31, 1980, is:

Bonds payable (10 percent, due December 31, 1988) $100,000
Less, unamortized bond discount 9,935
    $ 90,065

At the end of the ten-year period, the bond discount will be reduced to zero and the balance sheet liability will increase to $100,000. Illustration 9–6 calculates the interest expense and the amortization of bond discount over the ten-year period using the compound interest method.

When the compound interest method of amortization is used, the bond liability is always the present value of the future (interest and principal payments) cash flows.

The liability account always reflects the initial amount borrowed

ILLUSTRATION 9–6

	Interest Expense	Coupon Payment	Par Value	Bond Discount	Balance Sheet Liability
1- 1-79			$100,000	$11,300	$ 88,700
12-31-79	$10,644	$10,000		(644)	89,344
12-31-80	10,721	10,000		(721)	90,065
12-31-81	10,808	10,000		(808)	90,873
12-31-82	10,905	10,000		(905)	91,778
12-31-83	11,013	10,000		(1,013)	92,791
12-31-84	11,135	10,000		(1,135)	93,926
12-31-85	11,271	10,000		(1,271)	95,197
12-31-86	11,424	10,000		(1,424)	96,621
12-31-87	11,594	10,000		(1,594)	98,215
12-31-88	11,785	10,000		(1,785)	100,000

($88,700) plus the portion of the interest expense (amortized bond discount) that will not be paid until the maturity date.

For example, on December 31, 1983, the liability on the balance sheet is:

Bonds payable $100,000
Less, bond discount ($11,300 − $4,091) 7,209
$ 92,791

The present value of $10,000 for five annual
periods at 12 percent ($10,000 × 3.6048) 36,048
The present value of $100,000 to be paid in five
years at 12 percent ($100,000 × .56743) 56,743
$ 92,791

The liability on December 31, 1983, is made up of the $88,700 originally borrowed plus the amortized discount (additional interest expense) of $4,091 ($644 + $721 + $808 + $905 + $1,013).

If we had used the straight-line method of amortization, the liability on December 31, 1983, would have been $94,350 ($88,700 + $1,130 + $1,130 + $1,130 + $1,130 + $1,130) and the liability would not reflect an effective interest rate of 12 percent.

Illustration 9–7 shows the calculation of interest expense, amortization of bond premium, and the balance sheet liability throughout the life of the 10 percent bond issue assuming it was sold to yield 8 percent.

ILLUSTRATION 9–7

	Interest Expense	Coupon Payment	Par Value	Bond Premium	Balance Sheet Liability
1- 1-79			$100,000	$13,420	$113,420
12-31-79	$9,074	$10,000		(926)	112,494
12-31-80	9,000	10,000		(1,000)	111,494
12-31-81	8,920	10,000		(1,081)	110,414
12-31-82	8,833	10,000		(1,167)	109,247
12-31-83	8,740	10,000		(1,260)	107,987
12-31-84	8,639	10,000		(1,361)	106,626
12-31-85	8,530	10,000		(1,470)	105,156
12-31-86	8,413	10,000		(1,588)	103,568
12-31-87	8,285	10,000		(1,715)	101,853
12-31-88	8,147	10,000		(1,853)	100,000

The entries for the first two years of the bond issue are:

Cash..	113,420	
Bonds Payable		100,000
Bond Premium.............................		13,420

To record issuance of ten year, 10 percent bonds due 12/31/88.

Interest Expense (8 percent of $113,420)	9,074	
Bond Premium...................................	926	
Cash.......................................		10,000

To record 1979 interest.

Interest Expense (8 percent of $112,494)	9,000	
Bond Premium...................................	1,000	
Cash.......................................		10,000

To record 1980 interest.

BOND REDEMPTION

In addition to the two payment promises, many bonds have a call provision which enables the bonds to be retired prior to maturity. The redemption price usually includes a premium paid to bondholders for having their bonds called earlier than they had anticipated.

Assume at the time the bonds were redeemed the following accounts pertaining to the bond issue were on the books.

Bonds Payable

	200,000

Bond Discount

8,000	

The call (redemption) price is stated as a percentage of the par value. The entry to record the bond redemption, assuming a call price of 108, is:

Bonds Payable	200,000	
Loss on Bond Redemption	24,000	
Bond Discount		8,000
Cash (1.08 × $200,000)......................		216,000
To record redemption of $200,000 par value bonds.		

The loss on bond redemption is reported net of taxes on the income statement as an extraordinary loss.[5]

BOND CONVERSION

Convertible bonds give the bondholders the option of converting their bonds into common stock at a future date. This convertible feature gives the bondholder (investor) the opportunity to share in the growth (appreciation of the market price of the stock) of the company while maintaining a creditor (bond) position. The conversion feature usually enables the issuing company to sell the bonds in the market place at interest rates lower than interest rates of an equivalent issue without the conversion feature.

Assume that on January 1, 1978, the Yardley Corporation issues $1 million, 10 percent, 20-year convertible debentures for $920,000. The conversion option allows each $1,000 bond to be converted into 40 shares of common stock. On January 1, 1983, when the market price of Yardley common stock is $28, 30 percent of the bondholders decide to convert their bonds into common stock.

The relevant general ledger accounts on January 1, 1983, before the conversion are:

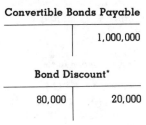

Convertible Bonds Payable

	1,000,000

Bond Discount*

80,000	20,000

* Straight-line amortization.

[5] Financial Accounting Standards Board *Statement No. 4,* "Reporting Gains and Losses from Extinguishment of Debt," March 1975.

The entry to record the conversion of 30 percent of the outstanding bonds is:

Bonds Payable	300,000	
Bond Discount		18,000
Common Stock		282,000
To convert $300,000 convertible bonds into 12,000 shares of common stock.		

This method (which is preferred) is different than for a redemption as it ignores the market value of the stock on the date of conversion. It considers the convertible bond as a device to issue common stock and states the common stock at the amount received from the original convertible bond issue.

An alternative treatment is to consider the market value of the bonds to be their conversion value.

Bonds Payable	300,000	
Loss on Bond Conversion	54,000	
Bond Discount		18,000
Common Stock (12,000 shares at $28)..........		336,000
To convert $300,000 convertible bonds into 12,000 shares of common stock.		

This method assumes that the common stock is sold at its market price and that the proceeds from the sale are used to redeem the convertible bonds.

LEASES

A lease is an agreement between the owner of an asset (lessor) and the user of the asset (lessee) in which the lessee pays the lessor for the right to use the asset.

Assume that on January 1, 1979, the Rogers Company leases an office copier from the SMD Corporation for 36 months. Rogers agrees to pay SMD $100 at the end of each month with the first payment due January 31, 1979.

Monthly Entry on Rogers's Books

Rent (lease) Expense	100	
Cash...		100
To record one month's rental expense for the office copier.		

Because the lease is for services (use of the office copier) to be rendered in the future, no asset or liability is recorded on Rogers's books on the date the lease is signed.

Many companies structured what were actually purchases of fixed assets financed with long-term debt as leases in order to avoid recording either the fixed asset or the corresponding long-term liability on the balance sheet. To prevent this practice and to promulgate the idea of recording transactions in accordance with their economic substance, the Financial Accounting Standards Board issued *Statement No. 13*, "Accounting for Leases."[6] This rule applies to *all* companies which prepare their financial statements in accordance with generally accepted accounting principles.

FASB *Statement No. 13* requires the capitalization (recording as assets) of all leases which are in substance purchases. These leases are defined as *capital* leases. All other leases are defined as operating leases. The lease payment in an operating lease is charged to rental expense as in the previous Rogers Company example.

According to FASB *No. 13*, if a lease meets *any* of the following criteria it is a *capital* lease:

1. Ownership is transferred to the lessee by the end of the lease.
2. There is a bargain (pay less than fair value) purchase option.
3. The lease term is 75 percent or more of the leased property's estimated economic life.
4. The present value of the minimum lease payments is 90 percent or more of the fair value of the leased property (less the investment credit if retained by the lessor).

The method for calculating the long-term liability of capital leases is the same as used in *APB No. 21* to calculate the liability for noninterest bearing long-term notes payable.

The lease is recorded at the lower of the fair value of the leased property or the present value of the minimum lease payments. The interest rate to be used by the leasee is the interest rate implicit in the lease (probably known only to lessor) or, if the implicit interest rate is not known, the lessee's incremental interest rate. The incremental interest rate is the rate the lessee company would pay if the funds were borrowed to purchase the asset and repaid over a period similar to the lease.

Assume that on January 1, 1979, the Santiago Corporation leases a large piece of equipment from the Roar Corporation. The terms of the lease require Santiago to pay $10,000 a year rental for ten years and to pay all related insurance, maintenance, and property taxes. The fair value of the equipment on January 1, 1979, is estimated to be $68,000, and it is expected to have an economic life of 12 years.

The lease is a capital lease because the lease term is at least 75 percent (10 years/12 years = 83.3 percent) of the economic life of the machine. Santiago has to record the asset and the liability at the

---

[6] November 1976.

lower of the fair value of the equipment or the present value of the lease payments. Santiago's incremental interest rate is determined to be 10 percent and the rate implicit in the lease is not known to them.

The present value of $10,000 a year at 10 percent for ten years is $61,450. (See the calculation under noninterest bearing long-term notes payable in the beginning of the chapter.)

The entry on January 1, 1979, is:

Capital Lease Asset	61,450	
Capital Lease Liability......................		61,450
To record ten-year lease at $10,000 per year.		

Capital Lease Asset is classified on the balance sheet as a fixed asset, and Capital Lease Liability is classified as a long-term liability.

December 31, 1979

Interest Expense (10 percent of $61,450)	6,145	
Capital Lease Liability.........................	3,855	
Cash......................................		10,000
To record lease payment for 1979.		
Depreciation Expense—Capital Lease Asset	6,145	
Accumulated Depreciation—Capital Lease		6,145
Asset		
To record depreciation (ten years straight line, 10 percent of $61,450).		

The lessee has the same option for using the straight-line or an accelerated depreciation method for leased assets as for purchased assets. For leased assets the lessee also has the option of directly decreasing the value of the asset account rather than creating an accumulated depreciation account.

Insurance, Maintenance,		
Property Tax Expenses......................	*XXXX*	
Cash (Payables)		*XXXX*
To record expenses related to leased equipment.		

December 31, 1980

Interest Expense (10 percent of $57,595)	5,759	
Capital Lease Liability.........................	4,241	
Cash......................................		10,000
To record lease payment for 1980.		

The amount of interest expense, which is calculated using the effective interest rate method, will decline each year because the liability is declining.

The allocation of the lease payments to interest expense and liability reduction for the entire ten-year period is shown in Illustration 9–8.

ILLUSTRATION 9–8

	Lease Payment	Interest	Principal Payment	Capital Lease Liability
1- 1-79				$61,450
12-31-79	$10,000	$6,145	$3,855	57,595
12-31-80	10,000	5,760	4,240	53,355
12-31-81	10,000	5,335	4,665	48,690
12-31-82	10,000	4,869	5,131	43,559
12-31-83	10,000	4,356	5,644	37,915
12-31-84	10,000	3,792	6,208	31,707
12-31-85	10,000	3,171	6,829	24,878
12-31-86	10,000	2,488	7,512	17,366
12-31-87	10,000	1,737	8,263	9,103
12-31-88	10,000	897*	9,103	—0—

* Adjusted for differences in rounding to the nearest dollar.

The accounting on the lessor's books will usually parallel the accounting on the lessee's books.

FASB *Statement No. 13*'s treatment for capital leases results in increasing both assets (the lease is capitalized) and the amount of debt outstanding. It has a direct impact on two ratios often used by financial analysts: the ratio of debt to equity (debt/equity ratio), and the ratio of net income to assets (rate of return on total assets).

STOCKHOLDERS' EQUITY

The claim of the owners (assets minus liabilities) of an enterprise is made up of two major sources: (1) the permanent capital contributed by the owners; and (2) earnings retained in the business.

In a proprietorship, the permanent capital is combined with the earnings and withdrawals of the owners in a single owner's equity account called *proprietor's capital*. In a partnership, the owners' equity account is called *partners' capital*. Capital contributions, withdrawals, and profit or loss are all recorded in the partners' capital account. It is not possible to distinguish between the permanent capital and retained earnings in the owner's equity account of a proprietorship or partnership.

A corporation, a legal entity separate from its owners, is required by state law to segregate amounts contributed as capital by its owners (stockholders) from its retained earnings. The state grants the corporation the right to exist and function within broad guidelines which are spelled out in the corporation's articles of incorporation and bylaws filed with the secretary of state. The state also authorizes the right to issue certificates of ownership (capital stock). The method by which capital stock may be sold to the public is regulated by both the state and federal (Securities and Exchange Commission) governments.

The owners of the common stock elect the board of directors of the corporation. The board of directors is responsible for the management of the corporation and hires the corporate officers to run it.

The entry to record the sale of 1,000 shares of common stock for $10,000 is

```
Cash.........................................     10,000
    Common Stock (Capital Contributed
        by Common Stockholders)..................            10,000
    To record the issue of 1,000 shares of common
    stock at $10 per share.
```

It has been the custom in accounting and law to assign a *par value* to stock. This par value is indicated in the certificate of incorporation filed with the secretary of state.

Assume that the 1,000 shares of common stock in the preceding example has a par value of $8.

```
Cash.........................................     10,000
    Common Stock  ...............................             8,000
    Paid-in Capital—Excess over Par Value........             2,000
    To record the issue of 1,000 shares of $8 par
    value stock.
```

There is no relationship between the par value and the amount received upon the issuance of the common stock. The only significance of par value is that it represents the minimum amount which must be legally contributed by the shareholders.

It is common procedure to indicate on the formal balance sheet the number of shares of stock authorized, as well as the number of shares issued and outstanding with excess over stated value entered in paid-in-capital.

```
        Common stock—par value $8 per share
            (authorized 3,000 shares: issued and out-
            standing 1,000 shares) .......................   $8,000
        Paid-in (additional) capital—excess over
            par value  ...................................    2,000
```

When some states enacted franchise taxes based on par value, there was a switch to the issuance of no-par (zero) value stock. The logical entry for the issuance of 1,000 shares of no-par value stock for $10,000 should be:

```
Cash ...........................................        10,000
    Common Stock .............................                    10,000
    To record the issue of 1,000 shares of no-par
    value stock at $10 a share.
```

In many cases a *stated value* is arbitrarily assigned to no-par value stock and the accounting procedure followed is the same as for par value stock.

TREASURY STOCK

In order to obtain stock for stock option plans, for employee purchase plans, for purchases of other corporations, for increases in earnings per share, or for other corporate purposes, companies repurchase their own stock. This reacquisition of a company's stock (treasury stock) is a decrease in both the assets and the stockholders' equity of a corporation.

If the corporation purchased 100 shares of its $8 par value stock for $15 (market value at date of purchase) a share, the entry would be:

```
Treasury Stock ................................        1,500
    Cash.......................................                    1,500
    To record the purchase of 100 shares of the
    corporation's stock at $15.
```

Treasury stock has no voting or dividend rights and is not included in the computation of earnings per share. It is the same as unissued stock except that it has been issued once and is being held for ultimate reissue (it is issued but not outstanding stock). In no sense should it be considered an asset of the corporation.

The formal balance sheet presentation would be:

```
Common stock—par value $8 per share
    (authorized 3,000 shares: issued 1,000 shares of
    which 100 are in the treasury) .................   $ 8,000
Paid-in capital—excess over par value ..........     2,000
                                                     $10,000
    Less, common stock held in the treasury
        (at cost 100 shares).......................     1,500
                                                     $ 8,500
```

If the treasury stock is reissued at a later date for $16, the entry is:

```
Cash.........................................        1,600
    Treasury Stock ............................                    1,500
    Paid-in Capital—Treasury Stock Transactions .                   100
    To record the sale of 100 shares of treasury stock for
    $16 a share.
```

If the treasury stock was reissued at a price less than its purchase price, the difference should be charged to *paid-in capital—treasury stock transactions* if such an account existed. If not, the entry should be made to retained earnings. In no case should the difference between the cost of the treasury stock and the proceeds on the reissue be recorded on the income statement.

If the purpose in reacquiring stock is to reduce the total number of shares outstanding, the stock should be formally cancelled and not kept in the treasury. The entry would be:

Common Stock	800	
Paid-in Capital—Excess Over Par Value	200	
Retained Earnings	500	
Cash		1,500

    To record the purchase at $15 and retirement of 100 shares of common stock.

PREFERRED STOCK

Preferred stock is another type of capital stock. It does not have the ownership rights of the common stock, but it usually has the first claim on dividends and a preference over common stock in liquidation. The exact rights of each type of preferred stock (also common stock) can be obtained only by reading the contract (small print on the stock certificate) between the corporation and its preferred stockholders.

Typical rights and terms of preferred stock are:

1. The first right to dividends if they are declared. The amount of the dividend is usually stated on the stock certificate.
2. The cumulative right, which requires that all preferred dividends including those passed in prior years must be paid prior to the declaration of any common stock dividends.
3. The preferred usually has preference over common stockholders in case of liquidation.
4. Many preferred stocks have a call provision. They may be retired at the option of the corporation at a price set in the contract. For example, a $100 par value, cumulative preferred stock paying a $6 annual dividend might be callable at $105.

Other features sometimes found in preferred stocks are:

1. The convertible feature that allows the preferred stockholders to convert their preferred stock to common stock sometime in the future. The convertible feature is based on the market value of the common stock rising in the future.
2. The participating feature, which allows preferred stockholders

some participation in the earnings of the corporation over and above the fixed preferred dividend rate.
3. A sinking fund provision which requires guaranteed amounts to be set aside to retire the preferred stock. Preferred stock with this feature have many of the characteristics of bonds.

The corporation will determine, based on an analysis of financial market conditions, which features it needs to include in order to sell the stock.

The entry to record the sale of 100 shares of the corporation's $100 par value, $6, cumulative preferred stock at $110 a share is:

Cash...	11,000	
Preferred Stock		10,000
Preferred Stock—Premium (Excess over Par Value)		1,000
To record the issuance of 100 shares of the $100 par value, $6 preferred at $110.		

Even though the account *paid-in capital—excess over par value* is more descriptive and informative, it has been the custom to use the account *preferred stock—premium* for preferred issues. If less than par value is received, the account has been called *preferred stock—discount*.

The formal balance sheet with the issued common and preferred is:

Shareholders' Equity

Preferred stockholders' equity:

Preferred stock—$6, cumulative $100 par value: (authorized 1,000 shares: issued and outstanding 100 shares)	$10,000	
Premium on preferred stock	1,000	$11,000

Common stockholders' equity:

Common stock—par value $8 per share (authorized 3,000 shares: issued 1,000 shares of which 100 are in the treasury)..............	$ 8,000	
Paid-in capital—excess over par value	2,000	10,000
		$21,000
Less, common stock held in the treasury (at cost, 100 shares)		1,500
		$19,500

CASH DIVIDENDS

Cash dividends represent a distribution to the stockholders. They result in a decrease in stockholders' equity (retained earnings) and a decrease in assets (cash). Many states require that a corporation have retained earnings (earnings in excess of the original investment) in order to declare cash dividends. In addition to retained earnings, the corporation must also have cash in order to pay a cash dividend.

Dividends become a legal liability at the time the board of directors declares the dividend (declaration date). If a dividend of $1 was declared on 20,000 shares of common stock, the entry made on the date of declaration would be:

Retained Earnings	20,000	
Dividends Payable		20,000
To record declaration of $1 dividend on outstanding common stock.		

The declaration states that the dividend will be paid to all stockholders who own the stock on a specific date (record date). The dividend is declared on December 15, 1978, to be paid on January 2, 1979, to stockholders of record on December 28, 1978.

On January 2, 1979, when the dividend is paid, the entry is:

Dividends Payable	20,000	
Cash		20,000
To record payment of cash dividends declared December 15, 1978.		

STOCK SPLITS

A stock split is the issuance of additional shares of stock to the current stockholders at no cost. There is no change in assets or shareholders' equity. The only change is in the number of shares outstanding.

If a corporation declares a three-for-one stock split when it has 100,000 common shares outstanding, it will issue 300,000 new shares of common stock and retire the 100,000 old shares. If it is a par value stock, the par value usually will be changed to accommodate the split. No accounting entry is necessary for a stock split because there has been no change in the shareholders' equity (assets minus liabilities). The stockholders have three times as many shares but the same percentage of ownership after the split as they had before the split. If the market price of the stock before the split was $75, it should be $25 after the split.

STOCK DIVIDENDS

A stock dividend (dividend paid in stock) is a pro rata distribution of a corporation's stock to its stockholders. The payment of a stock dividend does not result in a change in corporate assets or stock-holders' equity. It is no different than a small (usually less than 20 percent) stock split.

In practice, however, an accounting entry is made for stock dividends. Retained earnings are capitalized at the market price on the date the stock dividend is declared. Let us assume that the market price of the corporation's common stock is $20 on the date it declares and pays a stock dividend of 5 percent on its 10,000 outstanding shares of $10 par value common stock.

The required entry is:

Retained Earnings (500 Shares at $20).............	10,000	
Common Stock—Par Value...................		5,000
Paid-in Capital—Excess over Par Value.......		5,000
To record payment of a 5 percent stock dividend.		

The above entry treats a stock dividend as if it were a cash dividend that was paid and then reinvested in the corporation's stock.

The shareholders have exactly the same percentage interest in the corporation *after* the stock dividend as they did *before* the stock dividend. In the above example, a shareholder who owned 1,000 shares of stock before the stock dividend had a 10 percent, 1,000/10,000, ownership interest in the corporation. After the stock dividend it is still a 10 percent, 1,050/10,500, interest in the corporation. Generally the market price of the stock declines in proportion to the additional shares issued. Stock dividends and splits are not taxable for income tax purposes because they do not represent a distribution of income.

In most cases, companies that issue stock dividends do so because they want to conserve cash and still give the stockholders "something." They could accomplish the same thing by indicating to investors that it is the policy of the company to reinvest its earnings and not pay cash dividends.

RETAINED EARNINGS

Retained earnings is the portion of stockholders' equity derived from earnings. In its simplest form, it should consist of earnings accumulated since the inception of the company less dividends paid (earnings returned to the stockholders). If there have been losses over the years, and liabilities plus capital contributed by stockholders exceed total assets, this account is called *deficit* (negative retained earnings). Retained earnings, formerly called *earned surplus,* is not a tangible item but is part of the stockholders' claim against assets.

State laws and business contracts often require that a portion of the retained earnings should be restricted so that it is not available for the declaration of dividends. For example, an agreement with the bondholders requires that $100,000 of retained earnings must be restricted until the bonds are retired.

An entry disclosing this fact could be made as follows:

Retained Earnings	100,000	
Retained Earnings Restricted (Appropriated) for		
Payment of Bondholders		100,000
To record appropriation of retained earnings.		

Upon retirement of the bonds an entry would be made to reverse the above entry since the appropriation is no longer necessary.

Retained Earnings Restricted (Appropriated) for		
Payment of Bondholders	100,000	
Retained Earnings		100,000
To return to unappropriated retained earnings the		
amount appropriated for retirement of bonds.		

The same disclosure could be obtained by a footnote to the financial statements instead of a formal journal entry. For example:

> The agreement with the bondholders requires that $100,000 of retained earnings must be restricted until the payment of the bonds in 1978. Unrestricted retained earnings available for the payment of dividends amounted to $1 million.

In addition to the income statement and balance sheet, the financial statements will include a statement of the changes in retained earnings for the year. (See Illustration 9–9).

ILLUSTRATION 9–9

XYZ CORPORATION
Statement of Retained Earnings
Fiscal Year Ended June 30, 1981

Balance, July 1, 1980	$1,000,000
Add: Net income for the fiscal year ended	
June 30, 1981	300,000
	$1,300,000
Less: Dividends paid on common stock at	
$2 per share	200,000
Balance, June 30, 1981	$1,100,000

BOOK VALUE OF COMMON STOCK

The book value of a share of common stock is calculated by dividing common stockholders' equity by the number of common shares outstanding.[7] It is also the net asset (assets − liabilities = stockholders' equity) value per common share. The market price of a share of common stock is the amount for which it can be sold (usually on a securities exchange) and should be equal to the present value of the company's expected future cash flows to stockholders divided by the number of shares outstanding. Market value may or may not bear a relationship to book value.

SUMMARY

In practice, there are many diverse ways of classifying the effects of various transactions on the stockholders' equity section. The im-

ILLUSTRATION 9-10 _____

Stockholders' equity		
Preferred stockholders' equity:		
Preferred stock—$6 cumulative $100 par value (authorized 1,000 shares: issued and outstanding 100 shares—Note 1)	$10,000	
Premium on preferred stock	1,000	$11,000
Common stockholders' equity:		
Common stock—par value $8 per share (authorized 3,000 shares: issued 1,000 shares of which 100 are in the treasury)	$ 8,000	
Paid-in capital—excess over par value	2,000	
	$10,000	
Retained earnings (Note 2)	25,000	35,000
		$46,000
Less, common stock held in the treasury (at cost, 100 shares)		1,500
		$44,500

Note 1: The preferred stock may be redeemed at a price of $105 beginning July 1, 1985. There are no preferred dividends in arrears.

Note 2: Under the terms of an agreement with bondholders, $12,000 of the retained earnings is unavailable for dividend declaration, and $1,500 of retained earnings equal to the cost of the treasury stock is restricted in accordance with state statutes.

_____

[7] If there is any preferred stock outstanding, any portion of the retained earnings that belongs to the preferred stockholders (cumulative preferred dividends in arrears) must be deducted before calculating the book value of common stockholders.

portant consideration in analyzing these financial transactions should be whether they affect permanent capital or earnings.

The formal balance sheet presentation of the stockholders' equity section should include full disclosure of how all major changes in the stockholders' equity accounts are reflected. This may be done in the body of the statement, in separate schedules, or in the footnotes to the financial statements.

An acceptable balance sheet format for the stockholders' equity section is shown in Illustration 9–10.

CASES FOR CHAPTER 9

Case 9–1

Present Value and Bonds[1]

1. What is the most you would be willing to pay today for the privilege of receiving $10,000 five years from now? Assume you could earn 10 percent per year return on your money.

2. What is the most you would be willing to pay today for the privilege of receiving $1,000 at the end of each of the next five years? Assume you could earn 10 percent per year return on the money.

3. What is the most you would be willing to pay for a $10,000 face value, 10 percent annual coupon rate bond with a five year maturity? Assume you could earn 10 percent per year return on your money in an alternative investment. What is the present value of the $10,000 you would receive in five years? What is the present value of the five $1,000 annual interest payments?

4. Suppose you could earn 15 percent per year on an alternative investment. Now how much would you be willing to pay for the $10,000, five-year bond with a 10 percent annual coupon rate?

5. Suppose a corporation issued this $10,000 bond, which yields 15 percent, for $8,324.

Make the journal entry to record the issue of the bond.

Make the journal entry for the first year's interest payment assuming (a) straight-line amortization of bond discount, and (b) effective interest method amortization of bond discount.

---

[1] Calculators with financial functions may be used to calculate present value of $1, present value of $1 per period, future value of $1, and so forth.

Case 9–2

Expanso Corporation (A)

Mr. Jasper, president of Expanso Corporation, a rapidly expanding company, negotiates an agreement with Standard Insurance Company under which the insurance company is to lend Expanso $1 million on a 12 percent basis. The insurance company offers Expanso three options as to the method of repayment. The effective rate of interest for each option is 6 percent per half-year.

Option 1—Expanso to receive $1 million now; Expanso to pay 6 percent interest at the end of each six months for 20 years, and to pay $1 million at maturity 20 years hence.

Option 2—Expanso to receive $1 million now; Expanso to pay $10,285,717.94 at the end of 20 years, and to make no other payments of interest or principal during the 20-year term of the loan ($1 at 6 percent will accumulate to $10.28571794 at the end of 40 periods).

Option 3—Expanso to receive $1 million now; Expanso to pay $66,461.54 at the end of each six months for 20 years, and to make no other payments of interest or principal during or at the end of the 20-year period (the present value of $.06646154 per period for 40 periods at 6 percent is $1.00).

Required:

1. Jasper asks you to make the following computations for *each* option.
   a. The amount of the liability at the date of the loan.
   b. The amount of interest expense for the first year.
   c. The total interest expense for the entire 20-year period.
   d. The cash flow (inward and outward) for the first year.
   e. The cash flow (inward and outward) for the 2d and 20th years.
2. Which option should Mr. Jasper take? Why?

Case 9–3

Expanso Corporation (B)

After reviewing the three options in Expanso A, the controller of Expanso suggests an entirely different arrangement. He says that what Expanso wants is not money as such, but a method of paying the $1 million purchase price of a new papermaking machine which has just been installed. He suggests that the Standard Insurance

Company buy the papermaking machine and lease it to Expanso for 20 years for $66,461.54, rent to be paid at the end of each six months.

The Standard Insurance Company agrees with the controller and purchases the papermaker on January 1, 1980, and immediately leases it to Expanso at the terms suggested by Expanso's controller. The economic life of the papermaker is determined to be 25 years, and Expanso's incremental interest rate is 12 percent per annum (compounded semiannually).

Required:

1. Make the journal entry to record the lease agreement on January 1, 1980. (See requirements under FASB *Statement No. 13.*)
2. Make the entry to record the lease payments on June 30, 1980, and December 31, 1980.
3. Make the entry to record depreciation expense for 1980. Expanso uses the double-declining balance method for both its books and tax returns.
4. Is it more advantageous for Expanso to lease the papermaker from Standard Insurance or to borrow from Standard in accordance with option 2 and buy the papermaker?

Case 9– 4

MPB Corporation

MPB Corporation issued $1 million of 8 percent, 20-year bonds to yield 9 percent on January 1, 1975. It uses the effective interest method of amortization of bond discount and premium.

Refer to the bond table (Exhibit 1) and answer the following questions.

a. What were the proceeds of the bond issue?
b. Five years later the effective interest rate on bonds of this type had declined to 8.4 percent. What was the market price at that date?
c. What was the balance in the bond discount account at January 1, 1980?
d. Assume, contrary to fact, that the balance in the bond discount account at January 1, 1979, was $100,000. What was the amount of interest expense recognized at June 30, 1979?
e. Continuing the assumption of (d), what would be the balance of bond discount at July 1, 1979?
f. Continuing the assumption of (d), what would be the amount of interest expense recognized at December 31, 1979?

EXHIBIT 1

Bond Values in Percent of Par: 8-Percent Semiannual Coupons

Market Yield (percent per year compounded semiannually)	Years to Maturity							
	½	5	10	15	19½	20	30	40
5.0	101.463	113.128	123.384	131.396	137.096	137.654	146.363	151.678
5.5	101.217	110.800	119.034	125.312	129.675	130.098	136.528	140.266
6.0	100.971	108.530	114.877	119.600	122.808	123.115	127.676	130.201
6.5	100.726	106.317	110.905	114.236	116.448	116.656	119.690	121.291
7.0	100.483	104.158	107.106	109.196	110.551	110.678	112.472	113.374
7.1	100.435	103.733	106.367	108.225	109.424	109.536	111.113	111.898
7.2	100.386	103.310	105.634	107.266	108.314	108.411	109.780	110.455
7.3	100.338	102.889	104.908	106.318	107.220	107.303	108.473	109.044
7.4	100.289	102.470	104.188	105.382	106.142	106.212	107.191	107.665
7.5	100.241	102.053	103.474	104.457	105.080	105.138	105.934	106.316
7.6	100.193	101.638	102.767	103.544	104.034	104.079	104.702	104.997
7.7	100.144	101.226	102.066	102.642	103.003	103.036	103.492	103.706
7.8	100.096	100.815	101.371	101.750	101.987	102.009	102.306	102.444
7.9	100.048	100.407	100.683	100.870	100.986	100.997	101.142	101.209
8.0	100	100	100	100	100	100	100	100
8.1	99.9519	99.5955	99.3235	99.1406	99.0279	99.0177	98.8794	98.8170
8.2	99.9039	99.1929	98.6529	98.2916	98.0699	98.0498	97.7798	97.6589
8.3	99.8560	98.7924	97.9882	97.4528	97.1257	97.0962	96.7006	96.5253
8.4	99.8081	98.3938	97.3294	96.6240	96.1951	96.1566	95.6414	95.4152
8.5	99.7602	97.9973	96.6764	95.8052	95.2780	95.2307	94.6018	94.3282
8.6	99.7124	97.6027	96.0291	94.9962	94.3739	94.3183	93.5812	93.2636
8.7	99.6646	97.2100	95.3875	94.1969	93.4829	93.4191	92.5792	92.2208
8.8	99.6169	96.8193	94.7514	93.4071	92.6045	92.5331	91.5955	91.1992
8.9	99.5692	96.4305	94.1210	92.6266	91.7387	91.6598	90.6295	90.1982
9.0	99.5215	96.0436	93.4960	91.8555	90.8851	90.7992	89.6810	89.2173
9.5	99.2840	94.1378	90.4520	88.1347	86.7949	86.6777	85.1858	84.5961
10.0	99.0476	92.2783	87.5378	84.6275	82.9830	82.8409	81.0707	80.4035
10.5	98.8123	90.4639	84.7472	81.3201	79.4271	79.2656	77.2956	76.5876
11.0	98.5782	88.6935	82.0744	78.1994	76.1070	75.9308	73.8252	73.1036

g. Assume, contrary to fact, that the balance in the bond discount account on July 1, 1982, would be $80,000. At that date, MPB Corp. buys $50,000 par value of the bonds on the market for $44,000. Is there a gain or loss on the transaction and how much?

h. Continue the assumption of (g). In what category on MPB's income statement would the gain or loss on retirement be shown?

i. Continue the assumption of (g). What would be the net balance of the liability shown for bonds payable on a July 1, 1983, balance sheet?

j. Assume, contrary to (g), that no bonds have been retired before maturity. What would interest expense for the final six months be?

k. Assuming no bonds were retired before maturity, what was the effect of the retirement at maturity on net working capital? Answer by indicating increase or decrease and an amount. (Net working capital = current assets − current liabilities.)

l. Assuming no bonds were retired before maturity, what was the total interest expense over the life of the bond issue?

Case 9–5

IBM Notes—Issued October 3, 1979[1]

On October 3, 1979, a meeting was held in the conference room of the investment banker Salomon Brothers. Present at the meeting were representatives of Salomon Brothers and Merrill Lynch, another investment banker, and financial executives of International Business Machines (IBM).

The purpose of the meeting was to price an IBM offering of $500 million, seven-year notes with a coupon rate of 9½ percent (4.75 percent semiannually) and $500 million of 25-year debentures which bore a coupon rate of 9⅜ percent (4.6875 percent semiannually).

The IBM notes and bond issue were rated triple A (the highest rating) by both Standard and Poor's and Moody's and would be considered prime corporate paper. U.S. Treasury issues of comparable maturities are usually used as a key benchmark in pricing prime corporate paper.

Salomon Brothers, as the leader of the underwriting, wanted to price the bond and note issues so that they would both sell quickly and give IBM the lowest possible interest cost. Their immediate con-

---

[1] This case relies heavily on the article "The Bomb Dropped on Wall Street," by Walter Guzzardi, Jr., published in the November 19, 1979, issue of *Fortune*.

cern was that on October 3, 1979, interest rates were rising, the value of the dollar was declining, the value of gold was increasing, and bond and stock prices were falling.

After much negotiation the underwriters and IBM agreed at 12:40 P.M. on a yield to investors (interest cost to IBM) of seven basis points (a basis point is 1/100 of a percent) above U.S. Treasury notes for the IBM notes and 12 basis points above U.S. Treasury bonds for the IBM debentures. The effective interest (yield) rates for the notes was 9.62 percent (4.81 percent semiannually) and 9.41 percent (4.705 percent semiannually) for the debentures.

The price to buyers on a note was set at $994 per $1,000 note with $987.75 of that amount going to IBM. The difference of $6.25 went to the underwriting syndicate for selling the issue ($1.25 went to Salomon and Merrill Lynch as managers of the issue, $1.25 to each underwriter, and $3.75 was paid as a selling concession to the sellers of the note).

Required:

1. Make the journal entry on IBM's books to record the proceeds they received from the underwriters on the sale of the $500 million, seven-year notes.

2. Make the journal entry on IBM's books to record the first six months interest expense and amortization of note issue costs. IBM used the straight-line method to amortize note issue costs ($6.25 per $1,000 note) and the compound (effective) interest method to amortize note discount. (For purposes of this journal entry disregard the fact that IBM reports on a calendar year basis and would have to make an adjusting entry on December 31, 1979. You should also *assume* that the first coupon interest payment will be made one day after your entry.)

3. During the next two days interest rates rose (four-year U.S. Treasury notes sold to yield 9.79 percent on October 4) and on Monday, October 8, the Federal Reserve Board introduced strong anti-inflationary measures which resulted in large increases in interest rates.

   On Wednesday, October 10, the underwriting syndicate was no longer able to sell the IBM notes and bonds at the original yield rates. The syndicate was disbanded, and the bonds were allowed to sell at the market price. The market price of the notes fell about $5 each, and the yield rose to 10.65 percent. By November 1, the notes were selling for 92¼ bid and 92½ asked, a yield of approximately 10.98 percent.

   a. What journal entry should IBM make on their books on November 1 to reflect the 92¼–92½ note price?

   b. What journal entry would an investor make to reflect the purchase of $10,000 face amount of notes on November 1, 1979, at 92⅜ (notes and bonds sell at a price which includes accrued interest from the last interest payment date to the date of purchase)?

Case 9–6

Town of Grenoble[1]

The Town of Grenoble is planning to issue $1 million par value of bonds. The market (effective) rate will be determined by market conditions at the time that the issue is floated, but the nominal or coupon rate is to be fixed by town officials in consultation with the underwriters.

The town officials and the underwriters agreed at the beginning of May 1980, that a coupon rate of 6 percent (3 percent semiannually) was appropriate, and they proceeded to have bonds printed in $1,000 denominations with 20 coupons of $30 attached to each bond.

At the time the bonds were actually issued on June 1, 1980, the market rate of interest rose above 6 percent for commitments of this type and the bonds were sold at a price to yield investors 7 percent per annum (compounded semiannually). The underwriter who handled the issue charged a fee of 2 percent of par value to cover all costs involved in putting out the issue.

Interest Tables and Facts

Bonds authorized: $1,000,000. Date: June 1, 1980.

Term: Ten years. Interest payable: June 1st and December 1st.

Present value of $1 payable at the end of 20 periods with interest at:

3.00%	$ .5536758
3.50%	.5025659

Present value of $1 per period for 20 periods with interest at:

3.00%	14.8774749
3.50%	14.2124033

Required:

1. Prepare the journal entry on the Town of Grenoble books to record the issue of the bonds on June 1, 1980.
2. Prepare the journal entry on December 1, 1980, to accrue and pay interest. Use both the straight-line and compound interest methods of amortization.
3. Prepare the journal entry to accrue interest on December 31, 1980. (Town of Grenoble reports on a calendar year basis.) Use both the straight-line and compound interest methods of amortization.

---

[1] Interest on municipal bonds is exempt from federal taxes.

Case 9–7

Seitz, Incorporated

On December 31, 1978, the Seitz Corporation issued 10 percent subordinate debenture (unsecured) bonds with a face (par) value of $6 million and a maturity date of December 31, 1986. The coupon interest of 10 percent is paid semiannually (5 percent) on July 1 and January 1.

Listed below is the long-term debt section of the balance sheet and the related footnotes.

LONG-TERM DEBT

Long-term debt consists of the following:

Note payable to bank due in monthly installments of $6,180, including interest, to December 31, 1984	$2,949,140
10 percent subordinated debenture (with conversion privilege) due December 31, 1986	6,000,000
Less: Unamortized bond discount	(200,000)
	$8,749,140

FOOTNOTES ON LONG-TERM DEBT

The note payable to the bank has an interest rate of 8¼ percent and is secured by inventory, property, and equipment, by the unlimited guarantee of T. Seitz and R. Seitz and by the assignment of life insurance policies on the lives of those individuals (face value $1,750,000 each).

The 10 percent subordinated debentures are subordinated (come after) in payment to any debt to any financial institution engaged in the business of lending money and may be converted at any time prior to December 31, 1985, into the company's common stock at the rate of one share of stock for each $25 of unpaid principal amount of the debentures. The company has agreed to reserve and keep available, out of authorized but unissued common stock or common stock held in the treasury, the full number of shares of common stock issuable upon the conversion of all outstanding debentures.

The 10 percent subordinated debentures are also redeemable, at Seitz's option, at any time until maturity at a price of $102 per bond.

The company has agreed that, so long as the debentures are outstanding, it will not declare or pay any dividends (other than dividends payable in common stock of the company).

On December 31, 1980, bonds having a face value of $1 million were converted into common stock.

On December 31, 1981, bonds having a face value of $400,000 were redeemed by bondholders. The redeemed bonds were retired immediately.

Required:

1. Make the journal entry to record the issue of the 10-percent subordinated debenture bonds on December 31, 1978.
2. Record the journal entries for interest expense on the 10 percent subordinated debentures for 1979 (assume straight-line amortization of bond discount).
3. Make the journal entry on December 31, 1980, to reflect the conversion of bonds to common stock.
4. Make the journal entry to record the retirement of the 10 percent subordinated debenture bonds on December 31, 1981.

Case 9–8
Purcell, Inc.

Purcell, Inc., planned to add to its existing manufacturing capacity. Its proposed expansion will require $8 million of new long-term capital. The creation of the additional manufacturing capacity would increase *pre-tax net income* (before deducting additional interest in the event bonds are issued) to $3.9 million from its present annual level of $2.1 million.

The funds needed could be obtained by issuing 20-year bonds at par with a coupon rate of 10 percent or by issuing common stock at its current market price of $10. The company's relevant balance sheet information is:

Long-term debt.............................	$ —0—
Common stock, authorized 2.5 million shares, issued and outstanding—	
1 million shares, $5 par value	5,000,000
Additional paid-in capital	1,200,000
Retained earnings	2,300,000

Required:

1. Calculate the effect on net income per share (net income after tax divided by number of shares outstanding) if the funds are obtained by issuing the long-term bonds. Assume a tax rate of 50 percent.

2. Calculate the effect on net income per share if the funds are obtained by issuing common stock.

3. Which plan should the present stockholders favor? Why?

Case 9–9

P. R. Corporation

Shareholders' Equity
December 31, 1980

Capital stock:

Preferred, $6, $100 par value
350,000 shares, issued 275,000 shares $27,500,000

Common, par value $10, authorized
2.5 million shares, issued 1.5 million
shares   15,000,000

Additional paid-in capital   900,000

Retained earnings   6,100,000

Total shareholders' equity $49,500,000

During 1981 the following transactions occurred:

January 1   The P. R. Company sold 100,000 shares of common stock at $14 a share. The proceeds of the stock sale were received in cash.

January 25   The P. R. Company declared and paid its quarterly cash dividends: $1.50 on the preferred stock, and $.10 on the common stock outstanding.

March 15   A 5 percent common stock dividend was declared and distributed to the common stockholders. (Each shareholder received one share for each 20 shares owned.) The market price of the P. R. Company on March 15, 1981, was $14.50.

April 25   The P. R. Company declared and paid its quarterly cash dividend: $1.50 on the preferred stock, and $.10 on the common stock outstanding.

May 1   The P. R. Company purchased 5,000 shares of the company's common stock at $15 a share on the American Stock Exchange. This stock was to be held as treasury stock.

May 31   The P. R. Company purchased and retired 1,000 shares of its preferred stock at $110 per share.

July 25	The P. R. Company declared and paid its quarterly cash dividends: $1.50 on the preferred stock and $.10 on the common stock outstanding.
August 29	The board of directors appropriated $4 million of retained earnings for plant expansion.
October 25	The P. R. Company declared and paid its quarterly dividend: $1.50 on the preferred stock, and $.10 on the common stock.
November 18	The common stock was split 2 for 1. The new stock had a par value of $5.

Required:

1. Prepare journal entries to record each of the above transactions.
2. Present the shareholders' equity section of the balance sheet as it would appear on December 31, 1980. The net income for the year ended December 31, 1980, was $2 million.
3. Calculate the book value per share of common stock on December 31, 1980. Book value is the common stockholders' equity ÷ number of shares of common stock outstanding.
4. Calculate the earnings per share on common stock for the year ended December 31, 1980. (Use a weighted average of shares outstanding for the year in making your computation. Stock distributions made during the year should become retroactive to the beginning of the year in making the weighted average computation.)

Case 9–10

The Case of Disguised Debt

A number of companies have recently issued a preferred stock which must be repurchased by the company with guaranteed sinking fund deposits within a stated time period. The stock also provides for a stated dividend to be paid periodically. Many companies have utilized this type of stock instead of cash in connection with the buy-out of all of the shares of another corporation.

The Securities and Exchange Commission (SEC), the federal regulatory body that prescribes certain reporting conventions for public companies, recently proposed to change the rules which govern how such preferred stock is presented on financial statements "to give a better picture of the capital structure of companies." Specifically, the proposal would require companies to break all stock into three categories:

1. Preferred shares that must be redeemed.
2. Preferred shares that can't or may be redeemed at the option of the company.
3. Common stock.

Required:

1. What is the rationale underlying the SEC proposal?
2. Do you agree with the proposal?
3. Are there steps that should be taken beyond merely restating the equity section of the balance sheet to further reflect the different nature of this type of preferred stock?

10

The All-Inclusive Income Statement: A Closer Look

Events of an unusual (nonroutine) nature which affect owners' equity require special accounting treatment. Prior period adjustments, extraordinary items, and discontinued operations are examples of such unusual events. Special accounting treatment is also required when enterprises change their methods of accounting for particular types of events or report income for federal tax purposes which is different than reported financial statement income.

Proper disclosure of unusual (nonroutine) events and changes in accounting method is based on the accounting profession's current answers to two very general questions: Should the current income statement include the effects of all events that increase or decrease owners' equity during the accounting period with the exception of dividend distributions and capital transactions? This is a question of inclusion. How should we disclose the effects of these events in a particular income statement? This is a question of format.

Investors can best estimate the future results and cash flows of a firm if the nature and amount of income generated by unusual (nonroutine) events is reported separately from income from continuing (normal) operations.

ALL-INCLUSIVE INCOME STATEMENT

The 1976 annual report of the Wallace Murray Corporation (WMC) contains the accompanying note:

WALLACE MURRAY CORPORATION

Notes to Financial Statements

Litigation. A number of civil antitrust actions purporting to be class actions alleging price fixing of gas vent pipe are pending against the company and other manufacturers of gas vent pipe. The actions relate to the indictment and conviction after *nolo contendere* pleas in the U.S. District Court in Los Angeles in 1973 of five manufacturers of gas vent pipe. The company was not charged in that case. A tentative settlement covering all five of the alleged classes that have sued has been agreed upon and conditionally approved by the U.S. District Court for the Northern District of California. The settlement is subject to a number of contingencies, including final court approval.

Suppose WMC's accountants agreed that because of the likely unfavorable outcome of the action, a $100,000 liability for damages existed and had to be disclosed on the balance sheet. The account, Liability for Damages, was created and appropriately credited. The debit half of the entry was less obvious. Since the decrease in owners' equity arising out of the settlement was *first recognized* in 1976, one possible alternative was to show a loss in the 1976 income statement. The journal entry would be:

Loss from Lawsuit 100,000
    Liability for Damages   100,000

The loss would appear in WMC's 1976 income statement and reduce pretax income by $100,000.

The other possible alternative is not to show any of the $100,000 loss in the 1976 income statement since the loss is a direct result of events which occurred in accounting periods prior to 1976. The only effect in the 1976 statements would be a reduction in the beginning balance of retained earnings. The 1976 journal entry using this alternative would be:

Retained Earnings 100,000
    Liability for Damages   100,000

WMC's December 31, 1976, balance sheets would be identical under these alternative treatments since the loss appearing in the 1976 income statement under the first alternative would be closed to retained earnings at the end of 1976. The pretax income for 1976 would be $100,000 smaller under the first alternative.

The FASB *requires that with few exceptions all items of income and loss recognized during a period should be included in the income statement for the period.*[1] WMC *must* show the loss resulting from the damage settlement in its 1976 income statement. Such gains or losses, whether directly or indirectly related to events of the current period, affect the long run profitability of the firm. They are best brought to the attention of financial statement readers if they are completely and objectively disclosed in the income statement. This is an *all-inclusive* view of the income statement.

---

[1] FASB *Statement No. 16,* "Prior Period Adjustments," October 15, 1977.

PRIOR PERIOD ADJUSTMENTS

The only items of income and loss which are treated as *prior period adjustments* and excluded from the income statement by making an entry directly to retained earnings are correction of errors found in prior statements, recognition of an income tax loss carry forward acquired through purchase of a subsidiary, and compliance with a FASB or APB statement or opinion dealing with the reporting of a change in accounting method which permits or requires such treatment.

Errors may be mathematical in nature or result from the incorrect application of an accounting principle or misuse of information which existed at the time of statement preparation.

Suppose ABC Co. forgot to include $2,000 of depreciation on office equipment as an expense in its 1981 income statement. The error is discovered in 1982 at which time the correcting entry would be:

Retained Earnings	2,000	
Accumulated Depreciation—		
office equipment		2,000

The change from Lifo to some other cost flow assumption (change in accounting method) is disclosed as a prior period adjustment. Usually the adjustment is substantial and showing it in the current income statement would severely distort income for the current period.

FASB *Statement No. 13*, "Accounting for Leases," requires com-

ILLUSTRATION 10–1

TRW INCORPORATED
Change in Accounting Method

In compliance with a recent pronouncement of the Financial Accounting Standards Board, the company in 1977 changed its method of accounting for certain leases in which it is the lessee. The new method, which requires that amounts related to lease agreements meeting the criteria for classification as capital leases be recorded as assets with the related lease obligations recorded as liabilities, has been applied retroactively to lease agreements in existence prior to January 1, 1977. Retained earnings at January 1, 1976, have been reduced by $8.1 million and net earnings and earnings per share as previously reported for 1976 have been reduced by $.9 million and $.03, respectively. See note entitled "Long-Term Lease Commitments."

panies to restate retained earnings as of January 1, 1976, as if the new methods of lease accounting had been in effect prior to 1976. Subsequent years' income statements are reported in conformity with the new methods. Changes in accounting methods must be described in a footnote to the financial statements.

In 1977 the annual report of TRW Incorporated contained a footnote (Illustration 10–1) and statement of retained earnings (Illustration 10–2).

ILLUSTRATION 10–2

TRW INCORPORATED
Statement of Changes in Consolidated Shareholders' Investment
($000)

	Years Ended December 31	
	1977	1976 (restated)
Retained Earnings		
Balance at January 1, as previously reported	$650,183	$582,674
Retroactive adjustment for capitalizing leases ...	—	(8,050)
Balance at January 1, as restated	$650,183	$574,624
Net earnings	154,217	132,169
	$804,400	$706,793
Deduct dividends declared:		
Preference stock	17,522	17,966
Common stock	44,895	38,644
	$ 62,417	$ 56,610
Balance at December 31	$741,983	$650,183

EXTRAORDINARY ITEMS

Extraordinary items are an important class of items which are *disclosed separately* in the income statement after net income from operations. Any material item is an extraordinary item if it is *both unusual* in nature and *infrequent* in occurrence.[2] Losses resulting from earthquakes or expropriations would *usually* be considered extraordinary for U.S. firms because they are unusual and infrequent. However, flood damage suffered by a business located in the flood

---

[2] *Accounting Principles Board Opinion No. 30,* "Reporting the Results of Operations," effective September 30, 1973.

plain of a river is not extraordinary. The loss may be infrequent, but it is not unusual. Whether a particular gain or loss is extraordinary depends on a firm's individual operating environment. Items which are either infrequent but usual, or frequent but unusual, are disclosed as other revenue or other expense in the recurring revenue and expense section of the income statement. Only rarely do items meet both conditions for classification as an extraordinary item.

Gains or losses associated with litigation incidental to the business of a company are not usually reported as extraordinary items. Illustration 10–3 is an exception. In 1978 Diamond International Corporation was a defendant in a lawsuit which it considered to be both *unusual* in nature and *infrequent* in occurrence. It reported the effects of the suit as an extraordinary item and included an explanatory footnote in its annual report.

ILLUSTRATION 10–3

DIAMOND INTERNATIONAL CORPORATION
Consolidated Income

	Year Ended December 31, 1978
Revenues	$1,112,236
Costs and expenses	1,020,325
Income before income taxes and extraordinary item	$ 91,911
Income taxes	38,000
Income before extraordinary item	$ 53,911
Extraordinary item (Note 10)	(9,005)
Net income	$ 44,906

Note 10. Extraordinary Item. The extraordinary charge of $9,005,000 or $.77 per share net of the related tax reduction of $2,201,000 is in connection with the settlement of two unrelated antitrust treble damage class action litigations described in Note 11—Litigation.

Note 11. Litigation. The company and other business concerns are defendants in treble damage actions, most of which purport to be class actions and the remainder of which are individual actions, alleging a conspiracy in the folding carton business in violation of the federal antitrust laws but not specifying the amount of damages. On October 13, 1978, the company agreed to settle these class actions for $10,206,000. The settlement is subject to court approval and other conditions. The company still is a defendant in the individual actions. All these actions were filed subsequent to, and are based generally on, the same facts alleged in a criminal indictment brought in February 1976, against 23 corporations and 50 individuals, including the company, two of its officers, and five of its other employees. The company and its seven employees plead *nolo contendere* and were sentenced in the criminal action.

The company, 32 other business concerns, and the Fibre Box Association are defendants in treble damage actions, most of which purport to be class actions and the remainder of which are individual actions, alleging that the defendants combined and conspired to fix the prices of corrugated containers in violation of the federal antitrust laws and demanding unspecified treble damages and other relief. On December 22, 1978, the company agreed to settle the class actions for $1 million. This settlement is also subject to court approval and other conditions.

Although the outcome of the pending individual actions is uncertain, the company, after consultation with outside counsel, believes that the settlement of all the individual actions will not have a material adverse effect on the company's financial statements.

In 1977, the Sundstrand Corporation suffered a material loss when it disposed of machine tools. Although infrequent, such disposals are not unusual. Sundstrand disclosed the loss as an "other expense" in the operating section of its income statement. (Illustration 10–4.)

ILLUSTRATION 10–4

SUNDSTRAND CORPORATION AND SUBSIDIARIES (SNS)
Consolidated Statement of Earnings
($000)

	Year Ended December 31, 1977
Net sales	$649,903
Costs and expenses	
Costs of products sold	463,396
Marketing and administration	110,322
	$573,718
Earnings before other income (deductions)	$ 76,185
Other income (deductions)	
Royalties and commissions	$ 5,070
Interest expense	(18,080)
Interest income	460
Loss on disposal of machine tool assets	(9,200)
Unclassified—net	522
	$ (21,228)
Earnings before income taxes	$ 54,957
Income taxes	19,686
Net earnings	$ 35,271

The FASB may also *require* extraordinary item presentation for items which are not both infrequent and unusual in order to highlight specific items which might otherwise be overlooked if listed as a component of operating income. Currently, utilized tax loss carryforwards (FASB *Statement No. 4*) and gains or losses on premature retirement of debt (Accounting Interpretation of *APB Opinion No. 11*) are to be classified as extraordinary items. In the early 1970s corporate bonds outstanding generally had market values that were much less than their book values because interest rates had increased since the time the bond was issued. A company could realize large gains by buying back its bonds in the open market. These gains inflated their operating incomes. Since such gains (or losses) aren't attributable to normal operations the FASB decided to alert the readers of financial statements by requiring that the gains be disclosed as extraordinary items.

In 1977, the American Greetings Corporation paid $21,909,000 to retire notes payable with a book value of $20,000,000 (see Illustration 10–5). The $1,909,000 loss was disclosed net of tax effects as an extraordinary charge (loss).

ILLUSTRATION 10–5

AMERICAN GREETINGS CORPORATION

Year Ended
February 28, 1978

Net sales	$309,428
Other income	6,216
Total revenue	$315,644
Costs and expenses:	
Material, labor, and other production costs	$131,769
Selling, distribution, and marketing	88,282
Administrative and general	42,245
Depreciation and amortization	7,544
Interest	3,935
	$273,775
Income before income taxes and extraordinary charge	$ 41,869
Income taxes applicable to income before extraordinary charge	20,950
Income before extraordinary charge	$ 20,919
Extraordinary charge—Note C	(993)
Net income	$ 19,926

Note C. Extraordinary Charge. On April 29, 1977, the corporation prepaid the entire $20 million principal amount of its 9¾ percent Notes. The excess of the prepayment price over the carrying amount of the Notes, $1,909,000, less the related income tax benefit of $916,000, is included in consolidated net income for 1978 as an extraordinary charge.

ACCOUNTING CHANGES

The FASB requires special disclosure (net of tax effects and after operating income) of several other items not meeting the unusual and infrequency criteria for classification as extraordinary items. The cumulative effects of changing from one generally accepted accounting principle to another generally accepted accounting principle (if not required or permitted by an FASB Statement, FASB Interpretation, or APB Opinion to be reported in some other manner) are to be shown in their entirety *in the income statement* of the period in which the switch occurs. Changing from an unacceptable accounting principle to GAAP should be considered as an error correction to be treated as a prior period adjustment.

Ale Co. acquired an asset with a useful life of four years and zero salvage value for $1,000. Ale used sum-of-years'-digits depreciation for the first two years (for both taxes and financial statements) resulting in depreciation expense of $400 (4/10 × $1,000) in year 1 and $300 (3/10 × $1,000) in year 2. At the start of the third year Ale and Ale's auditor agreed that a switch to straight-line depreciation would be appropriate for this particular asset. Straight-line depreciation would have resulted in a total of $500 in depreciation expense for the first two years. Therefore Ale reported $200 more depreciation expense (and less income) over the first two years than would have been shown if straight-line depreciation had been used. The pretax cumulative effect of the switch is $200. Assuming a 40 percent tax rate the switch should be disclosed in Ale's third year income statement (along with a footnote explaining and justifying the change if necessary).

ALE CO.
Abbreviated Third Year Income Statement

Net income from operations	XXX
Add: Cumulative effect on prior years of switch in method of depreciation (net of $80 tax effect).........................	$120
Net income.......................................	XXX

Since Ale would have reported $200 more income during the first two years had it used straight-line depreciation, after tax financial statement income would have been $120 more. The cumulative effect of the restatement of prior years' income due to the depreciation method switch is shown in the third year.

Prior to January 1, 1977, Mountain Fuel Supply Company (MFSC) reduced financial statement income tax expense by the amount of the investment tax credit earned during the period. Beginning in 1977 MFSC elected to defer investment tax credits in the financial statements equally over the useful life of the asset which generated the credit. This is a change from one generally accepted accounting principle to another generally accepted accounting principle and was reported as in Illustration 10–6.

ILLUSTRATION 10–6

MOUNTAIN FUEL SUPPLY COMPANY AND SUBSIDIARIES
Consolidated Statements of Income
($000)

	Year Ended December 31	
	1978	1977
Income before federal income taxes and cumulative effect of change in accounting principle	$37,497	$40,701
Total federal income taxes	16,567	13,768
Income before cumulative effect of change in accounting principle	20,930	26,933
Cumulative effect to December 31, 1976, to defer investment tax credits on nonutility properties (Note B)	—	1,688
Net income	$20,930	$25,245
Dividends on preferred stock	869	661
Income available to common stock	$20,061	$24,584

Note B. Changes in Accounting for Investment Tax Credits. The company elected to defer the investment tax credits for nonutility properties, beginning January 1, 1977. The cumulative effect of the change to December 31, 1976, of $1,688,000 ($.27 per share) was included as a reduction of net income in 1977. The effect of this change in 1977 was to decrease net income $878,000 ($.14 per share). The change will relate the investment tax credits to the estimated remaining lives of the respective properties.

CHANGES IN ACCOUNTING ESTIMATES

There are many estimates inherent in the accounting process. Depreciation accounting relies on estimates of useful lives and future salvage values. Accounting for doubtful accounts relies on an estimate of future bad debts.

Changes in estimates are not considered to be errors (treated as prior period adjustments) or changes in accounting principles (treated as cumulative effects of accounting changes). The proper accounting treatment of changes in estimates is prospective—the change in estimate is adjusted for in future periods.

Suppose XYZ Co. acquired a piece of equipment two years ago at a cost of $500. The useful life is estimated to be five years, and the salvage value is zero. After two years of straight-line depreciation the net book value of the equipment is $300. At the beginning of the third year XYZ's accountants realize that the equipment has a remaining useful life of two rather than three years. The depreciation expense recognized in each of the subsequent two years will be $150 ($300 ÷ 2). No adjustment to retained earnings is made at the time the estimate of the useful life is revised to correct for the underdepreciation of the first two years. The *change in estimate* is adjusted for in the current and future periods.

DISCONTINUED OPERATIONS

Firms that dispose of an *entire* segment of a business or an *entire* product line (discontinued operations) must disclose the gain or loss on the disposal in a fashion similar to the disclosure required for extraordinary items (*APB Opinion No. 30*).

Gains on disposal of a discontinued operation are recognized on the disposal date, the date on which the sale is closed, or the property abandoned. Losses which are anticipated on the date management commits itself to a formal disposal plan (measurement date) are recognized as of the measurement date. This is consistent with the principle of conservatism.

The results of the discontinued operations for the current accounting period are also disclosed separately. Deciding if a particular disposal qualifies for discontinued operations treatment is a complicated and subjective process. The assets and activities of a segment are physically and operationally distinct from the other assets and activities of the business. The incomes should also be distinct. The Rockwell International Corporation disposed of *substantially all* of its industrial components group. The disposal qualified for discontinued operations treatment and was presented in the 1976 annual report. (See Illustration 10–7).

ILLUSTRATION 10-7

ROCKWELL INTERNATIONAL CORPORATION
AND CONSOLIDATED SUBSIDIARIES
Consolidated Income
(in millions)

	Years Ended September 30	
	1976	*1975*
Income from continuing operations before U.S. and foreign income taxes	$214.4	$162.2
U.S. and foreign income taxes	93.3	68.2
Income from continuing operations	$121.1	$ 94.0
Discontinued operations, net of applicable income taxes:		
Income from operations of discontinued units	0.7	7.6
Gain on sale of discontinued units	1.6	—
Net income	$123.4	$101.6

Discontinued Operations. On December 17, 1975, the company sold, substantially for cash, most of its Industrial Components Group of the Utility and Industrial Operations. The statement of consolidated income has been reclassified to exclude sales, costs, and expenses of the discontinued units and to set forth separately their net results as income from discontinued operations. Sales recorded by these units were $25.1 million for the period October 1, 1975, through December 17, 1975, and $139.5 million for fiscal 1975. A provision of $6 million has been made for income taxes related to the gain on sale of discontinued units. Such provision includes the effect of investment tax credit and depreciation recapture, state income taxes, and income taxes on undistributed earnings of foreign subsidiaries sold. Included in the consolidated balance sheet at September 30, 1975, are the following assets and liabilities of the units sold (in millions):

Current assets	$61.6
Current liabilities	(17.3)
Working capital	$44.3
Property and other noncurrent assets	34.7
Noncurrent liabilities and deferred income taxes	(2.2)
Net assets	$76.8

252

Uniroyal Incorporated closed and disposed of several individual facilities, none of which represented an entire segment of their business. Gains or losses on such disposals are shown as other income or other expense (similar to disclosure of unusual but frequently occurring items) in net income from operations in Illustration 10–8.

ILLUSTRATION 10–8

UNIROYAL, INC., AND SUBSIDIARY COMPANIES
Statements of Consolidated Income
($000)

	Fiscal Year Ended	
	January 1, 1978	January 2, 1977
Net sales	$2,581,927	$2,314,841
Cost of goods sold	$2,071,802	$1,847,127
Selling, administrative, and general expenses	399,850	390,596
Interest expense	49,810	44,083
(Gain) or loss on closed facilities	(3,826)	3,025
Other (income)—expense	309	(8,259)
Total costs and expenses	$2,517,945	$2,276,572
Income before income taxes	$ 63,982	$ 38,269
Federal and foreign income taxes	29,191	18,137
Net income	$ 34,791	$ 20,132

Gain or Loss on Closed Facilities. Operations in 1977 reflect a net pretax gain of $3,826,000 applicable to closed facilities. Included in this gain are the pretax profits of $4,124,000, recorded in the first quarter of 1977 applicable to the company's sale of its 51 percent interest in Latex Fiber Industries, Inc.

The fourth quarter of 1977 includes the effect of gains totaling $5,708,000 on the sale of certain properties; however, this gain was offset by additional provisions of $6,006,000 to cover the disposal of footwear operations in Naugatuck, Conn., and the planned closing of tire operations in Los Angeles, Calif., as well as adjustments to previous accruals to bring them in line with actual disposals or current estimates of the costs remaining to be incurred. The sale of facilities included a former manufacturing facility in Santa Ana, Calif., which for the last several years has been used only for warehousing and computer operations; a warehouse in Philadelphia, Pa., which was no longer required and had been subleased; the Fabric Fire Hose operations and equipment located in Sandy Hook, Conn.; and the auto tube manufacturing facility in Indianapolis, Ind.

ACCOUNTING FOR INCOME TAXES

Income for federal income tax purposes may not be the same as income before taxes on the financial statements because the rules in the Internal Revenue Code for determining taxable income differ from the generally accepted accounting principles used to construct financial statement income.

Interperiod income tax allocation is the process of computing and accounting for the difference between taxes due the IRS and income tax expense reported in the financial statements in a particular accounting period.

Some items considered to be revenues and expenses in determining accounting income are not ever considered to be revenues and expenses in computing taxable income.

Interest earned on most municipal securities and life insurance proceeds paid to a corporation upon the death of one of its officers are revenues included in accounting income but are not included in taxable income. Fines a company pays for violation of pollution emission standards and amortization of goodwill are expenses in the financial statements but are not allowable deductions (expenses) in determining taxable income. The differences between taxable income and accounting income caused by such items are called *permanent differences.*

Permanent differences are also caused by items considered to be revenues or expenses for tax purposes but not for financial statement purposes.

Berly Corporation's 1981 taxable income is computed below:

Sales revenue	$5,000
Costs of goods sold	2,000
Gross margin	$3,000
Interest expense	500
Taxable income	$2,500

Since Berly Corp. pays taxes to the IRS at the rate of 40 percent of taxable income, its 1981 income tax is $1,000 (.4 × $2,500).

Berly's 1981 income statement is shown below:

Sales revenue	$5,000
Cost of goods sold	2,000
Gross margin	$3,000
Interest expense	500
Amortization of goodwill	500
Income before taxes	$2,000
Income tax expense	1,000
Net income	$1,000

Except for amortization of goodwill all revenues and expenses are identical for tax and accounting purposes. Because amortization of goodwill will *never* be deductible for tax purposes, it creates a permanent difference between taxable income and accounting income. Income tax expense for financial statement purposes is computed *after* adjusting net income before taxes for all permanent differences (Berly's 1981 income tax expense on both the financial statements and income tax returns is 40 percent of $2,500).

Many transactions affect taxable income and accounting income in different accounting periods. These *timing differences* originate in one period and "turn around" in another period.

Sales on account, with the buyer agreeing to pay in several separate payments, are called installment sales. Installment sales usually are recognized as revenues for financial statement purposes in the period the sale is made. For tax purposes the revenue on installment sales may be recognized as the cash is collected. This creates a timing difference between taxable and accounting income.

Company Z sells $500 worth of merchandise (cost $280) for cash and $100 worth of merchandise (cost $20) under an installment purchase plan. Installments of $50 each will be received in 1982 and 1983. Company Z has no other revenues or expenses and pays income taxes amounting to 40 percent of taxable income. Assume that in both 1982 and 1983 Company Z makes no further installment sales, sells $700 of merchandise for cash (cost $500), and collects the installments due. Their taxable and accounting income for the three years will appear as follows:

COMPANY Z
Income Tax Returns

	1981	1982	1983
Revenues	$500	$750 (700 + 50)	$750 (700 + 50)
Cost of goods sold	280	510 (500 + 10)	510 (500 + 10)
Taxable income	$220	$240	$240
Taxes	88 (.4 × $220)	96 (.4 × $240)	96 (.4 × $240)
After tax income	$132	$144	$144

COMPANY Z
Income Statements

	1981	1982	1983
Revenues	$600 (500 + 100)	$700	$700
Cost of goods sold	300 (280 + 20)	500	500
Income before taxes	$300	$200	$200
Income tax expense	120 (.4 × $300)	80 (.4 × $200)	80 (.4 × $200)
Net income	$180	$120	$120

A timing difference of $80 ($300 accounting income − $220 taxable income) originates in 1981 and reverses itself in 1982 and 1983 when taxable income exceeds accounting income by $40 ($240 − $200).

Timing differences also arise because firms may use different methods of depreciation for tax and accounting purposes, because rents collected in advance are included in taxable income before they are included in accounting income, and because estimated warranty costs appear as expenses earlier in accounting income than in taxable income. Many other items may also cause timing differences.

Deferred income tax accounts are used to record the effects of all timing differences in an accounting period.

If a timing difference results in income tax expense which exceeds income taxes payable for the period, the difference is credited to the deferred income tax account.[3] In the previous installment sales example Company Z makes the following entry to record income tax expense, income taxes payable, and the effect due to the timing difference in 1981:

Income Tax Expense	120	
Income Taxes Payable		88
Deferred Income Taxes—Current		32

In 1982 and 1983 when the timing difference is reversed Company Z makes the following entry:

Deferred Income Taxes—Current	16	
Income Tax Expense	80	
Income Taxes Payable		96

The balance in the deferred income tax account at the end of 1983 is zero since the timing difference has been completely reversed. Deferred income taxes—current is classified as a current liability because the asset related to the timing difference (installment sales receivable) is a current asset.

If in 1982 and 1983 Company Z makes new installment sales at the 1981 rate, the tax and accounting income will be equal in 1983, and the deferred income tax account will still have a credit balance. The balance in deferred income tax will remain as long as Company Z continues to make installment sales at or above the 1981 level. Because of these phenomena some accountants question the classification of deferred income taxes as a liability in the balance sheet.

Every timing difference must be accounted for as in the above

---

[3] Income taxes payable denotes all taxes due the IRS for the period. Usually taxes are paid monthly in the year in which they are due.

example.[4] The tax rate in effect when the timing difference originates is used to compute the entry to the deferred taxes account. The deferred tax account associated with a particular timing difference is classified as a short-term or long-term asset or liability depending on whether it has a debit or a credit balance and how the assets and liabilities related to the timing difference are classified. For instance, a deferred tax account originating because depreciation expense in the financial statements *exceeded* the depreciation charge for tax purposes has a debit balance and is classified as a long-term asset (since depreciation relates to long-term assets).

Since permanent differences are never reversed, an accounting entry to deferred taxes is unnecessary.

DISCLOSURE

Investors and potential investors are concerned with the quality of a firm's earnings and the cash flows of a firm. In addition to the above deferred tax treatment of timing effects required by the FASB, the SEC requires disclosure of other tax information which aids investors in their assessments of the value of a firm.

The SEC requires firms to report (in the 10-K) the tax effects of timing differences of the current period, to disclose that portion of income tax expense which is currently payable, and to reconcile the statutory corporate tax rate with the effective tax rate shown in the financial statements.

The first two disclosures provide information about the necessary current and probable future cash flows required to discharge tax obligations. A reconciliation of the effective tax rate with the statutory rate makes investors aware of abnormally high or low current rates. If temporary in nature, the tax rate might change materially in future periods, leading to a material increase or decrease in earnings and cash flow.

The footnote in Illustration 10–9 is taken from the 1977 annual report of Sears, Roebuck & Company. Income tax expense was $356 million for the year ending January 31, 1978 when $110 million was deferred due to various short-term and long-term timing differences. Of the $262 million not deferred only $246 million is currently payable ($262 − $16) because of the $16 million investment tax credit. Sears' effective tax rates were 49.5 percent and 49.6 percent. Adjusted for state income taxes and miscellaneous items they were 45.8 percent (49.5 − 3.2 − .5) and 46.6 percent (49.6 − 2.6 − .4)—very close to the statutory rate of 48 percent.

---

[4] *APB Opinion No. 11,* "Accounting for Income Taxes," December 1967.

ILLUSTRATION 10-9
Income Taxes
(millions)

	Year Ended January 31	
	1978	1977
Federal and State Income Taxes on Current Operations		
Current portion	$262	$341
Investment tax credit (flow-through method)....	(16)	(13)
Deferred tax expense		
Current		
Installment sales	96	93
Receivable reserves	6	(8)
Maintenance agreement income	(8)	(11)
Supplemental pension costs	—	9
Other	(9)	(4)
Long-term		
Depreciation	21	28
Other	4	—
Total deferred	$110	$107
Financial statement income tax provisions.....	$356	$435

The financial statement tax expense for 1977 and 1976 includes state income tax expense of $44 million ($12 million deferred) and $43 million ($11 million deferred), respectively. A reconciliation of effective rates, based upon income before taxes, equity in net income of unconsolidated subsidiaries, and the Belgian subsidiary loss, with the statutory federal tax rate is:

	Year Ended January 31	
	1978	1977
Statutory federal income tax rate	48.0%	48.0%
State income taxes, net of federal income taxes.....................................	3.2	2.6
Investment tax credit (flow-through method)....	(2.2)	(1.4)
Miscellaneous items	.5	.4
Effective income tax rate	49.5%	49.6%

CASES FOR CHAPTER 10

Case 10–1

Allegheny Ludlum

1. What was the loss before taxes on the August 2, 1976, sale of the net assets of the Bar Products Division?

2. Why isn't the loss on discontinued operations disclosed as an unusual item in the operating section of the income statement? What useful information does the reader of Allegheny Ludlum's statements obtain from the disclosure of discontinued operations data in the required manner?

ALLEGHENY LUDLUM INDUSTRIES, INC., AND CONSOLIDATED SUBSIDIARIES
Consolidated Statements of Earnings
Years Ended January 1, 1978, and December 31, 1976
($000)

	1977	1976
Net sales	$1,002,065	$888,956
Equity in net earnings of unconsolidated subsidiaries and affiliated companies	2,080	9,866
Other income, net	5,318	3,272
	1,009,463	902,094
Costs and expenses:		
Cost of goods sold	838,995	746,424
Depreciation and amortization	22,483	19,195
Selling, general and administrative expenses	96,400	77,087
Interest expense	16,796	13,784
	974,674	856,490
Earnings from continuing operations before income taxes	34,789	45,604
Income taxes	9,357	14,880
Earnings from continuing operations	25,432	30,724
Losses from discontinued operations	—	(23,723)
Net earnings	$ 25,432	$ 7,001

	1977	1976
Earnings (loss) per share of common stock:		
Primary:		
Earnings from continuing operations	$2.53	$ 3.41
Losses from discontinued operations	—	(3.27)
Net earnings	$2.53	$ .14
Fully diluted:		
Earnings from continuing operations	$2.34	$ 2.93
Losses from discontinued operations	—	*
Net earnings	$2.34	$ *

* Amounts are antidilutive and accordingly are not shown.

Discontinued Operations. On August 2, 1976, the corporation completed a transaction announced on April 6, 1976, whereby its Dunkirk and Watervliet, New York, plants and related assets (the "Bar Products Division") were sold to a new company, AL Tech Specialty Steel Corporation ("AL Tech"), formed by officers and employees of the Bar Products Division.

The sale of the Bar Products Division was for cash, a subordinated term note, and shares of preferred stock of AL Tech aggregating $25,419,000, and the assumption of certain current liabilities, and resulted in a nonrecurring loss to the corporation of $21,800,000 million. As part of the agreement, AL Tech agreed to become successor employer and to become responsible for unfunded pension and other liabilities for active employees of the Bar Products Division in an approximate amount of $37 million.

Net sales of the Bar Products Division in 1976 to the date of sale amounted to $40,390,000. Losses from discontinued operations in the 1976 consolidated statement of earnings are comprised of the following (in thousands of dollars):

Losses from operations to April 6, 1976, less income tax benefits of $1,341	$ 1,231
Subsequent operating losses and loss on sale:	
Losses from operations from April 7, 1976 to date of sale, less income tax benefits of $670	692
Loss on sale of net assets, less income tax benefits of $19,700	21,800
	22,492
Total losses from discontinued operations	$23,723

Case 10–2

LTV Corporation

Footnotes to financial statements are frequently difficult to read and interpret.

For each of the following items on the 1977 and 1978 income statements of LTV explain the events giving rise to the numbers, and explain why the results of the events are disclosed as they are: unusual items, discontinued operations, extraordinary items, and accounting changes.

What other accounting changes aren't disclosed in the income statements?

THE LTV CORPORATION AND SUBSIDIARIES
Statement of Consolidated Operations
Years Ended December 31, 1978 and 1977
(in thousands except per share data)

	1978	1977
Sales	$5,260,537	$4,703,296
Other income	17,544	16,136
Total sales and other income	$5,278,081	$4,719,432
Operating costs and expenses:		
Cost of products sold	$4,885,989	$4,400,942
Depreciation	83,257	70,857
Selling, administrative, and general expenses	195,206	190,133
Unusual items	(16,721)	(3,129)
Interest and debt discount	105,694	99,617
Minority interest in subsidiaries	572	572
Total costs and expenses	$5,253,997	$4,758,992
Income (loss) from continuing operations before income taxes	$ 24,084	$ (39,560)
Federal, state and foreign income tax (charge) credit	(4,100)	4,000
Income (loss) from continuing operations	$ 19,984	$ (35,560)
Discontinued operations	6,500	(38,270)
Income (loss) before extraordinary items and accounting change	$ 26,484	$ (73,830)
Extraordinary items	—	20,674
Cumulative effect on prior years of accounting change	13,119	—
Net Income (loss)	$ 39,603	$ (53,156)

	1978	1977
Income (loss) per share—primary		
Continuing operations	$ 1.07	$ (2.63)
Discontinued operations	0.42	(2.65)
Before extraordinary items and accounting change	$ 1.49	$ (5.28)
Extraordinary items	—	1.43
Accounting change	0.84	—
Net income (loss)	$ 2.33	$ (3.85)
Income (loss) per share—assuming full dilution		
Continuing operations	$ 1.09	$ (2.63)
Discontinued operations	0.33	(2.65)
Before extraordinary items and accounting change	$ 1.42	$ (5.28)
Extraordinary items	—	1.43
Accounting change	0.67	—
Net income (loss)	$ 2.09	$ (3.85)

Note B. Receivables and Inventories. Approximately $44,605,000 of total receivables at December 31, 1978, relate to long-term contracts, of which no material amount is due or billable after one year. Receivables have been reduced for allowances for possible losses of $6,202,000 at December 31, 1978, and $1,874,000 at December 31, 1977.

Inventories at December 31 include the following (in thousands):

	1978	1977
Products	$ 503,090	$226,665
Contracts in progress	121,179	146,743
Materials, purchased parts, and supplies	388,342	128,661
Unreimbursed costs and fees under cost-plus-fee contracts	15,174	15,247
	$1,027,785	$517,316
Less progress payments received	67,922	100,142
	$ 959,863	$417,174

Inventories by business segment at December 31, 1978 (in thousands), were:

Steel	$782,370
Aerospace	102,578
Meat and food processing	71,712
Shipping	3,203
	$959,863

At December 31, 1978, the excess of current cost over carrying value of inventories valued on the Lifo basis was approximately $352 million (1977—$319 million).

In 1978 the method of computing Lifo inventories was changed from the dollar value, single-pool method to the specific goods multiple-pool method. The company believes that the specific goods multiple-pool method is the prevalent method in the industry and is preferable to the method previously used. This change increased 1978 net income by $19 million ($1.22 per share). The liquidation of Lifo inventory quantities carried as though acquired at lower costs which prevailed in earlier years decreased cost of products sold by approximately $27 million in 1978, inclusive of the pre-tax effect ($21,055,000) of the change to the specific goods multiple-pool method.

Note C. Property, Plant, and Equipment. Property, plant, and equipment at cost is as follows (in thousands):

	1978	1977
Land and land improvements	$ 162,343	$ 54,285
Plants and equipment—steel manufacturing	2,422,112	2,101,162
Ocean shipping vessels and equipment	85,692	—
Equipment, furniture, and fixtures	131,027	129,906
Assets acquired under capitalized leases	115,218	108,894
Unexpended proceeds of pollution control bonds	41,211	17,542
Other	10,155	5,495
	$2,967,758	$2,417,284
Less allowances for depreciation	1,338,897	1,317,013
Net carrying value	$1,628,861	$1,100,271

The company adopted the policy in 1978 of charging steel mill roll costs, net of estimated salvage value, to operating expense over the estimated useful life of the roll ($9,019,000 amortization expense in 1978). Previously, such costs were charged to operating expense at the time the rolls were placed into service. The company believes the new method is preferable because it minimizes fluctuations in roll expense between periods. As a result of this change, 1978 results of operations include a pre-tax credit of $13,119,000 representing the unamortized cost of rolls in service at the beginning of 1978. The effect of this change on the results of operations for 1978, and on a pro forma basis for 1977, was immaterial.

Note D. Indebtedness and Dividend Restrictions.

	Average Effective Rate of Interest	Amounts (in thousands)	
		December 31, 1978	December 31, 1977
The LTV Corporation			
5% Subordinated debentures due 1988	7.3%	$ 181,646	$ 181,646
7½% Subordinated debentures due 1993 and 1994	12.0	206,114	—
11% Subordinated debentures due 2000 and 2007	11.6	92,038	65,079
9¼% Sinking Fund debentures due 1997	11.6	75,000	75,000
Subsidiaries			
6½% and 6¾% Subordinated debentures due 1988	10.2	63,899	67,500
6¾% Subordinated debentures due 1994	10.2	172,301	172,978
7⅞% and 8⅝% Sinking fund debentures due 1997...............	8.2	60,000	60,000
9½% Sinking fund debentures due 1984	9.5	14,374	15,972
3⅝% to 10½% Mortgage bonds due through 2005	9.1	498,482	320,190
5% Guaranteed convertible (Subordinated) debentures due 1988	5.0	68,973	70,950
4.20% to 8.30% U.S. government insured Merchant Marine Bonds due through 1991	9.5	47,447	—
6½% to 9% Pollution control obligations due 1983 through 2006	9.0	84,420	—
Notes payable to banks due 1979–83...		144,550	76,550
Sundry mortgage and other notes		11,433	15,811
		$1,720,677	$1,121,676
Less current portion		28,646	10,586
		$1,692,031	$1,111,090
Less unamortized discount		171,937	77,919
Total consolidated long-term debt		$1,520,094	$1,033,171

Each share of Series B preferred stock is convertible into 2.3 shares of common stock and .3 shares of Series 1 participating preference stock. Holders of the Series B preferred stock are entitled to receive cumulative cash dividends annually of $2.60 per share, payable quarterly. In the event of liquidation, they would be entitled to receive $60 per share plus dividends accrued. The aggregate amount of such liquidation preference in excess of par value amounted to $245,901,000 at December 31, 1978. The Series B preferred stock may be redeemed at $30 per share plus accrued dividends.

Under an exchange offer of January 26, 1979, the company has offered to exchange, through May 11, 1979, two shares of Series B stock for each share of Series A stock.

Each share of Class AA special stock is convertible into common stock at ratios increasing from 1.45 shares on December 31, 1978, to 1.50 shares in 1979. The shares of special stock are entitled to annual cumulative stock dividends of 3 percent payable in special stock through 1992.

Each share of Series 1 participating preference stock is convertible into one share of common stock. Holders are entitled to receive cash dividends equal to 110 percent of any cash dividend declared on the common stock. In the event of liquidation, after any preference in distribution in respect to the preferred stock, the holders of the Series 1 participating preference stock would be entitled to receive $10 per share plus accrued dividends.

The holders of the common stock, the Series A and B preferred stock and the Series 1 participating preference stock are entitled to one vote per share. The holders of the special stock are entitled to a number of votes equal to the number of common shares into which their stock is convertible.

Changes in capital surplus are (in thousands):

	1978	1977
Balance at beginning of year	$332,550	$321,080
Excess over par value of shares issued upon:		
Stock dividends on Class AA special stock	401	294
Exercise of stock options	—	73
Conversion of $5 Series A preferred	471	—
Acquisition of Lykes Corporation	158,453	—
Other issuances of common shares	1,887	11,113
Sundry (charges) credits	369	(10)
Balance at end of year	$494,131	$332,550

Changes in consolidated retained earnings are (in thousands):

	1978	1977
Balance at beginning of year, as previously reported		$67,788
Retroactive restatement for change in accounting for leases		(5,867)
Balance at beginning of year, as restated	$ 5,933	$ 61,921
Net income (loss)	39,603	(53,156)
Cash dividends on preferred stock	(5,029)	(2,524)
Stock dividends on special stock	(414)	(308)
Balance at end of year	$ 40,093	$ 5,933

Note H. Leases. During 1978, the company changed its method of accounting for leases to comply with *Statement of Financial Accounting Standards No. 13 (FAS 13)*. As a result, the assets and related obligations for property under capital leases have been recorded. The financial statements for 1977 have been restated with the result that the net loss for the year was increased by $3.2 million, due primarily to the cumulative effect of restating income in years prior to 1977, which reduced tax credits available in 1977 by $2.7 million. The effect of adopting *FAS 13* was not material to the results of operations in 1978.

Leased capital assets included in property and equipment are as follows (in thousands):

	December 31	
	1978	1977
Buildings...	$ 43,146	$ 45,085
Plants and equipment—steel manufacturing	49,561	32,672
Equipment, furniture and fixtures.....................	22,511	31,137
	$115,218	$108,894
Less accumulated depreciation.......................	37,598	41,182
	$ 77,620	$ 67,712

Future minimum lease payments for capital leases together with the present value of net minimum lease payments at December 31, 1978, are (in thousands):

1979..	$ 14,146
1980..	13,089
1981..	11,835
1982..	10,163
1983..	9,782
Later years	87,994
Total minimum lease payments	$147,009
Less amount representing interest	58,095
Present value of net minimum lease payments	$ 88,914
Less current portion...	7,735
Long-term obligations under capital leases	$ 81,179

The charges to operations for the rental expense for all operating leases, less sublease rentals, was $26,608,000 in 1978 and $28,557,000 in 1977.

Future minimum operating lease commitments, exclusive of taxes and insurance, as of December 31, 1978, are as follows (in thousands):

1979	$ 18,209
1980	14,626
1981	11,620
1982	10,180
1983	9,399
Later years	41,466
	$105,500

Note I. Unusual Items, Discontinued Operations, and Extraordinary Items.

1. The unusual credit for 1978 of $16,721,000 is comprised of the net gain from the sale of the company's poultry, gelatin, and steel service center operations and the disposition of certain iron ore and coal mine properties. The unusual credit for 1977 of $3,129,000 is comprised of a credit resulting from the settlement of a legal claim, a charge relating to plant closings and consolidations, and a charge for a legal dispute relating to poultry operations.

2. In September 1977, LTV decided to discontinue its hotel, resort, inter-island passenger service, and steel conduit operations. In addition to the net operating losses of these operations a provision of $32 million was made to cover losses on disposition and costs and losses through date of disposition. The discontinued operations credit of $6.5 million in 1978 represents the portion of the loss provision recorded in 1977 which is no longer necessary.

3. Extraordinary items for the year 1977 include a $26,574,000 gain from early extinguishment of debt and a loss of $5,900,000 from a coal mine fire.

Note J. Estimated Liability for Plant Closing Costs. The statement of consolidated financial position at December 31, 1978, includes the remaining noncurrent provision of $196,099,000 for estimated costs relating to the closing of facilities by Lykes in 1977 and 1978.

Case 10–3

SCM Corporation

Investors can best estimate a firm's future income and cash flows if recurring income (usually from operations) is separated from non-recurring (one-time) income (usually from nonroutine events).

SCM Corporation reported earnings per share of $3.75 in 1978 and $3.70 in 1977. Adjust SCM's figures to reflect just the income from operations (for example, adjust for the difference in the effective tax rates for the two years). How do the operating results for the two years compare?

SCM CORPORATION
Years Ended June 30
(in $ millions)

	Business Segments				
	1978	*1977*	*1976*	*1975*	*1974*
Net sales					
Chemicals	$ 190.5	$ 179.4	$ 155.9	$ 122.2	$ 116.7
Coatings and resins .	402.2	381.6	363.0	332.8	312.0
Paper products	184.6	168.6	161.7	165.7	141.1
Foods	390.4	347.6	320.3	343.0	289.2
Typewriters and appliances	273.1	228.7	216.0	181.1	203.1
Business equipment..	60.0	62.4	107.1	122.0	124.6
Other	28.8	29.5	28.6	34.9	30.6
	1,529.6	1,397.8	1,352.6	1,301.7	1,217.3
Eliminations*	(20.3)	(20.2)	(20.7)	(14.2)	(15.1)
Total	$1,509.3	$1,377.6	$1,331.9	$1,287.5	$1,202.2
Operating income					
Chemicals	$ 2.2	$ 14.7	$ 12.3	$ 11.3	$ 13.4
Coatings and resins .	32.3	28.4	23.0	17.1	26.3
Paper products	19.1	22.6	25.2	41.6	25.5
Foods	11.9	20.4	17.0	8.0	2.7
Typewriters and appliances	26.5	22.4	16.5	8.8	18.9
Business equipment..	4.5	(2.1)	(9.7)	(15.7)	(12.5)
Other	3.8	4.8	3.3	2.5	1.1
	100.3	111.2	87.6	73.6	75.4
Corporate expense	(27.5)	(20.9)	(13.8)	(11.8)	(12.2)
Total	$ 72.8	$ 90.3	$ 73.8	$ 61.8	$ 63.2
Total assets					
Chemicals	$ 187.6	$ 182.9	$ 169.8	$ 148.7	$ 90.4
Coatings and resins .	230.7	211.9	212.5	187.5	192.6
Paper products	98.8	83.5	69.8	54.7	58.7
Foods	140.8	136.7	110.0	104.4	112.0
Typewriters and appliances	163.8	131.3	129.9	120.9	110.3
Business equipment..	12.3	12.1	37.6	75.5	68.0
Other	10.6	9.5	10.5	12.4	14.7
Total	$ 844.6	$ 767.9	$ 740.1	$ 704.1	$ 646.7

* Represents primarily sales of titanium dioxide by the Chemicals segment to the Coatings and Resins and Paper Products segments.

268

SCM CORPORATION (*continued*)

| | *Business Segments* | | | | |
	1978	*1977*	*1976*	*1975*	*1974*
Depreciation expense					
Chemicals...........	$ 10.0	$ 7.2	$ 6.6	$ 5.4	$ 3.6
Coatings and resins .	4.5	3.4	3.9	3.7	3.7
Paper products	4.3	3.5	3.4	2.9	3.2
Foods	2.9	2.7	2.6	2.9	2.4
Typewriters and appliances	5.9	6.0	6.0	5.2	4.5
Business equipment..	2.1	7.6	15.1	12.2	12.2
Other	.7	.6	.6	.8	.7
Total	$ 30.4	$ 31.0	$ 38.2	$ 33.1	$ 30.3
Capital expenditures					
Chemicals...........	$ 17.5	$ 21.0	$ 10.6	$ 36.8	$ 7.5
Coatings and resins .	13.9	10.7	10.1	4.7	5.2
Paper products	13.3	17.4	7.8	6.0	13.2
Foods	5.9	9.3	2.1	2.6	3.9
Typewriters and appliances	11.7	5.6	5.1	11.2	9.9
Business equipment..	—	1.3	2.4	25.0	18.4
Other	.3	.8	.6	.8	1.0
Total	$ 62.6	$ 66.1	$ 38.7	$ 87.1	$ 59.1

FINANCIAL REVIEW

Sales

Net sales for fiscal 1978 increased 9.6 percent from fiscal 1977. Most of this increase was from Typewriters and Appliances and Foods. Typewriters and Appliances had increased sales because of higher volume in all major products, including a new appliance and because of the addition of typewriters manufactured at the Glssgow, Scotland, plant purchased during the year. Higher Foods sales resulted from increased edible oils prices and increased volume in consumer foods. Sales dollars of Coatings and Resins, Paper Products, and Chemicals also increased, mainly because of higher unit volume. Coatings and Resins was also aided by higher prices.

In fiscal 1977, net sales increased 3.4 percent from fiscal 1976. Increases in Foods, Chemicals, and Coatings and Resins resulted from both increased physical volume and higher selling prices. The gain in Typewriters and Appliances was primarily due to improved sales of top-of-the-line typewriters. There was a moderate increase in sales of Paper Products as gains in paper and business forms offset a decrease in pulp sales. Business Equipment sales decreased as a result of excluding the European copier operations which were in the process of disposition. If European copier sales and sales from the disposed Coatings and Resins operation in Germany had been excluded from both years, fiscal 1977 sales would have increased 8.0 percent rather than 3.4 percent from fiscal 1976.

Operating Income

Fiscal 1978 operating income decreased 19.4 percent from the prior year principally because of a loss in Chemicals' titanium dioxide operation and severe fluctuations in the prices for edible oils used in Foods. Operating income from Paper Products also decreased because the effect of lower pulp prices more than offset higher profits in business forms.

Decreased operating income in Chemicals, Foods, and Paper Products was partly offset by improvements in Business Equipment, Typewriters and Appliances, and Coatings and Resins. Business Equipment was profitable, following several years of losses, because of reduced depreciation charges and better than anticipated results on disposition of the European copier operations. The increase in operating income of Typewriters and Appliances was primarily due to increased sales of appliances and the portable typewriters produced in the United States and Singapore. The improvement in operating income from Coatings and Resins reflects reduced foreign exchange losses as well as gains on the sale of two Latin American paint plants.

Corporate expense includes the cost of SCM's lawsuit against Xerox Corporation, which was $10.3 million in fiscal 1978, compared to $7.0 million in fiscal 1977.

Operating income for fiscal 1977 increased 22.4 percent from the prior year as all lines of business except Paper Products had improved operating results. The largest improvements in operating income were in Typewriters and Appliances and Coatings and Resins. The increase in Typewriters and Appliances came from an improved mix of higher margin products in typewriters and improved performance of Proctor-Silex appliances. Although affected by substantial foreign exchange losses, Coatings and Resins had increased profits because of higher gross margins. Operating income of Foods increased primarily due to increased volume in spices. Chemicals operating income increased as the effect of improved demand for organic chemicals more than offset decreased margins in inorganic chemicals. Operating income from Paper Products declined because of a combination of weak prices for pulp and increased manufacturing costs. The Business Equipment loss was reduced substantially because depreciation and obsolescence charges decreased to $7.6 million in fiscal 1977 from $18.3 million in fiscal 1976.

Years Ended June 30
(in $000, except per share amounts)

	1978	1977
Net sales	$1,509,307	$1,377,644
Cost of sales	1,128,947	1,000,579
Gross profit	$ 380,360	$ 377,065
Selling, administrative, and research expenses	307,583	286,730
Operating income	$ 72,777	$ 90,335
Interest expense, net	21,470	19,860
Other (income) expense, net	(215)	1,130
Income before income taxes	$ 51,522	$ 69,345
Income taxes	13,942	31,933
Net income	$ 37,580	$ 37,412
Earnings per share:		
Net income	$ 4.03	$ 4.01
Net income assuming full dilution	$ 3.75	$ 3.70

Statements of Consolidated Retained Earnings
Years Ended June 30
(in $000 except per share amounts)

	1978	1977
Balance, beginning of year	$ 186,063	$ 156,457
Net income	37,580	37,412
Cash dividends (per share—$1.025, 1978; $.85, 1977)	(9,439)	(7,806)
Balance, end of year	$ 214,204	$ 186,063

NOTES TO FINANCIAL STATEMENTS

Accounting Policies

Principles of Consolidation: The consolidated financial statements include the accounts of all wholly-owned and majority-owned subsidiaries. Investments in minority-owned affiliates and joint ventures, included in other assets, are adjusted to recognize SCM's share of their income or losses where the investment is 20 percent or more.

Inventories: Inventories are generally priced at the lower-of-average-cost-or-market, except for inventories of pulp, paper, and the raw material content of edible oils which are priced at the lower of last-in, first-out (Lifo) cost or market.

Property, Plant, and Equipment: Depreciation is provided on a straight-line basis at rates based on estimated useful lives. At the time properties are retired or disposed of, the property and related accumulated depreciation accounts are relieved of the applicable amounts, and any profit or loss is included in operating income.

Maintenance and Repairs: Routine maintenance and repairs are charged against operations as incurred. Expenditures that materially increase capacities or extend useful lives are capitalized.

Income Taxes: Income taxes are provided for in the year transactions affect net income regardless of when such transactions are recognized for tax purposes. The tax effect of timing differences is accounted for as deferred taxes. Provision is also made for income taxes on undistributed earnings of foreign subsidiaries not considered to be permanently invested. Investment tax credits are included as reductions of income tax expense in the year such credits become deductible.

Retirement Plans: SCM has several retirement plans that provide pensions for substantially all of its employees. Pension plan provisions include normal cost, interest on unfunded prior service liabilities, and amortization of actuarial gains or losses including prior service costs arising from plan amendments. Contributions to pension funds are made when actuarial computations prescribe such funding.

Earnings per Share

Net income per share is computed by dividing net income by the weighted average number of common and common equivalent shares outstanding. Net income per share assuming full dilution is computed based on the assumption that convertible debt obligations were converted and dilutive outstanding stock options were exercised as of the beginning of the fiscal year.

Retirement Plans

Pension expense, including interest on unfunded prior service liabilities, was approximately $15 million and $14 million for the years ended June 30, 1978 and 1977, respectively. Unfunded prior service liabilities decreased to approximately $75 million at June 30, 1978, from $85 million at June 30, 1977, because of a change in actuarial assumptions, which also decreased pension expense for the year by approximately $1.3 million. The actuarially computed value of vested benefits exceeded the total of the trust fund assets and the consolidated balance sheet accruals by approximately $31 million and $22 million at June 30, 1978, and 1977, respectively.

Inventories

As of June 30, 1978, approximately 17 percent of SCM's total inventories were priced on the Lifo method. Had all inventories currently on Lifo been priced on a Fifo basis, inventories would have been approximately $18.5 million higher at June 30, 1978, and $17.6 million higher at June 30, 1977.

Other Assets

As of June 30, 1978, and 1977, other assets include production rights, patents, and other intangibles of $11 million and $1.4 million; investments in unconsolidated affiliates and joint ventures of $5.8 million and $4.8 million; and long-term receivables of $5.7 million and $6.3 million. The increase in production rights, patents, and other intangibles during 1978 was related principally to the acquisition of a typewriter plant in Glasgow, Scotland.

Research and Development

Research and development expense was $19.7 million and $16.5 million for the years ended June 30, 1978, and 1977, respectively.

Income Taxes

Years Ended June 30
($000)

	1978	1977
Income taxes consist of:		
Current		
United States	$12,787	$26,937
Investment credit	(8,016)	(3,052)
Foreign	2,931	3,108
State and local	1,369	2,774
Total current	$ 9,071	$29,767
Deferred		
United States	6,251	1,890
Foreign	(1,380)	276
Total deferred	$ 4,871	$ 2,166
Total income tax expense	$13,942	$31,933
Reconciliation of effective tax rate:		
Statutory U.S. income tax rate	48.0%	48.0%
Investment credit	(15.6)	(4.4)
Foreign operations	(4.5)	1.9
Other net	(.8)	.5
Effective tax rate	27.1%	46.0%
Deferred taxes result from timing differences relative to:		
Business realignment	$ 2,535	$ (117)
Foreign operations	2,377	(522)
Depreciation	2,577	4,447
Other, net	(2,618)	(1,642)
Total deferred taxes	$ 4,871	$ 2,166

At June 30, 1978, provision for U.S. income taxes has not been made on $50 million of undistributed earnings of subsidiaries and joint ventures since these earnings are considered to be permanently invested.

Business Segments

Information concerning the net sales, operating income, total assets, depreciation expense, and capital expenditures of SCM's business segments for the years ended June 30, 1978, and 1977 is included in the business segments table presented [in] this report.

Foreign Operations

Operations were charged with pretax foreign exchange losses of $2.8 million in fiscal 1978 and $6 million in fiscal 1977.

The total effect of operations outside the United States and its possessions on consolidated net sales, net income, and total assets for the years ended June 30, 1978, and 1977 was (in thousands):

	1978	1977
Net sales	$182,781	$165,140
Net income	$ 7,330	$ 388
Total assets	$158,540	$119,792

Long-Term Debt

Long-term debt (in thousands).

	June 30, 1978	June 30, 1977
5½% sinking fund debentures due 1980–1984	$ 6,175	$ 8,700
5¾% sinking fund debentures due 1980–1987	11,469	12,168
7¼% sinking fund debentures due 1980–1988	12,495	14,000
9¼% sinking fund debentures due 1980–1990	26,250	28,000
10% sinking fund debentures due 1982–1996	50,000	50,000
8⅞% note (Industrial Revenue Bonds) due 1991–2000	17,000	17,000
Lease obligation (6% Environmental Improvement Revenue Bonds, due 1984–1993)	10,000	10,000
Other loans from 4% to 14%	8,477	9,091
5½% convertible subordinated debentures due 1980–1988	34,106	37,948
5¼% convertible subordinated debentures due 1980–1989	13,648	14,256
Total long-term debt	$189,620	$201,163

Approximate long-term debt maturities, including the current portion of long-term debt, during the next five years will be: 1979—$3.4 million; 1980—$5.6 million; 1981—$9.8 million; 1982—$12.8 million; 1983—$12.7 million.

Under the most restrictive provisions of the indentures related to long-term debt, retained earnings of $93.6 million were available at June 30, 1978 for declaration of cash dividends.

Credit Lines and Compensating Balances

The maximum short-term borrowing outstanding at any month end during the year was $71.8 million at May 31, 1978. SCM's unsecured short-term credit lines at June 30, 1978, totalled $89.4 million of which $63.9 million was outstanding. The average short-term borrowing outstanding during the fiscal year was $43.3 million.

Quarterly Results (unaudited)

Unaudited financial results by quarter for the fiscal years ended June 30, 1978, and 1977 are summarized here, (in thousands except per share amounts).

					Earnings per Share	
Fiscal Quarter	Net Sales	Gross Profit	Income Taxes	Net Income	Net Income	Assuming Full Dilution
1978 First	$ 365,393	$ 96,100	$ 8,936	$10,281	$1.10	$1.02
Second	359,513	92,493	2,591	6,985	.75	.70
Third	365,791	86,524	(1,993)	5,103	.55	.53
Fourth	418,610	105,243	4,408	15,211	1.63	1.50
Total	$1,509,307	$380,360	$13,942	$37,580	$4.03	$3.75
1977 First	$ 335,629	$103,711	$10,183	$11,161	$1.20	$1.10
Second	337,607	87,611	6,965	8,503	.91	.84
Third	339,384	86,977	6,048	6,355	.68	.65
Fourth	365,024	98,766	8,737	11,393	1.22	1.11
Total	$1,377,644	$377,065	$31,933	$37,412	$4.01	$3.70

Net income for the fiscal 1978 first quarter includes approximately $1.5 million or $.16 per share from the sale of a facility and the favorable settlement of litigation on a disputed utility rate.

Results and tax benefits on the disposal of the European copier operations were better than anticipated contributing net income of $2.8 million or $.30 per share in fiscal 1978—$1.8 million or $.19 per share in the third quarter and the balance in the second and fourth quarters. Estimates of the effective tax rate for fiscal 1978 were adjusted quarterly to reflect changes in the anticipated level of operating income and investment tax credits. Results for the first quarter of fiscal 1977 reflect a net charge of $1.7 million or $.18 per share, the estimated loss on disposition of SCM's European copier operations and certain other European operations.

Case 10–4
Sears (A)

SEARS ROEBUCK, INC.
Statements of Income
($000)

	Year Ended January 31	
	1978	1977
Net sales	$17,224,033	$14,950,208
Cost of sales, buying, and occupancy expenses	11,172,965	9,399,491
Selling and administrative expenses	4,839,653	4,293,933
Operating income from sales and services	$ 1,211,415	$ 1,256,784
Other income	1,960	4,230
Equity in net income of		
Allstate Group		
Allstate Insurance Company		
In accordance with prescribed standards, un-		
realized net increases in market value of		
marketable equity securities of $26,249 and		
$129,564 are not included in the determination		
of net income	395,104	195,314
Allstate Enterprises, Inc.	21,881	15,015
Total Allstate Group	$ 416,985	$ 210,329
Other unconsolidated subsidiaries and affiliates	57,048	42,568
	$ 474,033	$ 252,897
General expenses		
Interest	353,131	270,122
Contribution to Employees' Profit Sharing Fund	140,276	114,455
Discontinued subsidiary loss	—	54,058
Income taxes (Note 8)		
Current operations...............................	356,019	434,806
Benefit from disposition of subsidiary	—	(53,652)
	$ 849,426	$ 819,789
Net income	837,982	694,122
Per share (average shares 319,925 and 317,798)*	$2.62	$2.18

* Adjusted for two-for-one stock split effective May 27, 1977.

SEARS ROEBUCK, INC.
Statements of Financial Position
($000)

	January 31	
	1978	*1977*
Assets		
Current assets		
Cash...	$ 237,382	$ 223,112
Receivables	6,671,402	5,672,270
Inventories	2,626,070	2,215,141
Prepaid advertising and other charges.................	106,821	90,445
Total current assets...........................	$ 9,641,675	$ 8,200,968
Investments		
Allstate Insurance Company (cost $62,156 and		
$62,072)	1,735,382	1,433,945
Other investments and advances	822,788	695,368
	$ 2,558,170	$ 2,129,313
Property, plant, and equipment	2,534,841	2,487,790
Deferred charges	11,561	8,935
Total assets	$14,746,247	$12,827,006
Liabilities		
Current liabilities:		
Short-term borrowings		
Commercial paper................................	$ 2,586,051	$ 1,940,578
Banks..	404,936	305,869
Agreements with bank trust departments	717,958	655,046
Current maturity of long-term debt	30,473	54,969
Accounts payable and accrued expenses	1,124,713	990,762
Unearned maintenance agreement income............	276,969	242,143
Deferred income taxes	917,645	855,893
Total current liabilities	$ 6,058,745	$ 5,045,260
Deferred income taxes	173,139	154,959
Long-term debt	1,990,295	1,706,099
Total liabilities	$ 8,222,179	$ 6,906,318
Shareholders' equity	$ 6,524,068	$ 5,920,688

Note 8. Income Taxes. Federal and state income taxes on current operations include (in millions):

	Year Ended January 31	
	1978	1977
Current portion	$262	$341
Investment tax credit (flow-through method)	(16)	(13)
Deferred tax expense		
Current		
Installment sales	96	93
Receivable reserves	6	(8)
Maintenance agreement income	(8)	(11)
Supplemental pension costs	—	9
Other	(9)	(4)
Long-term		
Depreciation	21	28
Other	4	—
Total deferred	$110	$107
Financial statement income tax provisions	$356	$435

The financial statement tax expense for 1977 and 1976 includes state income tax expense of $44 million ($12 million deferred) and $43 million ($11 million deferred), respectively. A reconciliation of effective rates, based upon income before taxes, equity in net income of unconsolidated subsidiaries, and the Belgian subsidiary loss with the statutory federal tax rate is:

	Year Ended January 31	
	1978	1977
Statutory federal income tax rate	48.0%	48.0%
State income taxes, net of federal income taxes	3.2	2.6
Investment tax credit (flow-through method)	(2.2)	(1.4)
Miscellaneous items	.5	.4
Effective income tax rate	49.5%	49.6%

Required:

1. What is Sears' pretax income for 1977? What percentage of pretax income is the $356 million of income taxes shown on the income statement? In Note 8 to their financial statements, Sears claims that their effective tax rate is 49.5 percent. Explain the difference.

2. If Sears were to report as income tax expense the amount of income taxes actually paid or payable (including the reduction caused by the investment tax credit), how much larger or smaller would their income for the year have been?

3. If Sears had reported income tax expense in every year equal to income taxes paid or payable, how much larger or smaller would their shareholders' equity have been?

4. How much higher would actual income taxes have been if Sears used the same depreciation methods on both its financial statement and income tax returns? How much more or less would depreciation expense be in Sears' 1977 income statement?

11

Intercorporate Investments and Business Combinations

Many corporations try to increase their profitability by investing in the common stock of other corporations. These investments can be either short-term or long-term in nature depending on the intention of corporate management at the time they make the investment.

The corporation's short-term or temporary investment objective is to earn a return on funds not immediately needed for current operations. The investment is made in securities which are readily marketable so that they may easily be converted to cash when needed.

Their long-term investment objective may be to increase the efficiency of their present operations (purchasing another company in the same line of business), to gain access to raw material sources, distribution services, or markets (purchasing a company that increases their control of vertical operations from the raw material to the sale of the product), or to spread risk (purchasing a company in a different business).

When one corporation purchases all or part of the common stock of another corporation it raises the accounting issue of what is the most appropriate method to disclose the implications of this investment on the financial statements. If the intention of the corporation is to invest excess cash on a temporary basis, the investment will be recorded as a marketable security (marketable equity security) in the current asset section of the balance sheet.[1] If it is a long-term investment, the method of recording it will depend primarily on the percentage of ownership acquired and the relationship between the acquiring (investor, parent) corporation and the acquired (investee, subsidiary) corporation.

---

[1] FASB *Statement No. 12*, "Accounting for Certain Marketable Securities," effective December 31, 1975. This statement defines marketable equity securities as ownership securities which trade on a national securities exchange.

SHORT-TERM INVESTMENTS

Marketable equity securities are recorded at their cost (*cost method*) at the time of their purchase.

The Elba Corporation made the following short-term investments in marketable equity securities in 1980:

> January 18, 1980—Purchased 1,000 shares of NE Industries, Inc., at a cost of $18,732.
>
> May 19, 1980—Purchased 10,000 shares of Berga Corporation at a cost of $53,642.
>
> August 31, 1980—Purchased 5,000 shares of Serab Corporation at a cost of $32,000.

The journal entries on Elba's books to record the purchases are:

Marketable Equity Securities	18,732	
Cash.......................................		18,732
To record purchase of 1,000 shares of NE Industries, Inc.		
Marketable Equity Securities	53,642	
Cash.......................................		53,642
To record purchase of 10,000 shares of Berga Corporation.		
Marketable Equity Securities	32,000	
Cash.......................................		32,000
To record purchase of 5,000 shares of Serab Corporation.		

The carrying value on the balance sheet of the *aggregate portfolio* of the marketable equity securities is cost or market, whichever is lower. If a write-down to market is necessary, a *charge to net income* is made and a valuation (contra asset) allowance is created on the balance sheet.

On December 31, 1980, the cost and market values of the Elba Corporation's portfolio of marketable equity securities are:

	Cost	Market	Unrealized Gain (loss)
NE Industries, Inc.	$ 18,732	$ 19,100	$ 368
Berga Corporation	53,642	50,000	(3,642)
Serab Corporation	32,000	32,000	—0—
	$104,374	$101,100	($3,274)

The December 31, 1980, journal entry to reduce the *aggregate* portfolio to market is:

Unrealized Loss—Marketable Equity Securities	3,274	
Allowance for Valuation Loss—Marketable		
Equity Securities		3,274

To recognize loss on write-down to market of
marketable equity securities.

The general ledger accounts on December 31, 1980, are:

Marketable Equity Securities

18,732	
53,642	
32,000	

**Unrealized Loss/Gain
Marketable Equity Securities**

| (a) | 3,274 | |

**Allowance for Valuation Loss—
Marketable Equity Securities**

| | (a) | 3,274 | |

Balance sheet disclosure would indicate that the temporary investment in marketable equity securities of $101,100 ($104,374 − $3,274) is carried at market value. If the market value of the portfolio increases in subsequent years, the temporary investment will be increased but only to the *extent of original cost.*

Gains or losses on the actual sale of temporary investments of marketable equity securities are recognized as the difference between the sales proceeds and the *original cost* of the security.

LONG-TERM INVESTMENTS

Cost Method

A corporation that has a long-term investment in less than 20 percent of the common stock of another corporation would ordinarily use the *cost method* shown below to record this investment on the books.

On January 1, 1980, Rogers Corporation purchases 10 percent (5,000 shares) of Rich Corporation's outstanding common stock for $50,000.

The journal entry on Rogers's books on the date of acquisition is:

| Investment in Rich Corporation................... | 50,000 | |
| Cash....................................... | | 50,000 |

To record purchase of 5,000 shares of Rich Corporation.

No entry is necessary on Rich's books as the only thing that has changed for them is the name of their stockholders.

Rich Corporation's net income for 1980 (both Rich and Rogers report on a calendar year basis) is $25,000. Rogers will not make an entry on its books to accrue any of Rich's 1980 net income, as their 10 percent ownership interest is not substantial enough to give them control over Rich's financial operations.

On January 31, 1981, Rich Corporation declares a cash dividend of 20 cents per share.

The entry on Rogers's books is:

Dividend Receivable	1,000	
Dividend Income (Revenue)		1,000
To record as income the dividend (20¢ ×		
5,000 shares) declared by Rich Corporation.		

On March 10, 1981, when the dividend is paid:

Cash...	1,000	
Dividend Receivable		1,000
To record receipt of a dividend from Rich Corporation.		

If the common stock of the investee (subsidiary) corporation is listed on a national securities exchange (marketable equity security), it must be reported on the balance sheet at cost or market, whichever is lower. Write-downs to market are charged to the *equity section* (not net income) of the balance sheet and shown as a separate item. The entries are made on an *aggregate portfolio* basis rather than by each individual security.

Assume that the Rich stock is the only long-term investment of Rogers Corporation and that the market value of the 5,000 shares on December 31, 1980, is $43,000. The required adjusting journal entry is:

Unrealized Loss on Noncurrent Marketable		
Equity Securities	7,000	
Allowance for Valuation Loss—		
Marketable Equity Securities		7,000
To record excess of cost over market of the non-		
current marketable equity securities.		

The *unrealized loss on noncurrent marketable equity securities* account is deducted from the stockholders' equity section in the same manner as the cost of treasury stock. The allowance account is contra to the long-term investment account. If the market value of the aggregate portfolio of the noncurrent marketable equity securities increases in subsequent years, the investment account will be increased, but only to the extent of original cost.

The impact of these entries is that long-term investments in noncurrent marketable equities, where the investments are initially recorded using the cost method, are carried on the balance sheet at cost or market, whichever is lower.

Equity Method

A corporation that owns 20 to 50 percent of another corporation is ordinarily required to use the *equity* method to record its investment on the balance sheet. The equity method assumes that the investor corporation has *significant* influence over the financial operations of the investee corporation and requires the investor corporation to accrue its pro-rata share of the investee corporation's net income in the accounting period in which it is earned. If significant influence exists with less than 20 percent ownership, the investor corporation should use the equity method in preference to the cost method. If the investor corporation can prove that it does not have significant influence over the investee corporation, even though it owns more than 20 percent, it may use the cost method.

On January 1, 1980, Torr Corporation purchases 40 percent (20,000 shares) of the common stock of Tee Corporation for $196,000.

The entry on Torr Corporation's books is:

Investment in Tee Corporation	196,000	
Cash......................................		196,000

To record purchase of 20,000 shares of Tee Corporation.

Tee Corporation's net income for the year ended December 31, 1980, is $25,000.

The entry on Torr Corporation's books is:

Investment in Tee Corporation	10,000	
Equity in Net Earnings of Unconsolidated Subsidiary*		10,000

To record as income for the year ended December 31, 1980, our share (40 percent) of Tee Corporation's net income.

* This entry assumes that Tee's book value was $490,000 (40 percent of $490,000 = $196,000) on the date Torr purchased the 20,000 shares of common stock. If the investor's purchase price is higher than the investee's book value, the difference is depreciated (difference attributable to excess of fair value over book value of fixed assets) and/or amortized (difference attributable to excess of purchase price over net assets at fair value) and charged to equity in net earnings of unconsolidated subsidiary. The equity method also requires an adjustment to current year's earnings and the investment account for any intercompany transactions.

Equity in net earnings of unconsolidated subsidiary is sometimes classified as *other income* on the income statement.

On January 31, 1981, Tee Corporation declares a dividend of $10,000. Torr makes the following entry.

Dividend Receivable............................	4,000	
Investment in Tee Corporation		4,000

To record declaration of dividend by Torr Corporation.

The Torr Corporation reduces its investment account because the dividend represents a return to it of a portion of its investment.

On March 10, 1981, when the dividend is paid:

Cash...	4,000	
Dividend Receivable		4,000

To record receipt of dividend from Tee Corporation.

These entries (*using the equity method*) are in accordance with the accrual method of accounting. They record the income on the investor corporation's books in the accounting period in which the income is earned by the investee corporation rather than in the accounting period in which the investee corporation declares a dividend (cost method). The investment account on the *investor's books* will always reflect the cost of the investment plus (minus if a deficit) the investor corporation's pro rata share of the investee corporation's retained earnings since the date of acquisition.[2]

Consolidation Method

If a corporation owns more than 50 percent of the common stock of any other corporation(s) it will ordinarily use the *consolidation method*.

This method requires that the financial statements (balance sheet, statement of income, and statement of financial condition) be prepared as if the parent (investor) corporation and the subsidiary (investee) corporation(s) were a single economic entity. It disregards the fact that each of the corporations in this group affiliated through common ownership is a separate legal entity and prepares its own financial statement.[3] Generally accepted accounting principles assume that the parent's consolidated financial statements provide better disclosure to the parent corporation's stockholders than the separate financial statements prepared by each corporation.

The parent corporation is not required to use the consolidation method if it does not provide better disclosure even if the parent owns more than 50 percent of the subsidiary. Foreign subsidiaries and domestic subsidiaries operating under the Federal Bankruptcy Act or under a consent decree of the Federal Trade Commission (legal restrictions) are often not consolidated for these reasons. Consolidation is also not required where the asset and liability structure of the subsidiary is significantly different in nature from that of the parent. An example would be a finance corporation which

---

[2] Adjusted, if necessary, for profits on intercompany transactions and amortization or depreciation on the excess of investment cost over investee's book value.

[3] The parent corporation will report the investment in the subsidiary on its own financial statements using the equity method.

is a subsidiary of a manufacturing corporation. In all of these cases, where the subsidiary is not consolidated, the parent corporation will report its investment using the equity method.

PREPARATION OF CONSOLIDATED STATEMENTS

The consolidation process consists of assembling and adjusting the balance sheet and income statement accounts of the parent and subsidiary corporations in a manner which makes it possible to prepare financial statements for a single economic entity which does not exist legally.

The consolidation elimination and adjusting entries are recorded *only on the worksheets* used to prepare consolidated financial statements. They are not recorded on the books and records of the affiliated companies.

CONSOLIDATED BALANCE SHEET

In order to illustrate the procedure for preparing a consolidated balance sheet let us assume that Torr Corporation purchased all the common stock of the Subb Corporation on December 31, 1980, for $100.

The procedure for preparing a consolidated balance sheet on December 31, 1980, would be as follows:

List the balance sheet accounts of each company on a worksheet and combine them. See Illustration 11–1.

Eliminate any intracompany accounts.

1. Our analysis reveals that on December 31, 1980, Subb Corporation owes Torr Corporation $10 for merchandise it purchased on credit. The appropriate elimination on the consolidated worksheet is:

Accounts Payable (Subb Corporation)	10	
Accounts Receivable (Torr Corporation)		10
To eliminate intracompany account.		

The result of this elimination is to reduce the combined accounts receivable of $89 to $79, the amount the *consolidated* entity is owed by customers. The consolidated accounts payable are reduced from the combined total of $95 to $85, the amount owed to outside creditors.

2. The note receivable represents a loan by Torr Corporation to Subb Corporation. The appropriate elimination is:

ILLUSTRATION 11–1

TORR CORPORATION
Worksheet—Consolidated Balance Sheet
December 31, 1980

	Individual Company Statements		Combined Balance Sheet	Eliminations		Consolidated Balance Sheet
	Torr	Subb		Dr.	Cr.	
Cash	$100	$ 20	$ 120			$120
Accounts receivable	54	35	89		(1) $ 10	79
Notes receivable	40		40		(2) 40	—
Inventory	100	85	185			185
Investment in Tee Corporation	206		206			206
Investment in Subb Corporation	100		100		(3) 100	—
Fixed assets (net of accumulated depreciation)	300	90	390			390
	$900	$230	$1130			$980
Accounts payable	$ 50	$ 45	$ 95	(1) $ 10		$ 85
Notes payable	40		40	(2) 40		—
Other current liabilities	40	10	50			50
Long-term liabilities	110	35	145			145
Common stock	300	70	370	(3) 70		300
Retained earnings	400	30	430	(4) 30		400
	$900	$230	$1130	$150	$150	$980

Notes Payable (Subb Corporation)	40	
Notes Receivable (Torr Corporation)		40
To eliminate intracompany loan.		

The consolidated balance sheet will not reflect this note as it is an intracompany item. The *consolidated entity* has neither a note receivable nor a note payable.

3. Eliminate parent corporation's investment in the subsidiary corporation.

Common Stock (Subb Corporation)................	70	
Retained Earnings (Subb Corporation)	30	
Investment in Subb Corporation		
(Torr Corporation).........................		100
To eliminate investment in Subb Corporation.		

The impact of this entry is the same as if the subsidiary corporation were *merged* into the parent corporation and no longer existed as a separate entity.

No adjustment is made to consolidate the Tee Corporation (see equity method example) as Torr Corporation only owns 40 percent of the common stock of the Tee Corporation and reports it on the *consolidated balance sheet* using the equity method.

FAIR VALUE OF FIXED ASSETS AND EXCESS OF PURCHASE PRICE OVER FAIR VALUE OF NET ASSETS (GOODWILL)

Suppose instead of $100 the Torr Corporation paid $125 in cash for all the common stock of the Subb Corporation. This is $25 more than Subb's book value of $100 (assets of $230 minus liabilities of $130) on December 31, 1980.

Assume further that an appraisal indicates that the fixed assets of Subb Corporation have a fair value of $115 ($25 more than their book value of $90). The journal entry to be made in the preparation of the consolidated balance sheet on December 31, 1980, is:

Fixed Assets	25	
Common Stock (Subb Corporation)................	70	
Retained Earnings (Subb Corporation)	30	
Investment in Subb Corporation		
(Torr Corporation).........................		125
To eliminate investment in Subb Corporation.		

The increase of $25 in fixed assets appears only on the *consolidated balance sheet*. Depreciation expense relating to this $25 increase in fixed assets will appear only on the *consolidated income statement*.

If the fair value of the assets are equal to the book value then the additional $25 would be allocated to an intangible asset, excess of purchase price over fair value of net assets, which is often labeled goodwill and will appear only on the *consolidated* balance sheet.[4]

If the $25 were attributed to goodwill the journal entry for *consolidated purposes only* would be:

```
Goodwill ........................................    25
Common Stock (Subb Corporation) ...............    70
Retained Earnings (Subb Corporation) ...........    30
   Investment in Subb Corporation
      (Torr Corporation) ..........................              125
   To eliminate investment in Subb Corporation.
```

Goodwill must be amortized over a period of not more than 40 years.[5]

The acquiring corporation is required *first* to allocate any excess of fair value over book value to identifiable assets and then assign any remaining balance to excess of purchase price over fair value of net assets (goodwill).

MINORITY INTEREST IN CONSOLIDATED SUBSIDIARY

Assume now that Torr Corporation pays $100 for 80 percent of the outstanding common stock of the Subb Corporation on December 31, 1980. Torr's consolidated balance sheet must now reflect the fact that 20 percent of Subb is owned by outsiders (the minority stockholders of Subb who are not part of the consolidated entity).

The journal entry to reflect the minority interest is:

```
Common Stock (Subb Corporation) ...............    14
Retained Earnings (Subb Corporation) ...........     6
   Minority Interest in Consolidated Subsidiary ..              20
   To record the minority interest in Subb Corpora-
   tion in 1/1/80.
```

The impact of this entry is to show that $20 of the consolidated entity belongs to the minority stockholders of Subb Corporation.

Since there is a disagreement as to whether it should be considered a liability or equity account, the account, *minority interest in consolidated subsidiary,* is usually classified on the consolidated balance sheet between the liability and equity sections.

4. The elimination entry on the consolidated worksheets for Torr's 80 percent investment in Subb is:

---

[4] *Accounting Principles Board Opinion No. 16,* "Business Combinations," effective October 31, 1970.

[5] *Accounting Principles Board Opinion No. 17,* "Intangible Assets," effective October 31, 1970.

Goodwill	20	
Common Stock (Subb Corporation)	56	
Retained Earnings (Subb Corporation)	24	
Investment in Subb Corporation		100
To eliminate investment in Subb Corporation.		

Subb Corporation		
Common stock		$ 70
Retained earnings		30
Book value..		$100
Price paid by Torr for 80% ownership interest of Subb		$100
80 percent of Subb's book value		80
Goodwill		$ 20

This entry assumes that the $20 in excess of book value could not be allocated to any identifiable tangible assets and is allocated to goodwill.

The consolidated worksheet and consolidated balance sheet on December 31, 1980, assuming Torr Corporation acquires an 80 percent equity (ownership) interest in Subb Corporation are shown in Illustrations 11–2 and 11–3.

This consolidated balance sheet is prepared from the perspective of the parent (Torr) corporation. Assets and liabilities of the parent and subsidiary are combined (after eliminating any intracompany accounts) as if the parent owned 100 percent of the subsidiary. The minority interest in the subsidiary (20 percent of its assets minus liabilities) is reflected as a claim against the consolidated entity.

COMPLETE CONSOLIDATION PROCESS

In order to illustrate the complete consolidation process, the balance sheet (Illustration 11–4) and income statement (Illustration 11–5) accounts for Torr and Subb for the subsequent year ended December 31, 1981, are listed in a worksheet format.

BALANCE SHEET ADJUSTMENTS AND ELIMINATIONS

1. Eliminate the investment of Torr Corporation in Subb Corporation at date of acquisition.

Goodwill..	20	
Common Stock (Subb Corporation)	56	
Retained Earnings (Subb Corporation)	24	
Investment in Subb Corporation		
(Torr Corporation)		100
To eliminate investment in Subb Corporation on December 31, 1980.		

ILLUSTRATION 11-2

TORR CORPORATION
Worksheet—Consolidated Balance Sheet
December 31, 1980

	Individual Company Statements		Combined Balance Sheet	Adjustments and Eliminations		Consolidated Balance Sheet
	Torr	Subb		Dr.	Cr.	
Cash	$100	$ 20	$ 120			$ 120
Accounts receivable	54	35	89		(1) $ 10	79
Notes receivable	40		40		(2) 40	—
Inventory	100	85	185			185
Investment in Tee Corporation	206		206			206
Investment in Subb Corporation	100		100		(4) 100	—
Goodwill				(4) $ 20		20
Fixed assets (net of accumulated depreciation)	300	90	390			390
	$900	$230	$1,130			$1,000
Accounts payable	$ 50	$ 45	$ 95	(1) 10		$ 85
Notes payable		40	40	(2) 40		—
Other current liabilities	40	10	50			50
Long-term liabilities	110	35	145			145
Minority interest					(3) 20	20
Common stock	300	70	370	(3) 14 (4) 56		300
Retained earnings	400	30	430	(3) 6 (4) 24		400
	$900	$230	$1,130	$170	$170	$1,000

ILLUSTRATION 11-3

TORR CORPORATION
Consolidated Balance Sheet
December 31, 1980

Assets

Current assets:

Cash...		$ 120
Accounts receivable		79
Inventory..		185
		$ 384

Investment in nonconsolidated subsidiary (Tee Corporation)		206
Fixed assets (net of accumulated depreciation)...........		390
Other assets:		
Excess of purchase price over fair value of net assets		20
		$1,000

Liabilities and Stockholders Equity

Current liabilities:

Accounts payable......................................		$ 85
Other current liabilities		50
		$ 135
Long-term liabilities		145
		$ 280
Minority interest in consolidated subsidiary.............		20
Stockholders' equity:		
Common stock..	$300	
Retained earnings	400	700
		$1,000

This entry reflects the fact that Torr purchased 80 percent of the common stock of Subb for $100 on December 31, 1980, when Subb's common stock was $70 and retained earnings was $30. The excess of purchase price [$100 − ($56 + $24)] over book value is reported on the consolidated balance sheet as *goodwill* as it could not be attributable to identifiable tangible assets.

2. Eliminate Torr's increase since the date of acquisition in its investment in Subb. Torr uses the equity method on its *own* books to record this investment.

ILLUSTRATION 11–4

TORR CORPORATION, Worksheet—Consolidated Balance Sheet (December 31, 1981)

	Individual Company Statements		Combined Balance Sheet	Adjustments and Eliminations		Consolidated Balance Sheet
	Torr	Subb		Dr.	Cr.	
Cash	$ 82	$100	$ 182			$ 182
Accounts receivable	70	69	139		(3) $ 12	127
Notes receivable	30		30		(4) 30	—
Inventory	160	70	230			230
Investment in Tee Corporation	228		228		(1) 100	228
Investment in Subb Corporation	120		120		(2) 20	—
Goodwill (excess of purchase price over fair value)				(1) $ 20	(5) 1	19
Fixed assets (net of accumulated depreciation)	350	88	438			438
	$1,040	$327	$1,367			$1,224
Accounts payable	$ 60	$ 70	$ 130	(3) 12		$ 118
Notes payable		30	30	(4) 30		—
Other current liabilities	30	12	42			42
Long-term liabilities	105	90	195			195
Minority interest in subsidiary corporation					(6) 20	25
					(7) 5	
Common stock	300	70	370	(1) 56		300
				(6) 14		
Retained earnings (12/31/81)	545	55	600	(1) 24		544
				(2) 20		
				(5) 1		
				(6) 6		
				(7) 5		
	$1,040	$327	$1,367	$196	$196	$1,224

ILLUSTRATION 11–5

TORR CORPORATION
Worksheet—Consolidated Statement of Income
1981

	Individual Company Statements		Combined Income Statements	Adjustments and Eliminations		Consolidated Statement of Income
	Torr	Subb		Dr.	Cr.	
Sales	$1,300	$600	$1,900	(1) $350		$1,550
Cost of sales	700	355	1,055		(1) $350	705
Gross margin	600	245	845			845
Selling and administrative expenses	266	185	451			451
Amortization of goodwill				(2) 1		1
Interest expense	11	10	21		(3) 3	18
Interest income	3		3	(3) 3		
Equity in income of Tee Corporation	22		22			22
Equity in income of Subb Corporation	20		20	(4) 20		
Minority interest in Subb Corporation's net income				(5) 5		5
Net income before income taxes	$ 368	$ 50	$ 418			$ 392
Income taxes	163	25	188			188
Net income	$ 205	$ 25	$ 230			$ 204

As of December 31, 1981, Torr Corporation made the following entry on its *own* books.

Investment in Subb Corporation	20	
Equity in Income of Subb Corporation		20

To pick up pro-rata share of Subb Corporation's
1981 earnings (80 percent of $25).

An entry is made for consolidated statement purposes to eliminate the entire investment account and make sure that the earnings for the year which will be reflected in the consolidated income statement are not double counted.

Retained Earnings (Torr Corporation)*	20	
Investment in Subb Corporation		20

To eliminate net earnings since date of acquisition.

  * The entry is made to retained earnings because all the income and expense accounts for the year ended December 31, 1981, have been transferred (closed) to retained earnings.

3.   Eliminate intracompany payables.

Accounts Payable...............................	12	
Accounts Receivable		12

To eliminate intracompany accounts.

4.   Eliminate intracompany borrowings.

Notes Payable	30	
Notes Receivable		30

To eliminate intracompany accounts.

5.   Amortize goodwill.

Retained earnings	1	
Goodwill		1

To amortize goodwill.

This entry is made to amortize the *consolidated goodwill*. The company elected to use a 20-year life for the goodwill.

6. Record minority interest in Subb Corporation *at date of acquisition.*

Retained Earnings	6	
Common Stock	14	
Minority Interest in Subsidiary Corporation ...		20

To reflect the 20% interest of minority stockholders
in Subb Corporation.

7.   Record minority interest in current year's net income:

Retained Earnings   5
    Minority Interest in Subsidiary Corporation . . .   5
    To reflect minority stockholders' 20 percent
    interest in 1981 earnings.

This entry gives the minority interest credit for their share of 1981 net income.

INCOME STATEMENT ADJUSTMENTS AND ELIMINATIONS

1. Eliminate intracompany sales and cost of sales. Torr sold merchandise which cost is $175 to Subb for $350. Subb sold this same merchandise to its customers for $750.

Sales (Torr Corporation)   350
    Cost of Sales (Subb Corporation)   350
    To eliminate intracompany sales.

As a result of this entry the consolidated entity will report sales of $750 ($350 Torr plus $750 Subb minus $350 elimination entry) and cost of sales of $175 ($175 Torr plus $350 Subb minus $350 elimination entry). If Subb had not sold all the inventory it purchased from Torr as of the balance sheet date, an adjusting entry to eliminate the intracompany profit in inventory would be made.

2. Record amortization of goodwill.

Amortization of Goodwill   1
    Goodwill   1
    To record amortization of goodwill of $20 over a
    20-year life.

The reduction in the asset account has already been reflected on the worksheet for the consolidated balance sheet.

3. Eliminate intracompany interest.

Interest Income (Torr Corporation)   3
    Interest Expense (Subb Corporation)   3
    To eliminate intracompany interest.

The consolidated income statement will only report the $18 interest expense to outsiders.

4. Eliminate increase in Torr's equity in Subb's earnings.

Equity in Income of Subb Corporation   20
    Investment in Subb Corporation   20
    To eliminate Torr Corporation's share of Subb
    Corporation's earnings.

We have to make this entry in order not to double count Subb's net income for 1981. The reduction in the asset account has already been reflected on the consolidated balance sheet.

5. To record the minority stockholders' (Subb Corporation) interest in net income for 1981.

```
Minority Interest in Subb
   Corporation's Net Income ....................      5
      Minority Interest in Subsidiary                         5
      Corporation
```

To record the expense for the minority interest in 1981 income.

Only $20, 80 percent of Subb Corporation's net income of $25, belongs to the consolidated company. The remaining $5, 20 percent, belongs to the minority stockholders of the Subb Corporation and is an expense of the consolidated entity.

We can now prepare the Consolidated Income Statement and Reconciliation of Retained Earnings for 1981 and the Consolidated Balance Sheet on December 31, 1981, from the worksheets. (Illustrations 11–6, 11–7, and 11–8).

ILLUSTRATION 11–6

TORR CORPORATION
Consolidated Statement of Income
For the Year Ended December 31, 1981

Sales		$1,550
Cost of sales		705
Gross margin		$ 845
Expenses:		
Selling and administrative expenses	$451	
Amortization of goodwill	1	
Interest expense	18	470
		$ 375
Other income:		
Equity in unconsolidated subsidiary (Tee Corporation)		22
		$ 397
Income tax		188
		$ 209
Less, minority interest in consolidated subsidiary (Subb Corporation)		5
Net income		$ 204

ILLUSTRATION 11–7 ────────────────────────

TORR CORPORATION
Consolidated Reconciliation of Retained Earnings
For the Year Ended December 31, 1981

Balance, January 1, 1981	$400
Consolidated net income for 1981	204
	$604
Dividends declared and paid by Torr	60
Balance, December 31, 1981	$544

ILLUSTRATION 11–8 ────────────────────────

TORR CORPORATION
Consolidated Balance Sheet
December 31, 1981

Assets

Current assets:		
Cash		$ 182
Accounts receivable		127
Inventory		230
Total current assets		539
Investment in unconsolidated subsidiary (Tee Corporation)		228
Fixed assets (net of accumulated depreciation)		438
Excess of purchase price over fair value of acquired subsidiary		19
		$1,224

Equities

Current liabilities:		
Accounts payable		$ 118
Other current liabilities		42
Total current liabilities		160
Long-term liabilities		195
Minority interest in subsidiary corporation (Subb Corporation)		25
Stockholders' equity:		
Common stock	$300	
Retained earnings.......................................	544	844
		$1,224

A consolidated statement of changes in financial position can be prepared from the consolidated balance sheets of December 31, 1980, and December 31, 1981, and the consolidated income statement for the year ended December 31, 1981, using the method described in Chapter 12.

DISCLOSURE OF PRINCIPLES OF CONSOLIDATION

The notes to the consolidated financial statements will disclose the details of the parent corporation's consolidation policy. Examples of various types of disclosure are:

General Motors Corporation—1976

Principles of Consolidation

The consolidated financial statements include the accounts of the corporation and all domestic and foreign subsidiaries which are more than 50 percent owned and engaged principally in manufacturing or wholesale marketing of General Motors products. General Motors' share of earnings or losses of nonconsolidated subsidiaries and of associates in which at least 20 percent of the voting securities is owned is generally included in consolidated income under the equity method of accounting. Intercompany items and transactions between companies included in the consolidation are eliminated and unrealized intercompany profits on sales to nonconsolidated subsidiaries and to associates are deferred.

Signor Corporation—1977

Principles of Consolidation

The consolidated financial statements include the accounts of all subsidiaries. All significant intercompany balances, transactions, and stockholdings have been eliminated.

During the year ended June 30, 1976, one of the company's wholly owned subsidiaries, Gensco, Inc., acquired 40 percent of the capital stock of a foreign corporation for a total consideration of $3.2 million. The current carrying value of this investment exceeds the underlying equity in the net assets acquired by $580,000. Such excess is being amortized over a 20-year period. The investment is accounted for under the equity method. The company's share of the net loss of $279,471 (including a loss of $349,507 from foreign currency translation) for the year ended June 30, 1977, and the net loss of $148,402 for the year ended June 30, 1976, are included in other income (expense) in the consolidated statement of income.

SUMMARY

Consolidated financial statements are prepared for an *economic*, rather than a *legal* entity, and do not purport to show the financial results of any of the individual corporations (legal entities) in the consolidated group. Creditors of and investors in subsidiary corporations have an interest in the liquidity and profitability of their subsidiary, not the consolidated group. A creditor of a subsidiary corporation wants to know its current ratio and debt/equity ratio rather than these ratios for the consolidated group (unless the parent is guaranteeing the subsidiary's debts). Similarly, investors (minority stockholders) in the subsidiary corporation look to its earnings as a source of potential dividends.

To be well-informed the reader of the consolidated financial statements should also consult the financial statements of each individual corporation in the consolidated group.

BUSINESS COMBINATIONS

A business combination occurs when a corporation and one or more incorporated or unincorporated businesses are brought together into one accounting entity. The single entity carries on the activities of the previously separate, independent enterprises.[6]

If one company *acquires* the assets or voting common stock of another company, the business combination is a *purchase*.

If there is *no acquisition* but a merger of common interests with only the voting common stock of one company being exchanged for at least 90 percent of the voting common stock of another company and the transaction meets all of the other criteria listed in *APB Opinion No. 16*, the business combination is called a *pooling of interests*.

Purchase Method

The purchase method, used in the previous consolidation example, records the acquisition at its cost to the acquiring corporation. Any excess of cost over the book value of the net assets of the acquired company is first assigned to the assets purchased and then to goodwill (*APB No. 16*). The earnings of the two companies are combined commencing with the date of acquisition.

---

[6] *Accounting Principles Board Opinion Number 16*, Business Combinations, effective October 31, 1970. Portions of the text of *APB No. 16* is reproduced as Exhibit 3 of the A. J. Johnson case (Case 11–2).

Pooling of Interests Method

The pooling of interests method assumes that the two corporations who have exchanged their common stock have combined (pooled their resources) into one *continuing entity* and that no purchase (acquisition) of one corporation by the other has taken place.

In that the pooling of interests method assumes continuing ownership, there is no revaluation of assets and equities as there is in the purchase method. The book values of the assets and equities of the two corporations are combined and become the balance sheet of the continuing entity. The earnings of the two corporations are combined commencing with the first day of the year in which the exchange of stock takes place. For example, if two corporations, both of whom report on a calendar year basis, exchange their common stock on November 1, 1980, and the exchange qualifies as a pooling of interests, they will combine their earnings as if they had been together on January 1, 1980.

To illustrate the difference in the consolidated financial statements using the purchase and pooling of interests methods, assume the following balance sheets for the Pace Corporation (Illustration 11–9) and Joy Corporation (Illustration 11–10).

ILLUSTRATION 11–9

PACE CORPORATION
Balance Sheet
December 31, 1980

Assets

Current assets		$ 5,000
Fixed assets (net of accumulated depreciation)		7,900
		$12,900

Equities

Current liabilities		$ 2,900
Stockholders' equity:		
Common stock—par value $5	$5,000	
Paid-in capital—excess over par value	900	
Retained earnings	4,100	10,000
		$12,900

ILLUSTRATION 11–10

JOY CORPORATION
Balance Sheet
December 31, 1980

Assets

Current assets	$ 900
Fixed assets (net of accumulated depreciation)	800
	$1,700

Equities

Current liabilities		$ 210
Stockholders' equity:		
Common stock—par value $1	$ 300	
Paid-in capital—excess		
over par value	100	
Retained earnings	1,090	1,490
		$ 1,700

Purchase Method

On January 1, 1981, the Pace Corporation *purchased* all the common stock of the Joy Corporation (from Joy Corporation stockholders) for $5,000 in cash. The entry on *Pace's books* to record this transaction (puchase method) is:

Investment in Joy Corporation	5,000	
Cash		5,000

To record acquisition of all of the outstanding
common stock of Joy Corporation.

If Pace had issued its own common stock instead of cash to the *Joy stockholders,* the purchase price would be the number of shares issued times the market price at the date of issue.

Assume Pace issued 200 shares of their $5 par value stock to Joy stockholders and that the market value on January 1, 1981, was $25 per share.

The entry would be:

Investment in Joy Corporation	5,000	
Common Stock—$5 Par Value		1,000
Paid-in Capital (Excess over Par Value)		4,000

To record the acquisition of the Joy Corporation
for 200 shares of $5 par value common stock.

The worksheet for the preparation of the consolidated balance sheet on January 1, 1981, (assume Joy is to continue as a separate legal entity and is not liquidated) after the acquisition has been recorded on Pace's books would be:

	Pace	Joy	Com- bined	Elimi- nation	Consolidated Balance Sheet
Current assets	$ 5,000	$ 900	$ 5,900		$ 5,900
Investment in Joy	5,000		5,000	(5,000)	—
Fixed assets (net)	7,900	800	8,700	2,510	11,210
Goodwill				1,000	1,000
	$17,900	$1,700	$19,600		$18,110
Current liabilities	$ 2,900	$ 210	$ 3,110		$ 3,110
Common stock	6,000	300	6,300	(300)	6,000
Paid-in capital	4,900	100	5,000	(100)	4,900
Retained earnings	4,100	1,090	5,190	(1,090)	4,100
	$17,900	$1,700	$19,600		$18,110

The elimination entry for the investment on the consolidated worksheet *assumes* that the $3,510 (5,000 − 1,490) excess of fair market value over book value is to be allocated $2,510 to fixed assets (the fair market value of the fixed assets was determined by an appraisal) and $1,000 to goodwill.

The appropriate elimination entry is:

Common stock....................................	300	
Paid-in capital	100	
Retained earnings	1,090	
Goodwill	1,000	
Fixed assets.....................................	2,510	
Investment in Joy Corporation		5,000

To eliminate the investment in Joy Corporation.

The *consolidated balance sheet* reflects the *fair market value* of the assets acquired and eliminates the stockholders' equity of the acquired company as of the date of acquisition. *Consolidated net income* after the acquisition will be reduced by the depreciation expense on the increased valuation ($2,510) of the fixed assets and the amortization of the goodwill ($1,000).

If the acquiring company purchases the net assets of another company for less than their fair market value (bargain purchase or because the expected future earnings justify a lower price), GAAP (cost principle) requires that the assets be reduced to the amount actually paid for them. Any residual amount, after the noncurrent assets are written down to zero, is recorded as a deferred credit (*negative goodwill*, excess of fair market value of net assets over purchase price) and is allocated to income over a period not to exceed 40 years.

Pooling of Interests Method

Assume that on January 1, 1980, Pace issued 200 shares of its $5 par value common stock to Joy stockholders in exchange for all of Joy's common stock, and this business combination meets all the specific criteria of *APB No. 16* and is required to be recorded as a *pooling of interests*. The journal entry to record the issuance of stock on Pace's books is:

Investment in Joy Corporation	1,490	
Common Stock—Par Value $5		1,000
Paid-in Capital (Excess over Par)		490

To record exchange of 200 shares of our common stock for all the common stock of Joy Corporation (Joy's book value is $1,700 − $210).

Because the business combination is a pooling of interests and is not a purchase, Pace will record the investment on its books at an amount equal to Joy's book value.

The worksheet for the preparation of the consolidated balance sheet on January 1, 1981, after this business combination has been recorded on Pace's books would be:

	Pace	Joy	Com-bined	Elimi-nation	Consolidated Balance Sheet
Current assets	$ 5,000	$ 900	$ 5,900		$ 5,900
Investment in Joy Corporation	1,490		1,490	(1,490)	
Fixed assets (net)	7,900	800	8,700		8,700
	$14,390	$1,700	$16,090		$14,600
Current liabilities	$ 2,900	$ 210	$ 3,110		$ 3,110
Common stock	6,000	300	6,300	(300)	6,000
Excess over par	1,390	100	1,490	(1,190)	300
Retained earnings	4,100	1,090	5,190		5,190
	$14,390	$1,700	$16,090		$14,600

The common stock ($300) of Joy is eliminated with the remainder of Joy's book value ($1,190) being offset against the pooled ($1,490) paid-in capital account (excess over par). The method of eliminating the *book value* of the pooled company is to first offset the par or stated value of common stock of the pooled company and then the combined (pooled) paid-in capital account with any remaining residual charged to the pooled retained earnings account.

An examination of the two consolidated balance sheets (purchase and pooling of interests) indicates that assets are $3,510 ($18,110 − $14,600) higher using the purchase method. The allocation of this additional asset cost to future periods (depreciation expense and amortization of goodwill) will result in lower reported earnings using the purchase method than the pooling of interests method.

The pooling of interests method also creates the opportunity to obtain "instant earnings" for the consolidated entity by selling at a much higher market value some of the assets which have been recorded at book value. For example, the sale of Joy's fixed assets by the consolidated entity on January 2, 1981, at their market value would result in "instant earnings" of $1,710 ($2,510 − $800). Separate disclosure is required on the financial statements if the profit or loss on disposal of pooled assets is material and occurs within two years of the consummation of the business combination.

It is also possible for the issuing (dominant) company to create earnings and increase earnings per share by combining at the end of the year with a company that has current earnings and a ratio of market price to earnings which is lower than theirs.[7]

These opportunities to increase reported earnings by treating what is really an acquisition as a pooling of interest resulted in many abuses and led to the issuing of *APB No. 16* in August 1970. *APB No. 16* requires that the pooling of interest method be used to account for *business combinations* when all 12 specific criteria of the opinion are met. These criteria relate primarily to the independence and autonomy of the companies prior to the business combination and the requirement that at least 90 percent of a company's voting common stock be exchanged for the voting common stock of the other company pursuant to a plan to be completed within one year. All business combinations that do not meet all the criteria of *APB No. 16* must be treated as purchases.

The purpose of the *Opinion* was to eliminate alternative accounting procedures for business combinations and to try to establish criteria which will allow the pooling of interests method to be used only when there is a bona fide merger of interests into one continuing entity.

---

[7] *APB No. 16* does not impose size restrictions on business combinations.

DISCLOSURE ON THE FINANCIAL STATEMENTS OF PURCHASE AND POOLING OF INTERESTS METHODS

The notes to the financial statements will disclose whether a business combination is recorded using the purchase or the pooling of interests method. If the pooling of interests method is used, restatement of earnings for prior periods is required. If the purchase method is used, no restatement of prior periods is required and it is more difficult to evaluate from the consolidated statements the earnings trend for the business combination.

Some examples of this type of disclosure (purchase and pooling of interests) quoted from published financial statements are:

TENNECO—1977

Acquisitions

In 1977, Tenneco Inc., acquired all of the outstanding common stock of Monroe Auto Equipment Company (Monroe) in exchange for 4,982,044 shares of Tenneco Inc., common stock. This transaction has been accounted for on the "pooling of interests" basis of accounting and accordingly the accompanying financial statements have been restated to include Monroe. The operating revenues and net income of Monroe included in 1976 were approximately $191 million and $5 million, respectively. The operating revenues and net income of Monroe prior to date of acquisition (six months ended June 30, 1977) included in the 1977 consolidated income statement were approximately $125 million and $5 million, respectively.

In June 1977, a subsidiary of Tenneco Inc., completed its acquisition of a 40 percent interest in Poclain, S.A., a French construction machinery firm, through the purchase of newly issued shares of Poclain capital stock, at a purchase price of approximately $40 million. In addition to acquisition of the Poclain stock, the subsidiary subsequently acquired certain subsidiaries of Poclain, at a purchase price of approximately $18 million.

In December 1977, Tenneco Inc., purchased the remaining 50 percent interest in Petro-Tex Chemical Corporation for approximately $35 million. Tenneco has owned 50 percent of Petro-Tex since its formation.

UNITED TECHNOLOGIES—1977

Merger with Otis Elevator Company

On July 7, 1976, Otis Elevator Company (Otis) became a wholly owned subsidiary of the corporation pursuant to a merger under terms of which 1,216,166 shares of the corporation's $7.32 Cumulative Dividend Convertible Preferred Stock ($7.32 Preferred Stock) were issued in exchange for the outstanding Otis common stock held by the minority shareholders of Otis and in substitution for shares of Otis common stock issuable under Otis stock purchase plans. In November 1975, the corporation had acquired approximately 70 percent of the outstanding common stock of Otis pursuant to a cash tender offer. Otis's principal business is the sale, engineering, manufacture, installation, and service of elevators and escalators.

The acquisition of Otis has been accounted for as a purchase. The aggregate purchase price of approximately $398 million, including approximately $122 million assigned to the $7.32 Preferred Stock on the basis of an estimate of market value provided by investment bankers, exceeded the fair values of the underlying net assets of Otis by approximately $5 million; such excess is included in deferred charges and is being amortized over ten years.

Pro forma amounts for 1976, as though the merger had taken place at the beginning of such year, would have been: Primary earnings per share—$5.11; and fully diluted earnings per share—$3.64.

SUMMARY

Whether a business combination is treated as a pooling of interests or a purchase is determined by the guidelines established in *APB Opinion No. 16*. If the business combination is structured to be a pooling of interests, it will probably result in higher current and future earnings and understated assets. The pooling of interests method does not record the net assets of the acquired company at their fair market value (understated assets) and, therefore, does not reduce future earnings by the amortization of acquired goodwill or the depreciation on the increased cost of the fixed assets acquired. Future earnings can also be enhanced under the pooling of interests method if acquired assets (recorded at net book value) are sold for their fair market value.[8] Net income in the year of acquisition will also be higher assuming a pooling of interests as earnings of the acquired company are picked up as of the first day of the year that the acquisition takes place rather than the date of the acquisition as is required in the purchase. Return on investment (net income divided by total assets) will also usually be higher using the pooling of interests method rather than the purchase method because net income will be higher and total assets will be lower. In the unusual case where there is substantial negative goodwill and the pooling of interests method would report lower earnings than the purchase method, the transaction would probably be structured as a purchase.

---

[8] If the combined companies intended to dispose of a *significant* part of these assets (except for duplicate facilities and excess capacity) within two years after the combination date, the business combination would not qualify for pooling of interests treatment.

CASES FOR CHAPTER 11

Case 11–1 _____

General Motors Corporation (A)

Refer to the 1978 financial statements of General Motors Corporation and answer the following questions:

1. What method did General Motors (GM) use to report their investment in General Motors Acceptance Corporation (GMAC) on their consolidated balance sheet?
2. Identify the items that were responsible for the increase in the Investment in GMAC account.
3. Assume that GM had reported their investment in GMAC using the cost method.
   a. How much larger or smaller would GM's earned on common stock for 1978 have been?
   b. What would be the amount in the Investment in GMAC account on December 31, 1978?
   c. Do you think the cost method provides better disclosure than the equity method?
4. Assume GM accounted for its investment in GMAC using the consolidation method instead of the equity method.
   a. How much larger or smaller would GM's earned on common stock for 1978 have been?
   b. How much more or less would the *total assets* be?
   c. How much more or less would the long-term debt (payable after one year) be?
5. Calculate the ratio of earned on common stock to total assets using (a) the equity method and (b) the consolidation method.
6. Calculate the ratio of earned on common stock to common stockholders' equity (stockholders' equity minus preferred stock) using (a) the equity method and (b) the consolidation method.
7. Calculate the ratio of long-term debt to long-term debt plus stock-

holders' equity using (a) the equity method and (b) the consolidation method.
8. Which method provides the best disclosure, the equity or the consolidation method?

CONSOLIDATED FINANCIAL STATEMENTS

RESPONSIBILITIES FOR FINANCIAL STATEMENTS

The following financial statements of General Motors Corporation and consolidated subsidiaries were prepared by the management which is responsible for their integrity and objectivity. The statements have been prepared in conformity with generally accepted accounting principles and, as such, include amounts based on judgments of management.

Management is further responsible for maintaining a system of internal controls, including internal accounting controls, that contains organizational arrangements that provide an appropriate division of responsibility and is designed to assure that the books and records reflect the transactions of the companies and that its established policies and procedures are carefully followed. The system is constantly reviewed for its effectiveness and is augmented by written policies and guidelines, a strong program of internal audit, and the careful selection and training of qualified personnel.

Deloitte Haskins & Sells, independent certified public accountants, are engaged to examine the financial statements of General Motors Corporation and its subsidiaries and issue reports thereon. Their examination is conducted in accordance with generally accepted auditing standards and includes a review of internal controls and a test of transactions. The Accountants' Report appears at the end of this report.

The Board of Directors, through the Audit Committee of the Board, is responsible for assuring that management fulfills its responsibilities in the preparation of the financial statements and for engaging the independent public accountants with whom the Committee reviews the scope of the audits and the accounting principles to be applied in financial reporting. The Audit Committee meets regularly (separately and jointly) with the independent public accountants, representatives of management, and the internal auditors to review the activities of each and to ensure that each is properly discharging its responsibilities. To ensure complete independence, Deloitte Haskins & Sells have full and free access to meet with the Audit Committee, without management representatives present, to discuss the results of their examination and their opinions on the adequacy of internal controls and the quality of financial reporting.

T. A. Murphy
Chairman

A. B. Smith
Chief Financial Officer

Statement of Consolidated Income*
For The Years Ended December 31, 1978, and 1977
(dollars in millions except per share amounts)

	1978	*1977*
Net sales	$63,221.1	$54,961.3
Equity in earnings of nonconsolidated subsidiaries and associates (dividends received amounted to $123.7 in 1978 and $110.3 in 1977)	253.0	222.1
Other income less income deductions—net (Note 2)	(141.4)	54.9
Total	$63,332.7	$55,238.3
Costs and expenses		
Cost of sales and other operating charges, exclusive of items listed below	51,275.7	44,427.9
Selling, general, and administrative expenses	2,255.8	1,997.3
Depreciation of real estate, plants, and equipment	1,180.6	974.0
Amortization of special tools	1,855.7	1,406.4
Provision for the Bonus Plan (Note 3)	168.4	161.0
United States, foreign, and other income taxes (Note 5)...	3,088.5	2,934.2
Total	$59,824.7	$51,900.8
Net income	3,508.0	3,337.5
Dividends on preferred stocks	12.9	12.9
Earned on common stock	$ 3,495.1	$ 3,324.6
Average number of shares of common stock outstanding (in millions)	285.5	286.1
Earned per share of common stock (Note 6)	$12.24	$11.62

* References should be made to Notes to Financial Statements.
Certain amounts for 1977 have been reclassified to conform with classifications for 1978.

Consolidated Balance Sheet*
December 31, 1978, and 1977
(dollars in millions)

	1978	1977
Assets		
Current assets:		
Cash...	$ 177.3	$ 293.4
United States Government and other marketable securities and time deposits—at cost, which approximates market:		
Held for payment of income taxes	791.3	715.3
Other	3,086.2	2,231.3
Accounts and notes receivable (Note 7)	5,638.7	4,681.1
Inventories	7,576.7	7,175.7
Prepaid expenses....................................	729.3	860.4
Total current assets...........................	$17,999.5	$15,957.2
Investments and miscellaneous assets (Note 8)..........	2,812.1	2,351.7
Common stock held for the incentive program (Note 3)...	181.1	146.5
Property		
Real estate, plants, and equipment (Note 10)	22,052.0	19,860.9
Less accumulated depreciation (Note 10)	13,438.8	12,679.4
Net real estate, plants, and equipment	8,613.2	7,181.5
Special tools—less amortization	992.4	1,021.4
Total property	$ 9,605.6	$ 8,202.9
Total assets	$30,598.3	$26,658.3
Liabilities and Stockholders' Equity		
Current liabilities:		
Accounts, drafts, and loans payable	$ 4,612.4	$ 3,719.1
United States, foreign, and other income taxes payable	944.8	887.5
Accrued liabilities	4,493.4	3,720.3
Total current liabilities	$10,050.6	$ 8,326.9
Long-term debt—less unamortized discount (Note 11)	978.9	1,068.2
Other liabilities	1,384.4	1,023.5
Deferred investment tax credits	519.9	368.2
Other deferred credits	94.6	104.6
Stockholders' equity (Notes 3 and 12)		
Preferred stock ($5.00 series, $183.6; $3.75 series, $100.0)	283.6	283.6
Common stock.......................................	480.1	479.5
Capital surplus (principally additional paid-in capital)	792.0	772.1
Net income retained for use in the business.............	16,014.2	14,231.7
Total stockholders' equity	$17,569.9	$15,766.9
Total liabilities and stockholders' equity	$30,598.3	$26,658.3

* Reference should be made to Notes to Financial Statements.

Statement of Changes in Consolidated Financial Position*
For The Years Ended December 31, 1978, and 1977
(dollars in millions)

	1978	1977
Source of Funds		
Net income	$3,508.0	$3,337.5
Depreciation of real estate, plants, and equipment	1,180.6	974.0
Amortization of special tools	1,855.7	1,406.4
Deferred income taxes, undistributed earnings of nonconsolidated subsidiaries and associates, etc.—net...	(64.6)	(157.9)
Total current operations	6,479.7	5,560.0
Proceeds from issuance of long-term debt	111.9	130.7
Proceeds from disposals of property—net................	125.5	110.7
Proceeds from sale of newly issued common stock	20.5	1.9
Other—net..	273.8	120.8
Total	$7,011.4	$5,924.1
Application of Funds		
Dividends paid to stockholders	1,725.5	1,957.7
Expenditures for real estate, plants, and equipment	2,737.8	1,870.9
Expenditures for special tools.........................	1,826.7	1,775.8
Investments in nonconsolidated subsidiaries and associates.......................................	201.6	139.5
Retirement of long-term debt	201.2	106.5
Total	$6,692.8	$5,850.4
Increase in working capital............................	318.6	73.7
Working capital at beginning of the year	7,630.3	7,556.6
Working capital at end of the year	$7,948.9	$7,630.3
Increase (decrease) in Working Capital by Element		
Cash, marketable securities, and time deposits	$ 814.8	($1,384.9)
Accounts and notes receivable	957.6	722.0
Inventories	401.0	847.9
Prepaid expenses	(131.1)	299.6
Accounts, drafts, and loans payable	(893.3)	(651.7)
United States, foreign, and other income taxes payable..	(57.3)	764.0
Accrued liabilities	(773.1)	(523.2)
Increase in working capital............................	$ 318.6	$ 73.7

* Reference should be made to Notes to Financial Statements.

NOTES TO FINANCIAL STATEMENTS

Note 1. Significant Accounting Policies

Principles of Consolidation. The consolidated financial statements include the accounts of the corporation and all domestic and foreign subsidiaries which are more than 50 percent owned and engaged principally in manufacturing or wholesale marketing of General Motors products. General Motors' share of earnings or losses of nonconsolidated subsidiaries and of associates in which at least 20 percent of the voting securities is owned is generally included in consolidated income under the equity method of accounting. Intercompany items and transactions between companies included in the consolidation are eliminated and unrealized intercompany profits on sales to nonconsolidated subsidiaries and to associates are deferred.

Income Taxes. Investment tax credits are deducted in determining taxes estimated to be payable currently and are deferred and amortized over the lives of the related assets. The tax effects of timing differences between pretax accounting income and taxable income (principally related to depreciation, sales, and product allowances, undistributed earnings of subsidiaries and associates, and benefit plans expense) are deferred, except that the tax effects of certain expenses charged to income prior to 1968 have not been deferred but are recognized in income taxes provided at the time such expenses become allowable deductions for tax purposes. Provisions are made for estimated U.S. and foreign taxes, less available tax credits and deductions, which may be incurred on remittance of the corporation's share of subsidiaries' and associates' undistributed earnings included in the consolidated financial statements.

Inventories. Inventories are stated generally at cost, which is not in excess of market. The cost of substantially all domestic inventories was determined by the last-in, first-out (Lifo) method, which was adopted in 1976. If the first-in, first-out (Fifo) method of inventory valuation had been used by the corporation for U.S. inventories, it is estimated they would be $1,097.7 million higher at December 31, 1978, compared with $697.3 million higher at December 31, 1977. The cost of inventories outside the United States was determined generally by the Fifo or the average cost method.

Property, Depreciation, and Amortization. Property is stated at cost. Maintenance, repairs, rearrangement expenses, and renewals and betterments which do not enhance the value or increase the basic productive capacity of the assets are charged to costs and expenses as incurred.

Depreciation is provided on groups of property using, with minor exceptions, an accelerated method which accumulates depreciation of approximately two thirds of the depreciable cost during the first half of the estimated lives of the property. The annual group rates of depreciation are as follows:

Classification of Property	Annual Group Rates (percent)
Land improvements	5
Buildings	3½
Machinery and equipment	8⅓ (average)
Furniture and office equipment	6 (average)

Expenditures for special tools are amortized, with the amortization applied directly to the asset account, over short periods of time because the utility value of the tools is radically affected by frequent changes in the design of the functional components and appearance of the product. Replacement of special tools for reasons other than changes in products is charged directly to cost of sales.

Pension Program. The corporation and its subsidiaries have a number of pension plans covering substantially all employees. Benefits under the plans are generally related to an employees length of service, wages and salaries, and, where applicable, contributions. The costs of these plans are determined on the basis of actuarial cost methods and include amortization of prior service cost over periods not exceeding 30 years. With the exception of certain overseas subsidiaries, pension costs accrued are funded.

Product-Related Expenses. Expenditures for advertising and sales promotion and for other product-related expenses are charged to costs and expenses as incurred; provisions for estimated costs related to product warranty are made at the time the products are sold.

Expenditures for research and development are charged to expenses as incurred and amounted to $1,633.1 million in 1978 and $1,451.4 million in 1977.

Foreign Exchange. All exchange and translation activity is included in cost of sales and amounted to a gain of $62.7 million in 1978 and a loss of $47.6 million in 1977.

Note 2. Other Income Less Income Deductions

(dollars in millions)

	1978	1977
Other income:		
Interest income	$357.5	$310.3
Other	67.2	54.2
Income deductions:		
Interest on long-term debt	(90.0)	(86.2)
Other interest	(265.9)	(195.5)
Other	(210.2)*	(27.9)
Net	($141.4)	$ 54.9

* Principally provision for cost of liquidation of Argentine automotive operations and discontinuance of appliance manufacturing at Frigidaire.

Note 3. Incentive Program

The Incentive Program consists of the General Motors Bonus Plan, first approved by stockholders in 1918, and the General Motors Stock Option Plans, adopted in 1957 and 1977. The By-Laws provide that the Plans shall be presented for action at a stockholders' meeting at least once in every five years. The Incentive Program was last approved by stockholders at the 1977 Annual Meeting.

The corporation maintains a reserve for purposes of the Bonus Plan to which may be credited each year an amount which the independent public accountants of the corporation determine to be 8 percent of the net earnings which exceed 7 percent but not 15 percent of net capital, plus 5 percent of the net earnings which exceed 15 percent of net capital, but not in excess of the amount paid out as dividends on the common stock during the year. However, for any year the Bonus and Salary Committee may direct that a lesser amount be credited. Bonus awards under the Bonus Plan and such other amounts arising out of the operation of the Incentive Program as the Committee may determine are charged to the reserve.

For the year 1978, the Bonus and Salary Committee directed a credit to the Reserve for the Bonus Plan of $168.4 million (the maximum permitted under the Bonus Plan formula as determined by the independent public accountants) as set forth in the accompanying table:

(dollars in millions except per share amount)

Computation of net capital
Stockholders' equity and long-term debt of General Motors
Corporation at December 31, 1977 .... $16,478.4
Add proportionate allowance for changes during 1978 in capital
stock, capital surplus, and long-term debt—net .... —

Net capital (as defined in the Bonus Plan) $16,478.4

Computation of net earnings
Net income for 1978 .... $ 3,508.0
Add provision for Bonus Plan 168.4
Add interest and discount on long-term debt 55.2
Deduct loss of rights to prior years' bonus awards and contingent
credits included in income................................... .5
Deduct prior unawarded bonus reserve restored to income 1.3

Net earnings (as defined in the Bonus Plan) .... $ 3,729.8
Deduct 7 percent of net capital (equivalent to $3.81 per share
of common stock)... 1,153.5

Net earnings for bonus credit calculation .... $ 2,576.3

Maximum amount which could be credited to reserve
8 percent of the net earnings between 7 percent and 15 percent
of net capital .... $ 105.5
5 percent of the net earnings which exceed 15 percent of
net capital 62.9

Total amount available in the reserve for awards under
the Bonus Plan .... $ 168.4

As indicated in the preceding table, the total unawarded reserve carried forward from 1977 in the amount of $1.3 million was, in accordance with action taken by the Bonus and Salary Committee, restored to income in 1978, but was not included in net earnings for that year in determining the provision for the Bonus Plan. As a result, the total amount available for distribution will be the aforementioned $168.4 million. Subject to final determination, the Committee has tentatively directed that the total of individual awards shall approximate the amount of the credit to the reserve related to 1978. As a result of tentative determinations of awards by the Committee, the amount provided was transferred to current liabilities and other liabilities at December 31, 1978.

If participants in the Bonus and Stock Option Plans fail to meet conditions precedent to receiving undelivered installments of bonus awards (and contingent credits related to the Stock Option Plan prior to 1977), the amount of any such installments is credited to income. Upon the exercise of stock options, any related contingent credits are proportionately reduced and the amount of the reduction is credited to income.

Changes during 1978 in the status of options granted under the Stock Option Plans are shown in the following table. The option prices are 100 percent of the average of the highest and lowest sales prices of General Motors common stock on the dates the options were granted as reported (1) on the New York Stock Exchange for options granted prior to 1976, and (2) on the Composite Tape of transactions on all major exchanges and nonexchange markets in the United States for options granted in 1976 and subsequent years. The options outstanding at December 31, 1978, expire ten years from date of grant. All options are subject to earlier termination under certain conditions.

The corporation intends to deliver newly issued stock upon the exercise of any of the outstanding options. The maximum number of shares for which additional options might be granted under the Plan was 2,211,335 at January 1, 1978, and 1,904,325 at December 31, 1978.

Shares under Option

			Changes during Year			
Year Granted	Option Price	January 1, 1978	Granted	Exercised	Terminated	December 31, 1978
1973	$73.38	175,614	—	—	41,508	134,106
1974	50.00	215,398	—	3,042	15,570	196,786
1976	65.19	139,308	—	—	9,522	129,786
1977	66.57	288,665	—	—	8,745	279,920
1978	63.75	—	316,060	—	305	315,755
Total		818,985	316,060	3,042	75,650	1,056,353

Common stock held for the Incentive Program is exclusively for payment of liabilities under the Incentive Program and is stated substantially at cost.

(dollars in millions)	1978		1977	
	Shares	Amount	Shares	Amount
Balance at January 1	2,136,633	$146.5	1,457,629	$ 99.6
Acquired during the year	1,338,698	81.6	1,186,731	81.9
Delivered to participants	(687,591)	(47.0)	(507,727)	(35.0)
Balance at December 31	2,787,740	$181.1	2,136,633	$146.5

Note 4. Pension Program

The total pension expense of the corporation and its consolidated subsidiaries amounted to $1,326.7 million in 1978 and $1,207.7 million in 1977. In the United States, the market value of trusteed pension funds totaled $7,143.8 million, and assets held under the insured part of the salaried employees' program totaled $2,290.3 million at December 31, 1978.

The actuarially computed value of vested benefits of all plans exceeded the total of pension funds, at market, and balance sheet accruals as of December 31, 1978, by about $3.9 billion. This amount represents the unfunded portion of the actuarially computed present value of pension benefits to which employees are entitled based on service as of December 31, 1978, and is calculated as if all employees were to terminate service as of that date. This figure is in excess of the estimated liability for benefits guaranteed under the Employee Retirement Income Security Act (ERISA) in the event of plan termination.

Note 5. U.S., Foreign, and Other Income Taxes (dollars in millions)

	1978	1977
Taxes estimated to be payable currently*		
U.S. federal	$2,259.3	$2,468.3
Foreign	511.0	430.3
Other	300.5	292.9
Total	$3,070.8	$3,191.5
Taxes deferred—net:		
U.S. federal	$ (159.3)	$ (231.7)
Foreign	41.3	(94.9)
Other	(16.0)	(12.7)
Total	$ (134.0)	$ (339.3)

	1978	1977
Investment tax credits deferred—net:		
U.S. federal	$ 149.7	$ 77.3
Foreign	2.0	4.7
Total	$ 151.7	$ 82.0
Total	$3,088.5	$2,934.2

* Investment tax credits deducted in determining taxes estimated to be payable currently amounted to $293.7 million in 1978 and $170.8 million in 1977.

Note 6. Earnings per Share

Earnings per share of common stock are based on the average number of shares outstanding during each year. The effect on earnings per share resulting from the assumed exercise of outstanding options and delivery of bonus awards and contingent credits under the Incentive Program is not material.

Note 7. Accounts and Notes Receivable (dollars in millions)

	1978	1977
GMAC and subsidiaries (relating to current wholesale financing of sales of GM products, etc.)	$2,893.5	$2,496.6
Other trade and sundry receivables (less allowances)	2,745.2	2,184.5
Total	$5,638.7	$4,681.1

Note 8. Investments and Miscellaneous Assets (dollars in millions)

	1978	1977
Nonconsolidated subsidiaries:		
GMAC and subsidiaries (Note 9)	$2,005.8	$1,688.2
Dealerships (retail companies)	113.5	110.4
Other domestic and foreign subsidiaries	60.9	53.8
Associates (interests in overseas companies)	95.6	92.6
Other investments and miscellaneous assets		
—at cost (less allowances)	536.3	406.7
Total	$2,812.1	$2,351.7

Note 9. General Motors Acceptance Corporation and Subsidiaries Condensed Consolidated Balance Sheet (dollars in millions)

	1978	1977
Cash	$ 484.5	$ 342.3
Marketable securities (market value, 1978—$579.4; 1977—$574.6)	552.5	532.7
Finance receivables (including installments maturing after one year: 1978—$10,343.0; 1977—$8,150.3; less unearned income: 1978—$1,977.8; 1977—$1,530.8; and allowance for financing losses: 1978—$216.9; 1977—$177.6)	25,622.7	22,582.6
Insurance receivables	45.0	36.8
Unamortized debt expense	42.2	41.3
Other assets	156.5	105.0
Total assets	$26,903.4	$23,640.7
Notes, loans, and debentures payable within one year (less unamortized discount)	$12,058.4	$10,480.0
Accounts payable and other liabilities General Motors Corporation and affiliated companies	$ 2,893.5	$ 2,496.6
Other	1,105.8	899.2
Total accounts payable and other liabilities	$ 3,999.3	$ 3,395.8
Notes, loans, and debentures payable after one year (maturing prior to 2009—less unamortized discount)	7,165.3	6,602.1
Subordinated indebtedness payable after one year (maturing prior to 1998—less unamortized discount)	1,674.6	1,474.6
Total liabilities	$24,897.6	$21,952.5
Stockholder's equity: Preferred stock, $100 par value (authorized and outstanding, 1,100,000 shares):		
6 percent cumulative	$ 75.0	$ 75.0
7¼ percent cumulative	35.0	35.0
Common stock, $100 par value (authorized and outstanding, 1978—9,650,000 shares; 1977—7,650,000 shares)	965.0	765.0
Net income retained for use in the business: Balance at beginning of the year	$ 813.2	$ 709.8
Net income	229.6	205.4
Total	$ 1,042.8	$ 915.2
Cash dividends	112.0	102.0
Balance at end of the year	$ 930.8	$ 813.2
Total stockholder's equity	$ 2,005.8	$ 1,688.2
Total liabilities and stockholder's equity	$26,903.4	$23,640.7

Note 10. Real Estate, Plants and Equipment and Accumulated Depreciation (dollars in millions)

	1978	*1977*
Real estate, plants, and equipment:		
Land	$ 268.0	$ 255.7
Land improvements	719.3	646.9
Leasehold improvements—less amortization	22.3	23.9
Buildings	4,975.4	4,643.3
Machinery and equipment	14,434.1	13,149.5
Furniture and office equipment	317.9	286.7
Construction in progress	1,315.0	854.9
Total	$22,052.0	$19,860.9
Accumulated depreciation:		
Land improvements	$ 430.6	$ 406.5
Buildings	2,964.9	2,837.6
Machinery and equipment	9,832.3	9,242.6
Furniture and office equipment	161.7	143.4
Extraordinary obsolescence	49.3	49.3
Total	$13,438.8	$12,679.4

Note 11. Long-Term Debt (excluding current portion) (dollars in millions)

		1978	*1977*
GM—U.S. dollars:			
8.05 percent notes	1985	$300.0	$ 300.0
8⅞ percent debentures	2005	300.0	300.0
Other	1980–2000	77.7	108.9
Consolidated subsidiaries:			
U.S. dollars	1980–86	231.9	256.0
British pounds	1987–92	30.6	59.5
Australian dollars	1980–83	34.5	34.2
Other currencies	1980–2004	10.0	16.7
Total		$984.7	$1,075.3
Less unamortized discount		5.8	7.1
Total*		$978.9	$1,068.2

* Maturities of long-term debt at December 31, 1978 for each of the five years through 1983 are (in millions): 1979—$137.8 (included in current liabilities); 1980—$53.5; 1981—$75.4; 1982—$72.2; and 1983—$50.8.

Note 12. Stockholders' Equity (dollars in millions except per share amounts)

	1978	1977
Capital stock:		
Preferred stock, without par value (authorized, 6 million shares), no change during the year:		
$5 series, stated value $100 per share, redeemable at $120 per share (issued, 1,875,366 shares; in treasury, 39,722 shares; outstanding, 1,835,644 shares)	$ 183.6	$ 183.6
$3.75 series, stated value $100 per share, redeemable at $100 per share (issued and outstanding, 1 million shares)	100.0	100.0
Common stock, $1⅔ par value (authorized, 500 million shares):		
Issued at beginning of the year (287,704,811 shares in 1978 and 287,674,147 shares in 1977)	479.5	479.4
Newly issued stock sold under provisions of the Stock Option Plans and Savings-Stock Purchase Program (365,029 shares in 1978 and 30,664 shares in 1977)	.6	.1
Issued at end of the year (288,069,840 shares in 1978 and 287,704,811 shares in 1977)	$ 480.1	$ 479.5
Total capital stock at end of the year	$ 763.7	$ 763.1
Capital surplus (principally additional paid-in capital):		
Balance at beginning of the year	772.1	770.3
Proceeds in excess of par value of newly issued common stock sold under provisions of the Stock Option Plans and Savings-Stock Purchase Program	19.9	1.8
Balance at end of the year	$ 792.0	$ 772.1
Net income retained for use in the business:		
Balance at beginning of the year	14,231.7	12,851.9
Net income	3,508.0	3,337.5
Total	$17,739.7	$16,189.4
Cash dividends:		
Preferred stock, $5.00 series, $5.00 per share	9.2	9.2
Preferred stock, $3.75 series, $3.75 per share	3.7	3.7
Common stock, $6.00 per share in 1978 and $6.80 per share in 1977	1,712.6	1,944.8
Total cash dividends	$ 1,725.5	$ 1,957.7
Balance at end of year	$16,014.2	$14,231.7
Total stockholders' equity	$17,569.9	$15,766.9

Note 13. Segment Reporting

General Motors Corporation is a highly vertically-integrated business operating primarily in a single industry consisting of the manufacture, assembly, and sale of automobiles, trucks, and related parts and accessories. Net sales, net income, total assets and average number of employees in the United States and in locations outside the United States for 1978 and 1977 are summarized here. Net income is after provisions for deferred income taxes on unremitted earnings of operations outside the United States, less available tax credits and deductions, and appropriate consolidating adjustments for the geographic areas set forth. Interarea sales are made at negotiated selling prices (dollars in millions).

1978	United States	Canada	Europe	Latin America	All Other	Total*
Net sales:						
Outside	$49,048.8	$3,362.9	$7,421.0	$1,784.5	$1,603.9	$63,221.1
Interarea	4,450.0	3,412.8	245.7	94.0	4.8	—
Total net sales	$53,498.8	$6,775.7	$7,666.7	$1,878.5	$1,608.7	$63.221.1
Net income (loss)	$ 3,073.2	$ 157.5	$ 376.2	($ 96.2)†	$ 15.6	$ 3,508.0
Net assets:						
Total current assets	$13,086.1	$ 947.4	$2,640.2	$ 788.4	$ 603.5	$17,999.5
Real estate, plants, and equipment	17,908.4	912.5	2,248.9	446.5	535.7	22,052.0
Accumulated depreciation	(10,821.2)	(545.7)	(1,472.2)	(211.1)	(388.6)	(13,438.8)
Special tools— less amortization	691.3	12.8	221.5	12.5	54.3	992.4
Other assets	3,395.9	16.7	216.0	106.0	71.2	2,993.2
Total assets	$24,260.5	$1,343.7	$3,854.4	$1,142.3	$ 876.1	$30,598.3
Loans payable	$ 95.1	$ —	$ 545.3	$ 310.3	$ 164.5	$ 1,115.2
Other current liabilities	6,635.6	469.6	1,315.6	324.8	189.8	8,935.4
Total current liabilities	$ 6,730.7	$ 469.6	$1,860.9	$ 635.1	$ 354.3	$10,050.6
Long-term debt	693.3	—	32.8	200.2	52.6	978.9
Other liabilities and deferred credits	1,387.0	149.6	634.6	22.4	47.5	1,998.9
Total liabilities	$ 8,811.0	$ 619.2	$2,528.3	$ 857.7	$ 454.4	$13,028.4
Allied accounts	$ 472.1	($ 123.3)	($ 106.4)	($ 67.4)	($ 175.0)	—
Net assets	$15,921.6	$ 601.2	$1,219.7	$ 217.2	$ 246.7	$17,569.9
Average number of employees (in thousands)	611	38	126	34	30	839

* After elimination of interarea transactions.
† Due principally to cost of liquidation of Argentine automotive operations.

1977	United States	Canada	Europe	Latin America	All Other	Total*
Net Sales:						
Outside	$43,514.3	$3,149.8	$5,573.3	$1,440.2	$1,283.7	$54,961.3
Interarea	4,036.7	2,594.1	150.0	39.0	5.6	—
Total net sales	$47,551.0	$5,743.9	$5,723.3	$1,479.2	$1,289.3	$54,961.3
Net income (loss)	$ 2,976.2	$ 116.7	$ 277.3	($ 4.9)	($ 19.9)	$ 3,337.5
Total assets	$20,452.7	$1,369.4	$2,892.1	$1,133.4	$ 891.8	$26.658.3
Net assets	$13,715.7	$ 605.8	$ 976.4	$ 134.9	$ 371.2	$15,766.9
Average number of employees (in thousands)	580	34	119	34	30	797

* After elimination of interarea transactions.

Note 14. Contingent Liabilities

There are various claims and pending actions against the corporation and its subsidiaries with respect to commercial matters, including warranties and product liability, governmental regulations including environmental and safety matters, civil rights, patent matters, taxes, and other matters arising out of the conduct of the business. Certain of these actions purport to be class actions, seeking damages in very large amounts. The amounts of liability on these claims and actions at December 31, 1978, were not determinable but, in the opinion of the management, the ultimate liability resulting will not materially affect the consolidated financial position or results of operations of the corporation and its consolidated subsidiaries.

ACCOUNTANTS' REPORT

Deloitte Haskins & Sells
Certified Public Accountants

1114 Avenue of the Americas
New York 10036

General Motors Corporation,
Its Directors and Stockholders:

February 14, 1979

We have examined the Consolidated Balance Sheet of General Motors Corporation and consolidated subsidiaries as of December 31, 1978, and 1977 and the related Statements of Consolidated Income and Changes in Consolidated Financial Position for the years then ended. Our examinations were made in accordance with generally accepted auditing standards and, accordingly, included such tests of the accounting records and such other auditing procedures as we considered necessary in the circumstances.

In our opinion, these financial statements present fairly the financial position of the companies at December 31, 1978, and 1977 and the results of their operations and the changes in their financial position for the years then ended, in conformity with generally accepted accounting principles applied on a consistent basis.

Deloitte Haskins & Sells

SUPPLEMENTARY INFORMATION

Lines of Business

General Motors is a highly integrated business engaged primarily in the manufacture, assembly and sale of automobiles, trucks, and related parts and accessories classified as automotive products. Substantially all of General Motors' products are marketed through retail dealers and through distributors and jobbers in the United States and Canada and through distributors and dealers overseas. To assist in the merchandising of General Motors products, General Motors Acceptance Corporation and its subsidiaries offer financial services and certain types of automobile insurance to dealers and customers. The amount of net sales attributable to U.S., Canadian, and overseas operations, and by class of product are summarized for the five years ended December 31, 1978 as follows:

	1978	1977	1976	1975	1974
Net Sales Attributable to:					
U.S. operations	$53,498.8	$47,551.0	$39,784.7	$28,917.8	$26,016.0
Canadian operations	6,775.7	5,743.9	5,263.0	4,263.3	3,693.7
Overseas operations	10,975.0	8,399.1	7,495.2	7,227.3	5,968.8
Elimination of interarea sales	(8,028.4)	(6,732.7)	(5,361.9)	(4,683.5)	(4,129.0)
Total	$63,221.1	$54,961.3	$47,181.0	$35,724.9	$31,549.5
Automotive products	$58,985.5	$51,429.5	$44,106.3	$32,536.0	$28,665.2
Nonautomotive products	$ 4,235.6	$ 3,531.8	$ 3,074.7	$ 3,188.9	$ 2,884.3

Because of the high degree of integration, substantial interdivisional and intercompany transfers of materials and services are made. Consequently, any determination of income by the classes of products or areas of operations shown above is necessarily arbitrary because of the allocation and reallocation of costs, including corporate costs, benefiting more than one division or product. Within these limitations, the corporation estimates that the percentage of net income attributable to the U.S., Canadian and overseas operations, and by class of product for the five years ended December 31, 1978, is as follows:

	1978	1977	1976	1975	1974
Percentage of Net Income Attributable to:					
U.S. operations	87%	89%	82%	85%	89%
Canadian operations	5	3	6	9	11
Overseas operations	8	8	12	6	—
Total	100%	100%	100%	100%	100%
Automotive products	96%	95%	97%	90%	92%
Nonautomotive products	4	5	3	10	8

Selected Quarterly Data
(dollars in millions)

	1978 Quarters				1977 Quarters			
	1st	2d	3d	4th	1st	2d	3d	4th
Net sales	$14,867.2	$17,026.1	$13,583.3	$17,744.5	$13,552.9	$14,880.6	$11,426.8	$15,101.0
Net income	869.6	1,106.3	527.9	1,004.2	903.4	1,096.6	402.0	935.5
Per share amounts								
Earned	3.03	3.86	1.84	3.51	3.14	3.82	1.40	3.26
Dividends	1.00	1.50	1.00	2.50	0.85	1.85	0.85	3.25
Stock price range*								
High	62.50	66.88	66.50	65.50	78.50	71.00	70.75	70.88
Low	57.13	59.25	58.00	53.75	66.38	65.88	64.75	61.13

* The principal market is the New York Stock Exchange and prices are based on the Composite Tape.

Replacement Cost Information

In compliance with regulations of the Securities and Exchange Commission, the corporation will include certain estimated replacement cost information for worldwide inventories, property, cost of sales, depreciation of plants and equipment, and amortization of special tools in its Form 10-K report to be filed with the Commission. Stockholders who wish to obtain such information should request a copy of Form 10-K in accordance with the instructions on the inside front cover.

1979 PUBLIC INTEREST REPORT

Additional information on GM operations in such areas as automotive emissions and fuel economy, automotive safety, industrial energy management, alternative auto engine developments, overseas operations, product quality and service, equal employment opportunities, and environmental control programs will be available in a supplemental booklet "1979 General Motors Public Interest Report" after April 1. Stockholders wishing to receive a copy of this booklet may write to: General Motors Corporation, Room 11-227, General Motors Building, Detroit, Michigan 48202.

Summary of Operations

($ millions except per share amounts)

	1978	1977	1976	1975	1974
Net sales	$63,221.1	$54,961.3	$47,181.0	$35,724.9	$31,549.5
Equity in earnings of nonconsolidated subsidiaries and associates, and other income—net	111.6	277.0	211.9	21.0	166.8
Cost of sales and selling, general, and administrative expenses, exclusive of items listed below	53,531.5	46,425.2	39,546.4	31,255.5	28,328.2
Depreciation of real estate, plants, and equipment	1,180.6	974.0	939.3	906.1	846.6
Amortization of special tools	1,855.7	1,406.4	1,296.9	1,180.1	858.4
Provision for the Bonus Plan	168.4	161.0	139.7	32.9	5.9
U.S., foreign, and other income taxes	3,088.5	2,934.2	2,567.8	1,118.2	727.1
Net income	$ 3,508.0	$ 3,337.5	$ 2,902.8	$ 1,253.1	$ 950.1
Dividends on preferred stocks	12.9	12.9	12.9	12.9	12.9
Earned on common stock	$ 3,495.1	$ 3,324.6	$ 2,889.9	$ 1,240.2	$ 937.2
Dividends on common stock	1,712.6	1,944.8	1,590.5	688.4	973.3
Net income retained in the year	$ 1,782.5	$ 1,379.8	$ 1,299.4	$ 551.8	($ 36.1)
Net income					
Percent of sales	5.5%	6.1%	6.2%	3.5%	3.0%
Percent of stockholders' equity	20.0%	21.2%	20.2%	9.6%	7.6%
Earned on common stock—per share	$ 12.24	$ 11.62	$ 10.08	$ 4.32	$ 3.27
Dividends on common stock—per share	6.00	6.80	5.55	2.40	3.40
Net income retained in the year—per share	$ 6.24	$ 4.82	$ 4.53	$ 1.92	($ 0.13)
Average shares of common stock outstanding (in millions)	285.5	286.1	286.7	286.8	286.3
Dividends on capital stock as a percentage of net income	49.2%	58.7%	55.2%	56.0%	103.8%

Note: Management's discussion and analysis of operations for 1978, 1977, and 1976; the impact of inflation in the Letter to Stockholders; and the Financial Review section are discussed elsewhere. Certain amounts have been reclassified to conform with classifications for 1978.

Additional Statistics ($ millions except per share amounts):

Expenditures for real estate, plants, and equipment	$ 2,737.8	$ 1,870.9	$ 998.9	$ 1,200.9	$ 1,458.5
Expenditures for special tools	$ 1,826.7	$ 1,775.8	$ 1,308.4	$ 1,035.6	$ 1,095.6
Worldwide average number of employees (in thousands)	839	797	748	681	734
Worldwide payrolls (including GMAC)	$17,195.5	$15,270.8	$12,908.5	$10,028.4	$ 9,771.4
Common and preferred stockholders					
Number (in thousands)	1,268	1,245	1,251	1,323	1,348
Equity	$17,569.9	$15,766.9	$14,385.2	$13,082.4	$12,530.6
Book value per share of common stock	$ 60.01	$ 53.82	$ 49.02	$ 44.50	$ 42.58
Working capital	$ 7,948.9	$ 7,630.3	$ 7,556.6	$ 6,394.0	$ 5,541.9

Worldwide Factory Sales of Cars and Trucks
(units in thousands):

Manufactured in the United States					
Passenger cars	5,292	5,259	4,883	3,680	3,592
Trucks and coaches	1,586	1,436	1,335	978	1,086
Total manufactured in the United States	6,878	6,695	6,218	4,658	4,678
Manufactured in Canada	853	777	715	595	642
Manufactured overseas*	1,751	1,596	1,635	1,376	1,370
Total factory sales of cars and trucks—all sources	9,482	9,068	8,568	6,629	6,690

* Includes units manufactured by Isuzu Motors Limited under contract for and marketed by GM.

Case 11–2

A. J. Johnson, Inc.

"To purchase or to pool—that is the question."

The following conversation took place on July 8, 1980, between Martha Cummings, vice president of finance, and Robert Sterling, controller for A. J. Johnson, Inc.

Cummings: Bob, I just heard from A. J. (A. J. Johnson, president of A. J. Johnson, Inc.) regarding the negotiations with Research Products, Inc. Research [a privately owned company] has agreed to accept our take-over bid. The price is $7 million. Their common stockholders will tender all their common stock in exchange for approximately 100,000 shares of our common stock provided our current price of $70 a share holds up through December 31, 1980, which is our tentative closing date. If the price of our stock drops below $70, we will have to issue additional stock to make up any price differential. We have the option at the closing of substituting cash for up to 11 percent of the $7 million.

A. J. asked me whether we should record the acquisition as a purchase or a pool [pooling of interest] and let her know later in the week. Her present intention is to run Research as a separate entity rather than merge it into A. J. Johnson, Inc. I'd like you to prepare an analysis and recommendation for me by tomorrow morning.

You should look at our file on the proposed acquisition which is on my desk. It contains pro forma [as if] balance sheets for both companies as of December 31, 1980 (Exhibit 1), and projected income and reconciliation of retained earnings statements for 1980 (Exhibit 2); a copy of *APB Opinion No. 16*, which lists the requirements for purchasing and pooling (Exhibit 3); and a memo written by A. J. (Exhibit 4) on what she considers the underlying value of Research's assets.

Required:

Prepare the analysis requested by Martha Cummings, assuming the closing takes place on December 31, 1980, and that A. J. Johnson, Inc.'s common is $70 on that date. It should include:

1. Pro forma consolidated balance sheet on December 31, 1980, assuming the acquisition is treated (a) as a pooling of interest or (b) as a purchase.[1]
2. Projected consolidated income statement for 1980, assuming the acquisition is treated (a) as a pooling of interest or (b) as a purchase.[2]
3. Calculate 1980 pro forma earnings per share for the consolidated entity, assuming the acquisition is treated (a) as a pooling of interest or (b) as a purchase.[3]
4. What would be the impact on 1981 earnings per share of the sale on January 2, 1981, of one half of the patents for $1.5 million, assuming that the acquisition is treated (a) as a pooling of interest (assume amortization of patents of $88,000 per year) or (b) as a purchase (amortization based on economic life at date of purchase).
5. Which method do you recommend?

EXHIBIT 1
Summary Pro Forma Balance Sheets—December 31, 1980
(000 omitted)

	A. J. Johnson, Inc. [*]	*Research Products, Inc.*
Current assets	$ 8,272	$1,350
Buildings and equipment (net of depreciation)	7,500	1,500
Patents	—	520
	$15,772	$3,370
Current liabilities	$ 1,000	$ 140
Common stock—$10 par value	4,000	—
Common stock—no par value	—	1,000
Paid-in capital (excess paid in over par value)	3,300	1,500
Retained earnings	7,472	730
	$15,772	$3,370

[*] Does not include acquisition of Research Products, Inc.

[1-3] Treatment as a purchase assumes cash is paid for 11 percent of the $7 million purchase price and 89,000 shares of A. J. Johnson, Inc., are issued for the balance of the $7 million.

EXHIBIT 2
Projected Income Statements and Reconciliation of Retained Earnings—1980
(000 omitted)

	A. J. Johnson, Inc.*	Research Products, Inc.
Sales	$60,000	$10,500
Expenses		
Cost of goods sold	$43,500	$ 4,300
Depreciation	400	92
Amortization of patents	—	88
Selling and general administrative expenses	10,000	1,200
	$53,900	$ 5,680
Income (loss) before income taxes	$ 6,100	$ 4,820
Income taxes	2,928	2,314
Net income	$ 3,172	$ 2,506
Retained earnings (deficit)—1/1/80	4,300	(1,776)
Retained earnings—12/31/80	$ 7,472	$ 730

* Does not include any income attributable to the acquisition of Research Products, Inc. There are no intracompany transactions projected for 1980.

EXHIBIT 3
Excerpts from *APB Opinion No. 16**

SUMMARY

Problem

1. A business combination occurs when a corporation and one or more incorporated or unincorporated businesses are brought together into one accounting entity. The single entity carries on the activities of the previously separate, independent enterprises.

2. Two methods of accounting for business combinations— "purchase" and "pooling of interests"—have been accepted in practice and supported in pronouncements of the Board and its predecessor, the Committee on Accounting Procedure. The accounting treatment of a combination may affect significantly the reported financial position and net income of the combined corporation for prior, current, and future periods.

3. The Director of Accounting Research of the American Institute of Certified Public Accountants has published two studies on accounting

EXHIBIT 3 (continued)

for business combinations and the related goodwill: Accounting Research Study No. 5, *A Critical Study of Accounting for Business Combinations*, by Arthur R. Wyatt and Accounting Research Study No. 10, *Accounting for Goodwill*, by George R. Catlett and Norman O. Olson.[1] The two studies describe the origin and development of the purchase and pooling of interests methods of accounting for business combinations. The studies also cite the supporting authoritative pronouncements and their influences on accounting practices and evaluate the effects of practices on financial reporting.

Scope and Effect of Opinion

4. The Board has considered the conclusions and recommendations of Accounting Research Studies Nos. 5 and 10, the discussions of the need for and appropriateness of the two accepted methods of accounting for business combinations, and proposals for alternative accounting methods. It has also observed the present treatments of combinations in various forms and under differing conditions. The Board expresses in this Opinion its conclusions on accounting for business combinations.

5. This Opinion covers the combination of a corporation and one or more incorporated or unincorporated businesses; both incorporated and unincorporated enterprises are referred to in this Opinion as companies. The conclusions of this Opinion apply equally to business combinations in which one or more companies become subsidiary corporations, one company transfers its net assets to another, and each company transfers its net assets to a newly formed corporation. The acquisition of some or all of the stock held by minority stockholders of a subsidiary is not a business combination, but paragraph 43 of this Opinion specifies the applicable method of accounting. The term business combination in this Opinion excludes a transfer by a corporation of its net assets to a newly formed substitute corporate entity chartered by the existing corporation and a transfer of net assets or exchange of shares between companies under common control (control is described in paragraph 2 of *ARB No. 51*), such as between a parent corporation and its subsidiary or between two subsidiary corporations of the same parent. This Opinion does not specifically discuss the combination of a corporation and one or more unincorporated businesses or of two or more unincorporated businesses, but its provisions should be applied as a general guide.

6. This Opinion applies to regulated companies in accordance with the provisions of the Addendum to *APB Opinion No. 2, Accounting for the "Investment Credit,"* 1962.

---

[1] Accounting research studies are not pronouncements of the Board or of the Institute but are published for the purpose of stimulating discussion in important accounting matters.

EXHIBIT 3 (continued) ────────────────────────────

7. The conclusions of this Opinion modify previous views of the Board and its predecessor committee. This Opinion therefore supersedes the following Accounting Research Bulletins (ARB) and Opinions of the Accounting Principles Board (APB):

ARB No. 43, Chapter 5, *Intangible Assets*, paragraph 10.
ARB No. 48, Business Combinations.
ARB No. 51, Consolidated Financial Statements, paragraphs 7 and 8.
. . .
APB Opinion No. 6, Status of Accounting Research Bulletins, paragraphs 12 c and—

APB Opinion No. 10, Omnibus Opinion—1966, paragraph 5. Since this Opinion supersedes those existing pronouncements, paragraph 87 of this Opinion should be substituted for the reference to *ARB No. 51* in paragraph 49 of *APB Opinion No. 11*.

Conclusions

8. The Board concludes that the purchase method and the pooling of interests method are both acceptable in accounting for business combinations, although not as alternatives in accounting for the same business combination. A business combination which meets specified conditions requires accounting by the pooling of interests method. A new basis of accounting is not permitted for a combination that meets the specified conditions, and the assets and liabilities of the combining companies are combined at their recorded amounts. All other business combinations should be accounted for as an acquisition of one or more companies by a corporation. The cost to an acquiring corporation of an entire acquired company should be determined by the principles of accounting for the acquisition of an asset. That cost should then be allocated to the identifiable individual assets acquired and liabilities assumed based on their fair values; the unallocated cost should be recorded as goodwill.

BACKGROUND

Present Accounting and Its Development

Development of Two Methods

9. Most business combinations before World War II were classified either as a "merger," the acquisition of one company by another, or as a "consolidation," the formation of a new corporation. Accounting for both types of combinations generally followed traditional principles for the acquisition of assets or issuance of shares of stock. The accounting adopted by some new corporations was viewed as a precedent for

EXHIBIT 3 (continued)

the combining of retained earnings and of amounts of net assets recorded by predecessor corporations as retained earnings and net assets of a new entity.

10. Emphasis shifted after World War II from the legal form of the combination to distinctions between "a continuance of the former ownership or a new ownership" (*ARB No. 40,* paragraph 1). New ownership was accounted for as a purchase; continuing ownership was accounted for as a pooling of interests. Carrying forward the stockholders' equity, including retained earnings, of the constituents became an integral part of the pooling of interests method. Significant differences between the purchase and pooling of interests methods accepted today are in the amounts ascribed to assets and liabilities at the time of combination and income reported for the combined enterprise.

Purchase Method[2]

11. The purchase method accounts for a business combination as the acquisition of one company by another. The acquiring corporation records at its cost the acquired assets less liabilities assumed. A difference between the cost of an acquired company and the sum of the fair values of tangible and identifiable intangible assets less liabilities is recorded as goodwill. The reported income of an acquiring corporation includes the operations of the acquired company after acquisition, based on the cost to the acquiring corporation.

Pooling of Interests Method

12. The pooling of interests method accounts for a business combination as the uniting of the ownership interests of two or more companies by exchange of equity securities. No acquisition is recognized because the combination is accomplished without disbursing resources of the constituents. Ownership interests continue and the former bases of accounting are retained. The recorded assets and liabilities of the constituents are carried forward to the combined corporation at their recorded amounts. Income of the combined corporation includes income of the constituents for the entire fiscal period in which the combination occurs. The reported income of the constituents for prior periods is combined and restated as income of the combined corporation.

---

[2] This Opinion refers to the "purchase method of accounting" for a business combination because the term is widely used and generally understood. However, the more inclusive terms "acquire" (to come into possession of) and "acquisition" are generally used to describe transactions rather than the more narrow term "purchase" (to acquire by the payment of money or its equivalent). The broader terms clearly encompass obtaining assets by issuing stock as well as by disbursing cash and thus avoid the confusion that results from describing a stock transaction as a "purchase." This Opinion does not describe a business combination accounted for by the pooling of interests method as an "acquisition" because the meaning of the word is inconsistent with the method of accounting.

EXHIBIT 3 (continued)

13. The original concept of pooling of interests as a fusion of equity interests was modified in practice as use of the method expanded.[3] The method was first applied in accounting for combinations of affiliated corporations and then extended to some combinations of unrelated corporate ownership interests of comparable size. The method was later accepted for most business combinations in which common stock was issued. New and complex securities have been issued in recent business combinations, and some combinations agreements provide for additional securities to be issued later depending on specified events or circumstances. Most of the resulting combinations are accounted for as poolings of interests. Some combinations effected by both disbursing cash and issuing securities are now accounted for as a "part purchase, part pooling."

14. Some accountants believe that the pooling of interests method is the only acceptable method for a combination which meets the requirements for pooling. Others interpret the existing pronouncements on accounting for business combinations to mean that a combination which meets the criteria for a pooling of interests may alternatively be accounted for as a purchase.

Appraisal of Accepted Methods of Accounting

15. The pooling of interests method of accounting is applied only to business combinations effected by an exchange of stock and not to those involving primarily cash, other assets, or liabilities. Applying the purchase method of accounting to business combinations effected by paying cash, distributing other assets, or incurring liabilities is not challenged. Thus, those business combinations effected primarily by an exchange of equity securities present a question of choice between the two accounting methods.

16. The significantly different results of applying the purchase and pooling of interests methods of accounting to a combination effected by an exchange of stock stem from distinct views of the nature of the transaction itself. Those who endorse the pooling of interests method believe that an exchange of stock to effect a business combination is in substance a transaction between the combining stockholder groups and does not involve the corporate entities. The transaction therefore neither requires nor justifies establishing a new basis of accountability for the assets of the combined corporation. Those who endorse the purchase method believe that the transaction is an issue of stock by a corporation for consideration received from those who become stockholders by the transaction. The consideration received is established by bargaining between independent parties, and the acquiring corpo-

---

[3] The origin, development, and application of the pooling of interests method of accounting are traced in Accounting Research Study No. 5 and summarized in Accounting Research Study No. 10.

EXHIBIT 3 (*continued*) _____

ration accounts for the additional assets at their bargained—that is, current—values.

Purchase Method

17. The more important arguments expressing the advantages and disadvantages of the purchase method and some of the practical difficulties experienced in implementing it are summarized in paragraphs 18 to 26.

18. *An acquisition.* Those who favor the purchase method of accounting believe that one corporation acquires another company in almost every business combination. The acquisition of one company by another and the identities of the acquiring and acquired companies are usually obvious. Generally, one company in a business combination is clearly the dominant and continuing entity and one or more other companies cease to control their own assets and operations because control passes to the acquiring corporation.

19. *A bargained transaction.* Proponents of purchase accounting hold that a business combination is a significant economic event which results from bargaining between independent parties. Each party bargains on the basis of his assessment of the current status and future prospects of each constituent as a separate enterprise and as a contributor to the proposed combined enterprise. The agreed terms of combination recognize primarily the bargained values and only secondarily the costs of assets and liabilities carried by the constituents. In fact, the recorded costs are not always known by the other bargaining party.

20. Accounting by the purchase method is essentially the same whether the business combination is effected by distributing assets, incurring liabilities, or issuing stock because issuing stock is considered an economic event as significant as distributing assets or incurring liabilities. A corporation must ascertain that the consideration it receives for stock issued is fair, just as it must ascertain that fair value is received for cash disbursed. Recipients of the stock similarly appraise the fairness of the transaction. Thus, a business combination is a bargained transaction regardless of the nature of the consideration.

21. *Reporting economic substance.* The purchase method adheres to traditional principles of accounting for the acquisition of assets. Those who support the purchase method of accounting for business combinations effected by issuing stock believe that an acquiring corporation accounts for the economic substance of the transaction by applying those principles and by recording:

a. All assets and liabilities which comprise the bargained cost of an acquired company, not merely those items previously shown in the financial statements of an acquired company.

b. The bargained costs of assets acquired less liabilities assumed, not the costs to a previous owner.

EXHIBIT 3 (continued)

c. The fair value of the consideration received for stock issued, not the equity shown in the financial statements of an acquired company.

d. Retained earnings from its operations, not a fusion of its retained earnings and previous earnings of an acquired company.

e. Expenses and net income after an acquisition computed on the bargained cost of acquired assets less assumed liabilities, not on the costs to a previous owner.

22. *Defects attributed to purchase method.* Applying the purchase method to business combinations effected primarily by issuing stock may entail difficulties in measuring the cost of an acquired company if neither the fair value of the consideration given nor the fair value of the property acquired is clearly evident. Measuring fair values of assets acquired is complicated by the presence of intangible assets or other assets which do not have discernible market prices. Goodwill and other unidentifiable intangible assets are difficult to value directly, and measuring assets acquired for stock is easier if the fair value of the stock issued is determinable. The excess of the value of stock issued over the sum of the fair values of the tangible and identifiable intangible assets acquired less liabilities assumed indicates the value of acquired unidentified intangible assets (usually called goodwill).

23. However, the fair value of stock issued is not always objectively determinable. A market price may not be available for a newly issued security or for securities of a closely held corporation. Even an available quoted market price may not always be a reliable indicator of fair value of consideration received because the number of shares issued is relatively large, the market for the security is thin, the stock price is volatile, or other uncertainties influence the quoted price. Further, the determinable value of one security may not necessarily indicate the fair value of another similar, but not identical, security because their differences affect the value—for example, the absence of registration or an agreement which restricts a holder's ability to sell a security may significantly affect its value.

24. Those who oppose applying the purchase method to some or most business combinations effected by stock also challenge the theoretical merits of the method. They contend that the goodwill acquired is stated only by coincidence at the value which would be determined by direct valuation. The weakness is attributed not to measurement difficulties (direct valuation of goodwill is assumed) but to the basis underlying an exchange of shares of stock. Bargaining in that type of transaction is normally based on the market prices of the equity securities. Market prices of the securities exchanged are more likely to be influenced by anticipated earning capacities of the companies than by evaluations of individual assets. The number of shares of stock issued in a business combination is thus influenced by values attributed to goodwill of the acquirer as well as goodwill of the acquired company.

EXHIBIT 3 (*continued*) _____

Since the terms are based on the market prices of both stocks exchanged, measuring the cost of an acquired company by the market price of the stock issued may result in recording acquired goodwill at more or less than its value determined directly.

25. A related argument is that the purchase method is improper accounting for a business combination in which a relatively large number of shares of stock is issued because it records the goodwill and fair values of only the acquired company. Critics of purchase accounting say that each group of stockholders of two publicly held and actively traded companies evaluates the other stock, and the exchange ratio for stock issued is often predicated on relative market values. The stockholders and management of each company evaluate the goodwill and fair values of the other. Purchase accounting is thus viewed as illogical because it records goodwill and values of only one side of the transaction. Those who support this view prefer that assets and liabilities of both companies be combined at existing recorded amounts, but if one side is to be stated at fair values, they believe that both sides should be recorded at fair values.

26. Criticism of the purchase method is directed not only to the theoretical and practical problems of measuring goodwill in combinations effected primarily by stock pooling of interests method believe that a departure from the traditional principles is justified only if evidence shows that financial statements prepared according to other principles better reflect the economic significance of a combination. In their opinion, the characteristics of a business combination do not justify departing from traditional principles of accounting to accommodate the pooling of interests method.

OPINION

Applicability of Accounting Methods

42. The Board finds merit in both the purchase and pooling of interests methods of accounting for business combinations and accepts neither method to the exclusion of the other. The arguments in favor of the purchase method of accounting are more persuasive if cash or other assets are distributed or liabilities are incurred to effect a combination, but arguments in favor of the pooling of interests method of accounting are more persuasive if voting common stock is issued to effect a combination of common stock interests. Therefore, the Board concludes that some business combinations should be accounted for by the purchase method and other combinations should be accounted for by the pooling of interests method.

43. The Board also concludes that the two methods are not alternatives in accounting for the same business combination. A single method should be applied to an entire combination; the practice now

EXHIBIT 3 (continued)

known as part-purchase, part-pooling is not acceptable. The acquisition after the effective date of this Opinion of some or all of the stock held by minority stockholders of a subsidiary—whether acquired by the parent, the subsidiary itself, or another affiliate—should be accounted for by the purchase method rather than by the pooling of interests method.

44. The Board believes that accounting for business combinations will be improved significantly by specifying the circumstances in which each method should be applied and the procedures which should be followed in applying each method. The distinctive conditions which require pooling of interests accounting are described in paragraphs 45 to 48, and combinations involving all of those conditions should be accounted for as described in paragraphs 50 to 65. All other business combinations should be treated as the acquisition of one company by another and accounted for by the purchase method as described in paragraphs 66 to 96.

Conditions for Pooling of Interests Method

45. The pooling of interests method of accounting is intended to present as a single interest two or more common stockholder interests which were previously independent and the combined rights and risks represented by those interests. That method shows that stockholder groups neither withdraw nor invest assets but in effect exchange voting common stock in a ratio that determines their respective interests in the combined corporation. Some business combinations have those features. A business combination which meets *all* of the conditions specified and explained in paragraphs 46 to 48 should be accounted for by the pooling of interests method. The conditions are classified by (1) attributes of the combining companies, (2) manner of combining interests, and (3) absence of planned transactions.

46. *Combining companies.* Certain attributes of combining companies indicate that independent ownership interests are combined in their entirety to continue previously separate operations. Combining virtually all of existing common stock interests avoids combining only selected assets, operations, or ownership interests, any of which is more akin to disposing of and acquiring interests than to sharing risks and rights. It also avoids combining interests that are already related by substantial intercorporate investments.

The two conditions in this paragraph define essential attributes of combining companies.

a. Each of the combining companies is autonomous and has not been a subsidiary or division of another corporation within two years before the plan of combination is initiated.

A plan of combination is initiated on the earlier of (1) the date that the major terms of a plan, including the ratio of exchange of stock, are

EXHIBIT 3 (*continued*) ───────────────────────────────

announced publicly or otherwise formally made known to the stock-holders of any one of the combining companies or (2) the date that stockholders of a combining company are notified in writing of an exchange offer. Therefore, a plan of combination is often initiated even though consummation is subject to the approval of stockholders and others.

A new company incorporated within the preceding two years meets this condition unless the company is successor to a part of a company or to a company that is otherwise not autonomous for this condition. A wholly owned subsidiary company which distributes voting common stock of its parent corporation to effect the combination is also considered an autonomous company provided the parent corporation would have met all conditions in paragraphs 46 to 48 had the parent corporation issued its stock directly to effect the combination.

Divestiture of assets to comply with an order of a governmental authority or judicial body results in an exception to the terms of this condition. Either a subsidiary divested under an order or a new company which acquires assets disposed of under an order is therefore autonomous for this condition.

b. Each of the combining companies is independent of the other combining companies.

This condition means that at the dates the plan of combination is initiated and consummated the combining companies hold as intercorporate investments no more than 10 percent in total of the outstanding voting common stock of any combining company.[4] For the percentage computation, intercorporate investments exclude voting common stock that is acquired after the date the plan of combination is initiated in exchange for the voting common stock issued to effect the combination. Investments of 10 percent or less are explained in paragraph 47-b.

47. *Combining of interests.* The combining of existing voting common stock interests by the exchange of stock is the essence of a business combination accounted for by the pooling of interests method. The separate stockholder interests lose their identities and all share mutually in the combined risks and rights. Exchanges of common stock that alter relative voting rights, that result in preferential claims to distributions of profits or assets for some common stockholder groups, or that leave significant minority interests in combining companies are incompatible with the idea of mutual sharing. Similarly, acquisitions of common stock for assets or debt, reacquisitions of outstanding stock for the purpose of exchanging it in a business combination, and other transactions that reduce the common stock interests are contrary to the

---

[4] An exception for common stock held on October 31, 1970, is explained in paragraph 99.

EXHIBIT 3 (continued) ────────────────────────────────

idea of combining existing stockholder interests. The seven conditions in this paragraph relate to the exchange to effect the combination.

a. The combination is effected in a single transaction or is completed in accordance with a specific plan within one year after the plan is initiated.

Altering the terms of exchange of stock constitutes initiation of a new plan of combination unless earlier exchanges of stock are adjusted to the new terms.[5]

A business combination completed in more than one year from the date the plan is initiated meets this condition if the delay is beyond the control of the combining companies because proceedings of a governmental authority or litigation prevent completing the combination.

b. A corporation offers and issues only common stock with rights identical to those of the majority of its outstanding voting common stock in exchange for substantially all of the voting common stock interest of another company at the date the plan of combination is consummated.[6]

The plan to issue voting common stock in exchange for voting common stock may include, within limits, provisions to distribute cash or other consideration for fractional shares, for shares held by dissenting stockholders and the like, but may not include a pro rata distribution of cash or other consideration.

Substantially all of the voting common stock means 90 percent or more for this condition. That is, after the date the plan of combination is initiated, one of the combining companies (issuing corporation) issues voting common stock in exchange for at least 90 percent of the voting common stock of another combining company that is outstanding at the date the combination is consummated. The number of shares exchanged therefore excludes those shares of the combining company (1) acquired before and held by the issuing corporation and its subsidiaries at the date the plan of combination is initiated, regardless of the form of consideration,[7] (2) acquired by the issuing corporation and its subsidiaries after the date the plan of combination is initiated other

---

[5] However, an adjustment after the effective date of this Opinion in the terms of exchange in a plan of combination initiated before and consummated after the effective date always constitutes initiation of a new plan. The one year specified in this condition is measured, therefore, from the date of adjustment of terms and all other conditions are evaluated for the new plan. (Paragraph 97 describes the application of this Opinion to a plan of combination initiated before the effective date of this Opinion and consummated later in accordance with the terms of exchange prevailing on the effective date.)

[6] A class of stock that has voting control of a corporation is the majority class.

[7] An exception for common stock held on October 31, 1970 is explained in paragraph 99.

EXHIBIT 3 (continued)

than by issuing its own voting common stock, and (3) outstanding after the date the combination is consummated.

An investment in stock of the issuing corporation held by a combining company may prevent a combination from meeting this condition even though the investment of the combining company is not more than 10 percent of the outstanding stock of the issuing corporation (paragraph 46-b). An investment in stock of the issuing corporation by another combining company is the same in a mutual exchange as an investment by the issuing corporation in stock of the other combining company—the choice of issuing corporation is essentially a matter of convenience. An investment in stock of the issuing corporation must be expressed as an equivalent number of shares of the investor combining company because the measure of percent of shares exchanged is in terms of shares of stock of the investor company. An investment in 10 percent or less of the outstanding voting common stock of the issuing corporation affects the measure of percent of shares exchanged in the combination as follows:

> The number of shares of voting common stock of the issuing corporation held by the investor combining company at the date the plan is initiated plus shares it acquired after that date are restated as an equivalent number of shares of voting common stock of the investor combining company based on the ratio of exchange of stock in the combination.
>
> The equivalent number of shares is deducted from the number of shares of voting common stock of the investor combining company exchanged for voting common stock of the issuing corporation as part of the plan of combination.
>
> The reduced number of shares is considered the number exchanged and is compared with 90 percent of the outstanding voting common stock of the investor combining company at the date the plan is consummated to determine whether the terms of condition 47-b are met.

Since the number of shares of voting common stock exchange is reduced for an intercorporate investment in voting common stock of the issuing corporation, the terms of condition 47-b may not be met even though 90 percent or more of the outstanding common stock of a combining company is exchanged to effect a combination.

A combination of more than two companies is evaluated essentially the same as a combination of two companies. The percent of voting common stock exchanged is measured separately for each combining company, and condition 47-b is met if 90 percent or more of the voting common stock of each of the several combining companies is exchanged for voting common stock of the issuing corporation. The number of shares exchanged for stock of the issuing corporation includes only shares exchanged by stockholders other than the several combin-

EXHIBIT 3 (*continued*) _____

ing companies themselves. Thus, intercorporate investments in combining companies are included in the number of shares of stock outstanding but are excluded from the number of shares of stock exchanged to effect the combination.

A new corporation formed to issue its stock to effect the combination of two or more companies meets condition 47-b if (1) the number of shares of each company exchanged to effect the combination is not less than 90 percent of its voting common stock outstanding at the date the combination is consummated and (2) condition 47-b would have been met had any one of the combining companies issued its stock to effect the combination on essentially the same basis.

Condition 47-b relates to issuing common stock for the common stock interests in another company. Hence, a corporation issuing stock to effect the combination may assume the debt securities of the other company or may exchange substantially identical securities or voting common stock for other outstanding equity and debt securities of the other combining company. An issuing corporation may also distribute cash to holders of debt and equity securities that either are callable or redeemable and may retire those securities. However, the issuing corporation may exchange only voting common stock for outstanding equity and debt securities of the other combining company that have been issued in exchange for voting common stock of that company during a period beginning two years preceding the date the combination is initiated.

A transfer of the net assets of a combining company to effect a business combination satisfies condition 47-b provided all net assets of the company at the date the plan is consummated are transferred in exchange for stock of the issuing corporation. However, the combining company may retain temporarily cash, receivables, or marketable securities to settle liabilities, contingencies, or items in dispute if the plan provides that the assets remaining after settlement are to be transferred to the corporation issuing the stock to effect the combination. Only voting common stock may be issued to effect the combination unless both voting common stock and other stock of the other combining company are outstanding at the date the plan is consummated. The combination may then be effected by issuing all voting common stock or by issuing voting common and other stock in the same proportions as the outstanding voting common and other stock of the other combining company. An investment in 10 percent or less of the outstanding voting common stock of a combining company held by another combining company requires special computations to evaluate condition 47-b. The computations and comparisons are in terms of the voting common stock of the issuing corporation and involve:

Stock issued for common stock interest. The total number of shares of voting common stock issued for all of the assets is

EXHIBIT 3 (continued)

divided between those applicable to outstanding voting common stock and those applicable to other outstanding stock, if any, of the combining company which transfers assets (transferor company).[8]

Reduction for intercorporate investments. The number of issued shares of voting common stock applicable to the voting common stock interests of the transferor combining company is reduced by the sum of (1) the number of shares of voting common stock of the issuing corporation held by the transferor combining company at the date the plan of combination is initiated plus shares it acquired after that date and (2) the number of shares of voting common stock of the transferor combining company held by the issuing corporation at the date the plan of combination is initiated plus shares it acquired after that date. The shares of the transferor combining company are restated as the equivalent number of shares of voting common stock of the issuing corporation for this purpose. Restatement is based on the ratio of the number of shares of voting common stock of the transferor combining company which are outstanding at the date the plan is consummated to the number of issued shares of voting common stock applicable to the voting common stock interests.

Comparison with 90 percent. The reduced number of shares of stock issued is compared with 90 percent of the issued number of shares of voting common stock applicable to voting common stock interests to determine if the transfer of assets meets the terms of condition 47-b.

c. None of the combining companies changes the equity interest of the voting common stock in contemplation of effecting the combination either within two years before the plan of combination is initiated or between the dates the combination is initiated and consummated; changes in contemplation of effecting the combination may include distributions to stockholders and additional issuances, exchanges, and retirements of securities.

Distributions to stockholders which are no greater than normal dividends are not changes for this condition. Normality of dividends is determined in relation to earnings during the period and to the previous dividend policy and record. Dividend distributions on stock of a combining company that are equivalent to normal dividends on the stock to be issued in exchange in the combination are considered normal for this condition.

d. Each of the combining companies reacquires shares of voting common stock only for purposes other than business combinations, and

[8] Including (for this computation) stock of the issuing corporation held by the transferor combining company.

EXHIBIT 3 (continued)

no company reacquires more than a normal number of shares between the dates the plan of combination is initiated and consummated.

Treasury stock acquired for purposes other than business combinations includes shares for stock option and compensation plans and other recurring distributions provided a systematic pattern of reacquisitions is established at least two years before the plan of combination is initiated. A systematic pattern of reacquisitions may be established for less than two years if it coincides with the adoption of a new stock option or compensation plan. The normal number of shares of voting common stock reacquired is determined by the pattern of reacquisitions of stock before the plan of combination is initiated.

Acquisitions by other combining companies of voting common stock of the issuing corporation after the date the plan of combination is initiated are essentially the same as if the issuing corporation reacquired its own common stock.

e. The ratio of the interest of an individual common stockholder to those of other common stockholders in a combining company remains the same as a result of the exchange of stock to effect the combination.

This condition means that each individual common stockholder who exchanges his stock receives a voting common stock interest exactly in proportion to his relative voting common stock interest before the combination is effected. Thus no common stockholder is denied or surrenders his potential share of a voting common stock interest in a combined corporation.

f. The voting rights to which the common stock ownership interests in the resulting combined corporation are entitled are exercisable by the stockholders; the stockholders are neither deprived of nor restricted in exercising those rights for a period.

This condition is not met, for example, if shares of common stock issued to effect the combination are transferred to a voting trust.

g. The combination is resolved at the date the plan is consummated and no provisions of the plan relating to the issue of securities or other consideration are pending.

This condition means that (1) the combined corporation does not agree to contingently issue additional shares of stock or distribute other consideration at a later date to the former stockholders of a combining company of (2) the combined corporation does not issue or distribute to an escrow agent common stock or other consideration which is to be either transferred to common stockholders or returned to the corporation at the time the contingency is resolved.

EXHIBIT 3 (continued) ─────────────────────────────────────

An agreement may provide, however, that the number of shares of common stock issued to effect the combination may be revised for the later settlement of a contingency at a different amount than that recorded by a combining company.

48. *Absence of planned transactions.* Some transactions after a combination is consummated are inconsistent with the combining of entire existing interests of common stockholders. Including those transactions in the negotiations and terms of the combination, either explicitly or by intent, counteracts the effect of combining stockholder interests. The three conditions in this paragraph relate to certain future transactions.

a. The combined corporation does not agree directly or indirectly to retire or reacquire all or part of the common stock issued to effect the combination.

b. The combined corporation does not enter into other financial arrangements for the benefit of the former stockholders of a combining company, such as a guaranty of loans secured by stock issued in the combination, which in effect negates the exchange of equity securities.

c. The combined corporation does not intend or plan to dispose of a significant part of the assets of the combining companies within two years after the combination other than disposals in the ordinary course of business of the formerly separate companies and to eliminate duplicate facilities or excess capacity.

Subsidiary Corporation

49. Dissolution of a combining company is not a condition for applying the pooling of interests method of accounting for a business combination. One or more combining companies may be subsidiaries of the issuing corporation after the combination is consummated if the other conditions are met.

Application of Pooling of Interests Method

50. A business combination which meets all of the conditions in paragraphs 45 to 48 should be accounted for by the pooling of interests method. Appropriate procedures are described in paragraphs 51 to 65.

Assets and Liabilities Combined

51. The recorded assets and liabilities of the separate companies generally become the recorded assets and liabilities of the combined corporation. The combined corporation therefore recognizes those assets and liabilities recorded in conformity with generally accepted accounting principles by the separate companies at the date the combination is consummated.

EXHIBIT 3 (*continued*) ───────────────────────

52. The combined corporation records the historical cost based amounts of the assets and liabilities of the separate companies because the existing basis of accounting continues. However, the separate companies may have recorded assets and liabilities under differing methods of accounting and the amounts may be adjusted to the same basis of accounting if the change would otherwise have been appropriate for the separate company. A change in accounting method to conform the individual methods should be applied retroactively, and financial statements presented for prior periods should be restated.

Stockholders' Equity Combined

53. The stockholders' equities of the separate companies are also combined as a part of the pooling of interests method of accounting. The combined corporation records as capital the capital stock and capital in excess of par or stated value of outstanding stock of the separate companies. Similarly, retained earnings or deficits of the separate companies are combined and recognized as retained earnings of the combined corporation (paragraph 56). The amount of outstanding shares of stock of the combined corporation at par or stated value may exceed the total amount of capital stock of the separate combining companies; the excess should be deducted first from the combined other contributed capital and then from the combined retained earnings. The combined retained earnings could be misleading if shortly before or as a part of the combination transaction one or more of the combining companies adjusted the elements of stockholders' equity to eliminate a deficit; therefore, the elements of equity before the adjustment should be combined.

54. A corporation which effects a combination accounted for by the pooling of interests method by distributing stock previously acquired as treasury stock (paragraph 47-d) should first account for those shares of stock as though retired. The issuance of the shares for the common stock interests of the combining company is then accounted for the same as the issuance of previously unissued shares.

55. Accounting for common stock of one of the combining companies which is held by another combining company at the date a combination is consummated depends on whether the stock is the same as that which is issued to effect the combination or is the same as the stock which is exchanged in the combination. An investment of a combining company in the common stock of the issuing corporation is in effect returned to the resulting combined corporation in the combination. The combined corporation should account for the investment as treasury stock. In contrast, an investment in the common stock of other combining companies (not the one issuing stock in the combination) is an investment in stock that is exchanged in the combination for the common stock issued. The stock in that type of intercorporate invest-

EXHIBIT 3 (*continued*) ——————————————————————————

ment is in effect eliminated in the combination. The combined corporation should account for that investment as stock retired as part of the combination.

Reporting Combined Operations

56. A corporation which applies the pooling of interests method of accounting to a combination should report results of operations for the period in which the combination occurs as though the companies had been combined as of the beginning of the period. Results of operations for that period thus comprise those of the separate companies combined from the beginning of the period to the date the combination is consummated and those of the combined operations from that date to the end of the period. Eliminating the effects of intercompany transactions from operations before the date of combination reports operations before and after the date of combination on substantially the same basis. The effects of intercompany transactions on current assets, current liabilities, revenue, and cost of sales for periods presented and on retained earnings at the beginning of the periods presented should be eliminated to the extent possible. The nature of and effects on earnings per share of nonrecurring intercompany transactions involving long-term assets and liabilities need not be eliminated but should be disclosed. A combined corporation should disclose in notes to financial statements the revenue, extraordinary items, and net income of each of the separate companies from the beginning of the period to the date the combination is consummated (paragraph 64-d). The information relating to the separate companies may be as of the end of the interim period nearest the date that the combination is consummated.

57. Similarly, balance sheets and other financial information of the separate companies as of the beginning of the period should be presented as though the companies had been combined at that date. Financial statements and financial information of the separate companies presented for prior years should also be restated on a combined basis to furnish comparative information. All restated financial statements and financial summaries should indicate clearly that financial data of the previously separate companies are combined.

Expenses Related to Combination

58. The pooling of interests method records neither the acquiring of assets nor the obtaining of capital. Therefore, costs incurred to effect a combination accounted for by that method and to integrate the continuing operations are expenses of the combined corporation rather than additions to assets or direct reductions of stockholders' equity. Accordingly, all expenses related to effecting a business combination accounted for by the pooling of interests method should be deducted in determining the net income of the resulting combined corporation for the period in which the expenses are incurred. Those expenses in-

EXHIBIT 3 (*continued*)

clude, for example, registration fees, costs of furnishing information to stockholders, fees of finders and consultants, salaries and other expenses related to services of employees, and costs and losses of combining operations of the previously separate companies and instituting efficiencies.

Disposition of Assets After Combination

59. A combined corporation may dispose of those assets of the separate companies which are duplicate facilities or excess capacity in the combined operations. Losses or estimated losses on disposal of specifically identified duplicate or excess facilities should be deducted in determining the net income of the resulting combined corporation. However, a loss estimated and recorded while a facility remains in service should not include the portion of the cost that is properly allocable to anticipated future service of the facility.

60. Profit or loss on other dispositions of assets of the previously separate companies may require special disclosure unless the disposals are part of customary business activities of the combined corporation. Specific treatment of a profit or loss on those dispositions is warranted because the pooling of interests method of accounting would have been inappropriate (paragraph 48-c) if the combined corporation were committed or planned to dispose of a significant part of the assets of one of the combining companies. The Board concludes that a combined corporation should disclose separately a profit or loss resulting from the disposal of a significant part of the assets or a separable segment of the previously separate companies, provided the profit or loss is material in relation to the net income of the combined corporation, and the disposition is within two years after the combination is consummated.

The disclosed profit or loss, less applicable income tax effect, should be classified as an extraordinary item.

Date of Recording Combination

61. A business combination accounted for by the pooling of interests method should be recorded as of the date the combination is consummated. Therefore, even though a business combination is consummated before one or more of the combining companies first issues its financial statements as of an earlier date, the financial statements issued should be those of the combining company and not those of the resulting combined corporation. A combining company should, however, disclose as supplemental information, in notes to financial statements or otherwise, the substance of a combination consummated before financial statements are issued and the effects of the combination on reported financial position and results of operations (paragraph 65). Comparative financial statements presented in reports of the resulting combined corporation after a combination is consummated

EXHIBIT 3 (*continued*)

should combine earlier financial statements of the separate companies.

62. A corporation may be reasonably assured that a business combination which has been initiated but not consummated as of the date of financial statements will meet the conditions requiring the pooling of interests method of accounting. The corporation should record as an investment common stock of the other combining company acquired before the statement date. Common stock acquired by disbursing cash or other assets or by incurring liabilities should be recorded at cost. Stock acquired in exchange for common stock of the issuing corporation should, however, be recorded at the proportionate share of underlying net assets at the date acquired as recorded by the other company. Until the pooling of interests method of accounting for the combination is known to be appropriate, the investment and net income of the investor corporation should include the proportionate share of earnings or losses of the other company after the date of acquisition of the stock. The investor corporation should also disclose results of operations for all prior periods presented as well as the entire current period as they will be reported if the combination is later accounted for by the pooling of interests method. After the combination is consummated and the applicable method of accounting is known, financial statements issued previously should be restated as necessary to include the other combining company.

Disclosure of a Combination

63. A combined corporation should disclose in its financial statements that a combination which is accounted for by the pooling of interest method has occurred during the period. The basis of current presentation and restatements of prior periods may be disclosed in the financial statements by captions or by references to notes.

64. Notes to financial statements of a combined corporation should disclose the following for the period in which a business combination occurs and is accounted for by the pooling of interests method.

a. Name and brief description of the companies combined, except a corporation whose name is carried forward to the combined corporation.
b. Method of accounting for the combination—that is, by the pooling of interests method.
c. Description and number of shares of stock issued in the business combination.
d. Details of the results of operations of the previously separate companies for the period before the combination is consummated that are included in the current combined net income (paragraph 56). The details should include revenue, extraordinary items, net income, other changes in stockholders' equity, and amount of and manner of accounting for intercompany transactions.

EXHIBIT 3 (*continued*)

e. Descriptions of the nature of adjustments of net assets of the combining companies to adopt the same accounting practices and of the effects of the changes on net income reported previously by the separate companies and now presented in comparative financial statements (paragraph 52).

f. Details of an increase or decrease in retained earnings from changing the fiscal year of a combining company. The details should include at least revenue, expenses, extraordinary items, net income, and other changes in stockholders' equity for the period excluded from the reported results of operations.

g. Reconciliations of amounts of revenue and earnings previously reported by the corporation that issues the stock to effect the combination with the combined amounts currently presented in financial statements and summaries. A new corporation formed to effect a combination may instead disclose the earnings of the separate companies which comprise combined earnings for prior periods.

The information disclosed in notes to financial statements should also be furnished on a pro forma basis in information on a proposed business combination which is given to stockholders of combining companies.

65. Notes to the financial statements should disclose details of the effects of a business combination consummated before the financial statements are issued but which is either incomplete as of the date of the financial statements or initiated after that date (paragraph 61). The details should include revenue, net income, earnings per share, and the effects of anticipated changes in accounting methods as if the combination had been consummated at the date of the financial statements (paragraph 52).

Application of Purchase Method

Principles of Historical Cost Accounting

66. Accounting for a business combination by the purchase method follows principles normally applicable under historical cost accounting to recording acquisitions of assets and issuances of stock and to accounting for assets and liabilities after acquisition.

67. *Acquiring assets.* The general principles to apply the historical cost basis of accounting to an acquisition of an asset depend on the nature of the transaction:

a. An asset acquired by exchanging cash or other assets is recorded at cost—that is, at the amount of cash disbursed or the fair value of other assets distributed.

b. An asset acquired by incurring liabilities is recorded at cost—that is, at the present value of the amounts to be paid.

EXHIBIT 3 (*continued*)

    c. An asset acquired by issuing shares of stock of the acquiring corporation is recorded at the fair value of the asset[9]—that is, shares of stock issued are recorded at the fair value of the consideration received for the stock.

    The general principles must be supplemented to apply them in certain transactions. For example, the fair value of an asset received for stock issued may not be reliably determinable, or the fair value of an asset acquired in an exchange may be more reliably determinable than the fair value of a noncash asset given up. Restraints on measurement have led to the practical rule that assets acquired for other than cash, including shares of stock issued, should be stated at "cost" when they are acquired and "cost may be determined either by the fair value of the consideration given or by the fair value of the property acquired, whichever is the more clearly evident."[10] "Cost" in accounting often means the amount at which an entity records an asset at the date it is acquired whatever its manner of acquisition, and that "cost" forms the basis for historical cost accounting.

    68. *Allocating cost.* Acquiring assets in groups requires not only ascertaining the cost of the assets as a group but also allocating the cost to the individual assets which comprise the group. The cost of a group is determined by the principles described in paragraph 67. A portion of the total cost is then assigned to each individual asset acquired on the basis of its fair value. A difference between the sum of the assigned costs of the tangible and identifiable intangible assets acquired less liabilities assumed and the cost of the group is evidence of unspecified intangible values.

    69. *Accounting after acquisition.* The nature of an asset and not the manner of its acquisition determines an acquirer's subsequent accounting for the cost of that asset. The basis for measuring the cost of an asset—whether amount of cash paid, fair value of an asset received or given up, amount of a liability incurred, or fair value of stock issued—has no effect on the subsequent accounting for that cost, which is retained as an asset, depreciated, amortized, or otherwise matched with revenue.

Acquiring Corporation

    70. A corporation which distributes cash or other assets or incurs liabilities to obtain the assets or stock of another company is clearly the acquirer. The identities of the acquirer and the acquired company are usually evident in a business combination effected by the issue of stock. The acquiring corporation normally issues the stock and com-

---

[9] An asset required may be an entire entity which may have intangible assets, including goodwill.

[10] ARB No. 24; the substance was retained in slightly different words in Chapter 5 of ARB No. 43 and ARB No. 48.

354

EXHIBIT 3 (*continued*)

monly is the larger company. The acquired company may, however, survive as the corporate entity, and the nature of the negotiations sometimes clearly indicates that a smaller corporation acquires a larger company. The Board concludes that presumptive evidence of the acquiring corporation in combinations effected by an exchange of stock is obtained by identifying the former common stockholder interests of a combining company which either retain or receive the larger portion of the voting rights in the combined corporation. That corporation should be treated as the acquirer unless other evidence clearly indicates that another corporation is the acquirer. For example, a substantial investment of one company in common stock of another before the combination may be evidence that the investor is the acquiring corporation.

71. If a new corporation is formed to issue stock to effect a business combination to be accounted for by the purchase method, one of the existing combining companies should be considered the acquirer on the basis of the evidence available.

Determining Cost of an Acquired Company

72. The same accounting principles apply to determining the cost of assets acquired individually, those acquired in a group, and those acquired in a business combination. A cash payment by a corporation measures the cost of acquired assets less liabilities assumed. Similarly, the fair values of other assets distributed, such as marketable securities or properties, and the fair value of liabilities incurred by an acquiring corporation measure the cost of an acquired company. The present value of a debt security represents the fair value of the liability, and a premium or discount should be recorded for a debt security issued with an interest rate fixed materially above or below the effective rate or current yield for an otherwise comparable security.

73. The distinctive attributes of preferred stocks make some issues similar to a debt security while others possess common stock characteristics, with many gradations between the extremes. Determining cost of an acquired company may be affected by those characteristics. For example, the fair value of a nonvoting, nonconvertible preferred stock which lacks characteristics of common stock may be determined by comparing the specified dividend and redemption terms with comparable securities and by assessing market factors. Thus although the principle of recording the fair value of consideration received for stock issued applies to all equity securities, senior as well as common stock, the cost of a company acquired by issuing senior equity securities may be determined in practice on the same basis as for debt securities.

74. The fair value of securities traded in the market is normally more clearly evident than the fair value of an acquired company (paragraph 67). Thus, the quoted market price of an equity security issued to effect a business combination may usually be used to ap-

EXHIBIT 3 *(continued)*

proximate the fair value of an acquired company after recognizing possible effects of price fluctuations, quantities traded, issue costs, and the like (paragraph 23). The market price for a reasonable period before and after the date the terms of the acquisition are agreed to and announced should be considered in determining the fair value of securities issued.

75. If the quoted market price is not the fair value of stock, either preferred or common, the consideration received should be estimated even though measuring directly the fair values of assets received is difficult. Both the consideration received, including goodwill, and the extent of the adjustment of the quoted market price of the stock issued should be weighed to determine the amount to be recorded. All aspects of the acquisition, including the negotiations, should be studied, and independent appraisals may be used as an aid in determining the fair value of securities issued. Consideration other than stock distributed to effect an acquisition may provide evidence of the total fair value received.

76. *Cost of acquisition.* The cost of a company acquired in a business combination accounted for by the purchase method includes the direct costs of acquisition. Costs of registering and issuing equity securities are a reduction of the otherwise determinable fair value of the securities. However, indirect and general expenses related to acquisitions are deducted as incurred in determining net income.

Contingent Consideration

77. A business combination agreement may provide for the issuance of additional shares of a security or the transfer of cash or other consideration contingent on specified events or transactions in the future. Some agreements provide that a portion of the consideration be placed in escrow to be distributed or to be returned to the transferor when specified events occur. Either debt or equity securities may be placed in escrow, and amounts equal to interest or dividends on the securities during the contingency period may be paid to the escrow agent or to the potential security holder.

78. The Board concludes that cash and other assets distributed and securities issued unconditionally and amounts of contingent consideration which are determinable at the date of acquisition should be included in determining the cost of an acquired company and recorded at that date. Consideration which is issued or issuable at the expiration of the contingency period or which is held in escrow pending the outcome of the contingency should be disclosed but not recorded as a liability or shown as outstanding securities unless the outcome of the contingency is determinable beyond reasonable doubt.

79. Contingent consideration should usually be recorded when the contingency is resolved and consideration is issued or becomes issuable. In general, the issue of additional securities or distribution of

EXHIBIT 3 (*continued*)

other consideration at resolution of contingencies based on earnings should result in an additional element of cost of an acquired company. In contrast, the issue of additional securities or distribution of other consideration at resolution of contingencies based on security prices should not change the recorded cost of an acquired company.

80. *Contingency based on earnings.* Additional consideration may be contingent on maintaining or achieving specified earnings levels in future periods. When the contingency is resolved and additional consideration is distributable, the acquiring corporation should record the current fair value of the consideration issued or issuable as additional cost of the acquired company. The additional costs of affected assets, usually goodwill, should be amortized over the remaining life of the asset.

81. *Contingency based on security prices.* Additional consideration may be contingent on the market price of a specified security issued to effect a business combination. Unless the price of the security at least equals the specified amount on a specified date or dates, the acquiring corporation is required to issue additional equity or debt securities or transfer cash or other assets sufficient to make the current value of the total consideration equal to the specified amount. The securities issued unconditionally at the date the combination is consummated should be recorded at that date at the specified amount.

82. The cost of an acquired company recorded at the date of acquisition represents the entire payment, including contingent consideration. Therefore, the issuance of additional securities or distribution of other consideration does not affect the cost of the acquired company, regardless of whether the amount specified is a security price to be maintained or a higher security price to be achieved. On a later date when the contingency is resolved and additional consideration is distributable, the acquiring corporation should record the current fair value of the additional consideration issued or issuable. However, the amount previously recorded for securities issued at the date of acquisition should simultaneously be reduced to the lower current value of those securities. Reducing the value of debt securities previously issued to their later fair value results in recording a discount on debt securities. The discount should be amortized from the date the additional securities are issued.

83. Accounting for contingent consideration based on conditions other than those described should be inferred from the procedures outlined. For example, if the consideration contingently issuable depends on both future earnings and future security prices, additional cost of the acquired company should be recorded for the additional consideration contingent on earnings, and previously recorded consideration should be reduced to current value of the consideration contingent on security prices. Similarly, if the consideration contingently issuable depends on later settlement of a contingency, an increase in

EXHIBIT 3 (*continued*)

the cost of acquired assets, if any, should be amortized over the remaining life of the assets.

84. *Interest or dividends during contingency period.* Amounts paid to an escrow agent representing interest and dividends on securities held in escrow should be accounted for according to the accounting for the securities. That is, until the disposition of the securities in escrow is resolved, payments to the escrow agent should not be recorded as interest expense or dividend distributions. An amount equal to interest and dividends later distributed by the escrow agent to the former stockholders should be added to the cost of the acquired assets at the date distributed and amortized over the remaining life of the assets.

85. *Tax effect of inputed interest.* A tax reduction resulting from imputed interest on contingently issuable stock reduces the fair value recorded for contingent consideration based on earnings and increases additional capital recorded for contingent consideration based on security prices.

86. *Compensation in contingent agreements.* The substance of some agreements for contingent consideration is to provide compensation for services or use of property or profit sharing, and the additional consideration given should be accounted for as expenses of the appropriate periods.

Recording Assets Acquired and Liabilities Assumed

87. An acquiring corporation should allocate the cost of an acquired company to the assets acquired and liabilities assumed. Allocation should follow the principles described in paragraph 68.

First, all identifiable assets acquired, either individually or by type, and liabilities assumed in a business combination, whether or not shown in the financial statements of the acquired company, should be assigned a portion of the cost of the acquired company, normally equal to their fair values at date of acquisition.

Second, the excess of the cost of the acquired company over the sum of the amounts assigned to identifiable assets acquired less liabilities assumed should be recorded as goodwill. The sum of the market or appraisal values of identifiable assets acquired less liabilities assumed may sometimes exceed the cost of the acquired company. If so, the values otherwise assignable to noncurrent assets acquired (except long-term investments in marketable securities) should be reduced by a proportionate part of the excess to determine the assigned values. A deferred credit for an excess of assigned value of identifiable assets over cost of an acquired company (sometimes called "negative goodwill") should not be recorded unless those assets are reduced to zero value.

Independent appraisals may be used as an aid in determining the fair values of some assets and liabilities. Subsequent sales of assets may also provide evidence of values. The effect of taxes may be a

EXHIBIT 3 (*continued*) ————————————————————————————

factor in assigning amounts to identifiable assets and liabilities (paragraph 89).

88. General guides for assigning amounts to the individual assets acquired and liabilities assumed, except goodwill, are:

a. Marketable securities at current net realizable values.

b. Receivables at present values of amounts to be received determined at appropriate current interest rates, less allowances for uncollectibility and collection costs, if necessary.

c. Inventories: (1) Finished goods and merchandise at estimated selling prices less the sum of (a) costs of disposal and (b) a reasonable profit allowance for the selling effort of the acquiring corporation; (2) work in process at estimated selling prices of finished goods less the sum of (a) costs to complete, (b) costs of disposal, and (c) a reasonable profit allowance for the completing and selling effort of the acquiring corporation based on profit for similar finished goods; (3) raw materials at current replacement costs.

d. Plant and equipment: (1) to be used, at current replacement costs for similar capacity[11] unless the expected future use of the assets indicates a lower value to the acquirer, (2) to be sold or held for later sale rather than used, at current net realizable value, and (3) to be used temporarily, at current net realizable value recognizing future depreciation for the expected period of use.

e. Intangible assets which can be identified and named, including contracts, patents, franchises, customer and supplier lists, and favorable leases, at appraised values.[12]

f. Other assets, including land, natural resources, and nonmarketable securities, at appraised values.

g. Accounts and notes payable, long-term debt, and other claims payable at present values of amounts to be paid determined at appropriate current interest rates.

h. Liabilities and accruals—for example, accruals for pension cost,[13] warranties, vacation pay, deferred compensation—at present values of amounts to be paid determined at appropriate current interest rates.

i. Other liabilities and commitments, including unfavorable leases, contracts, and commitments and plant closing expense incident to

———————

[11] Replacement cost may be determined directly if a used asset market exists for the assets acquired. Otherwise, the replacement cost should be approximated from replacement cost new less estimated accumulated depreciation.

[12] Fair values should be ascribed to specific assets: identifiable assets should not be included in goodwill.

[13] An accrual for pension cost should be the greater of (1) accrued pension cost computed in conformity with the accounting policies of the acquiring corporation for one or more of its pension plans or (2) the excess, if any, of the actuarially computed value of vested benefits over the amount of the pension fund.

EXHIBIT 3 (continued) ————————————————————————

the acquisition, at present values of amounts to be paid determined at appropriate current interest rates.

An acquiring corporation should record periodically as a part of income the accrual of interest on assets and liabilities recorded at acquisition date at the discounted values of amounts to be received or paid. An acquiring corporation should not record as a separate asset the goodwill previously recorded by an acquired company and should not record deferred income taxes recorded by an acquired company before its acquisition. An acquiring corporation should reduce the acquired goodwill retroactively for the realized tax benefits of loss carryforwards of an acquired company not previously recorded by the acquiring corporation.

89. The market or appraisal values of specific assets and liabilities determined in paragraph 88 may differ from the income tax bases of those items. Estimated future tax effects of differences between the tax bases and amounts otherwise appropriate to assign to an asset or a liability are one of the variables in estimating fair value. Amounts assigned to identifiable assets and liabilities should, for example, recognize that the fair value of an asset to an acquirer is less than its market or appraisal value if all or a portion of the market or appraisal value is not deductible for income taxes. The impact of tax effects on amounts assigned to individual assets and liabilities depends on numerous factors, including imminence or delay of realization of the asset value and the possible timing of tax consequences. Since differences between amounts assigned and tax bases are not timing differences (*APB Opinion No. 11, Accounting for Income Taxes,* paragraph 13), the acquiring corporation should not record deferred tax accounts at the date of acquisition.

Amortization of Goodwill

90. Goodwill recorded in a business combination accounted for by the purchase method should be amortized in accordance with the provisions in paragraphs 27 to 31 of *APB Opinion No. 17 Intangible Assets.*

Excess of Acquired Not Assets over Cost

91. The value assigned to net assets acquired should not exceed the cost of an acquired company because the general presumption in historical cost based accounting is that net assets acquired should be recorded at not more than cost. The total market or appraisal values of identifiable assets acquired less liabilities assumed in a few business combinations may exceed the cost of the acquired company. An excess over cost should be allocated to reduce proportionately the values assigned to noncurrent assets (except long-term investments in marketable securities) in determining their fair values (paragraph 87). If the allocation reduces the noncurrent assets to zero value, the remainder

EXHIBIT 3 *(continued)*

of the excess over cost should be classified as a deferred credit and should be amortized systematically to income over the period estimated to be benefited but not in excess of forty years. The method and period of amortization should be disclosed.

92. No part of the excess of acquired net assets over cost should be added directly to stockholders' equity at the date of acquisition.

Acquisition Date

93. The Board believes that the date of acquisition of a company should ordinarily be the date assets are received and other assets are given or securities are issued. However, the parties may for convenience designate as the effective date the end of an accounting period between the dates a business combination is initiated and consummated. The designated date should ordinarily be the date of acquisition for accounting purposes if a written agreement provides that effective control of the acquired company is transferred to the acquiring corporation on that date without restrictions except those required to protect the stockholders or other owners of the acquired company—for example, restrictions on significant changes in the operations, permission to pay dividends equal to those regularly paid before the effective date, and the like. Designating an effective date other than the date assets or securities are transferred requires adjusting the cost of an acquired company and net income otherwise reported to compensate for recognizing income before consideration is transferred. The cost of an acquired company and net income should therefore be reduced by imputed interest at an appropriate current rate on assets given, liabilities incurred, or preferred stock distributed as of the transfer date to acquire the company.

94. The cost of an acquired company and the values assigned to assets acquired and liabilities assumed should be determined as of the date of acquisition. The statement of income of an acquiring corporation for the period in which a business combination occurs should include income of the acquired company after the date of acquisition by including the revenue and expenses of the acquired operations based on the cost to the acquiring corporation.

Disclosure in Financial Statements

95. Notes to the financial statements of an acquiring corporation should disclose the following for the period in which a business combination occurs and is accounted for by the purchase method.

a. Name and a brief description of the acquired company.
b. Method of accounting for the combination—that is, by the purchase method.
c. Period for which results of operations of the acquired company are included in the income statement of the acquiring corporation.

EXHIBIT 3 *(concluded)* ————————————————————

   d. Cost of the acquired company and, if applicable, the number of shares of stock issued or issuable and the amount assigned to the issued and issuable shares.

   e. Description of the plan for amortization of acquired goodwill, the amortization method, and period *(APB Opinion No. 17,* paragraphs 27 to 31).

   f. Contingent payments, options, or commitments specified in the acquisition agreement and their proposed accounting treatment.

Information relating to several relatively minor acquisitions may be combined for disclosure.

96. Notes to the financial statements of the acquiring corporation for the period in which a business combination occurs and is accounted for by the purchase method should include as supplemental information the following results of operations on a pro forma basis:

   a. Results of operations for the current period as though the companies had combined at the beginning of the period, unless the acquisition was at or near the beginning of the period.

   b. Results of operations for the immediately preceding period as though the companies had combined at the beginning of that period if comparative financial statements are presented.

The supplemental pro forma information should as a minimum show revenue, income before extraordinary items, net income, and earnings per share. To present pro forma information, income taxes, interest expense, preferred stock dividends, depreciation and amortization of assets, including goodwill, should be adjusted to their accounting bases recognized in recording the combination. Pro forma presentation of results of operations of periods prior to the combination transaction should be limited to the immediately preceding period.

EXHIBIT 4 _____

From: A. J. Johnson, Inc., President   July 5, 1980
   To: Board of Directors
   Re: Purchase of Research Products, Inc.

My analysis of Research indicates that, with the exception of
the patents, the net book value of their assets on December 31,
1980, will be about equal to their fair market value. We estimate
that as of December 31, 1980, the patents will have a market
value of $3 million. At that point they will have a legal and
economic life of ten years. In fact, my strategy is to sell approximately one half of the patents early in 1981 for $1.5 million, which
should more than offset our projected decrease in earnings for
1981. The remaining excess of $1.29 million of purchase price
over fair market value should be allocated to goodwill. If we
structure the deal as a purchase, we'll amortize the goodwill over
a 20-year period.

Case 11–3 _____

Chesebrough-Pond's, Inc.

Refer to Chesebrough-Pond's, Inc.'s financial statements and
Notes 1 and 2 for the year ended December 31, 1978, and answer the
following questions:

1. Where does the $13,238,000 excess of purchase price over the fair
   value of assets acquired from G. H. Bass and Company (Note 2)
   appear on Chesebrough-Pond's, Inc.'s consolidated balance
   sheet?
2. How much higher or lower would earnings per share have been
   for 1978 if the combination had been treated as a pooling of interests rather than a purchase? For purposes of this question, assume that the fair value of Bass's net assets is equal to their book
   value.
3. Why do you think this business combination was structured as a
   purchase rather than a pooling of interests?

CHESEBROUGH-POND'S, INC.
Consolidated Balance Sheet*

	December 31, 1978	December 31, 1977
Assets		
Current assets:		
Cash and time deposits	$ 28,109,000	$ 19,940,000
Marketable securities, at cost which approximates market	2,320,000	1,045,000
Accounts receivable	194,882,000	152,802,000
Inventories	233,189,000	202,633,000
Prepaid expenses	15,279,000	9,835,000
Total current assets	$473,779,000	$386,255,000
Property, plant, and equipment:		
At cost......................................	236,131,000	198,252,000
Less accumulated depreciation	80,946,000	69,600,000
Net property, plant, and equipment	$155,185,000	$128,652,000
Investments and other assets	23,020,000	19,394,000
Goodwill and trademarks	54,271,000	41,128,000
	$706,255,000	$575,429,000
Liabilities and Shareholders' Equity		
Current liabilities:		
Notes payable	$ 40,517,000	$ 26,929,000
Accounts payable and accrued liabilities	105,395,000	83,870,000
Income taxes payable	21,744,000	17,395,000
Long-term debt due within one year..........	7,390,000	3,665,000
Total current liabilities	$175,046,000	$131,859,000
Long-term debt.............................	120,900,000	75,382,000
Deferred income taxes.......................	9,038,000	8,539,000
Other non-current liabilities	10,139,000	8,798,000
Shareholders' equity:		
Common stock	32,466,000	32,427,000
Additional paid-in capital	46,386,000	45,139,000
Retained earnings	316,523,000	277,199,000
	$395,375,000	$354,765,000
Less treasury stock, at cost	4,243,000	3,914,000
Total shareholders' equity	$391,132,000	$350,851,000
	$706,255,000	$575,429,000

* See accompanying notes.

CHESEBROUGH-POND'S INC. AND SUBSIDIARIES
Consolidated Statement of Income*
Year Ended December 31

	1978	1977
Net sales	$969,833,000	$807,997,000
Royalties	2,760,000	2,610,000
Operating revenues	$972,593,000	$810,607,000
Cost of products sold	461,338,000	383,189,000
Selling, advertising, and administrative expenses	365,872,000	303,216,000
Operating costs and expenses	$827,210,000	$686,405,000
Income from operations	$145,383,000	$124,202,000
Other income (expense):		
Interest expense	(12,229,000)	(9,735,000)
Interest income	3,018,000	1,477,000
Loss on foreign exchange	(3,353,000)	(1,331,000)
Miscellaneous—net	(1,978,000)	(815,000)
	$(14,542,000)	$(10,404,000)
Income before provision for taxes	$130,841,000	$113,798,000
Provision for income taxes	61,127,000	53,708,000
Net income	$ 69,714,000	$ 60,090,000
Earnings per share	$2.16	$1.86

* See accompanying notes.

CHESEBROUGH-POND'S INC. AND SUBSIDIARIES
Consolidated Statement of Shareholders' Equity*
Year Ended December 31

	1978		1977	
	Shares	*Amount*	*Shares*	*Amount*
Preferred stock—1 million shares authorized and unissued; par value $1 per share	—	—	—	—
Common stock—50 million shares authorized; par value $1 per share				
Balance at January 1	32,427,050	$ 32,427,000	32,312,478	$ 32,312,000
Issued under the stock and stock option plans	38,576	39,000	112,369	113,000
Debenture conversions	—	—	2,203	2,000
Balance at December 31	32,465,626	$ 32,466,000	32,427,050	$ 32,427,000
Additional paid-in capital				
Balance at January 1		$ 45,139,000		$ 42,454,000
Common shares issued under the stock and stock option plans		1,549,000		2,903,000
Other		(302,000)		(218,000)
Balance at December 31		$ 46,386,000		$ 45,139,000
Retained earnings				
Balance at January 1		$277,199,000		$244,181,000
Net income		69,714,000		60,090,000
Dividends paid—$.94 per share (1977—$.84)		(30,390,000)		(27,072,000)
Balance at December 31		$316,523,000		$277,199,000
Treasury stock, at cost				
Balance at January 1	183,237	$ 3,914,000	101,394	$ 1,945,000
Issued under the stock plan	(98,033)	(2,100,000)	(3,421)	(73,000)
Issued under the executive incentive profit-sharing plan	(12,617)	(280,000)	(14,736)	(310,000)
Purchased for cash	109,400	2,709,000	100,000	2,352,000
Balance at December 31	181,987	$ 4,243,000	183,237	$ 3,914,000

* See accompanying notes.

CHESEBROUGH-POND'S INC. AND SUBSIDIARIES
Consolidated Statement of Changes in Financial Position*
Year Ended December 31

	1978	1977
Sources of working capital		
Net income	$ 69,714,000	$ 60,090,000
Depreciation	12,664,000	11,238,000
Deferred income taxes	499,000	2,701,000
Other expenses not involving working capital.....	2,972,000	1,751,000
Provided from operations	$ 85,849,000	$ 75,780,000
Common shares issued under the stock and stock option plans	3,688,000	3,089,000
Increase in long-term debt	52,804,000	3,939,000
Book value of disposed assets	1,637,000	1,558,000
	$143,978,000	$ 84,366,000
Applications of working capital		
Dividends paid	$ 30,390,000	$ 27,072,000
Additions to property, plant, and equipment	34,913,000	17,951,000
Decrease in long-term debt......................	10,913,000	729,000
Purchase of treasury stock	2,709,000	2,352,000
Net non-current assets of G.H. Bass & Co., at date of acquisition	17,580,000	—
Increase in investments and other assets—net	1,606,000	14,657,000
Other—net	1,530,000	957,000
	$ 99,641,000	$ 63,718,000
Increase in working capital	$ 44,337,000	$ 20,648,000
Changes in components of working capital		
Increase (decrease) in current assets:		
Cash and time deposits........................	$ 8,169,000	$ 286,000
Marketable securities	1,275,000	(154,000)
Accounts receivable	42,080,000	12,925,000
Inventories	30,556,000	25,824,000
Prepaid expenses.............................	5,444,000	1,906,000
	$ 87,524,000	$ 40,787,000
Increase (decrease) in current liabilities:		
Notes payable	$ 13,588,000	$ 3,723,000
Accounts payable and accrued liabilities	21,525,000	19,312,000
Income taxes payable.........................	4,349,000	(2,901,000)
Long-term debt due within one year	3,725,000	5,000
	43,187,000	20,139,000
Increase in working capital	$ 44,337,000	$ 20,648,000

* See accompanying notes.

NOTES TO CONSOLIDATED FINANCIAL STATEMENTS

1. SUMMARY OF SIGNIFICANT ACCOUNTING POLICIES

Principles of Consolidation

The consolidated financial statements include the accounts of all domestic and majority-owned foreign subsidiaries. Intercompany accounts and material intercompany transactions have been eliminated in consolidation.

Inventories

Inventories are valued at the lower-of-cost (first-in, first-out)-or-market. Market is estimated net realizable value.

Property, Plant, and Equipment

Property, plant, and equipment are stated at cost. Depreciation, which includes amortization of assets recorded under capital leases, is provided on a straight-line basis for financial accounting purposes, while accelerated methods are used for income tax purposes. Maintenance and repairs are expensed as incurred and additions and major improvements are capitalized. Upon the sale or retirement of property, the property accounts and the related accumulated depreciation are adjusted and any profit or loss is reflected in income.

Income Taxes

Deferred income taxes result from timing differences between the amounts reported for financial accounting and income tax purposes, primarily related to accelerated methods of depreciation for tax purposes. Investment tax credits are applied as a reduction of the provision for income taxes in the year the related property is placed in service.

Goodwill and Trademarks

Costs in excess of net assets of acquired companies (goodwill) and trademarks acquired under agreements entered into prior to November 1, 1970, are not being amortized since there is no present indication of any permanent impairment in the value of these assets. All significant goodwill and trademarks acquired after October 31, 1970, are being amortized on a straight-line basis over periods not exceeding 40 years.

Advertising and Sales Promotion Costs

Advertising costs are expensed as incurred, while sales promotion costs are expensed during the period of the promotional program.

Retirement Plans

The company has various retirement plans covering the majority of its employees worldwide. The company's policy is to fund current service costs each year and to amortize prior service costs over 30 years.

Earnings per Share

The computation of earnings per share is based on the weighted average number of shares outstanding (32,311,000 in 1978 and 32,222,000 in 1977). Dilution relating to convertible debentures and other rights was not material.

Reclassifications

Certain 1977 amounts have been reclassified to conform to the 1978 presentation, principally related to investments in Puerto Rico, which the Company now intends to hold to maturity.

2. ACQUISITION

On July 31, 1978, the company acquired all of the outstanding stock of G. H. Bass & Co. (Bass), a domestic manufacturer of casual footwear, for a cash purchase price of $27,064,000, including expenses of the acquisition. The acquisition has been accounted for as a purchase and, accordingly, the operations of Bass have been included since the acquisition date. The excess of the purchase price over the fair value of the net assets acquired amounted to $13,238,000 and is being amortized on a straight-line basis over forty years.

The following pro forma summary presents the results of the company's operations as if Bass had been acquired on January 1, 1977:

	1978	*1977*
Net sales	$1,000,094,000	$846,097,000
Net income	71,333,000	61,737,000
Earnings per share	2.21	1.92

3. PROPERTY, PLANT, AND EQUIPMENT

Property, plant, and equipment at December 31 follows:

	1978	1977
Land	$ 10,289,000	$ 9,416,000
Buildings and building improvements	82,112,000	71,544,000
Machinery and equipment	124,835,000	109,847,000
Leasehold improvements	5,295,000	4,563,000
Construction in progress	13,600,000	2,882,000
	236,131,000	198,252,000
Less accumulated depreciation	80,946,000	69,600,000
Net property, plant, and equipment	$155,185,000	$128,652,000

Included above is net property, plant, and equipment relative to capital leases of $12,704,000 in 1978 and $7,641,000 in 1977.

Case 11–4

Owens-Corning Fiberglas

A note to the 1977 annual report of Owens-Corning Fiberglas Corporation makes the following disclosure:

> *Purchase of Fry Roofing and Trumbull Asphalt.* On April 20, 1977, the company acquired substantially all of the assets and certain liabilities of the Lloyd A. Fry Roofing Company and Trumbull Asphalt Company (Fry) in exchange for approximately $108,749,000 in cash. Fry is a manufacturer of roofing and asphalt materials, with numerous locations throughout the country. This transaction has been accounted for as a purchase. The purchase price approximates the estimated fair value of the assets acquired.

The journal entry to record this purchase was as follows:

Investment in Fry:		
Current assets (net of current liabilities)	41,398,000	
Plant and equipment	67,351,000	
Cash		108,749,000

Required:

1. Make the journal entry that would have been required if Owens-Corning had made the purchase half in cash and half by issuing Owens-Corning common stock to Fry shareholders. (Owens-Corning common stock was selling for $69 per share on the New York Stock Exchange at the time of the

purchase. The common stock had a par value of $1 per share with 20 million shares authorized and 15,079,258 outstanding on April 20, 1977.)

2. Suppose that Owens-Corning had issued stock for the entire purchase price, and was required to treat the acquisition as a pooling of interests. Make the journal entry to record Owens-Corning investment in Fry, assuming that the book value of Fry's plant and equipment was $30 million less than their fair market value, and that for all other assets Fry's book value is equal to fair market value.

3. How much larger or smaller will reported net income be over the life of the assets under the purchase method that Owens-Corning used than under the pooling of interests method? (Owens-Corning's tax rate is 48 percent.)

12

Statement of Changes in
Financial Position

The statement of changes in financial position, sometimes called a *funds statement*, reports the financing and investing activities of an enterprise and the changes in its financial position during an accounting period.[1] It explains how an enterprise obtains its resources (source of funds) and how it invests these resources (use of funds).

Funds are usually defined either as *working capital* (current assets minus current liabilities) or as *cash*. In practice most firms select the broader definition, working capital, in order to emphasize management's longer term decisions.

Major sources of an enterprise's funds *defined as working capital* are operations, sale of fixed assets, long-term borrowing, and issuance of capital stock. Major uses of funds *defined as working capital* are purchase of noncurrent assets, retirement of debt, purchase of capital stock, and the payment of dividends.

MAJOR SOURCES OF FUNDS

1. Operations. An enterprise's operations generally are its largest source of funds. Funds from operations are defined as the amount of working capital generated from operations. If working capital consumed by expenses is greater than working capital generated from revenues, funds from operations is a *use* rather than a *source* of funds. This is not the same figure as net income because there are expenses such as depreciation, depletion, amortization, and loss on sale of fixed assets which do not use working capital, as well as revenues such as the increase in undistributed earnings of subsidiaries and gain on sale of fixed assets which do not provide working capital.

---

[1] Accounting Principles Board, *Opinion No. 19* (September 30, 1971) requires that the Statement of Changes in Financial Position be an integral part of an enterprise's financial report.

Listed in Illustration 12–1 is the income statement of the Texas Bookstore, Inc., for the year ended December 31, 1979.

ILLUSTRATION 12–1 _____

TEXAS BOOKSTORE, INC.
Statement of Income
For the Year Ended December 31, 1979

Sales		$100,000
Cost of sales		60,000
Gross margin		$ 40,000
Expenses:		
Wages and salaries	$15,500	
Rent	3,600	
Depreciation expense	2,880	
Amortization of copyright	1,800	
Selling and administrative expenses	10,120	33,900
Net income		$ 6,100

Funds (working capital) from operations are:

Working capital (accounts receivable, cash) received from sales		$100,000
Less, working capital consumed by expenses:		
Cost of sales (inventory)	$60,000	
Wages and salaries (cash or wages payable)	15,500	
Rent (cash or rent payable)	3,600	
Selling and administrative expenses (cash or accounts payable)	10,120	89,220
Funds (working capital) from operations		$ 10,780

Neither depreciation expense nor amortization of copyright are part of the calculation of funds from operations as they do not consume working capital. The offsetting credit in the depreciation expense entry is accumulated depreciation, a contra-fixed asset (nonworking capital) account. Similarly, the credit in the entry to amortize the copyright is the fixed asset (nonworking capital) account, copyright.

Another method of *calculating* funds from operations is to start with net income as reported and add back any expenses that do not reduce working capital.

Net income		$ 6,100
Add back expenses that do not require an outlay of working capital:		
Depreciation	$2,880	
Amortization of copyright	1,800	4,680
Funds (working capital) from operations		$10,780

The method which adds back depreciation expenses and other nonworking capital expenses to net income is the one that is most frequently seen in practice. Unfortunately, this reporting procedure has created one of the most misunderstood concepts in financial analysis, the idea that depreciation expense is a source of funds because it is added back to net income to calculate funds from operations.

2. *Sale of Noncurrent Assets.* The sale of fixed assets will result in an increase in funds (cash, accounts receivable) equal to the net proceeds received from the sale. The treatment of gain or loss on sale of fixed assets as part of the calculation of funds from operations is explained later in the chapter.

3. *Long-Term Borrowing.* An increase in long-term borrowing will result in an increase in funds (working capital) to the extent of the net proceeds borrowed. Short-term borrowing is not an increase in funds because it increases the current liability, notes payable, as well as the current asset, cash, and results in no change in funds (working capital).

4. *Issuance of Capital Stock.* If the enterprise issues capital stock it will increase funds by an amount equivalent to the net proceeds received.

MAJOR USES OF FUNDS

1. *Purchase of Noncurrent Assets.* One of the major uses of funds by an enterprise are expenditures for noncurrent assets. Typical expenditures would be land, buildings, equipment, investments in other companies, patents, and so forth. The decrease in funds is measured by the amount paid for the asset.

2. *Retirement of Long-Term Debt.* The decrease in the long-term debt account is usually attributable to either a cash payment or the transfer to current liabilities of the current portion of the long-term

debt due within one year of the balance sheet date. Both are uses of funds as they reduce working capital.

3. *Purchase of Capital Stock.* When a company purchases its own capital stock either for the treasury or retirement, it is a use of funds.

4. *Payment of Cash Dividends.* The payment of dividends is a major use of funds. The dividends are a use of funds when they are declared because the current liability, dividends payable, is increased and working capital is decreased.

SCHEDULE OF WORKING CAPITAL ACCOUNTS

A separate schedule detailing the changes in all the individual working capital accounts is an integral part of the Statement of Changes in Financial Position.

ALL RESOURCES CONCEPT OF STATEMENT OF CHANGES IN FINANCIAL POSITION

In order to meet its objectives of disclosing all significant financing and investing activities of the enterprise, this statement will have to report certain transactions which do not *directly* affect funds. For example, the Samson Company issues $1 million in common stock in exchange for property. The entry on Samson's books is:

Property...	1,000,000	
Common Stock		1,000,000

There is no entry to a working capital item, and this transaction would not appear on the funds statement if it is viewed in its narrowest sense. The broader interpretation of this transaction by the Accounting Principles Board in *Opinion No. 19* requires that it be reflected on the statement of changes in financial position. The substance of the transaction is an issue of common stock for cash (source of funds) and an expenditure of the cash for the property (use of funds). Similar financing and investing transactions which do not directly affect funds and which would be included in the statement are the conversion of long-term debt or preferred stock to common stock and the acquisition or disposal of property for long-term debt, preferred or common stock.

Examples of two different formats for a Statement of Changes in Financial Position are shown in Illustrations 12–2 and 12–3.

ILLUSTRATION 12–2

XYZ CORPORATION*
Statement of Changes in Financial Position
Fiscal Year Ended June 30, 1980

Source of funds:

From operations:

Sales	$33,100,000

Costs and expenses (consuming funds):

Cost of sales	$26,900,000
Selling, general and administrative	2,500,000
Interest	30,000
Income taxes (current)	1,400,000
	$30,830,000
Total from operations	$ 2,270,000
Increase in long-term debt	120,000
Decrease in long-term note receivable	50,000
	$ 2,440,000

Use of funds:

Additions to property, plant, and equipment	$ 878,000
Cash dividend declared	536,000
Payment of long-term debt	330,000
Purchase of treasury stock	31,000
	$ 1,775,000
Increase in working capital	$ 665,000

Statement of Changes in Working Capital Items
Fiscal Year Ended June 30, 1980

	June 30, 1980	1979	Increase	Decrease
Cash and treasury bills	$ 346,000	$ 413,000	$	($ 67,000)
Accounts receivable	3,900,000	3,451,000	449,000	
Inventories	6,500,000	5,294,000	1,206,000	
Prepaid expenses	304,000	277,000	27,000	
Total current assets	$11,050,000	$9,435,000	$1,682,000	($ 67,000)
Notes payable to bank	$ 750,000	$	($ 750,000)	$
Accounts payable	926,000	830,000	(96,000)	$
Accrued and other liabilities	1,265,000	1,192,000	(73,000)	
Accrued federal and state income tax	454,000	360,000	(94,000)	
Current portion of long-term debt	60,000	123,000		63,000
Total current liabilities	$ 3,455,000	$2,505,000	$1,013,000	$ 63,000
Working capital	$ 7,595,000	$6,930,000	$ 669,000	$ 4,000
Increase in working capital		665,000		665,000
	$ 7,595,000	$7,595,000	$ 669,000	$669,000

* For purposes of this statement funds were defined as working capital.

ILLUSTRATION 12–3

XYZ CORPORATION*
Statement of Changes in Financial Position
Fiscal Year Ended June 30, 1980

Source of funds:

Net income	$1,460,000
Add: Expenses not requiring working capital	
Depreciation and amortization	810,000
Total from operations	$2,270,000
Increase in long-term debt	120,000
Decrease in long-term note receivable	50,000
	$2,440,000

Use of funds:

Additions to property, plant, and equipment	$ 878,000
Cash dividends declared	536,000
Payment of long-term debt	330,000
Purchase of treasury stock	31,000
	$1,775,000
Increase in working capital	$ 665,000

Changes in working capital consist of:

Cash and treasury bills	($ 67,000)
Accounts receivable	449,000
Inventories	1,206,000
Prepaid expenses	27,000
Notes payable to bank	(750,000)
Accounts payable	(96,000)
Accrued and other liabilities	(73,000)
Accrued federal and state income taxes	(94,000)
Current portion of long-term debt	63,000
Increase in working capital	$ 665,000

* For purposes of this statement, funds were defined as *working capital*. Figures in parentheses represent *decreases in working capital*.

This statement (Illustration 12–3) reveals that the XYZ Corporation generated $2,440,000 of funds (working capital) in 1980. Of this amount, $2,270,000 came from operations, $120,000 from an increase in long-term debt, and $50,000 from a decrease in a long-term note receivable. The XYZ Corporation used this $2,440,000 to purchase $878,000 of property, plant, and equipment; declare dividends of $536,000; retire long-term debt of $330,000; purchase treasury stock in the amount of $31,000; and increase its working capital by $665,000.

The changes in the individual working capital accounts totaling $665,000 are shown in the other segment of the statement.

METHOD OF PREPARING A STATEMENT OF CHANGES IN FINANCIAL POSITION

The statement of changes in financial position is prepared from information obtained from the statement of income and reconciliation of retained earnings, the comparative balance sheets, and other financial data.

In preparing the statement of changes in financial position, we use the same journal entry method of analyzing transactions and adjustments as we did in preparing the balance sheet and income statement. The only difference is that our emphasis is on the effect of each entry on funds which we define as working capital. If the entry increases or decreases working capital, it becomes part of our statement of changes in financial position and is recorded in the *working capital summary* at the bottom of the worksheets.

The comparative balance sheet and statement of income and reconciliation of retained earnings of the Roberts Corporation for the years ended December 31, 1980, and December 31, 1979, are shown in Illustration 12–4 and Illustration 12–5.

ILLUSTRATION 12–4

THE ROBERTS CORPORATION
Comparative Balance Sheet
December 31, 1980 and 1979

	1980	1979
Assets		
Current assets:		
Cash	$ 60,000	$ 50,000
Accounts receivable	40,000	35,000
Inventory	50,000	55,000
Prepayments	10,000	8,000
Total current assets	$160,000	$148,000
Fixed assets	$ 40,000	$ 45,000
Less: Accumulated depreciation	20,000	15,000
	$ 20,000	$ 30,000
Total assets	$180,000	$178,000

ILLUSTRATION 12–4 (*continued*)

	1980	1979
Equities		
Current liabilities:		
Accounts payable..............................	$ 32,500	$ 43,000
Income tax payable............................	7,500	5,000
Total current liabilities	$ 40,000	$ 48,000
Long-term liabilities:		
Bonds payable	45,000	50,000
Total liabilities	$ 85,000	$ 98,000
Owners' equity:		
Common stock..................................	$ 75,000	$ 70,000
Retained earnings	20,000	10,000
Total owners' equity	$ 95,000	$ 80,000
Total equities	$180,000	$178,000

ILLUSTRATION 12–5 ————————————————————————

THE ROBERTS CORPORATION
Statement of Income and Reconciliation of Retained Earnings
For the Year Ended December 31, 1980

Net sales		$140,000
Expenses:		
Operating expenses (except depreciation)..............	$105,000	
Depreciation	10,000	115,000
		$ 25,000
Provision for federal income taxes		7,500
		$ 17,500
Gain on sale of fixed assets*		2,500
Net income		$ 20,000
Retained earnings—January 1, 1980....................		10,000
		$ 30,000
Deduct:		
Cash dividend.......................................	$ 5,000	
Stock dividend	5,000	10,000
Retained earnings—December 31, 1980		$ 20,000

* The company sold fixed assets with an original cost of $8,000 on December 31, 1980.

A six-column worksheet can be used to obtain the information necessary to prepare the statement of changes in financial position.

The first two columns are for the balance sheet accounts at the beginning of the year, and the last two columns are for the balance sheet accounts at the end of the year. The two middle columns are for transactions. The lower half of the worksheet will contain statement of changes in financial position (funds) entries only. For purposes of this problem we have *defined funds as working capital.*

Calculate from the comparative balance sheets the working capital (current assets minus current liabilities) at the end of each year, and put these figures on the worksheet (see Illustration 12–6, page 384). Then insert all other balance sheet (nonworking capital items) accounts on the worksheet. Foot (add) the worksheet to make sure it is in balance.

Start with the income statement and record journal entries as they occur. Post all entries which affect any current asset or current liability in the working capital summary.

1. Sales for the Year, $140,000

Accounts Receivable/Cash	140,000	
Sales		140,000

The increase in accounts receivable/cash increases working capital and is recorded in the working capital summary. The sales (revenue account) is part of the computation of the net income for the year which has been closed to retained earnings.

Entry (1) on the funds statement worksheet (Illustration 12–6) is:

Working Capital Summary (Funds from Operations)	140,000	
Retained Earnings		140,000

2. Operating Expenses for the Year, $105,000

Operating Expenses	105,000	
Accounts Payable, Accrued Expenses,		
Prepayments, and so forth		105,000

The increase in payables, or decrease in prepayments, is a reduction in working capital.

The operating expenses are a decrease in net income and are reflected in Retained Earnings. The entry for the worksheet is:

Retained Earnings	105,000	
Working Capital Summary		
(Funds from Operations)		105,000

3. Depreciation Expense, $10,000

Depreciation Expense	10,000	
Accumulated Depreciation		10,000

The depreciation expense is a decrease in net income and is reflected in retained earnings. The credit is to accumulated depreciation which is not a working capital item. The entry for the worksheet is:

Retained Earnings	10,000	
Accumulated Depreciation		10,000

4. Federal Income Tax, $7,500

Federal Income Tax Expense	7,500	
Federal Income Tax Payable		7,500

The income tax expense reduces net income and is reflected in retained earnings. The payable increases current liabilities (decreases working capital). The entry for the worksheet is:

Retained Earnings	7,500	
Working Capital Summary		
(Funds from Operations)		7,500

5. Gain on Sale of Fixed Assets, $2,500

The company sold fixed assets which cost $8,000 and realized a gain of $2,500. To make the entry we have to deduce both the accumulated depreciation on the $8,000 fixed asset which was sold and the cash received on the sale. Analysis of the accumulated depreciation account shows that the balance at the beginning of the year was $15,000, that depreciation for the year was $10,000 so that the balance at the end of the year, assuming no further transactions, should be $25,000. The actual balance is $20,000, so some transaction must have occurred to reduce the balance by $5,000 to $20,000. The most logical explanation (we know an asset with a cost of $8,000 was sold) is that this $5,000 is the accumulated depreciation on the fixed asset sold.

Cash...	5,500	
Accumulated Depreciation	5,000	
Fixed Assets		8,000
Gain on Sale		2,500

The cash figure is derived from the other three figures. In that cash is a working capital item, it will go in the working capital summary as proceeds from sale of fixed assets. The gain on sale, a revenue account, is an increase in net income and retained earnings. The worksheet entry is:

Working Capital Summary		
(Proceeds of Sale of Fixed Assets)	5,500	
Accumulated Depreciation	5,000	
Fixed Assets		8,000
Retained Earnings		2,500

An analysis of retained earnings reveals the following facts:

6. Paid a Cash Dividend, $5,000

Retained Earnings	5,000	
Cash/Dividends Payable....................		5,000

The decrease in cash or increase in dividends payable is a decrease in working capital. The worksheet entry is:

Retained Earnings	5,000	
Working Capital Summary (Paid Cash Dividends)		5,000

7. Paid a Stock Dividend, $5,000

Retained Earnings	5,000	
Common Stock		5,000

Since there is no effort on working capital, the entry is recorded in the upper portion of the worksheet.

The retained earnings account had a beginning balance of $10,000. Increases for the year amounted to $142,500, and decreases to $132,500, resulting in an ending balance of $20,000. This explains all the entries in the retained earnings account. Similarly, we can explain the $5,000 increase in the capital stock account.

The procedure to be followed now is to search for any hidden transactions which might affect working capital. Start by analyzing all other balance sheet accounts on the worksheet.

8. Retired Bonds, $5,000

The bonds payable account has a decrease of $5,000 for the year. The most logical explanation for this change would be the retirement of bonds.

Bonds Payable	5,000	
Cash..		5,000

On the worksheet:

Bonds Payable	5,000	
Working Capital Summary (Retired Bonds)		5,000

9. Purchased Fixed Assets, $3,000

The fixed assets account had a beginning balance of $45,000; it decreased $8,000 because of the sale of a fixed asset, reducing it to $37,000. At the end of the period it was $40,000. The most logical explanation of the $3,000 increase in this account is the purchase of

ILLUSTRATION 12–6

THE ROBERTS CORPORATION
Worksheet for Statement of Changes in Financial Position
Year Ended December 31, 1980

	12/31/79 Debit	12/31/79 Credit	Transactions Debit		Transactions Credit		12/31/80 Debit	12/31/80 Credit
Working capital	100,000		(10) 20,000				120,000	
Fixed assets	45,000		(9) 3,000		(5) 8,000		40,000	
Accumulated depreciation		15,000	(5) 5,000		(3) 10,000			20,000
Bonds payable		50,000	(8) 5,000					45,000
Common stock		70,000			(7) 5,000			75,000
Retained earnings		10,000	(2) 105,000		(1) 140,000			20,000
			(3) 10,000		(5) 2,500			
			(4) 7,500					
			(6) 5,000					
			(7) 5,000					
	145,000	145,000					160,000	160,000

	Working Capital Summary Increase	Working Capital Summary Decrease
Funds from operations		
Sales	(1) 140,000	
Operating expenses		(2) 105,000
Income tax.........................		(4) 7,500
Financial and other effects		
Proceeds on sale of fixed assets	(5) 5,500	
Paid dividends.....................		(6) 5,000
Retired bonds		(8) 5,000
Purchased fixed assets		(9) 3,000
	145,500	125,500
Increase in working capital		(10) 20,000
	145,500	145,500

fixed assets, which would result in a $3,000 decrease in working capital.

Fixed Assets	3,000	
Cash/Accounts Payable		3,000

The worksheet entry is:

Fixed Assets	3,000	
Working Capital (Purchase of Fixed Assets) ...		3,000

We have now explained all the differences in the nonworking capital accounts. If we have proceeded correctly, the increase or decrease in working capital should agree with the balance in the working capital summary. See journal entry Number 10 recorded directly on the worksheet in Illustration 12–6.

We can now prepare a statement of changes in financial position (funds flow) from the bottom half of the worksheet (Illustration 12–6). This formal statement should include the changes in each working capital account. (See Illustration 12–7.)

ILLUSTRATION 12–7

THE ROBERTS CORPORATION
Statement of Changes in Financial Position
For the Year Ended December 31, 1980

Source of funds:		
Operations	$27,500	
Sale of fixed assets	5,500	$33,000
Uses of funds:		
Paid dividends	$ 5,000	
Retired bonds	5,000	
Purchased fixed assets	3,000	13,000
Increase in working capital		$20,000
Changes in working capital consist of:		
Cash		$10,000
Accounts receivable		5,000
Inventory		(5,000)
Prepayments		2,000
Accounts payable		10,500
Income tax payable		(2,500)
Increase in working capital		$20,000

Other possible formats for the *funds from operations* portion of the statement are:

Funds from operations:

Sales		$140,000
Operating expenses	$105,000	
Federal income tax	7,500	112,500
Funds from operations		$ 27,500

Funds from operations:

Net income	$ 20,000
Add back expenses which do not require an outflow of funds—Depreciation	10,000
	30,000
Deduct revenues which did not provide funds—Gain on sale of fixed assets	2,500
	$ 27,500

CASH DEFINED AS FUNDS

If funds are defined as cash instead of as working capital, the changes in *all* the working capital accounts must be presented separately in the body of the statement of changes in financial position and the statement is essentially one of cash flows. Financial analysts find this cash flow (funds defined as cash) statement particularly useful in judging an enterprise's current liquidity.

In the Roberts Corporation case, the increase in accounts receivable from $35,000 (12/31/79) to $40,000 (12/31/80) would represent $5,000 of sales that were not collected in cash. To get cash inflow from sales we would have to reduce the $140,000 charge sales by the $5,000 that was not collected. Cash inflow from sales would be $135,000; $35,000 (collection of 12/31/79 accounts receivable) plus $100,000 ($140,000 sales minus $40,000 12/31/80 accounts receivable). Similar analysis could be made of all the other working capital items by listing them as individual line items in the funds worksheet and including them in the formal statement which is presented in Illustration 12–8.

USES OF THE STATEMENT OF CHANGES IN FINANCIAL POSITION

The statement of changes in financial position indicates the strategy the firm has used in obtaining and employing its resources. Management's current decisions about the sources and uses of their resources are probably the best predictor of what they will do in the future. This statement can, therefore, be very useful in estimating the policy the firm will follow for dividend payments, capital expenditures, and financing by debt and equity.

This statement also enhances the comparability of different enterprises as the funds from operations figure is not as distorted by inflation and alternative accounting policies as is net income.

ILLUSTRATION 12–8

ROBERTS CORPORATION
Statement of Changes in Financial Position*
For the Year Ended December 31, 1980

Sources of cash:
From operations:

Sales	$140,000	
Cash basis adjustments		
Increase in accounts receivable	(5,000)	
Cash inflow from sales		$135,000
Operating expenses	$105,000	
Cash basis adjustments		
Decrease in inventory	(5,000)	
Increase in prepayments	2,000	
Decrease in accounts payable	10,500	
Cash outflow for operating expenses	$112,500	
Income tax expense	$ 7,500	
Cash basis adjustments		
Increase in income taxes payable	(2,500)	
Cash outflow for income taxes	$ 5,000	
Cash outflow for operating expenses and income taxes		117,500
Cash from operations		$ 17,500
Sale of fixed assets		5,500
		$ 23,000
Uses of cash:		
Paid dividends	$ 5,000	
Retired bonds	5,000	
Purchased fixed assets	3,000	13,000
Increase in cash		$ 10,000

* For purposes of this statement funds are defined as cash.

Case 12–1

SSC Corporation

Comparative balance sheets of the SSC Corporation as of December 31, 1980, and December 31, 1979, an income statement, and a statement of changes in stockholders' equity for the year ended December 31, 1980, are shown below.

SSC CORPORATION

Comparative Balance Sheets

(000s omitted)

	December 31, 1980	December 31, 1979
Assets		
Cash	$ 230	$ 319
Accounts receivable	2,388	1,616
Inventories	2,492	1,449
Prepaid expenses	62	78
Total current assets	$5,172	$3,462
Property, plant and equipment, at cost:		
Land	$ 186	$ 94
Buildings	968	570
Machinery and equipment	865	583
	$2,019	$1,247
Less: Accumulated depreciation	528	416
	$1,491	$ 831
Excess of purchase price over net assets of companies acquired	1,224	1,227
	$7,887	$5,520

	December 31, 1980	December 31, 1979
Equities		
Notes payable—current portion	$1,118	$ 628
Accounts payable	880	417
Accrued liabilities	963	532
Total current liabilities	$2,961	$1,577
Notes payable after one year	314	291
	$3,275	$1,868
Stockholders' equity:		
Common stock	$ 22	$ 25
Paid-in capital	2,426	2,916
Retained earnings	2,164	711
Total stockholders' equity	$4,612	$3,652
	$7,887	$5,520

Statement of Income
For the Year Ended December 31, 1980

Sales	$11,988
Cost and expenses:	
Cost of sales*	$ 5,280
Selling and administrative*	4,428
Interest	93
	$ 9,801
	$ 2,187
Other income:	
Gain on sale of equipment†	19
Income before income taxes	$ 2,206
Provision for income taxes	753
Net income	$ 1,453

Statement of Changes in Stockholders' Equity
For the Year Ended December 31, 1980

	Common Stock	Paid-In Capital	Retained Earnings (deficit)
Balance, January 1, 1980	$25	$2,916	$ 711
Repurchase of common stock	(3)	(490)	
Net income			1,453
Balance, December 31, 1980	$22	$2,426	$2,164

* Includes depreciation of $126 and amortization of goodwill of $3.
† The only equipment sold in 1980 was fully depreciated.

Required:

1. Prepare a statement of changes in financial position worksheet. Assume funds are defined as working capital. Make sure you cross-reference each entry on the worksheet.
2. Prepare a statement of changes in financial position for the year ended December 31, 1980.

Case 12–2

The Orange Bowl Corporation

The Orange Bowl Corporation is a Miami-based operator and franchiser of Orange Bowl snack bars. Since its inception the company has located its fast-food outlets exclusively in the enclosed, air-conditioned malls of major regional shopping centers. Orange Bowl stores were designed to provide quick, convenient, and economical snack service for shoppers in high traffic areas. The company actively cultivated a reputation of cleanliness, courtesy, and efficiency for its stores.

In 1970, Walter O'Connell purchased 125,000 shares of the Orange Bowl Corporation common stock at a price of $287,500. He had been extremely impressed by the energy and creativity of the company's management and by the bright growth prospects for Orange Bowl stores.

In the next three years, O'Connell's investment judgment seemed to be vindicated as the Orange Bowl Corporation proceeded to fulfill his high-growth expectations. By the middle of 1973, the value of O'Connell's investment had more than doubled.

The performance of the Orange Bowl Corporation had been particularly good in the fiscal year ending July 31, 1973. The number of Orange Bowl snack bars increased to 71, an increase of 45 percent over the year before. Twenty were company-owned, 46 franchised, and 5 were joint ventures. In addition, another 15 Orange Bowl stores were under construction. During the period, net income before taxes jumped 48 percent to $235,000 in 1973, from $159,000 in 1972. Total assets climbed 52 percent to $1,901,000 in 1973, from $1,252,000 in 1972 (see Exhibits 1 and 2).

O'Connell, however, was worried. His optimism had been tempered by several recent cases in which aggressive "go-go" companies had succumbed to too rapid growth. These companies had placed excessive reliance on external financing in years of profit and growth, and subsequently encountered difficulty in meeting debt repayments and obtaining new loans when a bad year occurred.

EXHIBIT 1

THE ORANGE BOWL CORPORATION AND SUBSIDIARIES
Consolidated Balance Sheets
July 31, 1973 and 1972

	1973	1972
Assets		
Current assets:		
Cash	$ 297,000	$ 248,000
Due from franchises	401,000	223,000
Miscellaneous receivables	31,000	55,000
Inventory	23,000	14,000
Prepaid expenses	31,000	27,000
Total current assets	$ 783,000	$ 567,000
Long-term assets:		
Land	$ 190,000	$ 12,000
Building and improvements	66,000	66,000
Equipment and furniture	432,000	352,000
Leasehold improvements	420,000	220,000
	$1,108,000	$ 650,000
Less: Accumulated depreciation	(169,000)	(124,000)
	$ 939,000	$ 526,000
Marketable securities	6,000	—
Investments in joint ventures	92,000	79,000
Investments in subsidiary	44,000	44,000
Other assets	37,000	36,000
Total assets	$1,901,000	$1,252,000
Liabilities and Stockholders' Equity		
Current liabilities:		
Notes and mortgages payable (current portion)	$ 147,000	$ 116,000
Accounts payable	270,000	86,000
Accrued expenses	46,000	36,000
Accrued income taxes	82,000	40,000
Reserve for loss on lease settlements	15,000	2,000
Other current liabilities	82,000	102,000
Total current liabilities	$ 642,000	$ 382,000
Long-term liabilities:		
Notes and mortgages payable	$ 354,000	$ 148,000
Deposits from franchises	42,000	22,000
Deferred franchise fees	85,000	51,000
Total long-term liabilities	$ 481,000	$ 221,000
Stockholders' equity:		
Common stock ($.10 par value, authorized 1,000,000 shares, issued 490,000 shares)	$ 49,000	$ 49,000
Paid-in surplus	462,000	462,000
Retained earnings	267,000	138,000
Total stockholders' equity	$ 778,000	$ 649,000
Total liabilities and equity	$1,901,000	$1,252,000

EXHIBIT 2 _____

THE ORANGE BOWL CORPORATION AND SUBSIDIARIES
Consolidated Statement of Income
Fiscal Year Ended July 31, 1973

Income from operations:

Sales of food and beverages	$1,601,000
Less: Cost of goods sold	554,000
Gross profit from operations	$1,047,000

Other Income:

Sales of franchises	194,000
Franchise royalties	154,000
Gross income	$1,395,000

Expenses:

Selling, general and administrative Expenses (includes depreciation of $50,000 and amortization of leasehold improvements of $11,000)	$1,125,000
Provision for loss on lease settlements	35,000
Net income before taxes	$ 235,000
Provision for income taxes	106,000
Net income after taxes	$ 129,000

O'Connell feared that the Orange Bowl Corporation might fit such a pattern. He was particularly concerned with the 140 percent increase in company borrowings, from $148,000 in 1972, to $354,000 in 1973. In addition, working capital had declined by $44,000.

Owning 25 percent of the company's outstanding stock, O'Connell had considerable influence on management. He communicated his anxiety to Leonard Turkel, the president of the company, who attempted to show O'Connell that the company was pursuing a prudent growth policy. He contended that the company was generating over half its cash needs internally, and that the sharp increase in the company's debt account was due to the purchase of 2.75 acres of unimproved land in Dade County, Florida, which the company planned to hold as an investment.

Required:

1. As the company's accountant, prepare a statement of changes in financial position for 1973. Also provide a written analysis of the statement, keeping in mind Turkel's contention that the company generates over half of its cash needs internally.
2. If you were Turkel, what other facts would you present to convince O'Connell that you are a prudent manager?
3. If you were O'Connell, what would you do? Would you sell your stock? Why, or why not?

Case 12–3

Wright Electronics Corporation

In his annual letter to shareholders forwarding the 1975 corporate annual report and financial statements (see Exhibits 1 and 2), Chairman of the Board Samuel P. Molane stated the following:

> The general recession affected business conditions in the consumer and industrial sectors of the electronics industry as well as incoming orders in manufacturing operations, causing Wright Electronics to miss sales and earnings targets established at the beginning of the year. Despite the weakened business environment beginning in the fall of 1974, pretax profits from operations, before goodwill write-off, reached $2,567,122, an increase of 24 percent over fiscal 1974. Close attention to inventories and receivables enabled us to achieve a positive cash flow and improved return on assets. After considerable thought and discussion, our board approved the write-off of all the company's goodwill which amounted to $5,828,262. The intangible asset represented purchase price paid in excess of net worth for six separate companies acquired during the years 1967 through 1970. Although all six operations are profitable, the action taken was based on the desire to present Wright's financial position in terms of realistic values in view of current economic conditions and to purify the company's balance sheet to the point where only hard dollar values are the elements used in computing the company's shareholders' equity. The company's book value after the write-off is $1.58 per share.

In the corpus of the annual report, the treasurer of the corporation commented:

> The action by our Board of Directors to write off all the company's goodwill shows Wright's assets, liabilities, and equity in true relationship as used in daily operations. Accounting principles treat this write-off as a charge to operating income. Since cash was not affected by the write-off, net income contribution to Wright's cash flow amounted to $2,034,843 in 1975, compared with $1,928,411 in 1974.
>
> Working capital at the end of March 1975 was $13,601,608, an increase of $1,239,444 from a year earlier. Current assets decreased $583,929 while current liabilities decreased $1,843,373. Quick assets consisting of cash and cash equivalents, and trade receivables, exceeded total current liabilities by $2,183,281.

In the long-term debt subsection of the notes accompanying the financial statement, two additional interesting paragraphs were included.

> The 7 percent note payable to an insurance company (aggregating $3.7 million of the $8.4 million in long-term debt), which is due in installments to 1983, provides that the lender can require the Company

EXHIBIT 1 _____

WRIGHT ELECTRONICS CORPORATION
Balance Sheet
March 31, 1975, and 1974
(in millions, rounded)

	1975	1974
Assets		
Current:		
Cash...	$ 1.9	$ 1.8
Accounts receivable, net	6.8	7.6
Inventories	11.2	11.1
Prepaid expenses............................	.2	.2
	$20.1	$20.7
Property, plant, and equipment	$ 5.1	$ 5.7
Less: Accumulated depreciation	3.3	3.6
	$ 1.8	$ 2.1
Other assets (patents)........................	$ .8	$ .7
Cost of purchased subsidiaries in excess of tangible asset value at date of acquisition (goodwill)	$ —	$ 5.8
Total assets	$22.7	$29.3
Liabilities and Shareholders' Equities		
Current:		
Accounts payable...........................	$ 5.5	$ 7.2
Income taxes payable.......................	.1	.1
Current portion of long-term debt.............	.9	1.0
Total current liabilities	$ 6.5	$ 8.3
Long-term debt	$ 8.4	$ 9.4
Deferred taxes..............................	$ 1.5	$ 1.5
Shareholders' equity:		
Preferred stock	$ .1	$ .1
Common stock..............................	2.0	2.0
Additional paid-in capital....................	8.6	8.6
Retained earnings (deficit)	(4.0)	(.2)
	$ 6.7	$10.5
Less: Treasury stock at cost	.4	.4
Total shareholders' equity..............	$ 6.3	$10.1
Total equities	$22.7	$29.3

EXHIBIT 2 _____

WRIGHT ELECTRONICS CORPORATION
Statement of Income (Condensed)
For the Years Ending March 31, 1975, and 1974
(in millions, rounded)

	1975	1974
Net sales	$62.5	$60.3
Cost of sales	45.3*	44.0
Gross profit	$17.2	$16.3
Selling and administrative expenses	13.7	13.4
Interest expense	.9	.8
Income from operations	$ 2.6	$ 2.1
Income tax expense (net of tax loss carry-forwards of .7 and 1.0 in 1975 and 1974)	.6	.2
Write-off of goodwill	5.8	—
Net income	($ 3.8)	$ 1.9
Earnings per share (based on 3,984,472 average common shares outstanding each year)	($ .95)	$ .48

* Includes depreciation expense for the year totalling $.8 million.

to pay the unpaid balance on such note in full within one year after Samuel P. Molane, Chairman of the Board and Chief Executive Officer of the company, ceases to be engaged in the active management of the company.

The agreements relating to the long-term debt payable to banks ($4.7 million) provide for compensating balances equal to 15 percent of the debt to the banks, require the maintenance of specified amounts of working capital and shareholders' equity by the company, restrict the amounts which can be incurred for property and inventories, limit the amount of additional indebtedness and lease commitments which can be incurred, and restrict the amounts which can be paid for dividends and principal and interest on subordinated notes. At March 31, 1975, the working capital and shareholders' equity amounts of the company were 129 percent and 116 percent, respectively, of the minimum amounts required by the loan agreements during the 1976 fiscal year, or $3,100,000 and $840,000, respectively, in excess of the minimum amounts. The minimum requirements for working capital increase by $1,000,000 and $500,000, and the minimum requirements for shareholders' equity increase by $1,150,000 and $1,250,000, respectively, during the 1977 and 1978 fiscal years.

The notes to the financial statements further disclosed that the Wright Corporation disposed of certain equipment during the year for its net book value of $200,000 (rounded). In addition, purchases of transportation equipment and machinery totaling $700,000 were made during the period.

Required:

1. Prepare a statement of change in financial position for the year ended March 31, 1975.
2. Relate the work done in 1 above to the following questions:
   a. What did you think of Chairman Molane's and the treasurer's comments? What is meant by "purifying the company's balance sheet to the point where only hard dollar values are the elements used in computing the company's shareholders' equity?"
   b. Why does the treasurer place great emphasis on cash flow and working capital? Do the covenants to the long-term debt loan agreement bear on the question?
   c. Given the financial situation of Wright in March 1975, do the loan covenants appear reasonable?

Case 12–4

Asarco Incorporated and Consolidated Subsidiaries (B)

Required:

1. What significant changes took place in the first quarter of 1979?
2. Management indicated in a letter to Asarco stockholders that one of the reasons they could not increase dividends more was that only a small portion of the $30,146,000 reported as equity in earnings of nonconsolidated associated companies on the income statement was actually cash. Do you agree?
3. How does Asarco define funds?
4. What would be the increase in funds for the period if Asarco defined funds as working capital?

FIRST QUARTER 1979

The consolidated statement of changes in financial position for the quarter ended March 31, 1979, is listed below.

Consolidated Statement of Changes in Financial Position (unaudited)
(dollars in thousands)

	Three Months Ended March 31	
	1979	1978
Sources (uses) of Cash		
Operations:		
Net earnings (loss)	$ 37,345	$(11,129)
Noncash items included in net earnings (loss):		
Depreciation and depletion	12,681	12,781
Deferred income taxes	3,353	611
Equity in earnings of nonconsolidated associated companies, in excess of dividends received	(27,468)	(9,423)
Other	(1,568)	(1,408)
Cash provided from (used for) operations	$ 24,343	$ (8,568)
Cash dividends declared and paid on common stock	$ (3,051)	$ (2,672)
Investment activities:		
Property	$(12,354)	$(19,801)
Other	(1,076)	(6,426)
Cash used for investment activities	$(13,430)	$(26,227)
Working capital, exclusive of cash and current debt:		
Accounts receivable	$(25,531)	$ (6,975)
Inventories	(24,238)	(495)
Materials, supplies, and prepaid expenses	2,167	2,871
Accounts payable	60,454	2,923
Other current liabilities	9,133	3,272
Cash provided from working capital	$ 21,985	$ 1,596
Increase (decrease) in cash before financing activities	$ 29,847	$(35,871)
Financing activities:		
Bank loans repaid	$ (2,488)	$ (1,193)
Long-term debt incurred	22	39,750
Long-term debt retired	(1,294)	(875)
Debt proceeds released from escrow for construction	2,668	3,648
Repayments of proceeds from sale of future production	(1,152)	—
Treasury stock used, net	99	9
Cash (used for) provided from financing activities	$ (2,145)	$ 41,339
Increase in cash and marketable securities	$ 27,702	$ 5,468
Cash and marketable securities, beginning of period	27,456	9,112
Cash and marketable securities, end of period	$ 55,158	$ 14,580

13

Changing Prices and Foreign Currency Translations

FINANCIAL REPORTING AND CHANGING PRICES

Generally accepted accounting principles require financial statements to be prepared using the historical cost model. The balance sheet and income statement accounts are valued at their historical cost measured in dollars.[1] No adjustments are made to financial statements to reflect an increase (inflation) or decrease (deflation) in the general price level or to reflect increases or decreases in the prices of specific assets (specific price changes).

Inflation or deflation results in a change in the purchasing power of the dollar. Adding the historical costs of asset acquisitions made at different points in time (different purchasing power sacrifices) is similar to adding German marks and French francs. Each measuring unit has a different value. The more severe the inflation or deflation, the greater will be the change in the purchasing power of the dollar and the more likely financial statements prepared using the historical cost model (which assumes all dollars are the same) will be misleading.

Constant dollar (general price level) accounting restates historical cost financial statements in a common measuring unit in order to correct for the impact of inflation or deflation on the financial statements.

Historical cost financial statements which do not consider increases or decreases in the *specific prices* of assets may also be misleading. The prices of specific assets may fluctuate for reasons other than changes in the general price level. Technology and changes in supply and demand may cause the prices of specific items to move contrary to the general price level. For example, over the past decade, when inflation was significant, the price of computers decreased rather than increased.

---

[1] Some exceptions to the cost principle are inventories which are valued at lower of cost or market and short-term marketable equity securities which are valued at lower of cost or market on a portfolio basis.

Historical cost financial statements fail to record these changes in specific prices of assets or management's decision to hold rather than sell assets. When assets are sold the gains or losses from holding the assets in prior periods are reflected in the *current* income statement. Unrealized gains or losses (increases or decreases in the specific prices of assets held) are not recognized in the periods in which they occur.

Current cost methods attempt to adjust historical cost financial statements for specific price changes. Their objective is to have the balance sheet reflect current market values and to have the income statement include the effects of unrealized gains and losses due to the increase or decrease in the specific prices of assets held.

GENERAL PRICE LEVEL ACCOUNTING (CONSTANT DOLLAR ACCOUNTING)

The objective of general price level accounting is to restate the historical cost values of conventional accrual accounting in a common measuring unit and to calculate the purchasing power gain or loss on the enterprise's monetary position. All accounts are translated into constant (same unit of general purchasing power) dollars using a general price level index.[2] No accounting principles are changed, but the change to a uniform measuring unit insures that the resulting financial statements are objective, comparable, and verifiable.

BALANCE SHEET ACCOUNTS

It is not necessary to restate monetary assets and monetary liabilities as they are already stated in constant dollars (dollars of the balance sheet date). *Monetary assets* are cash and fixed obligations to receive cash, such as accounts receivable and notes receivable. *Monetary liabilities* are fixed obligations to pay cash, such as accounts payable and long-term debt. Net monetary assets are monetary assets minus monetary liabilities.

A building is not a monetary asset since it is neither an obligation

---

[2] The constant dollar chosen is usually the most recent balance sheet date dollar. A general price level index is used to measure the value (general purchasing power) of the dollar at different points in time. Two such indices are the Consumer Price Index (CPI) and the Gross National Product Implicit Price Deflator (GNPIPD). The CPI tracks the price level of a basket of goods and services purchased by a typical consumer. The GNPIPD tracks the price level of all goods and services making up the GNP.

to pay or to receive cash. Suppose Company A acquired a building ten years ago at a cost of $10,000 when the general price level index was 50. The building has no salvage value and is being depreciated on a straight-line basis over 20 years. The general price level index on the current balance sheet date is 100. Over the past ten years the general price level has increased by 100 percent (50/50). A dollar expenditure ten years ago is equivalent in terms of general purchasing power to a current expenditure of two dollars. The acquisition cost of the building is restated to $20,000 ($10,000 × 100/50). The $20,000 is the purchasing power sacrifice measured in constant (balance sheet date) dollars which had to be expended to obtain the building ten years ago. The $20,000 is the original cost of the building converted into constant (current balance sheet date) dollars. It is *not* the current market value of the building. The market price of the building may have changed in a different direction and magnitude than the *general* price level index.

Under constant dollar accounting all other nonmonetary accounts (for example, land, inventory, common stock) are restated in a manner similar to the building account. The constant dollar retained earnings account is obtained by subtracting all the constant dollar liability and stockholder equity accounts from the constant dollar asset accounts. The retained earnings account will reflect all prior years' earnings minus dividends expressed in constant dollars.

If companies do not adjust their balance sheets for changes in the value of the measuring unit (the dollar), their asset and liability valuations will not present an accurate picture of their financial position. This is particularly true for companies that have large inventories (particularly Lifo inventories) and are capital intensive.

INCOME STATEMENT

The methodology for restatement of income statement accounts is similar to that for balance sheet accounts.

Suppose Company C has historical cost sales revenue of $88,000 (sales occur evenly throughout the year) in a year when the general price level index rose from 200 to 220. To convert sales to constant end-of-year dollars, historical cost sales are multiplied by 1.05. The sales occurred uniformly throughout the year, and the relationship of the end-of-year dollar to the average dollar of the year is 220/210 (approximately 1.05). Price level adjusted sales revenue is $92,000 (1.05 × $88,000).

All other revenue and expense items occurring evenly throughout the year are similarly adjusted.

Depreciation expense and cost of goods sold may require much larger adjustments. Historical cost depreciation expense on the building acquired by Company A in the previous example is $500 ($10,000 × 1/20). The building would be restated on the balance sheet date at $20,000 ($10,000 × 100/50) and price level adjusted depreciation expense is $1,000 ($20,000 × 1/20).

If a company uses an inventory flow assumption other than Lifo, the cost of goods sold is likely to be measured in dollars from a prior accounting period (when goods were purchased), and the adjustment to current dollars can be substantial.

When the general price level rises, a company loses purchasing power on all monetary assets it holds (the monetary assets will purchase fewer goods and services). It gains, and its creditors lose purchasing power on its monetary liabilities. A company with positive net monetary assets will lose purchasing power during inflationary periods. Companies with monetary liabilities in excess of monetary assets will gain purchasing power during inflationary periods. They will pay off their debt with "cheaper" dollars.

The purchasing power gain or loss on net monetary assets can be computed as follows: Suppose Company B has average net monetary assets of $12,000 for the year and that the general price level index rose from 150 at the beginning of the year to 165 at the end of the year. Because the general price level index rose 10 percent (15/150) Company B experienced a purchasing power loss of $1,200 ($12,000 × 15/150) by being a net creditor during the year.

Purchasing power gains on debt should be considered when figuring a firm's real cost of borrowing money. If purchasing power gains on debt equal the reported historical cost interest expense for the period, both the company and its creditors agreed to interest rates which just offset the general rise in prices over the period. (The creditors are probably upset over such an outcome. More than likely their expectation at the beginning of the period was for a real return—interest earned in excess of general price level rises.) If interest expense exceeds the purchasing power gain on debt for the period, the company paid more than the general price level inflation rate in interest and the creditors of the company "earned more" than the inflation rate.

If companies do not adjust their income statements for changes in the value of the measuring unit (the dollar) their net income figures will not be an accurate measure of the results of operations. This is particularly true for companies that have a large fixed asset base, that do not use the Lifo inventory flow assumption, and that have a large net monetary position.

AN EXAMPLE—GENERAL PRICE LEVEL ADJUSTMENT

For the past several years Shell Oil Company included price level adjusted figures as a supplement to their historical cost financial statements. Except for depreciation all income statement items are adjusted upward by about 3 percent. Note the large adjustment for depreciation. This is typical since the average age of depreciable assets is much greater than one year. The much larger adjustment for depreciation causes price level adjusted net income (before gains or losses on monetary items) to be lower than historical cost income. Since Shell uses Lifo, the adjustment to cost of goods sold (operating and selling costs) is not as large as it would have been if they had used Fifo. Since Shell is a large net debtor, the purchasing power gain on monetary items compensates for the decline in translated preliminary income. The difference between price level adjusted net income and historical cost net income is 9.1 percent for Shell. Depending on the nature of its revenues and expenses and the size of its monetary assets and liabilities, a company may report price level adjusted income which is greater or less than historical cost net income (see Illustration 13–1).

ILLUSTRATION 13–1

SHELL OIL COMPANY
1978 Income Statement
(in millions)

	Historical Cost	Price Level Adjusted	Percent Change
Sales	$11,123	$11,446	2.9
Costs:			
Depreciation	597	869	45.6
Interest	112	115	2.7
Taxes	779	802	3.0
Operating and selling	8,821	9,106	3.2
Total costs	($10,309)	($10,892)	
Preliminary income	814	554	(31.9)
Purchasing power gain	—	186	
Net income	$ 814	$ 740	(9.1)

SPECIFIC PRICE LEVEL ADJUSTMENTS

This method of measurement emphasizes specific price changes of assets rather than price changes caused by general inflation (constant dollar accounting). It values individual assets at the cost to replace them as of the current balance sheet date.

BALANCE SHEET

The two major methods for obtaining specific price level adjusted asset values are *current cost* and *current replacement cost*.[3] The current cost approach values assets at the current cost to produce an *identical asset* (whether or not in actuality an identical asset would ever be used to replace the current one). The current replacement cost approach values assets at the current cost of replacing the *existing productive capacity* of the asset. Consider the current valuation of a steel mill in operation since 1950. The *current cost* of the mill is an estimate of the cost to construct a mill identical in all respects to the existing mill (even though the existing mill is technologically outdated and would probably never be replaced with a new mill of the same type). The *current replacement cost* valuation would first develop an estimate of the capacity of the existing mill and then a determination of the cost to build a new mill (based on new technology) of similar capacity. In the current balance sheet both the current cost and current replacement cost of the new mill would be adjusted for approximately 30 years of straight-line depreciation. If technology is not changing, current cost and current replacement cost valuations are likely to be almost identical. In the steel industry, where technology has changed dramatically over the past 30 years, the valuation under the two methods would be substantially different.

Current costs and current replacement costs are much more subjective estimates of value than are historical costs or historical costs adjusted for changes in the general price level. It is particularly difficult to determine the current cost of specially designed assets.

INCOME STATEMENT

Current cost revenues are equal to historical cost revenues. Current cost expenses are stated at the cost of replacing the asset at the

---

[3] The Securities and Exchange Commission's *Accounting Series Release 190* required companies (nonfinancial public companies whose inventories and gross plant, property, and equipment total $100 million and for whom that total is at least ten percent of all assets) to include current replacement cost data in annual 10-K reports filed with the SEC for fiscal years ending after December 25, 1976. The current replacement cost of inventories, cost of goods sold, depreciable, depletable or amortizable productive assets, and the related depreciation, depletion or amortization expense had to be disclosed. Subsequently the FASB issued *Statement No. 33*, "Financial Reporting and Changing Prices," (effective for fiscal years ending on or after December 25, 1979), and the SEC dropped their required current replacement cost disclosures. Disclosures required by *Statement No. 33* are illustrated later in this chapter.

moment in time it is consumed in the generation of a revenue. Suppose an item in inventory acquired one year ago for $25 is sold for $75. At the time of the sale, price lists show that it would cost $45 to obtain an identical item for inventory. The current cost of goods sold is $45. The current operating income realized on the sale is $30 ($75 − $45). Historical cost income is $50 ($75 − $25). The $20 difference in income results because the current cost of inventory has gone up by $20.

The difference between the current cost of an asset (for example, $45 inventory item) and the historical cost of an asset ($25 inventory item) is a *holding gain*. The holding gain or loss on the item in inventory is realized when the item is sold.

The current cost method attempts to decompose historical cost income into two components, current operating income and realized holding gains.

Historical Cost		*Current Cost*	
Revenue	$75	Revenue	$75
Cost of goods sold	25	Cost of goods sold	45
Net income	$50	Current operating income	$30
		Realized holding gain	20
		Realized income	$50

Current operating income is the difference between historical cost revenue (which equals current cost revenue) and current cost expenses. Realized holding gains measure the holding gains present in the assets used up or sold during the period. Current operating income (distributable income) is an informative measure of income. If the firm wishes to maintain operations at its current level and replenish its inventory at current cost, no more than $30 should be paid out in taxes and dividends.

Current cost depreciation expense is also likely to exceed historical cost depreciation expense since current costs of assets are likely to exceed historical costs of assets. Suppose Company X acquired an asset five years ago at a cost of $1,000. The asset has a ten-year life, zero salvage value, and is being depreciated on a straight-line basis. Historical cost depreciation is $100. If the current value of a similar new asset is $3,000, current cost depreciation expense will be $300 for the period.

In addition to realized holding gains, current cost methods usually propose that the unrealized holding gains of the period (changes in current values from the beginning of the period to the end of the period for assets not sold) be reported. In the preceding example, if the item was not sold, the $20 would be reported as an unrealized rather than realized holding gain of the period.

Current cost statements are generally viewed as providing a better economic measure of the success of operations in a period than historical cost statements. The rate of return on investment can be computed using current operating income in the numerator and current cost or current replacement cost of assets in the denominator. Unlike the standard rate of return measure (historical cost income/book value of assets), this measure is independent of realized holding gains and obsolete asset values. The measure is comparable across time and across firms.

FINANCIAL REPORTING AND CHANGING PRICES[4]

The FASB requires companies with inventories and gross fixed assets exceeding $125 million or with a book value of total assets in excess of $1 billion to provide supplementary financial statement information about the effects of inflation on its operations and financial position. *Both* general price level (constant dollar) and specific price level (current cost) information is required. This requirement is intended to help readers assess the performance, the status of operating capability, and the future cash flows of an enterprise.

The FASB defines current cost as the current cost of acquiring the same service potential (indicated by operating costs and physical output capacity) embodied by the asset owned. Current costs may be determined by applying specialized indexes to the historical cost of assets, by obtaining readily available current purchase prices of some standard assets, or by any other method appropriate to the circumstances.

The Consumer Price Index is to be used for restatement to constant dollars since it is published monthly and is better understood than other alternative indices such as the GNP Implicit Price Deflator.

The FASB requires both numerical data and verbal explanations of the data. The price level adjusted statements for the Inland Steel Company in Illustration 13–2 show compliance with FASB *Statement No. 33*.[5]

Constant dollar income from continuing operations must be disclosed. Only restatement of historical cost depreciation, depletion and amortization expense, and cost of goods sold is required. Sales and other expenses need not be restated because the restated amounts are not likely to differ materially from historical cost

---

[4] FASB *Statement No. 33*, "Financial Reporting and Changing Prices," October 1979.

[5] Illustration of Financial Reporting and Changing Prices, Statement of Financial Accounting Standards No. 33, FASB (Stamford), December 1979.

ILLUSTRATION 13-2 _____

INLAND STEEL COMPANY AND SUBSIDIARY COMPANIES
Statement of Income from Continuing Operations, Adjusted for Changing Prices
For the Year Ended December 31, 1978
(In thousands of average 1978 dollars)

Income from continuing operations, as reported in the Consolidated Statement of Income	$158,310
Adjustment to restate costs for the effect of general inflation: Depreciation, amortization, and depletion	(75,000)
Income from continuing operations adjusted for general inflation ..	$ 83,310
Adjustment to reflect the difference between general inflation and changes in specific prices (current costs): Depreciation, amortization, and depletion	(36,000)
Income from continuing operations adjusted for changes in specific prices	$ 47,310
Gain on net monetary liabilities due to decline in purchasing power of the dollar in 1978.....................................	$ 64,000
Total increase in specific prices (current cost) of inventories and property, plant, and equipment held during the year*...........	$217,000
Less: Effect of increase in general price level	159,000
Excess of increase in specific prices over the increase in the general price level	$ 58,000

* At December 31, 1978, the current cost of inventory was $738 million and the current cost of property, plant, and equipment, net of accumulated depreciation was $2,444 million.

amounts. Inland Steel's constant dollar income from continuing operations is less than historical cost income from continuing operations by $75 million. The total difference is attributed to the excess of general price level adjusted depreciation over historical cost depreciation. In its historical cost statements Inland Steel uses Lifo to compute cost of goods sold. Cost of goods sold using Lifo is sufficiently close to the general price level adjusted cost of goods sold so that no adjustment is necessary.

Current cost income from continuing operations must also be computed. As in the constant dollar information only cost of goods sold and depreciation, depletion, and amortization expenses need to be restated. For Inland Steel current cost depreciation *exceeded* general price level adjusted depreciation by $36 million. Inland Steel used the Consumer Price Index to compute general price level adjusted asset values and the *Engineering News Record* Construction Cost Index to compute the current cost of assets. Inland felt that this particular index closely reflected changes in the replacement cost of its assets. Because specific price level adjusted asset values exceed the general price level adjusted asset values, current cost depreciation expense exceeds general price level adjusted depreciation expense for the year.

The purchasing power gain or loss on net monetary items must be computed. Inland Steel held more monetary liabilities than monetary assets during the year. It showed a purchasing power gain of $64 million for the year.

FASB *Statement No. 33* also requires firms to compute current cost holding gains or losses on inventory and fixed assets. The gains or losses are to be reported both gross and net of general inflation. The current cost of Inland Steel's inventory and assets held during the year increased by $217 million. Of this amount $159 was attributed to general price level inflation.

The following simple example illustrates the computation of holding gains. A company acquires two assets for $50 and $100 at the beginning of the current year when the general price level index is 100. It sells the $50 asset midway through the period for $75 when the current cost is $60 and the general price level index is 110. At the end of the year the current cost of the $100 unsold asset is $140 and the general price level index is 120.

At the end of the year there is an unrealized holding gain of $40 ($140 − $100) on the unsold asset. $20 of this gain is attributable to inflation because the general price level went up 20 percent. The realized holding gain on the asset sold during the year is $10 ($60 − $50). Of this, $5 is attributed to general price level inflation.

Total holding gains ($40 + $10) (realized and unrealized)	$50
Less:	
Inflation component of holding gain ($20 + $5)	25
Holding gain (net of inflation)	$25

This disclosure indicates the portion of the holding gain attributable to inflation (increase in the general price level) and the portion of the holding gain attributable to specific price changes.

The current cost of year-end inventory and fixed assets also must be disclosed (see footnote in Inland Steel's income statement).

In addition to inflation adjusted information for the current period, companies are required to present a five-year summary similar to Illustration 13–3 (see footnote 5).

Note that cash dividends and market price per common share are reported as adjusted for changes in the general price level. This enables readers to focus on real changes in dividend payments and market prices.

ILLUSTRATION 13–3

INLAND STEEL COMPANY AND SUBSIDIARY COMPANIES

Five-Year Comparison of Selected Supplementary Financial Data Adjusted for Effects of Changing Prices

(in millions of average 1978 dollars)

(per share amounts in average 1978 dollars)

	Years Ended December 31				
	1974	1975	1976	1977	1978*
Net sales and other operating revenues					
at historical cost	$2,450	$2,107	$2,388	$2,682	$3,248
in average 1978 dollars	3,241	2,554	2,737	2,889	3,248
Historical cost information adjusted for general inflation					
Income (loss) from continuing operations					83
Income (loss) from continuing operations per common share					3.99
Net assets at year-end					2,088
Current cost information					
Income (loss) from continuing operations					47
Income (loss) from continuing operations per common share					2.26
Excess of increase in specific prices over increase in the general price level					58
Net assets at year-end					2,366
Gain on net monetary liabilities due to decline of purchasing power of dollar					64
Cash dividends declared per common share					
at historical cost	2.70†	2.40	2.50	2.60	2.80
in average 1978 dollars	3.57	2.91	2.87	2.80	2.80
Market price per common share at year-end					
at historical cost	32.00	40.75	50.88	38.50	35.00
in average 1978 dollars	42.34	49.39	58.30	41.46	35.00
Average consumer price index	147.7	161.2	170.5	181.5	195.4

Note: The reader is cautioned that all prior year's data are stated in terms of 1978 dollars except where noted otherwise.

* For purposes of this illustration it is assumed that the constant dollar and current cost methods are effective for the first time in 1978.

† Includes a year-end extra dividend of $.40 per share.

The two methods of accounting for inflation help intelligent readers of financial statements to better understand the operating performance and financial position of a firm. General price level (constant dollar) accounting allows adjustments for inflation or deflation and makes asset valuations comparable within a firm and across firms in the same industry. Current cost methods filter out the holding gains and losses due to price changes of individual assets and allow the readers to focus on operating income.

FOREIGN CURRENCY TRANSLATIONS

Many U.S. corporations are multinational. They enter into transactions that are denominated in foreign currencies, and they have foreign subsidiaries which generally prepare their financial statements in local currencies.

Foreign currency denominated transactions and foreign currency financial statements must be translated into dollars, the common measuring unit, if all transactions and operations of the parent company are to be reported in a single set of financial statements.

Exchange rates express the price of one U.S. dollar in terms of another country's currency. For example, the German mark might be worth $.50 at a given point in time. Exchange rates fluctuate (float) in response to changes in supply and demand for the currencies involved.

Foreign Currency Denominated Transactions

Foreign currency denominated transactions arise frequently in normal operations of U.S. corporations. Firms purchase or sell goods on account which are priced in a foreign currency. They also borrow or lend funds denominated in a foreign currency.

For example, suppose that on March 20, 1980, the Multicompany purchases goods on account from a German manufacturer for 3,000 marks. The exchange rate at the time of purchase is three marks to the dollar. Multicompany has an account payable, denominated in German marks, which it must express in dollars on its balance sheet. On the transaction date 3,000 marks are equivalent to $1,000. Multicompany makes the following journal entry:

Inventory... 1000
    Accounts payable (3,000 marks, 3 marks = $1).   1000

Even though Multicompany has listed the account payable in dollars, the obligation can only be discharged by paying the German company 3,000 marks. Multicompany has to settle its account on

July 20, 1980, when the exchange rate is two marks to the dollar (the mark has strengthened relative to the dollar). It now takes $1,500 to obtain 3,000 marks to settle the account. The additional $500 represents an exchange loss. Multicompany makes the following journal entry to recognize the payment of the account payable.

Accounts payable.............................	1,000	
Currency exchange loss........................	500	
Cash.......................................		1,500

The weakness in the dollar relative to the mark has made it more costly to discharge its mark denominated account payable.

If the exchange rate was four marks to the dollar on July 20, 1980, then it would cost Multicompany $750 to obtain 3,000 marks to settle the account. In this case there would be a currency exchange gain of $250 ($1,000 − $750).

Since the account payable has been settled, the currency exchange loss recognized in the 1980 income statement has been realized. Suppose that Multicompany did not settle the account by December 31, 1980, the end of its fiscal year, and the exchange rate on December 31, 1980, is 2.5 marks to the dollar (3,000 marks is equivalent to $1,200).

Should the account payable be adjusted to reflect the currency fluctuation? The FASB has adopted the position that financial statement users should be informed of this economic event immediately and not have to wait until a future period when final settlement of the payable is made.[6]

Multicompany must translate all foreign currency denominated payables and receivables outstanding as of December 31, 1980. The following entry makes the revaluation and recognizes the *unrealized* currency exchange loss.

Currency exchange loss........................	200	
Accounts payable...........................		200

The unrealized currency exchange loss is part of 1980 income, and the account payable appears on the balance sheet at $1,200.[7]

---

[6] FASB *Statement No. 8*, "Accounting for the Translation of Foreign Currency Transactions and Foreign Currency Financial Statements," October 1975.

[7] No currency exchange gain or loss will be recognized (no restatement of the payable on the balance sheet is necessary) if the exchange exposure has been hedged. That is, the U.S. purchaser buys foreign currency with dollars on the transaction date or enters into a contract to exchange marks for dollars at a specified rate on a specified future date (the settlement date).

Translations

Consolidated statements report the results of operations and financial position of a parent and *all* of its subsidiaries.

The assets, liabilities, revenues, and expenses of a foreign subsidiary must be translated into dollars before the financial statements of the subsidiary can be consolidated with the parent or accounted for under the equity method.

On December 31, 1979, a French subsidiary of Multicompany began operations. Its balance sheet is presented in Illustration 13–4. On this date the exchange rate was two francs to the dollar.

ILLUSTRATION 13–4 _____

	Francs	$U.S.
FRENCH SUBSIDIARY		
Balance Sheet as of 12/31/79		
Assets		
Cash............................	1,000	500
Inventory.......................	500	250
Fixed assets....................	2,000	1,000
	3,500	1,750
Equities		
Short-term debt.................	750	375
Long-term debt..................	2,000	1,000
Shareholders' equity............	750	375
	3,500	1,750

The second column translates every item into dollars at the exchange rate in effect the day the company was organized.

During 1980 the French subsidiary was involved in the following transactions:

1. Inventory costing 500 francs was sold for 1,000 francs on June 30, 1980, when the exchange rate was 2.25 francs to the dollar.
2. Inventory in the amount of 700 francs is purchased for cash on July 3, 1980, when the exchange rate was 2.25 francs to the dollar.

The French subsidiary uses the Fifo inventory flow assumption. The fixed assets have a useful life of 20 years, have no salvage value, and are depreciated on a straight-line basis.

The 1980 financial statements (Illustration 13–5) of the French subsidiary reflect the above transactions.

On December 31, 1980, Multicompany must translate the statements of the French subsidiary into dollars before they can be con-

ILLUSTRATION 13-5

FRENCH SUBSIDIARY
Income Statement for 1980
(francs)

Sales revenue	1,000
Cost of goods sold	500
Gross margin	500
Depreciation	100
Net income	400

Balance Sheet as of 12/31/80
(francs)

Assets

Cash	1,300 (1,000 + 1,000 − 700)
Inventory	700 (500 − 500 + 700)
Fixed assets	1,900 (2,000 − 100)
	3,900

Equities

Short-term debt	750
Long-term debt	2,000
Shareholders' equity	1,150 (750 + 400)
	3,900

solidated. The exchange rate on December 31, 1980, is 2.5 francs to the dollar.

What rates should Multicompany use to translate each item on the balance sheet? A distinction is made between two types of accounts. Accounts denominated in foreign currency representing claims to money or stated at current market values are translated at current exchange rates (rates in effect on the balance sheet date). Cash, accounts receivable, securities at market, and accounts payable are in this category. These accounts are analogous to monetary accounts in general price level adjusted financial statements. Monetary items are stated in current dollars, and the above accounts are stated in current francs (translation at current exchange rates results in current dollar valuations).

All other accounts (nonmonetary accounts) are translated using historical exchange rates (rates in effect when the asset was acquired or the liability valued). Nonmonetary assets do not fluctuate in value since the expenditure to acquire the asset has already been made. Translation of nonmonetary items at historical rates is also consistent with the historical cost principle underlying U.S. corporate statements. Inventories, property, plant and equipment, and securities valued at cost are translated at historical rates.

All revenue and expense items are translated using the exchange rate in effect on the day the revenue was generated or the expense incurred. The exceptions are expenses representing expiration of assets which are translated using historical rates (for example, depreciation or cost of goods sold).

The translated income statement for the French subsidiary of Multicompany is presented in Illustration 13–6. Sales revenue is translated at the 6/30/80 rate. Depreciation expense is translated using the 12/31/79 historical rate (date asset was acquired). Since the French subsidiary uses Fifo, the cost of goods sold represents items purchased on 12/31/79 when the exchange rate was two francs to the dollar.

ILLUSTRATION 13–6 _____

| | Income Statement—1980 | | |
	Francs	$U.S.	Exchange Rate Used
Sales revenue.........	1,000	$444.44	2.25:$1
Cost of goods sold	500	250.00	2.00:$1
Gross margin	500	$194.44	
Depreciation	100	50.00	2.00:$1
Net income	400	$144.44	

Multicompany's French subsidiary balance sheet is given in Illustration 13–7.

ILLUSTRATION 13–7 _____

| | FRENCH SUBSIDIARY Balance Sheet, 12/31/80 | | |
	Francs	$U.S.	Exchange Rate
Cash	1,300	$ 520.00	2.50:$1
Inventory	700	311.11	2.25:$1
Fixed assets	1,900	950.00	2.00:$1
	3,900	$1,781.11	
Short-term debt	750	$ 300.00	2.50:$1
Long-term debt..............	2,000	800.00	2.50:$1
Shareholders' equity	1,150	681.11	
	3,900	$1,781.11	

The monetary items (cash, short-term, and long-term debt) are translated at the current rate. Inventory is translated at the rate in effect when the inventory was acquired (7/3/80), and fixed assets are translated at the 12/31/79 rate because they were acquired on this date.

The $681.11 balance in shareholders' equity is derived by subtracting translated liabilities ($1,100) from translated assets ($1,781.11). This balance can be justified in terms of income earned during the period, translation gains and losses on inventory items for the period, and the beginning balance in shareholders' equity.

The subsidiary held 2,750 francs of debt throughout the year. Because the dollar has strengthened against the franc it takes fewer dollars to discharge franc denominated debt at the end of the year than it did at the beginning of the year. The currency translation gain on debt is $275 ($1,375 − $1,100). Holding cash results in a currency translation loss: 1,000 francs were held in cash for an entire year resulting in a $100 ($500 − $400) currency translation loss; 300 francs were held for six months when the exchange rate went from 2.25 to 2.5 francs to the dollar. The resultant translation loss is $13.33 ($133.33 − $120). In addition the subsidiary earned $144.44 during the year.

Beginning shareholders' equity (12/31/79)	$375
Plus translation gains on debt	275
Minus translation losses on cash	113.33
Plus income	144.44
Ending shareholders' equity (12/31/80)	$681.11

Foreign exchange gains and losses currently may appear in various places on the parent's income statement. General Motors includes exchange gains and losses in cost of sales.

> *Foreign Exchange*—All exchange and translation activity is included in cost of sales and amounted to a gain of $62.7 million in 1978 and a loss of $47.6 million in 1977.

Hercules Corporation prefers to report exchange gains and losses in other income or other expense.

> *Foreign Exchange*—Exchange gains and losses, net of taxes, resulted in gains of $500 in 1978 and $1,000 in 1977, and are included in other income (deductions) and equity in net income of affiliated companies.

FASB *Statement No. 8* has caused firms to take actions to decrease their exposure to foreign currency fluctuations. Actions include operating with a different level of average inventory, changing collection procedures in foreign currency receivables, incurring more or less debt denominated in foreign currencies, and hedging.

Many business executives argue that these actions, brought about by FASB *Statement No. 8*, are not economical and that accounting for foreign currency translation should be changed. The FASB is currently (early 1980) considering revision of FASB *Statement No. 8*. Among the proposals under consideration are (a) translation of inventory at current rates, (b) excluding exchange and translation gains from the income statement, and (c) listing gains or losses as an extraordinary item in the income statement.

CASES FOR CHAPTER 13

Case 13–1
Toledo Edison

Balance Sheet
December 31, 1974
($000)

	Traditional Historical Cost Accounting	General Price-Level Accounting*
Assets		
Property, plant, and equipment:		
In service	$438,639	$747,442
Less, accumulated provision for depreciation	116,062	202,806
	$322,577	$544,636
Construction work in progress	276,157	315,853
	$598,734	$860,489
Current assets	41,179	41,373
Investments and other	15,070	17,049
Total assets.............................	$654,983	$918,911
Liabilities		
Capitalization:		
Common stock equity:		
Common stock	$ 40,801	$ 75,668
Premium on capital stock	60,216	79,086
Earnings reinvested	76,279	140,823
	$177,296	$295,577
Cumulative preferred stock	81,000	81,000
Long-term debt................................	299,172	299,172
Accumulated inflation effect from financing sources other than common stock equity	—	145,345
	$557,468	$821,094

* General price level values based on current purchasing power of the dollar as of December 31, 1974.

	Traditional Historical Cost Accounting	General Price-Level Accounting*
Current liabilities:		
Short-term notes payable	$ 38,500	$ 38,500
Other current liabilities	43,981	44,283
	$ 82,481	$ 82,783
Accumulated provision for deferred taxes and other	$ 15,034	$ 15,034
Total liabilities	$654,983	$918,911

Comparative Rate of Return Ratios

	Traditional Historical Cost Accounting	General Price-Level Accounting*
Return on net plant investment (year-end basis)	9%	5%
Return on common stock equity (year-end basis)	11%	6%

Note: The following pages are an integral part of these statements.
* General price level values based on current purchasing power of the dollar as of December 31, 1974.

Results of Operations
For the Year Ended December 31, 1974
($000)

	Traditional Historical Cost Accounting	General Price-Level Accounting
Operating Revenues	$147,794	$154,317
Operating expenses:		
Depreciation provisions	$ 13,089	$ 23,181
Less, amortization of inflation effect from financing sources other than common stock equity	—	5,417
	$ 13,089	$ 17,764
Taxes	13,863	14,193
Other operating expenses	91,562	95,637
Total operating expenses.................	$118,514	$127,594

	Traditional Historical Cost Accounting	General Price-Level Accounting*
Operating Income	$ 29,281	$ 26,723
Other income:		
Allowance for funds used during construction	$ 15,886	$ 16,587
Price level loss from other monetary items	—	(85)
Other income and deductions (net)..............	387	404
Total other income	$ 16,273	$ 16,906
Income before interest charges	$ 45,554	$ 43,629
Interest charges	20,904	21,846
Net income	$ 24,650	$ 21,783
Preferred stock monthly dividends accrued	4,964	5,183
Earnings on common stock	$ 19,686	$ 16,600

Earnings Reinvested
For the Year Ended December 31, 1974

Balance, beginning of year........................	$71,096	$139,336
Add net income..................................	$24,650	$ 21,783
Deduct:		
Preferred stock quarterly dividends declared	5,147	5,363
Common stock cash dividends declared	14,320	14,933
Earnings reinvested during the year	$ 5,183	$ 1,487
Balance, end of year.............................	$76,279	$140,823

NOTES TO GENERAL PRICE LEVEL FINANCIAL STATEMENT STUDY
December 31, 1974

1. Results of Operations

The comparative price level values of all items, except those detailed below, represent the amounts recorded in our traditional historical cost statement, which amounts generally occurred ratably throughout the year, converted to year-end 1974 purchasing power. This conversion was accomplished through the use of the Gross National Product Implicit Price Deflator (GNP Deflator) as recommended in the FASB exposure draft. No federal income tax benefits for any inflation adjustment are reflected since current tax law does not allow any consideration for the erosion of capital which exists during inflationary periods.

The significant items in the results of operations statement which are exceptions to the general explanation above are "price level loss from other monetary items" (see first two paragraphs of Note 3) and the following:

Depreciation Provisions. The 1974 depreciation provision was determined by applying the same average depreciation rate used in the historical cost financial statements (3.3 percent) to the average plant in service which has been price level adjusted to December 31, 1974. Such a provision reflects the actual year-end purchasing power applicable to current operations.

Amortization of Inflation Effect from Financing Sources Other than Common Stock Equity. Partially offsetting the impact of inflation on current depreciation the "accumulated inflation effect from financing sources, other than common stock equity" is being amortized into income at the same rate as the overall composite rate (3.3 percent) being used to determine the annual depreciation provision for property, plant, and equipment. In our opinion, treating the sources of property investment on the same basis as the property it finances results in a realistic presentation for evaluating the overall impact of inflation.

2. Earnings Reinvested

The 1974 beginning balance of earnings reinvested, as converted to year-end 1974 purchasing power, represents historical cost earnings reinvested along with the net impact of restating the 1973 balance sheet from historical cost to year-end 1974 purchasing power through the use of the GNP Deflator. The amounts for 1974 preferred, and common dividends declared, are the historical cost amounts converted to year-end 1974 purchasing power.

3. Balance Sheet

In developing the comparative price level values, the nature (that is, monetary or nonmonetary) of each asset and liability was determined based on the criteria set forth in the FASB exposure draft. Assets and liabilities are considered "monetary" if their amounts are fixed in terms of dollars regardless of changes in general price level.

Excluding the major "nonmonetary" items, such as property, plant, equipment, and common stock equity items, most of the other asset and liability accounts have been identified as "monetary." These accounts in the traditional historical cost statement are stated in dollars of current purchasing power. Consequently, although not apparent in every instance because of consolidations with minor nonmonetary items, the value of these monetary items remains at the same amounts on the comparative price level statements. During 1974 the net impact of inflation on holding these monetary items resulted in the price level loss, as reported in the income statement. This price level loss was determined as the difference between the historical value of the monetary items and the year-end 1974 purchasing power value of both the beginning of year balances and the net changes in these items which occurred ratably throughout the year.

The major items classified as nonmonetary assets and liabilities consist of earnings reinvested (see Note 2) and the following.

Property, Plant, and Equipment. The actual amounts of property, plant, and equipment in service, as shown in the company's historical cost balance sheet at the end of 1974, were analyzed using property records of surviving plant by vintage year. The continuing property records of the company classify the investment in facilities by the year they were placed in service. Therefore, to more closely determine the year expenditures were made, the year-to-year changes in the construction work in progress account (excluding the ending balance) were netted with the vintage year values of surviving plant in service. The results of this approach, representing amounts expended for property each year, were then restated to year-end 1974 purchasing power. The amounts invested in construction work in progress at the end of 1974 were vintaged and also restated to year-end 1974 purchasing power.

Accumulated Provision for Depreciation. The beginning 1974 comparative price level reserve was established at the same percentage relationship to price level plant in service as that which existed on the historical cost basis at December 31, 1973. This approach was used as the most logical and supportable alternative to the ideal approach as outlined in the FASB exposure draft. In establishing the starting point for beginning a restatement of the accumulated provision for depreciation for 1974, the ideal approach would have required us to have analyzed in detail the transactions against the accumulated reserve for each prior year. Such an approach under a composite depreciation method would be an extremely extensive and costly undertaking and require substantial time and effort. Several alternative methods were considered but the results (that is, providing lower ratios of reserve for depreciation to plant-in-service than being experienced on a historical basis) appeared to require further review and consideration.

Common Stock and Premium on Capital Stock. The values of common stock and premium on capital stock on the comparative price level statement were computed by restating the historical costs amounts, based on the year invested, to year-end 1974 purchasing power.

Accumulated Inflation Effect from Financing Sources Other than Common Stock Equity. Debt financing through the issuance of first mortgage bonds, short-term notes, and other obligations and funds secured through the issuance of preferred stock have been identified as "monetary" items (see first paragraph of Note 3). However, since these items comprise some of the sources of funds invested in property, plant, and equipment, they have been treated on a basis consistent with the property financed. The approach used was to restate the historical cost amounts for these sources, based on the year of investment, to year-end 1974 purchasing power. The excess amounts over historical cost are identified as the "accumulated inflation effect from financing sources other than common stock equity." A portion of this accumulated inflation effect, equivalent to the percentage of reserve for depreciation to the plant-in-service, was credited to earnings reinvested at the beginning of the year. (See Note 1 for current year amortization.)

Required:

1. The president of the Toledo Edison Company feels that heavily capitalized industries such as electric utilities should be allowed depreciation on the replacement cost of fixed assets to reflect the value of plant investment "used up." Do you agree? Would the replacement cost depreciation for 1974 be $23,181 (see results of operations)?
2. Which figures more fairly present the results of operations for the year ended December 31, 1974?
3. Do you think federal income taxes should be based on general price level accounting net income rather than on historical cost net income?
4. Are the stockholders earning a fair rate of return on their investment? If not, should utility rates be raised?
5. Do you agree with the treatment of the account "Amortization of inflation effect from financing sources other than common stock equity?"
6. Do you think the general price level accounting figures are as easily understood by investors as the historical cost figures?

Case 13–2

Bethlehem Steel Corporation[1]

THE YEAR IN REVIEW

Lewis W. Foy
Chairman

As expected, the demand for steel products improved during the first six months of 1976 from the low levels in the latter part of 1975. We had anticipated that this improvement would continue through the second half of the year. However, the strong economic recovery in the earlier part of the year slowed as the year progressed. As a result, there was a pronounced lag in the demand for steel to be used in the capital goods sector, and Bethlehem's shipments, revenues,

---

[1] Accounting Series Release 190 of the Securities and Exchange Commission (August 1975) contains detailed explanations of the current replacement cost reporting requirements which were formerly required.

and net income for the year were substantially lower than had been anticipated.

Production of raw steel in 1976 was 18.9 million net tons, a 7.9 percent increase over the 17.5 million net tons in 1975. Shipments of steel products were also better in 1976 than in 1975 with 12.8 million net tons being shipped in 1976 compared to 11.9 million net tons in 1975. Total revenues in 1976 were $5.3 billion, a 5.5 percent increase over the $5.03 billion in 1975. Pre-tax income declined 31.5 percent from $283 million to $194 million. Net income was $168 million in 1976 compared to $242 million in 1975, a 30.6 percent decrease. Net income per share decreased fom $5.54 to $3.85.

While the lower than anticipated net income for 1976 reflects in part the lack of demand in the capital goods sector of the economy, it also reflects the problems we continue to have with low profit margins. As indicated, we produced and shipped more steel in 1976 than in 1975, and our revenues were higher, but both pre-tax income and net income were lower in 1976 than in 1975. Our costs and expenses continued upward without adequate price adjustments to offset the increases. During the year we implemented price increases on a number of our products. Unfortunately, these price increases were not sufficient to attain a satisfactory level of profitability. We shall continue to take steps to control costs and improve profit margins.

Capital Expenditures

Capital expenditures during 1976 were $406.6 million, compared to the record $687.8 million spent in 1975. At December 31, 1976, the estimated cost of completing authorized projects was $1.16 billion, including $246 million for environmental control. We estimate that capital expenditures during 1977 will amount to approximately $680 million.

To assist in the generation of funds for capital investment, Bethlehem has been supporting the following federal tax measures: (1) a capital recovery system which would permit the cost of machinery, equipment, and industrial buildings to be recovered over a five-year period, with deductions beginning as the funds are expended rather than when the project is placed in service; (2) a permanent 12 percent investment tax credit; (3) immediate write-off of the costs of pollution control facilities at the option of the taxpayer; (4) elimination of double taxation of corporate earnings paid to shareholders in the form of cash dividends by granting a deduction to the corporation for dividend payments; and (5) the retention of the percentage depletion allowance.

Steel Operations

Two electro-slag refining furnaces were placed in operation at the Bethlehem Plant in 1976. These furnaces are designed for production of very high quality steel for the utility industry and other specialty customers. The electro-slag refining process is a recently developed process for the production of high quality steel in small quantities. One of the furnaces is the largest in the United States and is capable of producing an ingot for high quality forgings weighing up to 75 tons. The other furnace is designed primarily to produce ingots for tool steels and other special steels. The two furnaces together have a designed annual capacity of approximately 12,000 ingot tons.

A sinter plant was placed in full operation at the Sparrows Point Plant in 1976. It is designed to produce annually approximately 3.9 million net tons of fluxed sinter for the blast furnaces from iron ore fines, flue dust, mill scale, iron bearing pollution control sludges and dust, BOF slag, and limestone fines. This single strand unit replaces six existing strands.

Capability

In 1976, the American Iron and Steel Institute began reporting the steel industry's rate of utilization of its raw steel production capability. The Institute defines "capability" as the tonnage of raw steel that can be produced assuming a full order book and taking into account, at the time capability is determined, the availability of raw materials, fuels and supplies, facilitates for production of coke and iron, and steelmaking, rolling, and finishing facilities, and recognizing any limitations on production because of current environmental and safety requirements. The steel industry's raw steel production capability for 1976 was 158.3 million tons, and the average rate of industry utilization of that capability was 80.8 percent. Bethlehem's raw steel production capability for 1976 was 23.5 million tons, and its average rate of utilization of that capability was 80.2 percent.

Environmental Control

Bethlehem continues to recognize the very real public concern for improving the quality of the environment. All our new facilities are being designed to comply with applicable federal, state, and local environmental protection regulations. The costly problem of meeting mandated environmental quality control deadlines and regulations is, however, still with us and will remain with us for years. We have already spent more than $400 million for environmental control equipment at our various operations. We expect to spend more than $700 million in the next five years to comply with current laws and regulations. In addition to these capital costs, annual maintenance and operating costs for pollution control equipment are currently about $50 million, which includes the cost of valuable energy consumed in operating these facilities.

Capital investments of the size needed to meet environmental requirements, as well as the operating costs of environmental control equipment, cut drastically into funds needed to improve or expand production facilities and provide job opportunities. Furthermore, some pollution control regulations and proposed legislation would severely limit expansion of steelmaking facilities at existing plants and the construction of additional facilities at new sites. In our view, therefore, it is vital that a reasonable balance between environmental and economic concerns be achieved.

We believe that old facilities with a limited life should be permitted to operate under less stringent regulations for a limited period if air quality standards can be met in the area in which the facilities are located. We also believe that industry should be allowed under the federal tax laws to write off expenditures for pollution control facilities, which are nonincome producing, immediately or over such other period of time as the taxpayer may elect rather than over the longer periods established for productive facilities. Finally, we believe that the adoption and enforcement of overly stringent regulations and legislation which achieve only marginal additional control of pollution are unnecessary and counterproductive.

Imports

Steel imports, particularly from Japan, continue to be a problem for the domestic steel industry. The industry maintains that these imports are being stimulated by subsidies and other trade practices which Congress declared unfair in the Trade Act of 1974 and which violate the General Agreement on Tariffs and Trade. The domestic industry has urged that the U.S. government, during the current round of talks under such General Agreement, attempt to negotiate solutions to the problem of cyclical distortions in steel trade while liberalizing steel trade conditions and providing safeguard mechanisms to deal with temporary distortions. Pending international agreements, the industry has urged that the President utilize remedies for unfair trade practices provided by Congress in the Trade Act. Bethlehem supports these industry positions.

Marine Construction

During 1976, the second and third of five 265,000 deadweight ton tankers being built at the Sparrows Point Shipyard were delivered. These are the largest ships ever built in the United States. The two remaining ships in this series are scheduled for delivery in March and July of 1977.

In June, Bethlehem was awarded a $156.7 million contract for the construction of two 27,340 deadweight ton container ships, which will also be built at the Sparrows Point Shipyard. These ships are scheduled for delivery in July and November of 1978. They will be the largest container ships ever built in the United States.

Our Beaumont Shipyard delivered three jack-up drilling platforms during the year. One of these platforms was the first of a new patented design developed by Bethlehem which is capable of operating in water depths up to 375 feet. In addition, four jack-up drilling platforms were delivered from the Singapore Shipyard during 1976.

Raw Materials

Initial production of iron ore pellets from the new taconite mine and pellet plant at Hibbing, Minnesota, commenced in August. The first phase of this project is expected to have an annual production capacity of 6 million net tons by 1978. Construction of a second phase, which will increase production capacity to 9 million net tons per year, is under way, with start-up presently expected to occur in 1979. Bethlehem has a 75 percent interest in the first phase of the Hibbing project and an 85 percent interest in the second phase.

During 1976 Bethlehem rehabilitated and put into operation an inactive coal mine in Nicholas County, West Virginia, which is expected to reach a full annual production capacity of 425,000 tons in 1978. Production of coal also began at a new mine in the Kayford Division of Bethlehem, in West Virginia, which is expected to reach a full annual production capacity of 125,000 tons in 1978, and at a new mine in Cambria County, Pennsylvania, which is expected to reach a full annual production capacity of 400,000 tons in 1979. Two new coal preparation plants were also completed in West Virginia in 1976.

Energy

A national energy policy is urgently needed. How that policy is shaped will have considerable impact on Bethlehem's operating costs and on the economic health of the nation.

Steelmaking, by its nature, is energy intensive. Some critical problems facing us in this regard include the lack of effective national policies to stimulate domestic production of gas, oil, and coal; the declining availability of natural gas for industrial use; and the risk of another Mideast oil embargo.

In dealing with these problems, Bethlehem supports policies that will both conserve and develop the nation's energy resources and that will insure adequate supplies of energy for all of us.

Financing

In February of 1976, Bethlehem sold $200 million principal amount of its 8⅝ percent Debentures, due March 1, 2001, through a public offering by a group of investment banking firms. The net proceeds received by Bethlehem from the sale of the Debentures are being used for general corporate purposes, including meeting the cost of additions and improvements to property.

Prospects for 1977

The pause in the economic recovery which slowed demand for many products in the second half of 1976 appears to be near its end, and we believe that steady and more balanced economic growth is likely in 1977. It is our current judgment that steel shipments in 1977 will move higher than in 1976, with actual growth depending on the degree to which capital spending is accelerated.

The key to our recovery is increased shipments resulting primarily from improved demand from the construction industry and expansion of the capital goods market, together with additional price increases. It does not appear that this recovery will occur in the first quarter. We believe, however, that such a recovery will commence during 1977.

Executive Office

For some time, I have been concerned about the expanding demands made on me in order to respond to increased government requirements on Bethlehem, the steel industry, and business generally. There is, consequently, a growing need for me to devote more time and thought to overall corporate matters. In order to make this possible and to distribute the functions of the Executive Office more effectively, the Board of Directors voted to reorganize that office and elected to the new office of Vice Chairman, effective January 26, 1977, Frederic W. West, Jr., formerly President, and C. William Ritterhoff and Richard M. Smith, formerly Executive Vice Presidents. I will continue as Chairman and chief executive officer. Each department head will report to one of the Vice Chairmen, with the exception of the Vice President, Law, and General Counsel, and the Secretary, who will continue to report to me.

The new organization is similar to those adopted successfully by a number of other major corporations. I am sure it will work out equally well for Bethlehem.

Lewis W. Foy

February 9, 1977

Consolidated Statements of Income and Income Invested in the Business
(in millions)

	1976	1975
Revenues:		
Net sales	$5,248.0	$4,977.2
Interest, dividends, and other income	56.7	51.1
	$5,304.7	$5,028.3
Costs and expenses:		
Cost of sales	$4,082.1	$3,854.3
Depreciation	275.6	234.2
Pensions (Note J)	261.2	198.4
Selling, administrative, and general expense	234.7	220.0
Interest and other debt charges	77.7	63.4
Taxes (including income taxes of $26,000,000 and $41,000,000) (Note K)	205.4	216.0
	$5,136.7	$4,786.3
Net income ($3.85 and $5.54 per share)	$ 168.0	$ 242.0
Income invested in the business, January 1	2,105.3	1,983.4
	$2,273.3	$2,225.4
Deduct: Dividends ($2.00 and $2.75 per share)	87.4	120.1
Income invested in the business, December 31	$2,185.9	$2,105.3

Consolidated Balance Sheets
(in millions)

	December 31, 1976	December 31, 1975
Assets		
Current assets:		
Cash..	$ 45.6	$ 59.7
Marketable securities, at cost (approximately market) ...	355.6	306.9
Receivables, less allowances of $6,100,000 and $5,800,000	421.5	401.7
Inventories (Note B)	834.1	619.9
Total current assets............................	$1,656.8	$1,388.2
Investments and long-term receivables:		
Investments in associated companies accounted for by equity method (Note D)...........................	116.9	114.3
Investments in other associated enterprises	97.4	94.1
Long-term receivables	24.8	23.9
Pollution control funds held in trust	35.6	58.3
Property, plant, and equipment (Note C)	2,963.4	2,854.3
Miscellaneous assets (Note E)	44.2	58.4
Total.......................................	$4,939.1	$4,591.5
Liabilities and Stockholders' Equity		
Current liabilities:		
Accounts payable.....................................	$ 274.8	$ 239.7
Accrued employment costs	241.5	234.6
Accrued taxes (Note K)	127.5	94.7
Debt due within one year	12.9	24.2
Other current liabilities	127.3	125.8
Total current liabilities	$ 784.0	$ 719.0
Liabilities payable after one year	140.8	140.0
Deferred income taxes (Note K)	298.6	263.6
Long-term debt (Note F)	1,023.1	856.9
Commitments (Note G)		
Stockholders' equity (Note H):		
Common Stock—$8 par value—		
Authorized 80,000,000 shares; issued 45,987,118 shares	$ 576.0	$ 576.0
Income invested in the business.......................	2,185.9	2,105.3
	$2,761.9	$2,681.3
Less—2,321,540 and 2,321,925 shares of common stock held in treasury, at cost	69.3	69.3
Total stockholders' equity	$2,692.6	$2,612.0
Total.......................................	$4,939.1	$4,591.5

Consolidated Statements of Changes in Financial Position
(in millions)

	1976	1975
Funds provided:		
Operations—		
Net income	$168.0	$ 242.0
Depreciation	275.6	234.2
Deferred income taxes	35.0	48.0
	$478.6	$ 524.2
Decrease in investments in associated enterprises	4.5	43.6
Use of pollution control funds held in trust	26.3	24.9
Sale of property	22.4	12.1
Decrease in miscellaneous assets	5.5	(10.8)
Increase in liabilities payable after one year	.8	13.0
Increase in long-term debt	200.0	250.0
Other	—	15.5
Total	$738.1	$ 872.5
Funds applied:		
Capital expenditures:		
Property, plant, and equipment	$396.2	$ 674.3
Investments in associated enterprises	10.4	13.5
Pollution control funds held in trust	3.6	4.8
Decrease in long-term debt	33.8	41.4
Payment of dividends	87.4	120.1
Other	3.1	—
Total	$534.5	$ 854.1
Net increase in working capital	$203.6	$ 18.4
Details of increase (decrease) in working capital:		
Cash and marketable securities	$ 34.6	$(308.5)
Receivables	19.8	(95.1)
Inventories	214.2	109.4
Accounts payable	(35.1)	52.1
Accrued employment costs	(6.9)	(20.4)
Accrued taxes	(32.8)	301.6
Debt due within one year	11.3	(16.4)
Other current liabilities	(1.5)	(4.3)
Total	$203.6	$ 18.4

NOTES TO CONSOLIDATED FINANCIAL STATEMENTS

A. Accounting Policies

Principles of Consolidation. All important majority owned subsidiaries of Bethlehem, except two ocean transportation subsidiaries, are consolidated. Investments in unconsolidated majority owned subsidiaries and joint ventures are accounted for by the equity method. Investments representing 50 percent or less of the voting interest are accounted for by the equity method or carried at cost or lower, as appropriate.

Inventories. Inventories, other than contract work in progress, are valued at the lower-of-cost-or-market using the last-in, first-out (Lifo) method, adopted in 1947, in costing the principal portion thereof and the first-in, first-out or average cost methods in costing the remainder. Contract work in progress is valued at cost less billings, adjusted for estimated partial profits and losses. Partial profits are not recognized until a contract has reached 75 percent completion and are generally limited to the percentage of completion or of contract price billed, whichever is lower, applied to the most recent estimate of total profit. Losses are recognized when first apparent.

Property, Plant, and Equipment. Property, plant, and equipment is valued at cost. Gains or losses on disposition of property, plant, and equipment are normally credited or charged to accumulated depreciation. Maintenance, repairs, and renewals which neither materially add to the value of the property nor appreciably prolong its life are charged to expense as incurred.

Mineral Exploration. Mineral exploration costs are charged to expense as incurred except for expenditures, such as those to acquire land and mining rights, which are capitalized and written off on the unit of production basis as the material is produced.

Depreciation. For financial accounting purposes depreciation is computed under the straight-line method and for income tax purposes substantially all depreciation is computed under accelerated methods. The depreciation rates used for both purposes are based on lives established by the U.S. Treasury Department in connection with guideline and asset depreciation range procedures, which reflect a factor for obsolescence.

Pensions. Pension costs under Bethlehem's Pension Plan for substantially all its employees include current service costs, which are accrued and funded on a current basis, and prior service costs, which are amortized and funded over periods of not more than 30 years. Pension costs are determined by an entry age normal actuarial cost method, using frozen unfunded prior service liability. Current service costs include adjustments for differences between actuarial assumptions and actual experience. Actuarial assumptions are reviewed periodically and revised as appropriate.

Income Taxes. Federal income tax expense for any year is reduced by the full investment tax credit for the year. Provision is made to reflect the tax effects of reporting income and expense at different times for financial accounting purposes and for income tax purposes.

B. Inventories

	December 31*	
	1976	1975
Ore, fluxes, fuel, and coal chemicals	$318.4	$186.9
Pig iron, alloys, scrap, and manufac-		
turing supplies	116.2	96.4
Finished and semifinished products	347.0	251.1
Contract work in progress	52.5	85.5
	$834.1	$619.9

* Dollars in millions.

During 1976, although inventories generally increased, certain Lifo quantities decreased below 1975 levels. Net income in 1976 benefited by approximately $15 million as a result of these decreases.

The amounts included in the above table for inventories valued by the Lifo method are less than replacement or current cost by approximately $721 million at December 31, 1976, and $624 million at December 31, 1975.

C. Property, Plant, and Equipment

	December 31*	
Gross	1976	1975
Class of Properties		
Steel producing and miscellaneous	$5,376.0	$5,197.7
Raw material (net of depletion)	708.3	623.1
Transportation	165.3	164.0
Marine construction	200.5	182.8
	$6,450.1	$6,167.6
Net of Accumulated Depreciation		
Steel producing and miscellaneous	$2,378.2	$2,349.0
Raw material (net of depletion)	417.1	360.3
Transportation	85.9	73.5
Marine construction	82.2	71.5
	$2,963.4	$2,854.3

* Dollars in millions.

D. Investments

Investments in associated companies accounted for by the equity method include advances of $23.2 million at December 31, 1976, and $30.4 million at December 31, 1975. Bethlehem's share in the earnings of such companies amounted to a profit of $5.6 million in 1976 and a loss of $1 million in 1975, which amounts are included in interest, dividends, and other income.

E. Miscellaneous Assets

On October 1, 1975, Bethlehem announced its decision to shut down its fabricated steel construction operations. The shutdown was substantially completed in 1976, and the effect on net income was not significant. The net book value of the remaining property, plant, and equipment was $13.9 million at December 31, 1976, and is included in miscellaneous assets.

Miscellaneous assets at December 31, 1976, and 1975, include $15.2 million and $21.3 million, respectively, representing the balance in a capital construction fund which has been set aside for investments in U.S. flag shipping operations.

F. Long-Term Debt

	December 31[*]	
	1976	*1975*
Consolidated mortgage bonds		
2¾%. Due 1976	—	$ 16.3
3%. Due 1979	$ 21.8	21.8
Debentures		
3¼%. Due 1980	3.1	3.1
5.40%. Due 1992	109.2	120.0
6⅞%. Due 1999	85.8	92.0
9%. Due 2000	144.0	144.0
8⅝%. Due 2001	200.0	—
8.45%. Due 2005	250.0	250.0
9¼% Notes Due 1977 through 1997	30.0	32.9
4½% subordinated debentures. Due 1990	94.5	99.2
5¼%–6% obligations related to pollution control revenue bonds. Due 1997 through 2002	100.0	100.0
4¾%–8% notes and lease obligations of consolidated subsidiaries. Due 1977 through 1989	3.2	6.6
	$1,041.6	$885.9
Less unamortized debt discount	8.1	5.4
	$1,033.5	$880.5
Less amounts due within one year	10.4	23.6
	$1,023.1	$856.9

[*] Dollars in millions.

The effective interest rate of any individual debt issue is not materially increased above the stated rate by the applicable debt discount.

The amounts shown above are net of securities owned. The aggregate of the excess of maturities and sinking fund requirements over securities owned and available therefor at December 31, 1976, was as follows in the next five years: $10.4 million in 1977, $14.0 million in 1978, $42.9 million in 1979, $24.3 million in 1980, and $21.1 million in 1981.

G. Commitments and Contingent Liabilities

Based on its proportionate stock interest in certain associated raw material enterprises, Bethlehem is entitled to receive its share of the raw materials produced by such enterprises and is committed to pay its share of their costs, including amortization of their long-term indebtedness. Bethlehem's share of such amortization averages approximately $6.4 million annually through 1983. In addition, Bethlehem has guaranteed indebtedness of various enterprises, including that of certain associated enterprises, aggregating $54.2 million at December 31, 1976.

Bethlehem has entered into noncancelable leases, principally for vessels, which at December 31, 1976, provided for aggregate minimum rental payments of $230.2 million as follows: $43.1 million in 1977, $41.9 million in 1978, $35.7 million in 1979, $29.2 million in 1980, $17.2 million in 1981, $39.2 million in the five years 1982 through 1986, and $23.9 million thereafter.

Bethlehem has placed purchase orders in respect of a substantial portion of the estimated cost of completion of authorized additions and improvements to its properties aggregating $1.1 billion at December 31, 1976.

H. Stockholders' Equity

During 1976 and 1975 Bethlehem reacquired 1,065 and 483 shares, respectively, of common stock.

At the 1975 annual meeting of stockholders, the stockholders approved the 1975 stock option plan providing for the granting, during each plan year (ending March 31) for five years, to certain employees, including officers, of options to purchase up to a maximum of 500,000 shares of common stock, but not exceeding an aggregate of 2 million shares for the five-year period. At December 31, 1976, options granted to 241 employees covering an aggregate of 753,050 shares were outstanding. Options covering 353,550 shares expire on April 30, 1985, and options covering 399,500 shares expire on April 28, 1986, subject in each case to earlier termination if the optionee dies or ceases to be an employee.

The following table sets forth data with respect to options outstanding under the 1975 stock option plan during 1975 and 1976:

	Number of Shares	Option Price
Balance, 1/1/1975	—	—
Granted	405,400	$38.875
Terminated or cancelled	(8,500)	38.875
Balance, 12/31/1975	396,900	38.875
Granted	407,100	41.50
Exercised or surrendered	(34,050)	38.875
Terminated or cancelled	(16,900)	*
Balance, 12/31/1976	753,050	*

* $38.875–$41.50.

The option price is in each case equal to the market price per share at the date of grant. Options are not exercisable for six months from the date of grant.

The common stock account is increased by the difference between the option price and the average cost of treasury shares used upon exercise of options.

The authorized stock includes 20 million shares of preferred stock, par value $1 per share, none of which has been issued.

I. Special Incentive Compensation Plan

Under the Special Incentive Compensation Plan provided for by Article Tenth of Bethlehem's Amended Certificate of Incorporation, certain executives and other important employees receive special incentive compensation in the form of dividend units. The aggregate number of dividend units credited for a year is determined by dividing an amount equal to 1.5 percent of the consolidated net income for the year by the market value per share of Bethlehem common stock at the beginning of the year. Each dividend unit entitles the holder to receive cash payments equal to cash dividends paid on a share of common stock after the crediting of the unit and during his life, but in any event until the 15th anniversary of the termination, by death or otherwise, of his service with Bethlehem, subject to earlier termination in certain circumstances. Charges to expense for the Plan in 1976 and 1975 were $2.0 million and $3.6 million, respectively.

J. Pensions

Pension costs for 1976 were increased by approximately $37 million to reflect the increases in pension benefits which became effective under the Pension Plan during 1975 and 1976, and by approximately $6 million to reflect revisions in actuarial assumptions. The remaining pension cost increase of $20 million was due mainly to increased employee compensation.

The actuarially computed value of vested benefits as of December 31, 1976, exceeded the market value of the Pension Trust Fund at that date by approximately $1,284 million. The unamortized balance of the actuarially computed value of prior service costs, including those related to vested benefits, was approximately $1,137 million at December 31, 1976.

K. Taxes

Tax expense, which excludes certain federal excise taxes and minor amounts of state and local taxes charged to cost of sales, includes the following:

	1976	1975
Income taxes:*		
Federal—current	$ (36.0)	$ (32.0)
—deferred	30.0	45.0
Foreign—current	20.0	12.0
State—current	7.0	13.0
—deferred	5.0	3.0
Total income taxes	$ 26.0	$ 41.0
Taxes—other than income:		
Employment taxes	$108.6	$106.9
Property taxes	45.6	43.1
State and foreign taxes	25.2	25.0
Total taxes—other than income	$179.4	$175.0
Total tax expense	$205.4	$216.0

* Dollars in millions.

The credits for the current portions of federal income tax expense for 1976 and 1975 result primarily from estimated refunds of prior years' taxes due to the carryback of investment tax credits.

Total income tax expense was less than the amount computed by applying the federal income tax rate of 48 percent to income before income taxes. That computed amount and the items which made total income tax expense vary from it are as follows (in millions):

	1976	1975
Computed amount	$93.1	$135.8
State income taxes	6.2	8.3
Investment tax credits	(38.4)	(59.6)
Percentage depletion on U.S. mineral properties	(33.3)	(38.2)
Foreign income	.5	(1.9)
Miscellaneous items	(2.1)	(3.4)
Total income tax expense	$26.0	$41.0

Deferred income tax expense results from differences in the time of recognition of income and expense for tax and financial statement purposes. Those differences and their effect on deferred income tax expense are as follows (in millions).

	1976	1975
Excess of tax depreciation over book depreciation ...	$28.6	$29.7
Earnings under Merchant Marine Act of 1970	5.2	5.4
Miscellaneous items	1.2	12.9
	$35.0	$48.0

Federal income tax returns of Bethlehem and its subsidiaries for the years 1961 through 1972 are under consideration by the Internal Revenue Service. Adjustments have been proposed by the Service for the years 1961 through 1970. Tentative agreement has now been reached on most of the adjustments proposed for 1961 and 1962. The resulting tax deficiencies and interest, which are expected to be paid in 1977, will be charged against reserves previously provided. Because of the complexity of the issues involved, it is not now possible to determine the amount of tax deficiencies which may ultimately be payable with respect to the remaining issues for 1961 and 1962 and with respect to the adjustments proposed for 1963 through 1970, the major portion of which are being contested by Bethlehem. However, Bethlehem believes that it has made adequate provision so that final settlement of its federal income tax liability for those years will not have any material adverse effect on its consolidated financial position at December 31, 1976.

Income Invested in the business at December 31, 1976, includes approximately $64 million of unremitted earnings of subsidiaries in respect of which income taxes on remittance have not been accrued. The subsidiaries have invested for indefinite periods amounts equal to those earnings and it is therefore expected that remittance thereof will be postponed indefinitely.

L. Supplementary Income Statement Information

Amounts charged to income in respect of the following items were (in millions):

	1976	1975
Maintenance and repairs	$682.0	$611.8
Mineral exploration	17.5	18.2
Rental expense		
Real estate, office machinery, and equipment	24.4	26.0
Vessels	17.4	30.6
Research and development	43.7	37.6

Interest, dividends, and other income includes $3.7 million in 1976 and $2.2 million in 1975 in respect of gains on the repurchase of long-term debt.

M. Replacement Cost Information (unaudited)

As required by Rule 3-17 of Regulation S-X of the Securities and Exchange Commission, Bethlehem's Annual Report on Form 10-K (a copy of which is available upon request) contains information (based on estimates) on the current replacement cost of inventories; the cost of sales on the basis of the replacement cost of the goods or services at the time of sale; gross (new) and depreciated replacement cost of productive capacity; and depreciation expense on a replacement cost basis. Such information (which must be read in conjunction with the explanations thereof contained in such Annual Report on Form 10-K and is expressly made subject to such explanations and the other qualifications set forth therein) shows that, on the basis of estimated replacement cost, inventories, property, plant, and equipment and depreciation expense would be significantly greater and cost of sales, as adjusted to reflect estimated cost savings, would be less than on the basis of historical cost.

N. Quarterly Financial Data (unaudited)

(\$ millions, except per share data)

1976 Quarters	Net Sales	Cost of Sales	Net In- come	Net In- come per Share
First	$1,278.1	$1,005.1	$ 28.4	$ .65
Second	1,435.9	1,126.3	54.4	1.25
Third	1,312.4	1,021.8	45.5	1.04
Fourth	1,221.6	928.9	39.7	.91
	$5,248.0	$4,082.1	$168.0	$3.85

REPORT OF INDEPENDENT ACCOUNTANTS

To the Board of Directors and Stockholders
of Bethlehem Steel Corporation:

In our opinion, the accompanying Consolidated Balance Sheets and the related Consolidated Statements of Income and Income Invested in the Business and of Changes in Financial Position present fairly the financial position of Bethlehem Steel Corporation and its consolidated subsidiaries at December 31, 1976, and 1975, and the results of their operations and the changes in their financial position for the years then ended, in conformity with generally accepted accounting principles consistently applied. Our examinations of these statements were made in accordance with generally accepted auditing standards and accordingly included such tests of the accounting records and such other auditing procedures as we considered necessary in the circumstances.

60 Broad Street
New York, N.Y. 10004
February 9, 1977

Price Waterhouse & Co.

Pension Trust Fund*
(in millions)

	December 31, 1976	December 31, 1975
Statements of Assets		
Cash and accrued interest receivable	$ 5.3	$ 5.3
Contributions receivable from employing companies	21.7	19.8
Investments, at cost:		
Short-term obligations	64.4	45.6
Long-term bonds, notes and other obligations	283.0	218.6
Preferred stocks	1.5	9.4
Common stocks	588.9	516.5
Total, at cost	$ 964.8	$815.2
Approximate market value	$1,119.0	$843.0
Statements of Changes in Fund		
Balance in Fund, January 1, at cost	$ 815.2	$731.6
Add:		
Contributions from employing companies	260.1	197.6
Income from investments	44.3	36.1
	$1,119.6	$965.3
Deduct:		
Net loss on disposition and write-down of investments	$ 3.0	$ 28.0
Pension payments	151.8	122.1
	$ 154.8	$150.1
Balance in Fund, December 31, at cost	$ 964.8	$815.2
Pensioners at year end	40,864	37,749

REPORT OF INDEPENDENT ACCOUNTANTS

To the Investment Committee and Trustees
Pension Trust of Bethlehem Steel Corporation
and Subsidiary Companies:

In our opinion, the accompanying Statements of Assets and Statements of Changes in Fund present fairly the assets of the Pension Fund under the Pension Trust of Bethlehem Steel Corporation and Subsidiary Companies at December 31, 1976, and 1975 and the changes in the Fund during the years, in conformity with generally accepted accounting principles consistently applied. Our examinations of these statements were made in accordance with generally accepted auditing standards and accordingly included such tests of the accounting records and such other auditing procedures as we considered necessary in the circumstances, including confirmation by the custodian of investments owned at December 31, 1976, and 1975.

60 Broad Street   Price Waterhouse & Co.
New York, N.Y. 10004
January 26, 1977

ASR 190 DISCLOSURE (FORM 10-K)

Information Based on Estimates of Replacement Cost (unaudited)

The statements below are made to comply with Rule 3-17 of Regulation S-X of the Securities and Exchange Commission, which requires disclosure of information (based on estimates) on the current replacement cost of inventories; the cost of sales on the basis of the replacement cost of the goods or services at the time of sale; gross (new) and depreciated replacement cost of productive capacity; and depreciation expense on a replacement cost basis; accompanied by a description of the methods employed in determining replacement costs and other information which the management believes is necessary to prevent the data from being misleading. The table below should be read in conjunction with the subsequent explanations and is expressly made subject to the entire narrative portion hereof, including such explanations (in millions).

Inventories valued on a Lifo basis, which account for approximately 85 percent of the consolidated book value of inventories, have been adjusted to estimated replacement cost by using the most recent purchase price or production cost. Other inventories have not been adjusted because it is estimated that book value approximates replacement cost.

The estimates of current replacement cost of present property,

	On Basis of	
	Estimated Replacement Cost (unaudited)	Historical Cost
At December 31, 1976		
Inventories	$ 1,555	$ 834
Property, plant, and equipment, excluding depletable mineral properties, land and construction in progress.........................		
Gross	$16,010	$5,839
Net of accumulated depreciation	$ 4,947	$2,352
For the year 1976		
Cost of sales (excluding estimated cost savings—see explanation below)	$ 4,132	$4,082
Depreciation, excluding depletion	$ 594	$ 274

plant, and equipment, excluding depletable mineral properties, land, and construction in progress, were determined as follows:

> Approximately 85 percent of such property, plant and equipment was valued by the use of estimated current facility replacement costs per ton of capacity. These estimates are based on a number of factors, such as actual construction costs of recent installations, estimated costs of authorized but incomplete projects, and quotations from vendors, and reflect the latest feasible technology and environmental controls as well as economic and commercial considerations.

> The estimates of current replacement cost of the remainder of such property, plant, and equipment were determined by indexing historical costs.

The cost of sales has not been adjusted to reflect $535 million of estimated cost savings which could reasonably be expected from the facilities utilized to calculate the estimated replacement cost of such property, plant, and equipment. The estimate of cost savings is based on efficiencies of new equipment actually installed or new equipment presently available from vendors and is consistent with the concepts and assumptions utilized in estimating such replacement cost. The estimate of cost savings does not take into account, among other things, the cost of the capital required to replace such property, plant, and equipment. Such estimate is based on present conditions and should not be considered indicative of any actual future cost savings or the possible effect thereof on financial results.

Current depreciated replacement cost and replacement cost depreciation were determined by the use of the historical ratios of accumulated depreciation to the cost of various groups of assets and of depreciation expense to the average balances of such costs at the beginning and end of the fiscal year, respectively.

The information set forth herein does not include information as to Bethlehem's share of property, plant, and equipment owned by the associated companies and enterprises reflected as investments in the 1976 Consolidated Balance Sheet.

Although it is believed that the estimates of replacement cost presented herein should be reasonably indicative of the magnitude of the difference between replacement cost and historical cost, it is emphasized that such estimates are subject to errors of estimation and are inherently imprecise because of the numerous assumptions and subjective decisions which were required in making them. For the same reasons, the information set forth herein may not be fully comparable with the corresponding information prepared by other companies in the industry.

Furthermore, it should not be assumed that Bethlehem has any present plans to replace completely its above-mentioned property, plant, and equipment or that replacement would actually take place in the manner implicit in the assumptions and decisions used in making the estimates. When any actual replacement takes place in the future, it will be accomplished under the economic, technological, competitive, and regulatory conditions existing at the time.

Because of the qualifications set forth above, it cannot be assumed that the replacement cost estimates necessarily represent the current value of existing property, plant, and equipment or that the difference between historical cost and the estimates of replacement cost represents additional book value for Bethlehem's common stock.

In the case of property, plant, and equipment, the estimated replacement cost data presented above does not take into consideration the capital requirements for any anticipated growth or other change in the demand for steel products or the future availability of funds and the costs thereof for any such capital requirements. The degree of such requirements and the availability of such funds depend, among other things, on the extent of future return on invested capital and the resulting degree of internal generation of funds, which in turn are influenced by a number of factors, including future government policies with respect to the encouragement of internal capital formation and related federal income tax policies. Neither the nature nor the effect of these factors in the future can be predicted at this time.

The information set forth herein should not be deemed to show the overall effect of inflation on net income or on the 1976 Consolidated Balance Sheet, because such information does not reflect the potentially significant effect of price level changes on assets and liabilities other than inventories and property, plant, and equipment, excluding depletable mineral properties, land, and construction in progress. In recognition of the substantial theoretical problems involved in determining the effect of price level changes on such assets and liabilities, the Securities and Exchange Commission intentionally determined not to require disclosure concerning such effect.

Required:

Read the case materials and answer the following questions.

1. The SEC indicated that the current replacement cost information required to be disclosed under ASR 190 will "enable investors to obtain more relevant information about the current economics of a business enterprise in an inflationary economy than that provided solely by financial statements prepared on the basis of historical cost." Do you agree?

2. How would an investor (you) use the current replacement cost information disclosed in Bethlehem Steel Corporation's Form 10-K for the year ended December 31, 1976? Does this disclosure correct for the distortion in the historical cost financial statement caused by inflation?

3. Would general purchasing power financial statements be more or less informative than the disclosure required by ASR 190?

4. How much less would the Bethlehem Steel Corporation pay in federal income taxes for the calendar year 1976 if they were allowed to deduct depreciation on replacement cost?

5. How much did the Bethlehem Steel Corporation really earn for the calendar year ended December 31, 1976?

Case 13–3
General Motors Corporation (B)

Required:

1. How does the method employed by GM in preparing its schedule on general price level adjustment for inflation presented in its 1978 annual report differ from the general price level (constant dollar) method of accounting described in this chapter?

2. Compute the profit margins using net income in constant dollars and sales in constant dollars. How do these compare to historical cost profit margins? Comment.

3. What are the major strengths and weaknesses of GM's approach to general price level adjustments for inflation?

THE IMPACT OF INFLATION ON ACCOUNTING DATA

In recent years, the accounting profession has given a great deal of consideration to the question of reporting the impact of inflation on accounting data.

The objective of financial statements, and the primary purpose of accounting, is to furnish, to the fullest extent practicable, objective, quantifiable summaries of the results of financial transactions to those who need or wish to judge management's ability to manage. The data are prepared by management and independently verified by the independent public accountants.

The present accounting system in general use in the United States, and the financial statements prepared by major companies from that system were never intended to be measures of relative economic value, but instead are basically a history of transactions which have occurred and by which current and potential investors and creditors can evaluate their expectations. There are many subjective, analytical, and economic factors which must be taken into consideration when evaluating a company. Those factors cannot be quantified objectively. Just as the financial statements cannot present in reasonable, objective, quantifiable form *all* of the data necessary to evaluate a business, they also should not be expected to furnish all the data needed to evaluate the impact of inflation on a company.

Financial reporting is, of necessity, stated in dollars. It is generally recognized that the purchasing power of a dollar has deteriorated in recent years and, accordingly, the costs of raw materials and other items as well as wage rates have increased and can be expected to increase further in the future to compensate for the decline. It is not as generally recognized, however, that profit dollars also are subject to the same degree of reduction in purchasing power. Far too much attention is given to the absolute level of profits rather than the relation of profits to other factors in the business and to the general price level. For example, as shown in the accompanying table, simply adjusting the annual amount of sales and net income to a constant 1973 dollar basis, using the Consumer Price Index, would demonstrate that constant dollar profits have not increased in recent years in line with the changes in sales volume. Expressed another way, net income, in constant dollars, has only held about even with 1973 even though sales, in constant dollars, have increased by 13 percent in 1977 and 20 percent in 1978, respectively, over 1973. The result has been a further erosion of GM's profit margin from 6.7 percent in 1973 to 5.5 percent in 1978.

General Price Level Adjustment for Inflation
($ millions except per share amounts)

	1978	1977	1976	1975	1974	Base Year 1973
Sales, as reported	$63,221.1	$54,961.3	$47,181.0	$35,724.9	$31,549.5	$35,798.3
Percent increase (decrease) over 1973	77%	54%	32%	—	(12%)	—
Sales in constant dollars*	43,086.2	40,305.0	36,831.6	29,497.4	28,430.9	35,798.3
Percent increase (decrease) over 1973	20%	13%	3%	(18%)	(21%)	—
Net income, as reported	3,508.0	3,337.5	2,902.8	1,253.1	950.1	2,398.1
Percent increase (decrease) over 1973	46%	39%	21%	(48%)	(60%)	—
Net income in constant dollars*	2,390.8	2,447.5	2,266.1	1,034.7	856.2	2,398.1
Percent increase (decrease) over 1973	—	2%	(6%)	(57%)	(64%)	—
Profit margin, as reported	5.5%	6.1%	6.2%	3.5%	3.0%	6.7%
Earnings per share—($ per share)						
As reported	12.24	11.62	10.08	4.32	3.27	8.34
Constant dollars*	8.34	8.51	7.86	3.56	2.95	8.34

* Adjustment to constant dollar basis has been determined by applying the Consumer Price Index to the data for 1974 through 1978 with 1973 as the base year.

Case 13–4

General Electric Company (C)

Required:

Explain which set of financial statements (historical cost, adjusted for general inflation, or adjusted for changes in specific prices) is the most useful to investors and creditors in estimating future cash flows.

FINANCIAL ISSUES: THE IMPACT OF INFLATION

Inflation is commonly defined as a loss in value of money due to an increase in the volume of money and credit relative to available goods and services, resulting in a rise in the level of prices. Inflation in the United States is generally recognized to be caused by a combination of factors, including government deficits, sharp increases in energy costs, and low productivity gains including the effect of proliferating government regulations.

Although loss of purchasing power of the dollar impacts all areas of the economy, it is particularly onerous in its effect on savings—of both individuals in forms such as savings accounts, securities and pensions, and of corporations in the form of retained earnings.

For the individual, with inflation of 6 percent a year, the dollar saved by a person at age 50 will have lost three fifths of its value by the time the person is age 65. With a 10 percent inflation rate, almost four fifths of the dollar's value is lost in 15 years. This problem affects almost everyone, including those presently working and especially those who are on fixed incomes.

The situation is rendered even more difficult by the progressive income tax system. A congressional staff study reports that a family of four with an income of $8,132 in 1964 would need a 1979 income of $18,918 to have kept pace with the increase in the Consumer Price Index over the years. However, the 1979 income of $18,918 puts the family into a higher tax bracket which, when coupled with increased Social Security taxes, reduces real after-tax income $1,068 below the equivalent 1964 level.

Your company and all U.S. businesses face a similar problem. Business savings are in the form of retained earnings—the earnings a company keeps after paying employees, suppliers, and vendors, and after payment of taxes to government and dividends to share owners. If a company is to continue in business, much less grow, it must be able to save or retain sufficient earnings, after providing a return to its share owners, to fund the cost of replacing—at today's inflated prices—the productive assets used up. Retention of capital in these inflationary times under existing tax laws is a challenge facing all businesses.

U.S. tax regulations permit recognition of the impact of inflation on a company's inventory costs by use of the Lifo (last-in, first-out) inventory method. In general, under the Lifo method, a company charges off to operations the current cost of inventories consumed during the year. With inflation averaging over 11 percent last year, the negative impact on operations of using current costs with respect to a supply of goods is substantial. Financial results are portrayed more accurately when the Lifo method is used in periods of high inflation, and GE has used Lifo for most of its U.S. manufacturing inventories for a quarter century. The Statement of Earnings is on that basis. As supplementary information to that Statement of Earnings: Use of the Lifo method increased 1979 and 1978 operating costs by $430.8 million and $224.1 million (to $20,330.7 million and $17,695.9 million), respectively, with a corresponding reduction of reported pre-tax profits.

Unfortunately, U.S. tax regulations fail to provide an equivalent to Lifo for the impact of inflation on a company's costs of property, plant, and equipment. Instead, deductions for wear and tear on these assets are based on original purchase costs rather than today's replacement costs. In general, the resulting shortfall must be funded from aftertax earnings.

The supplementary information shown in Table 1 restates operating results to eliminate the major effects of inflation discussed above. Table 1 compares GE operating results as reported with results adjusted in two ways. First, results are restated to show the effects of general inflation—the loss of the dollar's purchasing power—on inventories and fixed assets. The second restatement shows results restated for changes in specific prices—the current costs of replacing those assets. Your management feels that the last column in Table 1 is the more meaningful and has therefore shown, in Table 2 five years of results on that basis, also adjusted to equivalent 1979 dollars to make the years comparable. While the techniques used are not precise, they do produce reasonable approximations.

In these earnings statements, specific adjustments are made to (1) *cost of goods sold* for the current cost of replacing inventories and (2) *depreciation* for the current costs of plant and equipment. The restatements for inventories are relatively small because GE's extensive use of Lifo accounting already largely reflects current costs in the traditional statements. However, a substantial restatement is made for the impact of inflation on fixed assets, which have relatively long lives. The $624 million of depreciation as traditionally

TABLE 1

Supplementary Information—Effect of Changing Prices (Note A)
(in millions, except per share amounts)

For the Year Ended December 31, 1979

	As Reported in the Traditional Statements	Adjusted for General Inflation	Adjusted for Changes in Specific Prices (Current Costs) (Note B)
Sales of products and services to customers	$22,461	$22,461	$22,461
Cost of goods sold	15,991	16,093	16,074
Selling, general, and administrative expense	3,716	3,716	3,716
Depreciation, depletion, and amortization	624	880	980
Interest and other financial charges	258	258	258
Other income	(519)	(519)	(519)
Earnings before income taxes and minority interest	$ 2,391	$ 2,033	$ 1,952
Provision for income taxes	953	953	953
Minority interest in earnings of consolidated affiliates	29	16	13
Net earnings applicable to common stock	$ 1,409	$ 1,064	$ 986
Earnings per common share	$ 6.20	$ 4.68	$ 4.34
Share owners' equity at year end (net assets) (Note C)	$ 7,362	$10,436	$11,153

TABLE 2

Supplementary Information—Effect of Changing Prices (Note A)

(in millions, except per share amounts; all amounts expressed in average 1979 dollars)

Current Cost Information in Dollars of 1979 Purchasing Power (Note B)

	1979	1978	1977	1976	1975
Sales of products and services to customers	$22,461	$21,867	$20,984	$20,015	$19,022
Cost of goods sold	16,074	15,548	14,793	14,145	13,914
Selling, general, and administrative expense	3,716	3,566	3,606	3,360	3,018
Depreciation, depletion, and amortization	980	1,000	986	979	1,006
Interest and other financial charges	258	249	238	222	251
Other income	(519)	(466)	(467)	(350)	(235)
Earnings before income taxes and minority interest	$ 1,952	$ 1,970	$ 1,828	$ 1,659	$ 1,068
Provision for income taxes	953	995	926	853	620
Minority interest in earnings of consolidated affiliates	13	13	20	26	26
Net earnings applicable to common stock	$ 986	$ 962	$ 882	$ 780	$ 422
Earnings per common share	$ 4.34	$ 4.22	$ 3.88	$ 3.45	$ 1.88
Share owners' equity at year end (net assets) (Note C)	$11,153	$11,020	$10,656	$10,526	$10,056
Other Inflation Information					
Average Consumer Price Index (1967 = 100)	217.4	195.4	181.5	170.5	161.2
(Loss)/gain in general purchasing power of net monetary items	$(209)	$(128)	$ (61)	$ (20)	$ 19
Dividends declared per common share	2.75	2.78	2.52	2.17	2.16
Market price per common share at year end	47⅞	50½	58¼	69⅝	60¼

450

reported, when restated for general inflation, increases to a total of $880 million. But the restatement necessary to reflect replacement of these assets at current costs grows to $980 million. The net effect of these restatements lowers reported income of $6.20 a share to $4.68 on a general inflation-adjusted basis and $4.34 on a specific current cost basis.

It is significant to note that for the five years 1975–79, even after adjustment for inflation, your company has shown real growth in earnings and a steady increase in share owners' equity over the entire period. After adjusting earnings for current costs and restating all years to equivalent 1979 dollars, your company's average annual growth rate in real earnings was 21 percent since 1975 and 8 percent since 1976. This means that the growth in GE's earnings has been real, not just the product of inflation.

An important insight from these data is depicted in the pie charts. These show that, over the five years 1975–79, because of inflation 10 percent more of GE's earnings were taxed away than appeared to have been the case using traditional financial statements. While the traditional earnings statements indicated an effective tax rate of 41 percent over this period, the "real" tax rate averaged 51 percent of profits before taxes. Consequently, earnings retained for growth were cut in half to 16 percent of income before tax, not 32 percent as reflected in the traditional financial statements. Over the period, share owners received a measure of protection against inflation's impact as about two-thirds of after-tax earnings were distributed— equivalent to an average annual growth rate of about 8 percent in *real* dividends.

Use of Each Dollar of Earnings
(based on total earnings before taxes 1975–1979)

A. As reported

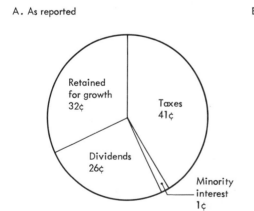

B. Adjusted for changes in specific prices (current costs)

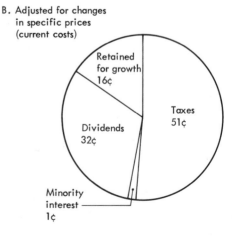

An area receiving special attention by management is experimentation with the use of inflation-adjusted measurements at the individual business and project level for capital budgeting. Since 1973, your company has been experimenting with various techniques to measure the impact of inflation, to incorporate the perspectives provided by such measurements into decision making, and to stimulate awareness by all levels of management of the need to develop constructive business strategies to deal with inflation. The objective is to ensure that investments needed for new business growth, productivity improvements, and capacity expansions earn appropriate *real rates of return* commensurate with the risks involved. Such supplemental measurements can assist in the entire resource allocation process, starting with initial project approval, implementation, and subsequent review.

Improving productivity to offset inflationary forces is a primary goal established by top management that is being stressed throughout General Electric. As discussed on the back cover of this Annual Report, the company has committed significant levels of resources to research and development activities to accelerate innovation and increase productivity. In addition, General Electric's production base continues to be expanded and modernized through increasing investments in plant and equipment. For example, $1,262 million and $1,055 million were spent on strengthening General Electric's production base in 1979 and 1978, respectively. Imaginative and diligent coupling of production techniques and equipment is critical to the maintenance and improvement of your company's profitability.

Notes to Supplementary Information—Tables 1 and 2

Note A. This information has been prepared in accordance with requirements of the Financial Accounting Standards Board (FASB). Proper use of this information requires an understanding of certain basic concepts and definitions.

The heading "As reported in the traditional statements" refers to information drawn directly from the financial statements. This information is prepared using the set of generally accepted accounting principles which renders an accounting based on the number of actual dollars involved in transactions, with no recognition given to the fact that the value of the dollar changes over time.

The heading "Adjusted for general inflation" refers to information prepared using a different approach to transactions involving inventory and property, plant, and equipment assets. Under this procedure, the number of dollars involved in transactions at different dates are all restated to equivalent amounts in terms of the general purchasing power of the dollar as it is measured by the Consumer Price index for all Urban Consumers (CPI-U). For example, $1,000 invested in a building asset in 1967 would be restated to its 1979 dollar purchasing power equivalent of $2,174 to value the asset and calculate depreciation charges. Similarly, 1978 purchases of non-Lifo inventory sold in 1979 would be accounted for at their equivalent in terms of 1979 dollars, rather than in terms of the actual number of dollars spent.

The heading "Adjusted for changes in specific prices (current costs)" refers to information prepared using yet another approach to transactions involving inventory and property, plant, and equipment assets. In this case, rather than restating to dollars of the same general purchasing power, estimates of current costs of the assets are used.

In presenting results of either of the supplementary accounting methods for more than one year, "real" trends are more evident when results for all years are expressed in terms of the general purchasing power of the dollar for a designated period. Results of such restatements are generally called "constant dollar" presentations. In the five-year presentations shown above, dollar results for earlier periods have been restated to their equivalent number of constant dollars of 1979 general purchasing power (CPI-U basis).

Since none of these restatements is allowable for tax purposes under existing regulations, income tax amounts are the same as in the traditional statements (but expressed in constant dollars in the five-year summary).

There are a number of other terms and concepts which may be of interest in assessing the significance of the supplementary information shown in Tables 1 and 2. However, it is management's opinion that the basic concepts discussed above are the most significant for the reader to have in mind while reviewing this information.

Note B. Principal types of information used to adjust for changes in specific prices (current costs) are (1) for inventory costs, GE-generated indices of price changes for specific goods and services, and (2) for property, plant, and equipment, externally generated indices of price changes for major classes of assets.

Note C. At December 31, 1979, the current cost of inventory was $5,251 million, and of property, plant, and equipment was $7,004 million. Estimated current costs applicable to the sum of such amounts held during all or part of 1979 increased by approximately $1,111 million, which was $329 million less than the $1,440 million increase which could be expected because of general inflation.

REPORT OF MANAGEMENT

To the Share Owners of General Electric Company:

We have prepared the accompanying statement of financial position of General Electric Company and consolidated affiliates as of December 31, 1979, and 1978, and the related statements of earnings, changes in financial position, and changes in share owners' equity for the years then ended, including the notes, industry, and geographic segment information, and supplementary information on the effect of changing prices. The statements have been prepared in conformity with generally accepted accounting principles appropriate in the circumstances, and include amounts that are based on our best estimates and judgments. Financial information elsewhere in this annual report is consistent with that in the financial statements.

Your company maintains a strong system of internal financial controls and procedures, supported by a corporate staff of traveling auditors and supplemented by resident auditors located around the world. This system is designed to provide reasonable assurance, at appropriate cost, that assets are safeguarded and that transactions are executed in accordance with management's authorization and recorded and reported properly. The system is time-tested, innovative, and responsive to change. Perhaps the most important safeguard in this system for share owners is the fact that the company has long emphasized the selection, training, and development of professional financial managers to implement and oversee the proper application of its internal controls and the reporting of management's stewardship of corporate assets and maintenance of accounts in conformity with generally accepted accounting principles.

The independent public accountants provide an objective, independent review as to management's discharge of its responsibilities insofar as they relate to the fairness of reported operating results and financial condition. They obtain and maintain an understanding of GE's accounting and financial controls, and conduct such tests and related procedures as they deem necessary to arrive at an opinion on the fairness of financial statements.

The Audit Committee of the Board of Directors, which is composed solely of directors from outside the company, maintains an ongoing appraisal of the effectiveness of auditors and the independence of the public accountants. The committee meets periodically with the public accountants, management, and internal auditors to review the work of each. The public accountants have free access to the committee, without management present, to discuss the results of their audit work and their opinions on the adequacy of internal financial controls and the quality of financial reporting. The committee also reviews the company's accounting policies, internal accounting controls, and the Annual Report and proxy material.

Your management has long recognized its responsibility for conducting the company's affairs in a manner which is responsive to the ever-increasing complexity of society. This responsibility is reflected in key company policy statements regarding, among other things, potentially conflicting outside business interests of company employees, proper conduct of domestic and international business activities, and compliance with antitrust laws. Educational, communication, and review programs are designed to ensure that these policies are clearly understood and that there is awareness that deviation from them will not be tolerated.

Chairman of the Board and Chief Executive Officer

Senior Vice President, Finance
February 15, 1980

REPORT OF INDEPENDENT CERTIFIED PUBLIC ACCOUNTANTS

To the Share Owners and Board of Directors of General Electric Company:

We have examined the statement of financial position of General Electric Company and consolidated affiliates as of December 31, 1979, and 1978, and the related statements of earnings, changes in financial position, and changes in share owners' equity for the years then ended. Our examinations were made in accordance with generally accepted auditing standards, and accordingly included such tests of the accounting records and such other auditing procedures as we considered necessary in the circumstances.

In our opinion, the aforementioned financial statements present fairly the financial position of General Electric Company and consolidated affiliates at December 31, 1979, and 1978, and the results of their operations and the changes in their financial position for the years then ended, in conformity with generally accepted accounting principles applied on a consistent basis.

Peat, Marwick, Mitchell & Co.

345 Park Avenue,
New York, N.Y. 10022
February 15, 1980

GENERAL ELECTRIC COMPANY AND CONSOLIDATED AFFILIATES
Statement of Earnings
For the years ended December 31
(in millions)

	1979	1978
Sales:		
Sales of products and services to customers	$22,460.6	$19,653.8
Operating costs:		
Cost of goods sold	15,990.7	13,915.1
Selling, general, and administrative expense	3,715.9	3,204.4
Depreciation, depletion and amortization	624.1	576.4
Operating costs	$20,330.7	$17,695.9
Operating margin	$ 2,129.9	$ 1,957.9
Other income	519.4	419.0
Interest and other financial charges	(258.6)	(224.4)
Earnings:		
Earnings before income taxes and minority interest	$ 2,390.7	$ 2,152.5
Provision for income taxes	(953.4)	(893.9)
Minority interest in earnings of consolidated affiliates . .	(28.5)	(28.9)
Net earnings applicable to common stock	$ 1,408.8	$ 1,229.7
Earnings per common share (in dollars)	$6.20	$5.39
Dividends declared per common share (in dollars)	$2.75	$2.50
Operating margin as a percentage of sales	9.5%	10.0%
Net earnings as a percentage of sales	6.3%	6.3%

GENERAL ELECTRIC COMPANY AND CONSOLIDATED AFFILIATES
Statement of Financial Position
At December 31
(in millions)

	1979	1978
Assets:		
Cash	$ 1,904.3	$ 1,992.8
Marketable securities	672.3	470.3
Current receivables	3,646.6	3,288.5
Inventories	3,161.3	3,003.4
Current assets	$ 9,384.5	$ 8,755.0
Property, plant, and equipment	$ 9,365.2	$ 8,328.2
Accumulated depreciation, depletion, and amortization	(4,752.4)	(4,305.6)
	$ 4,612.8	$ 4,022.6
Investments	1,691.5	1,410.5
Other assets	955.7	847.9
Total assets	$16,644.5	$15,036.0
Liabilities and equity:		
Short-term borrowings	$ 871.0	$ 960.3
Accounts payable	1,476.7	1,217.2
Progress collections and price adjustments accrued	1,957.0	1,667.3
Dividends payable	158.8	147.6
Taxes accrued	655.6	532.6
Other costs and expenses accrued	1,752.7	1,650.2
Current liabilities	$ 6,871.8	$ 6,175.2
Long-term borrowings	946.8	993.8
Other liabilities	1,311.9	1,129.5
Total liabilities	$ 9,130.5	$ 8,298.5
Minority interest in equity of consolidated affiliates	$ 151.7	$ 150.8
Preferred stock ($1 par value; 2 million shares authorized; none issued)	—	—
Common stock ($2.50 par value; 251,500,000 shares authorized; 231,463,949 shares issued 1979 and 1978)	$ 578.7	$ 578.7
Amounts received for stock in excess of par value	656.3	658.0
Retained earnings	6,307.6	5,552.4
	$ 7,542.6	$ 6,759.1
Deduct common stock held in treasury	(180.3)	(172.4)
Total share owners' equity	$ 7,362.3	$ 6,586.7
Total liabilities and equity	$16,644.5	$15,036.0

Commitments and contingent liabilities

GENERAL ELECTRIC COMPANY AND CONSOLIDATED AFFILIATES
Statement of Changes in Financial Position
For the years ended December 31
(in millions)

	1979	1978
Source of funds:		
From operations		
Net earnings	$1,408.8	$1,229.7
Less earnings retained by nonconsolidated		
finance affiliates	(16.8)	(15.7)
Depreciation, depletion, and amortization	624.1	576.4
Income tax timing differences	(37.2)	31.9
Minority interest in earnings of consolidated		
affiliates	28.5	28.9
	$2,007.4	$1,851.2
Increases in long-term borrowings	49.7	95.5
Newly issued common stock	—	2.6
Disposition of treasury shares	147.5	189.8
Increase in current payables other than short-term		
borrowings	785.9	570.0
Decrease in investments	—	22.8
Other—net	147.3	176.3
Total source of funds	$3,137.8	$2,908.2
Application of funds:		
Additions to property, plant, and equipment	$1,262.3	$1,055.1
Dividends declared on common stock	623.6	569.8
Increase in investments	281.0	—
Reduction in long-term borrowings	96.7	386.0
Purchase of treasury shares	155.4	195.7
Increase in current receivables	358.1	305.8
Increase in inventories	157.9	399.1
Total application of funds	$2,935.0	$2,911.5
Net change:		
Net change in cash, marketable securities and		
short-term borrowings	$ 202.8	$ (3.3)
Analysis of net change:		
Increase in cash and marketable securities	$ 113.5	$ 184.9
Decrease (increase) in short-term borrowings	89.3	(188.2)
	$ 202.8	$ (3.3)

GENERAL ELECTRIC COMPANY AND CONSOLIDATED AFFILIATES

Statement of Changes in Share Owners' Equity

For the years ended December 31

	Dollars (in millions)		Shares (in thousands)	
	1979	1978	1979	1978
Common stock issued:				
Balance January 1	$ 578.7	$ 578.5	231,464	231,410
New shares issued: Employee savings plans	—	0.2	—	54
Balance December 31	$ 578.7	$ 578.7	231,464	231,464
Amounts received for stock in excess of par value:				
Balance January 1	$ 658.0	$ 668.4		
Excess over par value of amounts received for newly issued shares	—	2.4		
Loss on disposition of treasury stock	(1.7)	(12.8)		
Balance December 31	$ 656.3	$ 658.0		
Retained earnings:				
Balance January 1	$5,522.4	$4,862.5		
Net earnings	1,408.8	1,229.7		
Dividends declared on common stock	(623.6)	(569.8)		
Balance December 31	$6,307.6	$5,522.4		
Common stock held in treasury:				
Balance January 1	$ (172.4)	$ (166.5)	(3,428)	(3,249)
Purchases	(155.4)	(195.7)	(3,155)	(3,838)
Dispositions:				
Employee savings plans	124.1	116.1	2,492	2,223
Employee Stock Ownership Plan	10.6	—	213	—
Incentive compensation plans	7.8	8.0	152	147
Stock options and appreciation rights	5.0	7.0	101	134
Business acquisitions	—	58.7	—	1,155
Balance December 31	$ (180.3)	$ (172.4)	(3,625)	(3,428)
Total share owners' equity December 31	$7,362.3	$6,586.7	227,839	228,036

Case 13–5

The Rouse Company

Required:

1. Comment on the economic difference (if any) between exchange gains or losses on foreign currency denominated transactions and exchange gains or losses resulting from translation of foreign currency financial statements into dollars.
2. Why is there an adjustment for gain or loss from translation of foreign debt in Rouse's statement of changes in financial position?
3. Do you agree with the position taken by Rouse in its petition to the FASB? Explain.
4. Suppose you were allowed to amend FASB *Statement No. 8*. What accounting treatment would you suggest for foreign currency exchange gains or losses on transactions? On translations? (*Rouse subsequently disposed of its two Canadian operations.*)

ACCOUNTING FOR CANADIAN CURRENCY EXCHANGE RATE FLUCTUATIONS

Results for both seven-month periods were affected by *Statement No. 8* of the Financial Accounting Standards Board (FASB) issued in October 1975. This ruling, which specifies the method for translating foreign operations for inclusion in financial statements of U.S. companies, has been applied to the financial statements of our retail centers in Montreal and Toronto, Canada. Translation gains or losses with respect to the debt of these centers are based upon changes in the exchange rates between the U.S. and Canadian dollars. For the seven months ended December 31, 1976, the translation of foreign debt produced a gain of $1,991,000, because of the sharp decline of the Canadian dollar during that period. For the comparable period ended December 31, 1975, there was a loss on translation of $406,000.

It is the company's belief, concurred in by our auditors, that no realistic circumstances exist in which the company could in fact realize either gains or losses from the effects of currency fluctuations on foreign debt. The debt of these two retail centers is substantially without recourse to The Rouse Company, is repayable in Canadian dollars from rental payments of the tenants, and is secured solely by Canadian operations. We and our auditors have presented our shared position to the FASB. However, while awaiting a final ruling from the FASB, translation gains and losses are being recorded with respect to the Canadian debt as required by *Statement No. 8*. The application of the ruling to this debt, although having no basis in economic reality, can significantly distort the company's reporting of its results of operations—as can be seen by reconstructing the effects of the ruling upon recent reporting periods:

Fiscal year ended May 31, 1974—$756,000 loss
Fiscal year ended May 31, 1975—$1,994,000 gain
Fiscal year ended May 31, 1976—$2,389,000 loss
Fiscal period ended December 31, 1976—$1,991,000 gain
Cumulative effect through December 31, 1976—$142,000 gain

SUMMARY

The seven-month period was a very satisfactory continuance of the progress reported for the previous year. Retail properties and the mortgage banking division performed very well. The projects in the development pipeline made excellent progress. Liquidation of Rouse Investing and Rouse-Wates continued on schedule. Shareholders' equity based on current values reached $137.9 million, up $10.8 million in the last seven months. We look forward to continuing increases in earnings and current value net worth during 1977.

Chairman of the Board

President

THE ROUSE COMPANY AND SUBSIDIARIES
Consolidated Cost Basis Statement of Operations
(in thousands)

	Seven Months Ended December 31, 1976	Year Ended May 31, 1976 (restated)
Revenues	$46,760	$73,712
Expense exclusive of interest, depreciation, and amortization	$27,455	$45,450
Interest expense	15,406	24,830
	$42,861	$70,280
	$ 3,899	$ 3,432
Depreciation and amortization	5,161	8,208
	$ (1,262)	$ (4,776)
Gain on sales of interests in retail centers	738	13,229
Gain (loss) from translation of foreign debt	1,991	(2,389)
Earnings before income taxes and extraordinary credit.........................	$ 1,467	$ 6,064
Federal and state income taxes: Current, state	$ 54	$ 97
Tax effect of accounting loss carryovers	—	4,000
	$ 54	$ 4,097
Earnings before extraordinary credit	$ 1,413	$ 1,967
Extraordinary credit—tax credit caused by availability of accounting loss carryovers	—	$ 4,000
Net earnings	$ 1,413	$ 5,967
Earnings per common share after provision for dividends on preferred stock: Earnings before extraordinary credit	$ .10	$ .14
Extraordinary credit	—	.31
Net earnings	$ .10	$ .45

THE ROUSE COMPANY AND SUBSIDIARIES
Consolidated Cost Basis Statement of Changes in Financial Position
(in $000)

	Seven Months Ended December 31, 1976	Year Ended May 31, 1976 (Restated)
Earnings before extraordinary credit	$ 1,413	$ 1,967
Depreciation and amortization	5,161	8,208
(Gain) loss from translation of foreign debt	(1,991)	2,389
	$ 4,583	$ 12,564
Tax credit caused by availability of accounting loss carryovers	—	4,000
Funds provided by operations after extraordinary credit	$ 4,583	$ 16,564
Less dividends on preferred stock...................	82	150
	$ 4,501	$ 16,414
Less mortgage principal payments—operating properties	2,262	3,641
Funds provided by operations after extraordinary credit. Preferred stock dividends and mortgage principal payments	$ 2,239	$ 12,773
Additions to reserves charged to operations, net of write-offs:		
Additions to development reserve, net	—	$ 950
Additions to reserve for possible investment losses, net..................................	$ (1,019)	1,545
Total additions to reserves charged to operations, net	$ (1,019)	$ 2,495
Funds provided (used) for projects:		
Borrowings of project related debt	$ 31,881	$ 45,568
Disposition of properties:		
Net book value of interests in retail centers sold	—	21,512
Net book value of other dispositions	3,606	2,744
Transfers to joint ventures, net	3,884	3,982
Total funds provided for projects..............	$ 39,371	$ 73,806
Construction and development of projects	$(20,404)	$(47,867)
Improvements to existing properties	(910)	(1,589)
Repayment of project debt other than mortgage principal payments	(17,366)	(13,331)
Mortgages assumed by purchasers of interests in retail centers	—	(23,832)
Total funds (used) for projects	$(38,680)	$(86,619)
Net funds provided (used) for projects	$ 691	$(12,813)

THE ROUSE COMPANY AND SUBSIDIARIES (continued)

	Seven Months Ended December 31, 1976	Year Ended May 31, 1976 (restated)
Other funds provided:		
Borrowings other than project related debt	$ 329	$ 6,992
Borrowings of investment operations	230	—
Increase in accounts payable and accrued expenses	2,897	—
Decrease in investment operations portfolio	1,274	8,606
Proceeds from exercise of stock options and sale of common stock	273	—
Total other funds provided	$ 5,003	$ 15,598
Other funds (used):		
Other property additions	$ (27)	$ (207)
Repayments of investment operations debt	—	(5,795)
Repayment of borrowings other than project related debt	(1,987)	(3,015)
Increase in advances to Rouse-Wates	(813)	(1,714)
Increase in other receivables	(1,194)	(7,726)
Decrease in accounts payable and accrued expenses	—	(1,609)
Other, net	(1,048)	(189)
Total other funds (used)	$ (5,069)	$(20,255)
Net other funds (used)	$ (66)	$ (4,657)
Increase (decrease) in cash and temporary investments	$ 1,845	$ (2,202)
Cash and temporary investments at beginning of period	3,805	6,007
Cash and temporary investments at end of period	$ 5,650	$ 3,305

TRANSLATION OF FINANCIAL STATEMENTS OF FOREIGN OPERATIONS

Beginning with the period ended December 31, 1976, the company has applied the Financial Accounting Standards Board's (FASB) *Statement No. 8* in translating the financial statements of two Canadian subsidiaries. These subsidiaries own two retail centers with non-recourse financing constituting over 90 percent of the total foreign debt financing the centers. The major change to the company's previous foreign currency translation policy as a result of applying *Statement No. 8* is the translation of foreign long-term debt at current exchange rates rather than at historic exchange rates. This change causes the company to report gains and losses from fluctuations in exchange rates as applied to long-term debt as part of its operating results. The consolidated financial statements for the prior year have been restated for the change in translation policy.

While *Statement No. 8* requires that unrealized gains and losses resulting from the translation of foreign debt be recognized in periodic operating results, the company believes that there are no realistic circumstances under which such gains or losses would be realized. This position is based on the following factors relating to this Canadian debt:

1. Over 90% of this debt is nonrecourse—debt secured *only* by the Canadian properties and operations with no recourse to the U.S. parent company.
2. Canadian revenues from tenants in these retail centers service the related Canadian debt.
3. Experience supports the company's position that tenants' leases can be renewed or replaced to provide continued servicing of the related Canadian debt.

Based on these economic realities, users of these financial statements should understand that the gains and losses relating to the translation of the Canadian debt at current exchange rates have no real economic impact on the company's current financial position or results of operations.

The accompanying table summarizes the impact on operating results and shareholders' equity of translating the Canadian debt at the current exchange rate as of the end of each period as required by *Statement No. 8* (in thousands):

	Seven Months Ended December 31,	Year Ended May 31 (restated)	
	1976	1976	1975
Net earnings (loss) before gain (loss) from Canadian debt translation	$ (578)	$ 8,356	$ (174)
Effect of translating Canadian debt at current rates	1,991	(2,389)	1,994
Net earnings after gain (loss) from Canadian debt translation	$1,413	$ 5,967	$1,820
Cumulative effect on debt and shareholders' equity at the end of the period	$ 142	$(1,849)	$ 540

The restatement has increased earnings per common share by $.16 for the year ended May 31, 1975, and reduced earnings per common share by $.19 for the year ended May 31, 1976.

The company and its auditors have petitioned the FASB to interpret

Statement No. 8 in a way which would reflect the economic realities of the Canadian operations. Until such time as the FASB acts, the company will translate the financial statements of its foreign operations in accordance with *Statement No. 8*. The company will continue to urge the FASB to remedy the unrealistic results of literally applying *Statement No. 8* to the company's foreign, nonrecourse debt.

There has been no change in the method of translating other accounts of the Canadian subsidiaries. The current assets and liabilities of the Canadian subsidiaries are translated at current exchange rates. Property and deferred costs are translated at the prevailing rates at the time the related transactions took place. The results of operations have been translated at the average exchange rate during the period except for depreciation and amortization which are based upon the translated property accounts. The resulting translation gains and losses are not material and are included in current operations.

14

Special Topics

SEGMENT REPORTING

In order to diversify, many corporations operate in more than one line of business and operate in many different foreign and domestic markets. To assess the growth and profit potentials of a diversified company an investor needs disaggregated marketing and operating data as well as information about the company's major customers.

For example, City Investing Corporation's domestic operations include the manufacture of heating and air conditioning units (Rheem Manufacturing), magazine printing (World Color Press), and the production of molded plastic products for the automobile and appliance industry (Alma Plastics). They also operate a budget motel chain (Motel 6), build single family homes in the west and southwest (Wood Bros. Homes), produce mobile homes (Guerdon Industries), and sell property and casualty insurance (City Home Corporation). They are involved in oil and gas exploration (Watson Oil Corporation) and have interests in oil reserves in the North Sea. Each of these markets differ in their supply, demand, and risk characteristics.

The FASB requires that financial statements include information pertaining to operations in different industries (reportable segments) and markets, and disclose the names of certain major customers of the firm.[1]

A particular segment is a reportable segment if any of the following conditions are met:

1. *The segment revenues exceed 10 percent of the combined revenues of all segments.*
2. *The assets used exclusively in segment operations (identifiable assets) exceed 10 percent of the identifiable assets of all segments.*

---

[1] FASB *Statement No. 14,* "Financial Reporting for Segments of a Business Enterprise," December 1976.

3. *The operating profit (loss) of the segment exceeds 10 percent of the combined operating profits (losses) of all profitable (unprofitable) segments.*

Although the 10 percent cutoff is somewhat arbitrary, the intent is to identify the major product lines that contribute to the firm's overall profitability. The determination of reportable segments is a subjective process because management must exercise judgment when grouping individual products and services into what they believe are the industry lines (segments) of its business.

In a footnote, in the body of the financial statements, or in a separate schedule in the annual report companies must disclose the revenues (including intersegment sales) and operating profits of each reportable segment. Identifiable assets, depreciation, depletion and amortization expense, capital expenditures, and the effects of accounting changes must also be presented for each segment.

If the corporation uses the equity method to account for an unconsolidated subsidiary whose operations are vertically integrated with the operations of a reportable segment, the firm's equity in net income and investment in net assets of the subsidiary is reported with the segment data.

Results of foreign operations are to be disclosed in aggregate or geographically if revenues from foreign operations exceed 10 percent of consolidated revenues, or if the identifiable assets of foreign operations exceed 10 percent of total assets. Firms that derive 10 percent or more of their revenue from sales to a single customer (or group of customers under common control) must disclose this information with the segment data. The federal government, a state or local government, or a foreign government are to be considered individual customers.[2]

Segment profitability data are useful in making year-to-year comparisons for each of the firm's major operations. When this material is used in conjunction with overall industry data, the reader of the statement can estimate the market share of the firm in particular industries. Combined with profitability information, the asset information is useful in computing rates of return.

Vertically integrated investments may insure raw material supplies or markets for final products of the segments.

Disclosure of any heavy dependence of revenues on a single customer is also very important to the readers of the statement so they can assess the probability that the customer will continue as a source of revenue in the future.

---

[2] FASB *Statement No. 30,* "Disclosure of Information about Major Customers," October 1979.

The 1977 annual report of the Mohasco Corporation discloses segment information in a footnote. (See Illustration 14–1.) Four segments are identified and their activities described. Corporate assets (assets not used in segment operations) consist principally of cash. Investments are another common corporate asset.

Corporate operating income consists of revenue and expense items not directly assignable to segments. These items include interest expense, general corporate expense, and income taxes. Any allocation of these to individual segments would be arbitrary and might distort the operating performance of the segments (the problem is similar to the problem faced when allocating fixed production costs to individual products and yearly operating costs to interim financial statements).

Transfer pricing policies on intersegment sales are usually described. Mohasco prices intersegment sales at prevailing market prices.

Mohasco must disclose the results of foreign operations since identifiable assets of foreign operations are approximately 14 per-

ILLUSTRATION 14–1 _____
Mohasco Corporation and Subsidiaries—1977 Annual Report

The revenue of the company has been grouped into four different industries which are listed below along with a description of the products and services from which the revenue of each industry is derived.

Carpet—Sales of a broad range of tufted, velvet, axminster, and knitted carpets and rugs.

Furniture—Sales of a variety of upholstered furniture, dining and family room furniture, office and institutional furniture, kitchen cabinets, and metal furniture components.

Distribution—Sales to retail outlets of a broad range of home furnishings. Products consist of carpets, resilient floor coverings, furniture, window coverings, and shades.

Rental—Leasing of furniture primarily to individuals renting apartments and to a lesser extent to major furniture users such as apartment complexes and offices.

Financial information regarding the above industries in which the company is engaged and its foreign operations as of and for the year ended December 31, 1977, is shown in the accompanying table.

ILLUSTRATION 14–1 (continued)

(in thousands except percentages)

	Carpet	Furni-ture	Distri-bution	Rental	Cor-porate	Consoli-dated
Total sales and other revenues	$204,909	$270,552	$228,153	$18,681	—	$653,390
Less intersegment sales*	68,440	465	—	—	—	
Net sales and other revenues	$136,469	$270,087	$228,153	$18,681	—	$653,390
Percent	21%	41%	35%	3%		
Operating income	$ 13,292	$ 17,209	$ 6,930	$ 2,131	($ 8,398)†	$ 31,164
Percent	34%	43%	18%	5%		
Total assets	$147,808	$130,496	$ 69,904	$ 20,097	$15,147†	$383,452
Additions to property, plant, and equipment	$ 6,554	$ 5,369	$ 372	$ 909	—	$ 13,204
Additions to rental furniture	$ —	—	—	$ 5,995	—	$ 5,995
Depreciation and amortization	$ 6,230	$ 3,903	$ 810	$ 2,462	—	$ 13,405

	United States	Foreign Opera-tions	Cor-porate	Consoli-dated
Net sales and other revenues	$596,309	$57,081	—	$653,390
Operating income	$ 32,181	$ 7,381‡	($8,398)	$ 31,164
Total assets	$314,459	$53,846‡	$15,147	$383,452

* Intersegment sales are priced the same as sales to unaffiliated customers. Adjustments to eliminate intercompany profit from year-end inventories are reflected in the operating income of the selling industry group.
† Amounts related to charges for corporate headquarters functions are stated separately to avoid possible inequities in allocation by industry grouping or foreign operations. Corporate assets are principally cash.
‡ Includes goodwill, and amortization thereof, relating to the company's investment in foreign operations.

cent ($53,846/$383,452) of total assets. This is required because foreign operations are inherently more risky than domestic operations.

Mohasco does not have unconsolidated subsidiaries whose operations are vertically integrated with the operations of the segments.
Allis Chalmers Corporation does. See Illustration 14–2 for a portion
of its 1978 disclosure on segment operations.

ILLUSTRATION 14–2

ALLIS-CHALMERS CORPORATION*
($000 omitted)

	1978		1977	
	Equity Investment at December 31	Equity in Net Income (loss)	Equity Investment at December 31	Equity in Net Income (loss)
Process equipment............	$ 3,555	$(631)	$2,901	$(1,054)
Agricultural equipment	2,213	(278)	1,032	(107)
Material handling and outdoor power equipment	10,620	619	7,972	456
Power generation and transmission	73	(443)	(684)	(910)

* The company's investments accounted for on the equity method include vertically integrated
companies operating primarily in the United States and Canada.

In 1977 Teledyne Incorporated disclosed its sales to the U.S. government as follows:

> Sales between business segments, which were not material, gener-
> ally were priced at prevailing market prices. In 1977, the Company's
> sales to the U.S. government were $519,317,000, including direct sales
> as prime contractor and indirect sales as subcontractor; the industrial
> and aviation and electronics segments made most of these sales. Sales
> by operations in the United States to customers in other countries were
> $193,963,000 in 1977.

INTERIM REPORTING

Interim reports are condensed financial statements covering portions of a company's annual accounting period.[3]

---

[3] Major stock exchanges and the SEC (Form 10-Q) require companies to issue quarterly interim reports.

In an attempt to provide investors with more timely information the FASB currently requires that interim reports to shareholders contain at least a condensed income statement with comparative figures for the corresponding interim period of the prior year.[4] An interim balance sheet and statement of changes in financial position is not required.

Each interim report should be viewed as an integral part of the annual report because in constructing the interim report it is necessary to anticipate the results of operations for the remainder of the year.

Interim reports are more subjective than annual reports because some revenues and expenses of the interim period can only be estimated. Items requiring special consideration include:

Operating Costs

Operating costs incurred throughout the year must be allocated to interim periods. How should annual rent payments on a firm's sales office be allocated to quarterly interim income statements? Should each quarter reflect 25 percent of the rent payment as rent expense or should rent payments be allocated to quarters on the basis of the percentage of quarterly revenue earned to total annual revenues earned? Either approach is acceptable. Costs (other than product costs or expenses directly related to revenues) may be expensed as incurred or allocated among interim periods using any reasonable basis. The difference in the quarterly net income can be significant for a company with a highly seasonal revenue pattern.

Income Tax Expense

Income tax expense for an interim period is based on the best estimate of the effective tax rate for the year. The annual effective rate depends on the types of income generated, investment and foreign tax credits earned, and tax loss carryforwards utilized during the *entire* year.

Lifo Inventories

Companies that *expect* to replace Lifo layers sold during an interim period by the end of the year should include the *expected*

---

[4] FASB *Statement No. 3*, "Reporting Accounting Changes in Interim Financial Statements," December 1974; *APB Opinion No. 28*, "Interim Financial Reporting," December 31, 1973.

cost to replace the liquidated layers (not the historical cost of the liquidated layers) in cost of goods sold.

Accounting Changes, Unusual Items, Extraordinary Items

All material unusual, infrequent, or extraordinary items are to be reported in their entirety in the interim period in which they occur. Changes in an accounting principle should be reported in the interim period in which the change occurs.

Assume that the Seabiz Company, which sells a single product, has just completed operations for the first quarter of 1981. Operating data for the first quarter and estimates for the subsequent three quarters are shown in Illustration 14–3.

ILLUSTRATION 14–3

SEABIZ COMPANY

	Quarter				Total for year
	1	*2*	*3*	*4*	
Estimated sales revenue ...	$100 (10 units at $10) (actual)	$200 (20 units at $10)	$400 (40 units at $10)	$100 (10 units at $10)	$800
Estimated operating costs (excluding product costs) .	$ 80 (actual)	$ 80	$ 80	$ 80	$320
Planned level of ending inventory (units)	35 (actual)	20	20	40	

Additional facts:

1. Seabiz uses the Lifo flow assumption. Beginning inventory consists of 40 units valued at $1/each. In the first quarter five units were purchased at a cost of $2/unit. The replacement cost of inventory units is expected to remain at $2/unit for the three subsequent quarters.
2. Seabiz *estimates* its effective annual tax rate to be 40 percent.
3. During the first quarter Seabiz realized an extraordinary loss of $10 (before taxes) on a premature retirement of debt.

Seabiz's first quarter interim income statement would be prepared in the following manner.

Sales

Interim sales revenue is the amount of sales revenue realized during the quarter. Seabiz Company's quarterly sales revenue is $100 (ten units at $10).

Lifo Inventory

Seabiz Company uses the Lifo flow assumption for inventory valuation. Beginning inventory was 40 units. The inventory level at the end of the first quarter dropped to 35 units (10 sold, 5 purchased), but *expectations are that by the end of the fourth quarter inventory levels will again be 40 units.*

If Seabiz computes cost of goods for the first quarter in the conventional Lifo manner the quarterly income statement will show a cost of goods sold equal to $15 (five units of currently purchased items at $2/unit plus five units of inventory purchased previously at $1/unit).

However, Seabiz *expects* to replace the liquidated base of five units in its inventory by the end of the year at a cost of $2/unit. On an annual basis they do not *expect* to use any of the inventory layer valued at $1/unit. Based on this replacement assumption, interim cost of goods sold should be $20 (five units purchased in first quarter at $2/unit plus five units *expected* to be purchased before year end at $2/unit).

Operating Costs

None of the operating costs of Seabiz Company are directly related to the generation of sales revenue. Seabiz Company allocates yearly operating costs to quarters in proportion to the percentage of estimated total yearly *sales* revenues earned during each quarter. Anticipated revenues for the year are $800. Revenues for the first quarter total $100 and total operating costs are estimated to be $320. Seabiz allocates $40 ($\frac{1}{8} \times$ $320) of operating costs to the first quarter. (A *valid alternative* is to show operating expenses of $80 in each quarter.)

Net income before taxes and extraordinary items is $40. The *estimated* annual tax rate of 40 percent is used to compute income tax expense of $16 (40 percent of $40) for the first quarter.

Extraordinary items are shown in their *entirety* in the quarter in which they are incurred. Seabiz Company must show the $6 after tax loss on premature retirement of debt in the first quarter statement.

In addition, Seabiz Company is required to disclose the seasonal nature of its business in a footnote to the quarterly statement of income (see Illustration 14–4.).

Review by Independent Certified Public Accountants

Interim financial statements are not subject to detailed audits by independent certified public accountants. Interim statements are re-

ILLUSTRATION 14-4 _____

SEABIZ COMPANY
Statement of Income for the First Quarter of 1981*

Revenue (10 units at $10)	$100
Cost of goods sold	20
Gross margin	$ 80
Operating expenses (⅛ × $320)	40
Net income before taxes and extraordinary item	$ 40
Income tax expense (40% of $40)	16
Net income before extraordinary item	$ 24
Extraordinary loss ($10 less tax effect of $4)	6
Net income	$ 18

* Historically sales for the four quarters have been in the approximate ratio 1:2:4:1. Expectations are that this ratio will continue.

The extraordinary loss resulted from premature retirement of long-term debt during the first quarter.

viewed by CPAs, but no opinion regarding the financial statements taken as a whole is rendered.[5] Price Waterhouse and Company audited United Technologies Corporation in 1979. They explained their *review* of UTC's first quarter summary of net income in the accompanying letter:

To the Shareholders of
United Technologies Corporation

We have made a review of the consolidated summary of income of United Technologies Corporation and subsidiaries for the three-month periods ended March 31, 1979, and 1978 in accordance with standards established by the American Institute of Certified Public Accountants. We did not review the financial information for the three-month period ended March 31, 1979, relating to the company's investment in Carrier Corporation, which constituted approximately 12 percent of the consolidated assets at March 31, 1979, and is accounted for under the equity method.

A review of interim financial information consists principally of obtaining an understanding of the system for the preparation of interim financial information, applying analytical review procedures to financial data, and making inquiries of persons responsible for financial and accounting matters. It is substantially less in scope than an exam-

_____
[5] *Statement on Auditing Standards No. 24,* "Review of Interim Financial Information," June 1979.

ination in accordance with generally accepted auditing standards, the objective of which is the expression of an opinion regarding the financial statements taken as a whole. Accordingly, we do not express such an opinion.

Based on our review, we are not aware of any material modifications that should be made to the accompanying consolidated summary of income for it to be in conformity with generally accepted accounting principles.

Hartford, Connecticut   Price Waterhouse & Co.
April 10, 1979

Summary

Quarterly information is best used to compare results of the current year with results of the corresponding quarters of prior years. Such comparisons can be deceptive, however, because the interim results are based on estimates of operating results for the entire year. Yearly net income should not be projected from quarterly net income by multiplying by four. The many estimates and arbitrary cost allocations used to construct quarterly income statements make such projections unreliable.

FORECASTS

Investors make decisions which are to a great extent based on the future performance of an enterprise.

Reliable expectations of the future are formed using historical information (financial statements) augmented by other financial and nonfinancial information about the future plans and environment of the firm. Planned capital expenditures, financing plans, production and backlog data, cash flow projections, and earnings projections are examples of useful supplemental information.

The SEC and FASB have recently taken steps to insure that users of financial statements and SEC reports obtain this supplemental information.

Two major problems must be solved in order to require and obtain high quality disclosure of soft (supplemental) financial information. Assurance that the preparation of supplemental information adheres to certain standards and rules to specify legal liability to all parties involved (management, auditor) should the disclosed forecasts prove to be inaccurate are needed.

SEC

The SEC has recently (June 1979) addressed the legal liability question. A rule covering all companies reporting to the SEC or filing registration statements with the SEC guarantees companies a "safe harbor" against fraud charges provided their disclosures are made in "good faith." Prior to this rule the burden of proof as to the fairness and reasonableness of the projections rested with the reporting company. Under the new rule any person or entity filing a complaint must prove the reporting company's intent to commit fraud.

This rule, which encourages (but does not require) disclosure of supplemental information, applies to all financial forecasts appearing as supplemental information to annual reports and 10-Ks.

FASB

Recognizing the need for more and better financial information, the FASB recently broadened its mission from that of setting standards (rule making) for financial statements to setting standards for financial reporting.

> Some useful information is better provided by financial statements and some is better provided, or can only be provided, by means of financial reporting other than financial statements.[6]

The FASB's recent statement on inflation accounting exemplifies this new mission. FASB *Statement No. 33* entitled "Financial Reporting and Changing Prices" (October 1979) requires current cost and constant dollar information from some 1,350 of the largest U.S. corporations. The information is supplemental to the annual report. It is not subject to audit although auditors would *review* the reasonableness of the disclosure.

The trend appears to be clear. Faced with an increasing demand by investors for supplemental financial and nonfinancial information, the SEC and FASB are moving in the direction of filling this need. It is likely that both bodies will require or recommend disclosure of supplemental information.

PENSIONS

A pension plan is an agreement between a company and its employees for the purpose of providing retirement income to the employees.

The agreement specifies:

1. The types and amounts of benefits the employees are to receive upon retirement.

---

[6] *Statement of Financial Accounting Concepts No. 1*, Objectives of Financial Reporting by Business Enterprises, November 1978.

2. The required contributions to the plan by the employer and employee.
3. How and when employees become vested.

There are two primary types of pension plans: *defined benefit* and *defined contribution*. The majority of private pension plans are defined benefit plans. The defined benefit is a specified or determinable amount that the employee receives upon retirement. The stated benefit (usually paid monthly) is calculated using a formula which reflects the employee's years of service, earnings, or a combination of years of service and earnings.

In defined contribution plans the employer agrees (the employee may also agree) to contribute a specified amount each year to the plan. There are no guaranteed benefit levels upon retirement.

Pension plans may be *contributory* or *noncontributory*. Contributory plans require that both employer and employees make payments to the pension fund. In noncontributory plans payments are only made by the employer. The discussion to follow will focus on *noncontributory, defined benefit plans*, the most common type of private sector pension plan.

Pension plans are usually managed by a trustee (for example, an insurance company). The employer makes periodic cash payments to the trustee according to funding provisions specified by the plan. A pension plan is *fully funded* if the cash value of the pension fund is equal to (or exceeds) the present value of all expected future obligations under the plan. Computation of the present value of all future pension fund obligations is a very difficult actuarial task. Assumptions must be made about employee turnover, the investment performance of the pension fund assets, future salary levels, and mortality rates.

Vested benefits are earned benefits that are not contingent on the employee's continuing in the service of the employer. Under most pension plans rights vest gradually until the employee becomes fully vested. For example, an employee may become 50 percent vested after five years service and receive an additional 10 percent vesting for each year's service beyond five years. At the end of ten years of service the employee is fully vested. Rights to benefits earned by the employee's contribution to the plan (if any) are always fully vested.

Accounting for pension plans is concerned with the recognition of pension costs as expenses. The *normal (current) pension service cost* of an accounting period is the present value of all future benefits earned by employees during the period. *Past service cost* is the present value of all future benefits granted to employees for years of service prior to the inception of a pension plan. *Prior service cost* includes the obligation created by the initiation of the plan (past service cost) plus the obligation created by events subsequent to the initiation of the plan.

Federal Pension Law

The Employee Retirement Income Security Act of 1974 (ERISA, Pension Reform Act of 1974) sets funding, coverage, and vesting requirements for private sector pension plans. The Act requires firms to fund normal pension costs as incurred, to fund past service costs systematically over a period not to exceed 30 years, to extend coverage to all employees in order for the employer's payments to the pension fund to be tax deductible, and to guarantee minimum vesting (specified in the Act) of benefits to employees.

ERISA protects employee benefits when a firm's pension plan is terminated and the pension fund is inadequate to insure payment of all earned benefits. It gives the government a claim against the assets of the firm (in addition to the pension fund assets) of up to 30 percent of the net worth of the company to insure payment of the pension benefits. This claim is senior to the claims of all other creditors.

GAAP for Pensions[7]

Normal service cost of a period is an expense of the period. Past service cost is systematically accrued as an expense over a period of 10 (minimum) to 40 (maximum) years. GAAP does not specify how or when the pension obligations are to be funded, and only the *accrued portion* of past service cost in excess of the amount of funded past service cost is shown as a liability on the firm's balance sheet. Payments to the pension fund reduce the pension liability.

On January 1, 1981, Generous Inc. established a defined benefit, noncontributory employee pension fund with a major insurance company as trustee. Actuarially computed current cost of benefits earned during the first year was $5,000. The following December 31, 1981, journal entry recognizes current pension cost as an expense of the period.

Current pension expense........................	5,000	
Pension liability		5,000

---

[7] *APB Opinion No. 8,* "Accounting for the Cost of Pension Plans," November 1966. FASB *Statement No. 36,* "Disclosure of Pension Information," May 1980.

The above plan also granted retirement benefits to employees for service performed prior to January 1, 1981. The insurance company estimated this past service cost to be $14,688.[8] Generous Inc. chooses to accrue past service cost as an expense systematically over the next three years (for computational efficiency we ignore the ten-year minimum accrual period required by GAAP in this example).

A three-year 6 percent annuity of $5,495 beginning December 31, 1981, has a present value of $14,688. On December 31, 1981, Generous Inc. makes the following journal entry to accrue past service cost as an expense.

Past service pension expense 5,495
    Pension liability   5,495

The pension liability account has a balance of $10,495 ($5,000 + $5,495). It will be reduced as the pension obligation is funded. Funding requirements are set by ERISA and not the FASB. Suppose, as many corporations do, Generous Inc. chooses to fund pension liabilities as they accrue. On December 31, 1981, Generous makes a cash payment of $10,495 to the pension fund trustee. This completely eliminates the liability that was just recognized.

Pension liability 10,495
    Cash   10,495

Although the cash payment discharges the accrued pension liability, the *yet to be accrued* portion of the past service obligation amounting to $10,074 (the present value of a two-period $5,495 annuity in arrears at 6 percent) does not appear as a liability on the December 31, 1981, balance sheet.

If the cash transfer to the fund trustee in the first year was less than $10,495, a pension liability for the difference between $10,495 and the amount transferred would appear on Generous's balance sheet. If the cash transfer to the fund trustee was greater than $10,495, a pension asset account (in spite of the existence of the yet unfunded and unrecognized $10,074 obligation) would appear on Generous's 1981 balance sheet.

Pension accounting is often criticized for not showing the unfunded portion of the pension obligation as a liability on a firm's balance sheet. Currently the FASB requires footnote disclosure in the financial statement of the actuarial present value of vested and nonvested benefits, the pension plans' net assets available to pay bene-

---

[8] This $14,688 is the amount of money which (given the actuarial assumptions of the insurance company) would have to be set aside on January 1, 1981, to guarantee that all the retroactively granted defined benefits could be paid as they come due. Assume the insurance company uses a 6 percent interest rate in its computations.

fits, the rates of return used in the computations, and the date as of which the benefit information was determined. The information can be disclosed for each individual company pension plan or in the aggregate for all plans.

The FASB also requires that a firm describe all of its pension plans, the employees covered, the funding policy, and the total pension cost for the period in a footnote to the financial statements.[9]

The 1978 United Technologies Corporation annual report contains the following footnote explaining its pension plans.

United Technologies Incorporated—1978

Note 14—Retirement Income and Incentive Compensation Plans

The corporation and its subsidiaries have a number of pension and retirement plans under which it is the corporation's general policy to fund current pension costs as accrued. Pension costs amounted to $127,263,000 and $121,603,000 in 1978 and 1977, respectively, including amortization of prior service costs over periods ranging from 14 years for the principal plans to 30 years for certain of the subsidiaries' plans. As of the latest valuation dates the actuarial value of vested benefits under pension plans of certain subsidiaries exceeded the totals of the related pension funds and balance sheet accruals by approximately $46 million. Liabilities under unfunded pension plans of certain international subsidiaries and for employee severance benefits, including those accruing to employees under foreign government regulations, are included in other long-term liabilities in the accompanying balance sheet.

For 1978, $11,687,000 ($10,636,000 in 1977) was authorized under the corporation's Incentive Compensation Plan for distribution among officers and employees designated by the Board of Directors.

Unfunded past service costs can be compared with current earnings to obtain an estimate of how future recognition of the unfunded obligations is likely to affect earnings.

In 1976 GM reported approximately $7.3 billion of unfunded past service costs and Chrysler reported about $2 billion. GM's unfunded obligation is equivalent to about 2 years of pretax earnings at the 1976 rate, while it would take approximately 30 years at its current earnings level for Chrysler to discharge its obligation.

---

[9] FASB *Statement No. 35*, "Accounting and Reporting by Defined Benefit Plan," March 1980, sets financial accounting and reporting standards for the annual financial statements of a defined benefits plan.

CASES FOR CHAPTER 14

Case 14–1

Inter Rim, Inc.

Inter Rim, Inc. wishes to present its senior corporate officials with quarterly net income figures which can be projected to obtain estimates of yearly net income.

Their plan is to allocate all fixed costs to quarters in proportion to the number of units expected to be sold in each quarter. The following formula is to be used to project annual net income from quarterly net income (and will be disclosed):

$$\text{Annual net income} = \frac{\text{Yearly unit sales}}{\text{Quarterly units sold}} \text{ (Quarterly net income)}$$

In addition the quarterly statement will contain the latest estimate of expected sales for the year.

Estimated Data

	Quarter			
	1	*2*	*3*	*4*
Sales price/unit.....................	$5 (actual)	$6	$5	$8
Expected sales (units)	100,000 (actual)	300,000	200,000	400,000
Expected costs:				
Variable manufacturing (unit)	$1			
Fixed manufacturing (year)	$600,000			
Variable selling (unit)	$2			
Fixed selling (year)	$200,000			

Required:

1. Compute net income for the first quarter. The actual variable manufacturing cost is $1/unit, the actual variable selling cost is $2/unit, and man-

482

agement's best estimates of total sales and total fixed costs for the year are still 1 million units and $800,000, respectively (ignore income taxes).

2. Using the above formula, project annual net income. Compute "actual" net income assuming that actual costs were the same as expected costs. Why aren't projected and "actual" net income equal?

3. Can you suggest an alternative allocation of fixed costs to quarters and an alternative equation for projecting annual net income from quarterly net income? Will your procedure always work?

Case 14–2

Sears (B)

Required:

1. Is the market value of Sears' pension plan assets larger or smaller than vested pension benefits?

2. What is the amount of unfunded vested benefits as a percentage of Sears' shareholders' equity? How many years of pretax profits at the 1977 rate would it take to fund all vested and nonvested benefits? Do you think vested benefits should be 100 percent funded? If you were due to receive a pension from Sears, would you be concerned?

3. At the end of fiscal year 1976, Wheeling-Pittsburgh Steel Corporation had unfunded vested benefits equal to 75 percent of stockholders' equity. Unfunded past service cost amounted to 838 percent of its average pretax profit for the previous three years. Why do you think these figures differ so much from Sears'?

4. What other disclosures about pension plans would you recommend?

SEARS ROEBUCK, INC
Statements of Income
($000)

	Year Ended January 31	
	1978	1977
Net sales	$17,224,033	$14,950,208
Cost of sales, buying and occupancy expenses	11,172,965	9,399,491
Selling and administrative expenses	4,839,653	4,293,933
Operating income from sales and services	$ 1,211,415	$ 1,256,784
Other income	1,960	4,230
Equity in net income of Allstate Group		
Allstate Insurance Company		
In accordance with prescribed standards, unrealized net increases in market value of marketable equity securities of $26,249 and $129,564 are not included in the determination of net income	395,104	195,314
Allstate Enterprises, Inc.	21,881	15,015
Total Allstate group	$ 416,985	$ 210,329
Other unconsolidated subsidiaries and affiliates	57,048	42,568
	$ 474,033	$ 252,897
General expenses		
Interest	353,131	270,122
Contribution to Employes' Profit-Sharing Fund (Note 11)	140,276	114,455
Discontinued subsidiary loss	—	54,058
Income taxes		
Current operations	356,019	434,806
Benefit from disposition of subsidiary	—	(53,652)
	$ 849,426	$ 819,789
Net income	$ 837,982	$ 694,122
Per share (average shares 319,925 and 317,798)*	$2.62	$2.18

* Adjusted for two-for-one stock split effective May 27, 1977. See accompanying notes to financial statements.

SEARS ROEBUCK, INC
Statements of Financial Position
($000)

	January 31	
	1978	*1977*
Assets		
Current assets:		
Cash	$ 237,382	$ 223,112
Receivables	6,671,402	5,672,270
Inventories	2,626,070	2,215,141
Prepaid advertising and other charges	106,821	90,445
Total current assets	$ 9,641,675	$ 8,200,968
Investments		
Allstate Insurance Company (cost $62,156 and $62,072)	1,735,382	1,433,945
Other investments and advances	822,788	695,368
	$ 2,558,170	$ 2,129,313
Property, plant, and equipment	2,534,841	2,487,790
Deferred charges	11,561	8,935
Total assets	$14,746,247	$12,827,006
Liabilities		
Current liabilities:		
Short-term borrowings		
Commercial paper	$ 2,586,051	$ 1,940,578
Banks	404,936	305,869
Agreements with bank trust departments	717,958	655,046
Current maturity of long-term debt	30,473	54,969
Accounts payable and accrued expenses	1,124,713	990,762
Unearned maintenance agreement income	276,969	242,143
Deferred income taxes	917,645	855,893
Total current liabilities	$ 6,058,745	$ 5,045,260
Deferred income taxes	173,139	154,959
Long-term debt	1,990,295	1,706,099
Total liabilities	$ 8,222,179	$ 6,906,318
Shareholders' equity	$ 6,524,068	$ 5,920,688

Note 11. Retirement Plans

The company provided $140.3 million for the Profit Sharing Fund and $44.3 million for the Supplemental Pension Plan for fiscal year 1977, and $114.5 million and $33.3 million for these plans, respectively, in 1976. Both of these employee benefit plans were modified as of the beginning of 1978.

The immediate effect of the plan changes is anticipated to be a significant increase in the provision for pensions which is expected to be partially offset by a reduction in the provision for profit sharing.

Profit Sharing: Under the new profit sharing plan, the company will contribute 6 percent of consolidated net income, as defined, before federal income taxes and profit-sharing contribution. Under the former plan, the company contributed 11 percent of consolidated net income, as defined, before federal income taxes, pension costs, and profit-sharing contribution.

Pension: The supplemental pension plan in effect in 1977 was a noncontributory plan which provided pension benefits for salaried employees based upon length of service and remuneration over $15,000 per year. At January 31, 1978, the actuarially computed value of vested benefits was $111.3 million in excess of the market value of the plan's assets. The actuarially computed unfunded past service costs, which includes provision for both vested and nonvested benefits, were $240.6 million at January 31, 1978.

Pension benefits under the new pension plan will be based on length of service, average annual compensation, and social security benefits received by the employee. All full-time employees as well as certain part-time employees will be entitled to participate after complying with conditions for vesting.

Case 14–3

Uniroyal, Inc.

Required:

How helpful is the segment data in Uniroyal's 1977 annual report in assessing the future earnings prospects and financial position of Uniroyal? Make a list of segment items you consider particularly important in your evaluation (be sure to indicate exactly why they are significant items).

BUSINESS SEGMENT AND INTERNATIONAL FINANCIAL RESULTS

Notes relating to Business Segments and International Operations

Major Customer—In 1977, sales to a single major customer exceeded 10 percent of company sales to unaffiliated customers and amounted to $425 million. These sales were generated by all business segments.

Export sales to unaffiliated customers are less than 10 percent of consolidated sales to unaffiliated customers.

To reconcile the business segment information with consolidated amounts, the following eliminations are required: $78.2 million of intersegment sales, $.3 million relating to the net change in intersegment operating profit in beginning and ending inventories; $7.7 million of intersegment receivables, and $1 million intersegment profit in inventory at January 1, 1978.

Intersegment sales and transfers between geographic areas are accounted for at market prices.

Operating profit represents total revenue less operating expenses. General corporate expense, foreign exchange, minority interests, gain or loss on closed facilities or investments, and interest are not included in operating expense.

The company has a 50 percent interest in Texas-U.S. Chemical Company, Rubicon Chemicals, Inc., and Monochem, Inc., the operations of which are considered to be vertically integrated with the Chemical, Rubber and Plastic Materials segment. Investment in these operations at year-end 1977 and 1976 was $21.1 million and $20.2 million, respectively. Income from these operations under the equity accounting method for 1977 and 1976 was $2.5 million and $1.5 million, respectively.

Identifiable assets by business are those assets that are used in the company's operations in each segment. Corporate assets are principally cash and marketable securities. Identifiable assets of geographic areas are those assets of the company identified with operations in such areas.

International Operations

Operating profit for international operations as determined for business segments and geographic areas was $43.8 million in 1977 and $50.8 million in 1976. Foreign sales were $867.9 million in 1977 compared with $829.1 million in 1976.

Consolidated net income includes approximately $8 million applicable to foreign subsidiaries and affiliates. For 1976 the comparable amount was $19 million.

Net assets outside the United States at year-end for 1977 and 1976 were as follows (in millions):

	1977	1976
Current assets	$362	$355
Current liabilities	274	205
Working capital	88	150
Property and other assets	291	268
Long-term debt and other liabilities	125	125
Net foreign assets	$254	$293

Included in Other Income-Expense is a loss of $3.5 million in 1977 compared with a gain of $.6 million in 1976 applicable to foreign currency transactions and translations. Write-down of foreign inventories to the lower-of-cost-or-market, which in 1976 was reported as foreign exchange, has been reclassified to cost of goods sold.

Financial Information Relating to Business Segments
($ in millions)

	Year	Tire and Related Products	Chemical, Rubber and Plastic Materials	Fabricated Rubber and Plastic Products	Leisure Sport and Other	Eliminations	Consolidated
Sales to unaffiliated customers	1977	$1,489.0	$391.4	$412.8	$288.7		$2,581.9
	1976	1,322.8	331.0	378.7	282.3		2,314.8
Intersegment sales	1977		70.4	.5	7.3	($78.2)	
	1976		50.9	2.4	8.9	(62.2)	
Total revenue	1977	1,489.0	461.8	413.3	296.0	(78.2)	2,581.9
	1976	1,322.8	381.9	381.1	291.2	(62.2)	2,314.8
Operating profit	1977	77.1	57.6	15.6	(2.7)	(.3)	147.3
	1976	57.3	39.5	16.0	.8	(.2)	113.4
Equity income	1977						4.1
	1976						3.7
General corporate expense	1977						37.6
	1976						34.7
Interest expense	1977						49.8
	1976						44.1
Income before income taxes	1977						64.0
	1976						38.3
Identifiable assets	1977	886.0	311.9	234.1	195.8	(8.7)	1,619.1
	1976	814.9	290.9	215.1	190.4	(5.3)	1,506.0
Investment in assets under equity accounting	1977						33.1
	1976						30.6
Corporate assets	1977						93.6
	1976						97.1
Total assets	1977						1,745.8
	1976						1,633.7
Depreciation	1977	40.9	15.1	8.6	5.8	.8	71.2
	1976	40.6	14.0	8.2	5.8	1.2	69.8
Capital expenditures	1977	54.7	17.4	17.5	10.2	1.8	101.6
	1976	36.1	26.2	18.4	6.2	.2	87.1

Domestic and International Operations
($ in millions)

		United States	Other North and South America	Europe and Asia	All Other	Eliminations	Consolidated
Sales to unaffiliated customers	1977	$1,714.0	$329.6	$446.1	$ 92.2		$2,581.9
	1976	1,485.7	334.7	401.1	93.3		2,314.8
Transfers between geographic areas	1977	37.4	19.1	24.7	8.9	($90.1)	
	1976	30.7	15.6	19.6	8.5	(74.4)	
Total revenue	1977	1,751.4	348.7	470.8	101.1	(90.1)	2,581.9
	1976	1,516.4	350.3	420.7	101.8	(74.4)	2,314.8
Operating profit	1977	103.9	1.8	29.5	12.5	(.4)	147.3
	1976	63.6	9.4	29.0	12.4	(1.0)	113.4
Identifiable assets	1977	1,022.2	238.3	324.3	83.4	(49.1)	1,619.1
	1976	975.5	218.8	281.7	70.4	(40.4)	1,506.0

UNIROYAL, INC. AND SUBSIDIARY COMPANIES
Statements of Consolidated Income
(dollars in thousands except per share amounts)

	Fiscal Year Ended	
	January 1, 1978	January 2, 1977
Net sales	$2,581,927	$2,314,841
Cost of goods sold	$2,071,802	$1,847,127
Selling, administrative, and general expenses	399,850	390,596
Interest expense	49,810	44,083
(Gain) or loss on closed facilities	(3,826)	3,025
Other (income)—expense	309	(8,259)
Total costs and expenses	$2,517,945	$2,276,572
Income before income taxes	63,982	38,269
Federal and foreign income taxes	29,191	18,137
Net income	$ 34,791	$ 20,132
Net income per common share:		
On average shares outstanding	$1.13	$.57
On a fully diluted basis*	$1.07	$.57

Consolidated Reinvested Earnings

Balance at beginning of year	$ 455,780	$ 453,819
Net income for the year	34,791	20,132
	$ 490,571	$ 473,951
Cash dividends:		
Preferred stock, $8.00 per share	4,889	4,889
Common stock, $.50 per share	13,283	13,282
	$ 18,172	$ 18,171
Balance at end of year	$ 472,399	$ 455,780

Consolidated Capital Surplus

Balance at beginning of year	$ 86,056	$ 86,034
Excess of consideration received over par value of common stock issued under stock option plans (3,500 shares, 1977; 3,000 shares, 1976)	26	22
Balance at end of year	$ 86,082	$ 86,056

* Conversion of the 5½ percent convertible subordinated debentures and the exercise of stock options considered in this calculation.

Case 14–4

Pennzoil Company

Required:

Project net income for the fiscal year ending December 31, 1979. Explain how you arrived at your projection. Be sure to list all the assumptions you are making. What other quantitative or qualitative information would you require in order to improve your earnings forecast?

PENNZOIL COMPANY AND SUBSIDIARIES
Condensed Consolidated Statement of Income (unaudited)
(expressed in thousands, except per share amounts)

	Three Months Ended March 31	
	1979	1978
Revenues	$433,421	$336,176
Costs and expenses		
Cost of goods sold and operating expenses	247,521	210,511
Selling, general, and administrative expenses	30,448	20,258
Depreciation, depletion, and amortization	53,545	44,295
Taxes, other than federal income	12,595	10,017
Interest charges, net	20,701	18,291
Interest capitalized	(3,472)	(2,519)
Federal income tax		
Current	27,064	12,499
Deferred	1,436	1,092
Investment tax credit	(2,539)	(1,813)
Minority interest	(51)	(106)
	$387,248	$312,525
Net income	$ 46,173	$ 23,651
Dividends on preferred stock	1,219	1,300
Earnings available for common stock	$ 44,954	$ 22,351
Earnings per share		
Primary	$ 1.36	$ .68
Fully diluted	1.32	.66
Dividends per share	.50	.50

PENNZOIL COMPANY AND SUBSIDIARIES
Consolidated Statement of Income
(expressed in thousands except per share amounts)

	Year Ended December 31	
	1978	*1977*
Revenues	$1,553,108	$1,280,432
Costs and expenses		
Cost of goods sold and operating expenses	943,584	809,767
Selling, general, and administrative expenses	95,461	78,843
Depreciation, depletion, and amortization	209,798	155,058
Taxes, other than federal income	45,292	40,943
Interest charges, net	78,962	66,133
Interest capitalized	(12,773)	(14,141)
Federal income tax		
Current	63,508	46,064
Deferred	8,566	9,088
Investment tax credit	(7,400)	(9,083)
Minority interest	(57)	(2,630)
	$1,424,941	$1,180,042
Net Income	$ 128,167	$ 100,390
Dividends on preferred stock	4,997	5,200
Earnings available for common	$ 123,170	$ 95,190
Earnings per share		
Primary	$ 3.74	$ 2.89
Fully diluted	3.64	2.82

PENNZOIL COMPANY AND SUBSIDIARIES
Consolidated Balance Sheet
(expressed in thousands)

	December 31	
	1978	*1977*
Assets		
Current Assets:		
Cash	$ 18,194	$ 37,026
Temporary cash investments	108,058	25,298
Trade accounts and notes receivable	270,575	221,751
Inventories:		
Crude oil, metals, sulphur, and potash	50,446	116,011
Manufactured products	47,799	49,290
Materials and supplies, at average cost	40,459	43,464
Other current assets................................	9,260	4,022
Total current assets	$ 544,791	$ 496,862
Property, plant and equipment, at cost:		
Oil and gas production (including $144,749,000 and $87,537,000 not being amortized in 1978, and 1977, respectively)—full cost method of accounting	1,935,812	1,644,488
Manufacturing and marketing	207,870	189,755
Mining	593,484	575,067
Other...	66,927	68,633
	$2,804,093	$2,477,943
Less—accumulated depreciation, depletion and amortization	1,330,929	1,139,071
	$1,473,164	$1,338,872
Excess of cost of predecessor company stock over underlying book value, being amortized	23,641	24,821
Other assets:		
Long-term receivables	22,133	26,165
Deferred charges	6,224	10,051
Other...	13,217	15,631
	41,574	51,847
	$2,083,170	$1,912,402

Consolidated Balance Sheet (*continued*)

	December 31	
	1978	*1977*
Liabilities and Shareholders' Equity		
Current liabilities:		
Convertible subordinated debentures of Pennzoil Louisiana and Texas Offshore, Inc., due May 1, 1979	$ 123,478	$ —
Sinking fund obligations and long-term debt due within one year	15,814	$ 19,170
Notes payable	4,000	19,550
Accounts payable	211,531	162,922
Exploration and development advances payable	—	7,610
Taxes accrued	39,962	22,957
Interest accrued	14,644	9,813
Dividends declared	1,219	1,438
Other current liabilities	35,552	7,326
Total current liabilities	$ 446,200	$ 250,786
Long-term debt, less amount due within one year	764,000	681,541
Convertible subordinated debentures, 6%, due May 1, 1979, of Pennzoil Louisiana and Texas Offshore, Inc., less unamortized discount of $3,327,000	—	120,151
Exploration and development advances payable	14,939	20,402
Proceeds from sale of production payments	—	51,264
Deferred federal income tax	164,780	156,214
Deferred credits	27,807	17,517
Minority interest	1,355	1,393
	$1,419,081	$1,299,268
Commitments and contingencies		
Shareholders' equity		
Capital stock	27,990	27,944
Additional capital	185,598	192,444
Retained earnings	450,501	392,746
Total shareholders' equity	$ 664,089	$ 613,134
	$2,083,170	$1,912,402

PENNZOIL COMPANY AND SUBSIDIARIES
Consolidated Statement of Changes in Financial Position
(expressed in thousands)

	Year Ended December 31	
	1978	*1977*
Financial resources provided by:		
Net income	$ 128,167	$100,390
Charges (credits) to income not requiring funds:		
Depreciation, depletion, and amortization	209,798	155,058
Deferred federal income tax	8,566	9,088
Interest capitalized	(12,773)	(14,141)
Minority interest	(57)	(2,630)
Funds provided from operations	$ 333,701	$247,765
Issuance of long-term debt	226,005	158,000
Decrease in long-term receivables	4,032	5,357
Sale of production payment	—	16,020
Noncash and other, net	10,930	8,010
Decrease in working capital...........................	147,485	—
	$ 722,153	$435,152
Financial resources used for:		
Additions to property, plant, and equipment, excluding interest capitalized of $12,773,000 and $14,141,000	$ 331,317	$244,290
Dividends	70,412	60,693
Retirement of long-term debt	143,546	79,040
Reduction of exploration and development advances	5,463	12,356
Reduction of production payments	51,264	28,836
Reclassification of convertible subordinated debentures	120,151	—
Increase in working capital	—	9,937
	$ 722,153	$435,152
Increase (decrease) in working capital:		
Cash...	$ (18,832)	$ (27,625)
Temporary cash investments	82,760	(13,472)
Receivables	48,824	31,539
Inventories	(67,056)	12,101
Materials and supplies	(3,005)	7,935
Other current assets	5,238	986
Convertible subordinated debentures	(123,478)	—
Current maturities of long-term debt	3,356	(8,711)
Notes payable	15,550	(18,000)
Accounts payable....................................	(48,609)	(31,527)
Advances payable	7,610	(7,610)
Taxes accrued	(17,005)	64,231
Interest accrued	(4,831)	(50)
Dividends declared	219	14
Other current liabilities	(28,226)	126
	$(147,485)	$ 9,937

15

Introduction to Financial Statement Analysis

Financial accounting information must be analyzed to predict the future performance of an enterprise. Astute investors will purchase a security with a dark past but a bright future in preference to one with a brilliant past but dim prospects. The history of an enterprise is studied to obtain clues about future results.

In analyzing financial statements, the investor must consider the strengths and weaknesses of generally accepted accounting principles (GAAP). Some major strengths are:

1. GAAP fosters comparison, both intrafirm and interfirm.
2. Financial statements are prepared on a consistent basis.
3. Business transactions are objectively measured in most cases.
4. A business firm is a complex organization. GAAP provides a way of summarizing numerous complex events into a few brief documents.

Conversely, some of the limitations are:

1. A business enterprise can apply acceptable but different accounting principles to a given situation, resulting in significant differences in reported net income.
2. The accounting measurement of assets reflects acquisition cost, not current value.
3. Financial statements are expressed in monetary terms, yet there are many valuable characteristics, such as the quality of management, that are not readily quantifiable.
4. Changes in the value of the dollar distort comparability over time.
5. Financial statements are necessarily influenced by estimates of future events.

Interested parties usually employ three general methods to interpret financial statements. One method, *funds flow analysis*, has been examined in the chapter on statement of changes in financial position. The other two methods are *comparative financial statement analysis* and *ratio analysis*.

COMPARATIVE FINANCIAL STATEMENT ANALYSIS

Financial statement analysis is best used in a relative sense. In practice four standards of comparison exist:

1. *Experience*—A subjective standard developed on the basis of past knowledge of similar situations. Frequently the experienced analyst obtains a "feel" for the "right" relationships. Often the "feel" of a competent analyst is more important than mechanical statistical comparison.

2. *Goals/Budgets*—Most business firms prepare budgets which indicate expected performance in advance of an accounting period. The periodic actual to budget comparison reveals how the firm actually performed relative to how the firm said it would perform.

This comparative technique relies on a careful setting of the budgeted figures. Economic circumstances can change rapidly, and the comparison of actual to budget must be modified to incorporate changes in underlying business assumptions.

3. *Industry Performance*—The third standard suggests the comparison of a company to either a similar company or to an industry average. Difficulties result from the diversity of accounting principles. The analyst must adjust for accounting differences, at least in an approximate way, to obtain an independent check on the performance of the enterprise.

Average ratios for companies in the same industry are published by many sources (Dun & Bradstreet, Robert Morris Associates, Moody's, Standard & Poor's). The use of industrywide averages includes all the difficulties associated with diverse accounting principles, plus the peculiar problems arising when figures for many companies are "averaged" into one number. Nevertheless, the industry ratios may present clues about the average situation in an industry.

4. *Historical Performance*—The most common comparative technique compares the current operating performance of the business firm with its prior operational results. The comparison eliminates problems associated with the use of differing accounting principles. It provides some basis for evaluation of progress, either improvement or deterioration, which cannot be gleaned from a review of the current period alone. The AICPA *Committee on Accounting Procedure Bulletin 43*, Chapter 2, recognized this point by stating:

> The presentation of comparative financial statements in annual and other reports enhances the usefulness of such reports and brings out more clearly the nature and trends of current changes affecting the enterprise. Such presentation emphasizes the fact that statements for a series of periods are far more significant than those for a single period

and that the accounts for one period are but an installment of what is essentially a continuous history.

When comparing results for a series of periods, the expression of relationships in terms of percentages of some base figure rather than in absolute figures permits measurement of proportional differences.

Percentage analysis depicts each item on a financial statement as a percent of a base figure. Net sales is usually the base figure on the income statement. Total assets or equities is the base figure on the balance sheet. Illustrations 15–1 and 15–2 show the most useful method of presentation.

ILLUSTRATION 15–1

THE REXELL DEERING CORPORATION
Comparative Income Statements (condensed)
For the Years Ended
June 30, 1974, and 1973
(in $000)

	1974		1973	
	Amount	Percent of Net Sales	Amount	Percent of Net Sales
Gross sales	$33,119	100.1	$28,267	100.2
Less: Sales returns and allowances	31	0.1	51	0.2
Net sales	$33,088	100.0	$28,216	100.0
Cost of goods sold	27,643	83.6	23,253	82.4
Gross margin	$ 5,445	16.4	$ 4,963	17.6
Expenses:				
Selling, general and administrative	$ 2,524	7.6	$ 2,456	8.7
Interest expense	92	0.3	75	0.3
Other deductions	20	0.1	126	0.5
Total expenses	$ 2,636	8.0	$ 2,657	9.5
Net income before taxes	$ 2,809	8.4	$ 2,306	8.1
Provision for income taxes	1,388	4.2	1,136	4.0
Net income	$ 1,421	4.2	$ 1,170	4.1

Percentage comparative analysis focuses on and *helps* to answer queries such as: Was the increase in profit due to an increase in sales volume, or were operating margins improved? Did operating expenses change in direct relation to sales? Did the sales increase result in a higher investment in inventories? In receivables? Did

ILLUSTRATION 15–2

THE REXELL DEERING CORPORATION
Comparative Balance Sheets (Condensed)
June 30, 1974, and 1973
(in $000)

	1974 Amount	1974 Per-cent	1973 Amount	1973 Per-cent
Assets				
Cash	$ 346	2	$ 414	3
Accounts receivable	3,891	22	3,442	22
Inventories	6,494	36	5,287	33
Prepaid expenses	303	2	276	2
Total current assets	$11,034	62	$ 9,419	60
Land and improvements.....................	$ 771	4	$ 705	5
Buildings and improvements	4,114	23	3,968	25
Machinery and equipment..................	7,266	40	6,724	43
Less: Accumulated depreciation	(5,546)	(31)	(5,446)	(35)
Total fixed assets, net	$ 6,605	36	$ 5,951	38
Other assets (patents, deferred charges)	383	2	376	2
Total assets	$18,022	100	$15,746	100
Equities				
Notes payable	$ 750	4	$ —	—
Accounts payable, trade	926	5	830	5
Taxes payable	454	3	359	2
Accrued salaries and wages...............	759	4	706	5
Other liabilities............................	566	3	609	4
Total current liabilities...............	$ 3,455	19	$ 2,504	16
Long-term debt	$ 1,447	8	$ 1,543	10
Common stock	$ 6,443	36	$ 6,443	41
Retained earnings	6,677	37	5,256	33
Total shareholders' equity	$13,120	73	$11,699	74
Total equities	$18,022	100	$15,746	100

liquid assets decline with the increase in sales volume? Did the investment in fixed assets increase? Were creditors used as a source of funds? Did the debt to equity relationship change significantly?

The exception principle, which suggests examination of non-routine variations, applies when interpreting comparative statements. In Rexell Deering, for example, inquiries about the decline in the gross margin, the increase in inventories, and the increase in short-term bank borrowing would be appropriate.

RATIO ANALYSIS

Ratios highlight, in arithmetical terms, the relationships between figures in the financial statements. A significant relationship between the numerator and the denominator must exist for the ratio to be useful. Commonly used ratios are of three types: ratios indicating profitability, ratios indicating current financial position (liquidity), and ratios indicating long-term financial position (solvency).

RATIOS INDICATING PROFITABILITY

Return on Investment.   An entrepreneur who has the opportunity to buy either of two businesses—Business X, promising an annual profit of $50,000 and requiring an investment of $400,000, or Business Y, promising an annual profit of $42,000 on an investment of $300,000—will invest in Business Y, assuming everything else is equal. The prospective annual rate of return on Business Y is 14 percent ($42,000/$300,000), a more attractive return than obtainable from Business X (12.5 percent). Return on invested funds is the substantive measure of financial performance because it focuses on the combination of the three principal factors that affect profit: *sales, costs, and total assets employed.*

The calculation for return on investment (ROI) is:

$$ROI = \frac{\text{Net income after taxes}}{\text{Total assets}}$$

In our entrepreneurial example, Business X had the higher annual return ($50,000 versus $42,000), but the assets needed to generate the higher return totaled $400,000 rather than $300,000.

A similar ratio focuses on the investment of the owners rather than on total assets. In the Rexell Deering Corporation (Illustrations 15–1 and 15–2) the return on investment on total assets (ROI) in 1974 was 8.5 percent ($1,421/$16,749[1]). The owners' return on investment (ROOI) was 11.5 percent ($1,421/$12,410[2]). The degree to which ROI differs from ROOI hinges solely on the relative mix of ownership and creditors' funds in the business. Put simply, if assets can be made to earn more than the cost of borrowing, financing through debt is profitable to the owners.

Other Profitability Indexes.   A widely used indicator of profitability is the ratio of net income to net sales, commonly called the *net*

---

[1] (18,022 + 15,746)/2 = Average assets for the year ended 12/31/74.

[2] (13,120 + 11,699)/2 = Average shareholders' equity for the year ended 12/31/74.

profit margin. While this ratio is helpful when used as a comparative tool relative to prior year performance or to competitor achievements, it does not include a consideration of the asset investment needed to generate the profits.

The sales to average net worth ratio may provide clues about managerial efficiency. Net worth is total assets minus all liabilities; it equals total shareholders' equity. In the Rexell Deering illustration, the ratio is: $33,088/$12,410 = 2.67 to 1.

Although the sales to net worth ratio will vary among industries, a range for manufacturing companies of 2 to 1 to 3.5 to 1 is generally acceptable. A 1 to 1 relationship may indicate the business firm is not aggressive in the pursuit of sales. A 5 to 1 ratio frequently is indicative of an equity base too small to finance the required working capital investment.

Another investor oriented ratio is the price-earnings (P/E) ratio. To illustrate its computation, assume the following:

Preferred stock—$8 cumulative—$100 par value (authorized 5,000 shares: issued and outstanding 2,000 shares)	$200,000
Common stock—par value $10 per share (authorized 100,000 shares: issued and outstanding 50,000 shares)	500,000
Retained earnings (not including current year's net income)	234,000
Net income	82,000
Market value per share of common stock	18

First, earnings per share (EPS) must be calculated:[3]

$$\frac{\text{Net income less preferred dividends}}{\text{Average common shares outstanding}} = \frac{\$82,000 - \$16,000}{50,000} = \$1.32 \text{ EPS}$$

The $1.32 is the profit earned on each share of common stock.

---

[3] The calculation of earnings per share becomes more difficult as a firm's capital structure becomes more complex. In the mid-1960s, a wave of business mergers financed by convertible debt or convertible preferred stock focused attention on the EPS computation. In May 1969, the *Accounting Principles Board* issued *Opinion No. 15,* which provided guidelines for complex situations and thoroughly dealt with the effect of convertible securities on EPS computations. *Opinion No. 15* requires two types of EPS data to be presented:

First, primary earnings per share—Calculation is based on the total of outstanding common shares and common stock equivalents (CSE). CSEs are those securities that are in substance equivalent to common shares and have the effect of diluting earnings. An example would be convertible bonds which are likely to be converted to common stock.

Second, fully diluted earnings per share—An EPS pro forma (as if) presentation which will "reflect the dilution of earnings per share that would have occurred if all contingent issuances of common stock that would individually reduce earnings per share had taken place."

The price-earnings ratio relates current market price to earnings per share:

$$\frac{\text{Market value per share}}{\text{Net income per share (EPS)}} = \frac{\$18}{\$1.32} = 13.6 \text{ to } 1$$

Common stocks trade at price-earnings multiples largely determined by current earning power and expectation of potential earnings and cash flows. The ability to estimate future earnings and cash flows accurately is the mark of the successful analyst.

RATIOS INDICATING CURRENT POSITION

Current position refers to the relationship of current assets to current liabilities. Current assets are assets readily convertible into cash (for payment of maturing obligations). Generally a company is weak financially if it does not have an adequate supply of liquid assets. The ratios listed below are indicators of the firm's liquidity.

Current Ratio. Probably the most popular liquidity ratio is the current ratio: current assets divided by the current liabilities. With the Rexell Deering figures, the current ratio is:

$$\frac{\text{Current assets}}{\text{Current liabilities}} = \frac{\$11,034}{\$3,455} = 3.2 \text{ to } 1$$

The ratio is an indicator of the safety margin a firm has in coping with the uneven flow of funds in the current accounts.

Acid-Test Ratio. One of the weaknesses of the current ratio is that it does not convey information about the composition of current assets. For example, a company with a high percentage of its current assets in cash is much more liquid than a firm with a high percentage in inventory. A measure designed to overcome this is the acid-test ratio: the ratio of quick assets (cash, marketable securities, and accounts receivable) to current liabilities. Inventories are excluded from quick assets because they must be sold and the cash collected before funds are available.

$$\text{Acid-test ratio} = \frac{\text{Quick assets}}{\text{Current liabilities}}$$

In Rexell Deering the acid ratio is 1.2 to 1 ($4,237/$3,455).

A current ratio of 2 to 1, and an acid test ratio of 1 to 1, are ordinarily adequate for industrial corporations. The ratios should be evaluated in light of industry characteristics, seasonal patterns, production fluctuations, and other factors. The financial analyst views a decline in the current ratio to 1.5 to 1 (or a decline in the acid-ratio to .8 to 1) as a signal to investigate *possible* liquidity problems.

Receivables Turnover. Accounts receivable turnover is the ratio of annual sales to average accounts receivable. The ratio using the illustrative statements is $33,088/$3,667 = 9.0. Receivables "turned over" nine times during the year.

A related statistic and perhaps more easily understood is the collection period. It is derived by dividing annual sales by 360 days, giving average daily sales. By dividing average daily sales into the year-end receivable balance we obtain the number of days' sales in accounts receivable. The calculation for Rexell Deering is: $33,088/ 360 = $91.91 average daily sales. The collection period of 42 days ($3,891/$91.91) can be related in a broad way to the credit policies of the company. The guiding rule is the collection period should not exceed 1.3 times the regular payment period. For example, if typical terms call for 30-day payment by customers, then the collection period should not exceed 40 days. Like all such rules, this one has many exceptions. However, changes in this ratio over time will indicate changes in the firm's credit policies or changes in its ability to collect receivables.

Inventory Turnover. Similar to receivables turnover, the inventory turnover ratio measures the speed at which merchandidse flows through the business. The calculation for inventory turnover is:

$$\frac{\text{Cost of goods sold}}{\text{Average inventory}} = \frac{\$27,643}{\$5,891} = 4.7 \text{ times}$$

This statistic is valuable for intercompany comparisons and for pointing out intracompany trends. Financial analysts generally consider a falling ratio to be a danger signal because of the decline in liquidity, the high carrying costs of inventory, and the potential future losses from obsolescence. For limited periods, however, a company may deliberately increase its inventory (resulting in a lower turnover ratio) to take advantage of "economy of scale" purchases or to obtain a large supply of a particularly critical raw material.

Ratios Indicating Equity Position

Two ways of measuring solvency[4] are the debt to asset ratio, (Total debts)/(Total assets), and the debt to equity ratio. (Long-term debt)/(Shareholders' equity[5]). In Rexell Deering, the debt to asset ratio is

---

[4] The terms *liquidity* and *solvency* differ in time horizon. A company experiencing a liquidity crisis has difficulty meeting its short-term obligations and may need to refinance by borrowing long-term money. A corporation experiencing solvency problems may be unable to meet its long-term debt principal repayments. Insolvency frequently leads to action under the bankruptcy statutes.

[5] An alternative expression of the debt-equity relationship is the ratio of long-term debt to total capital (long-term debt plus shareholders' equity).

27.2 percent ($4,902/$18,022), the debt-equity ratio is 11 percent ($1,447/$13,120). The debt to asset ratio indicates the proportion of the assets financed by outsiders. The debt-equity ratio focuses on the proportional amount of debt capital included as part of the permanent capital of the business.

Creditors and shareholders view the debt-equity relationship from their own perspective. The creditor prefers a large shareholders' equity. Ownership funds will serve as a buffer protecting the creditor from potential losses. The stockholder, however, may favor employing a relatively larger amount of debt capital since *"trading on the equity"* (*financial leverage*) may be advantageous. Trading on the equity occurs when a firm borrows money in anticipation of earning a return on the borrowed funds greater than the cost of borrowing. Any return over the cost of borrowing benefits the shareholders.

For the most part, manufacturing firms prefer "not to owe more than they own." This old Wall Street adage suggests that a 50-50 balance would be an appropriate outer limit for the debt-equity ratio. During recessionary or unstable periods, however, many corporations move to strengthen their balance sheets (that is, employ substantially less debt) on the theory that such a financial posture will gain them access to bank credit in an emergency ahead of other loan seekers.

Times Interest Earned. This ratio measures the amount by which earnings could decline without impairing the firm's ability to meet its fixed interest payments.

$$\text{Times interest earned} = \frac{\text{Net income before interest and income taxes}}{\text{Interest expense}}$$

The Rexell Deering Corporation is not highly leveraged. As a result, its interest earned ratio of 32 to 1, (2,809 + 92)/92, shows a substantial safety margin.

USES OF RATIO ANALYSIS

Ratios are mechanical tools of analysis. Because of their statistical aura they are mistakenly viewed to be an end or a standard in themselves. One writer has suggested that ratios are like a thermometer. Beyond a certain range the thermometer reading indicates that something is wrong but not exactly what it is.

Ratios are useful within relevant ranges. If, for example, the current ratio is too low, a liquidity problem may exist. If the current ratio is too high, the indicator may be pointing to the inefficient use of current assets.

Ratio analysis takes on more meaning when several years of a business firm are studied or when intercompany comparisons are made. Ratios are really helpful in pointing out trends; standing alone, any given ratio may be meaningless.

Sound business judgment is required in making comparisons and analyzing trends. For example, one firm may show a lower receivable turnover than its industry competitors. This may indicate the firm is guilty of lax credit policies, or the low ratio may be a reflection of a conscious management policy to compete for sales through liberal credit policies.

Industry characteristics also play an important role when analyzing businesses. For example, fast food companies are able to operate with current ratios of 1 to 1 because inventory turns over almost immediately and is sold for cash. Inventory for McDonald's Corp., the hamburger company, should be considered a quick asset.

Ratios are interrelated. A weak current position leads the analyst to an evaluation of the firm's long-term borrowing capacity. A low sales to net worth ratio leads to an analysis of profitability. A descriptive example is Schlumberger Limited, an offshore oil driller. In 1976 Schlumberger, had a sales to net worth ratio of only 1.7 to 1. Yet its net profit margin was 28.6 percent and its return on owners' investment was over 30 percent. It is hard to suggest that Schlumberger is inefficiently operated; more likely, Schlumberger has chosen to compete by accepting only highly profitable projects.

Lastly, ratios have been used in models designed to predict corporate failure. Research results indicate that the most successful predictors of bankruptcy are return on investment, debt to asset, and cash flow to total debt ratios.[6] Almost without exception, troubled companies experience severe declines in ROI and cash flow and rely more heavily on debt financing.

FINANCIAL REPORTING AND ANALYSIS IN PRACTICE

The stock market at times anticipates the deterioration of corporate earning capacity and financial strength before the actual publication of company statements. This anticipation is often caused by market analysts picking up accounting signals that may suggest a worsening situation before the net income figure becomes public information. The more serious signals arise when the management of a company sets out to manipulate reported profits.

"Management" of the profit figures can be accomplished by changing the timing of regular transactions, by choosing liberal accounting policies, and by altering presentation. Generally, a business

---

[6] Roughly, cash flow is defined as net income plus depreciation, depletion, and amortization.

firm wishing to report improved earnings in the short run will do so by using one or more of the following practices:

1. Choose inventory and depreciation methods which result in minimum current charges.
2. Decrease discretionary costs, for example, research and development, advertising, and maintenance expenditures, to the detriment of future earnings.
3. Amortize assets and defer costs over the longest possible period.
4. Capitalize where possible rather than expense administrative costs, taxes, and so forth.
5. Manipulate reserves to reduce expenses or increase income.
6. Choose the most accelerated methods of income recognition.
7. Inflate earnings by one-time profit generation opportunities.
8. Changing pension plan assumptions.

Because of management's choices, there is no single "right" net income figure. Analysts, therefore, make qualitative judgments about reported earnings.

Companies with high-quality earnings have these characteristics:

1. A set of conservative accounting policies, consistently applied.
2. A *recurring* stream of earnings.
3. Sales that quickly convert to cash after being reported.
4. An appropriate debt level.
5. A capital structure that has not been manipulated.
6. Earnings that have not been inflated.

Companies with low-quality earnings have several of the opposite characteristics.

An analysis of the choices management makes among alternative accounting policies is useful in evaluating the quality of management.

CASES FOR CHAPTER 15

Case 15–1

The United Electron Corporation and the Diode Manufacturing Corporation

James Gerber, a securities analyst with a well-known Wall Street firm, was studying the published annual reports of United Electron Corporation and Diode Manufacturing Corporation. Gerber specialized in the electronics industry and periodically issued comparative reports on various companies within the industry. His comments were highly regarded within the financial community and often created a flurry of activity among investment professionals and speculators.

Gerber has asked that you prepare a preliminary comparative report on United Electron Corporation and Diode Manufacturing Corporation for his review. The accompanying condensed data were taken from the published statements of the two companies:

($000 omitted)

	United Electron Corporation	Diode Manufacturing Corporation
Sales	$19,500	$36,000
Costs of goods sold	14,200	27,000
Selling, general and administrative expenses	2,800	6,000
Depreciation expense, included above	800	1,200
Interest expense	400	200
Extraordinary losses (gain)	100	(400)
Income taxes	1,000	1,600
Quick assets	800	3,500
Inventories	2,700	6,000
Fixed assets......................................	10,000	18,000
Accumulated depreciation	2,500	8,000
Investments	400	500
Other assets......................................	600	5,000
Current liabilities	1,200	2,700
Long-term debt	4,250	2,200
Capital stock ($10 par value)	5,000	15,000
Retained earnings	1,550	5,100
Current market value per share	30	10

Required:

1. Draft the comparative report for Gerber, specifically commenting on each corporation's:
   a. Profitability.
   b. Liquidity and solvency.
   Use relevant ratios to document your statements.
2. Which corporate security do you recommend as the better buy? Why?
3. What additional information might one seek before making a recommendation?

Case 15–2

Tribunal Printing Corporation

The Tribunal Printing Corporation was founded as a commercial printing business in New York City by Samuel J. Decker in 1935. While accepting almost any type of printing order, the company specialized in the production and printing of corporate annual reports. Over the years, the company has been very successful because of its quality printing and its ability to deliver orders on time to its major customers (nearby large Manhattan-based corporations).

In 1969, Decker died unexpectedly, leaving his majority interest in the corporation to his son, Michael. Michael Decker, employed at the time in his own venture capital firm, had been involved in the management of Tribunal on a part-time basis since graduating from college in 1955. Upon his father's death, he delegated complete operational responsibility to Peter Tedesco, who had joined the company as a managerial associate in 1962. Tedesco was given a three-year employment contract, which was renewable on December 31, 1972.

In mid-1972, Decker began to evaluate Tribunal's operational results to appraise the performance of Tedesco. As a basis for comparison, Decker obtained printing industry data for an average printing company. He believed that Tribunal's financial statements in 1971, as well as the 1971 industry data (See Exhibits 1 and 2) were representative of the financial statements of both the company and the industry for the past few years.

Required:

1. Do you think Decker should renew Tedesco's contract? Use the data in the financial statements to support your position.
2. What additional financial information would be helpful to confirm your impressions?

EXHIBIT 1

TRIBUNAL PRINTING CORPORATION
Condensed Comparative Income Statements
1971
(000s omitted)

	Tribunal Printing Corporation	Average Printing Industry Company
Sales	$2,091	$2,349
Cost of sales	1,388	1,588
Gross profit	$ 703	$ 761
Selling, general and administrative	526	602
Income from operations	$ 177	$ 159
Interest income	(3)	(6)
Interest expense	31	15
Net income before tax	$ 149	$ 150
Income tax	46	46
Net income	$ 103	$ 104
Dividends	$ 26	$ 43
Addition to retained earnings	$ 77	$ 61

EXHIBIT 2

TRIBUNAL PRINTING CORPORATION
Condensed Comparative Balance Sheets
December 31, 1971
(000s omitted)

	Tribunal Printing Corp.		Average Printing Industry Company	
	1970	*1971*	*1970*	*1971*
Assets				
Current assets:				
Cash...............................	$ 239	$ 301	$ 109	$ 71
Marketable securities	90	108	92	90
Accounts receivable	306	337	395	358
Inventory...........................	196	264	244	291
Total current assets	$ 831	$1,010	$ 840	$ 810
Fixed assets:				
Land..............................	$ 35	$ 35	$ 49	$ 42
Buildings and equipment	$1,090	$1,111	$1,218	$1,358
Less: Accumulated depreciation	563	640	657	741
	$ 527	$ 471	$ 561	$ 617
Total assets	$1,393	$1,516	$1,450	$1,469
Equities				
Current liabilities:				
Notes payable to bank	$ 178	$ 180	$ 111	$ 92
Accounts payable....................	76	79	158	180
Due to finance companies	138	178	31	12
Taxes payable......................	39	40	48	44
Total current liabilities	$ 431	$ 477	$ 348	$ 328
Long-term debt	—	—	140	118
Total liabilities	$ 431	$ 477	$ 488	$ 446
Shareholders' equity:				
Capital stock	$ 300	$ 300	$ 320	$ 320
Retained earnings	662	739	642	703
Total shareholders' equity......	$ 962	$1,039	$ 962	$1,023
Total equities	$1,393	$1,516	$1,450	$1,469

512

The Wolohan Lumber Company (B)

Reproduced as Exhibit 1 is the ten-year operating summary taken from the 1974 annual report of the Wolohan Lumber Company. Exhibit 2 is the most recent statement of changes in financial position. (Refer to the Wolohan Lumber Company (A) case for important additional operating and financial data.)

Required:

1. Analyze the company's performance in 1974 in comparison with the prior year(s).
2. Does the change in the inventory valuation method restrict your ability to draw comparisons? Should anything be done to resolve this difficulty?
3. What important trends have developed in the company over the past ten years? Insofar as past data is a reflection of future performance, where does Wolohan seem to be going?
4. Assess the business risks that Wolohan faces. What action might you take to reduce overall corporate risk?

EXHIBIT 1

THE WOLOHAN LUMBER COMPANY
Ten-Year Performance
($000)

Years Ended December 31	1974	1973	1972	1971	1970
Income statistics:					
Total sales	$72,349	$66,925	$51,627	$41,875	$30,371
Pre-tax earnings	2,009	2,432	3,012	2,636	1,692
Federal and state income taxes	1,001	1,232	1,492	1,335	864
Net income	1,008	1,200	1,520	1,301	828
Income per share*	.49	.59	.75	.74	.48
Average shares outstanding..........	2,040	2,040	2,040	1,762	1,710
Shares outstanding at December 31....	2,040	2,040	2,040	2,040	1,710
Income as a percentage of sales.......	1.4%	1.8%	2.9%	3.1%	2.7%
Return on assets employed...........	4.0%	5.4%	9.6%	11.9%	10.4%
Balance sheet statistics:					
Current asset totals..................	$13,284	$15,019	$12,237	$10,049	$ 5,588
Cash.............................	1,205	970	910	490	465
Marketable securities	—	—	—	1,232	—
Accounts receivable (net of reserve).......................	3,732	3,595	3,166	2,447	1,341
Inventories	8,335	10,405	8,139	5,855	3,764
Prepaid expenses and other current accounts	12	49	22	25	18
Other assets........................	78	56	67	39	59
Fixed assets (net)	9,613	8,935	5,647	3,486	2,683
Total assets	22,975	24,010	17,951	13,574	8,330
Current liability totals	4,093	8,006	6,622	3,830	3,681
Notes payable to banks	—	3,000	3,300	—	1,500
Trade accounts payable............	2,229	3,249	2,164	2,174	1,138
Federal and state income taxes	1	139	178	257	280
Other current liabilities	1,863	1,618	980	1,399	763
Long-term debt	5,401	3,427	—	10	433
Deferred credits	443	343	193	118	74
Total liabilities	9,937	11,776	6,815	3,958	4,188
Shareowners' equity	13,038	12,234	11,136	9,616	4,142
Stores and people:					
Number of stores	26	24	20	16	15
Number of employees	623	736	500	356	298
Number of employees eligible for profit sharing	437	322	242	205	181

* Based on average shares outstanding after giving retroactive effect to the merger of Wolohan Realty Co. and the 3-for-1 stock split in 1971.

EXHIBIT 1 (continued)

THE WOLOHAN LUMBER COMPANY
Ten-Year Performance
($000)

Years Ended December 31	1969	1968	1967	1966	196.
Income statistics:					
Total sales	$29,456	$26,617	$19,769	$16,912	$10,5
Pre-tax earnings	1,436	1,564	1,120	723	2
Federal and state income taxes	770	829	540	356	
Net income	666	735	580	367	2
Income per share*	.39	.44	.35	.24	
Average shares outstanding...........	1,696	1,680	1,673	1,559	8
Shares outstanding at December 31....	1,710	1,710	1,680	1,665	8
Income as a percentage of sales.......	2.3%	2.8%	2.9%	2.2%	1.!
Return on assets employed............	7.4%	10.2%	10.4%	8.5%	6.!
Balance sheet statistics:					
Current asset totals..................	$ 4,939	$ 5,140	$ 3,494	$ 2,765	$ 2,4
Cash.............................	477	348	242	272	
Marketable securities	—	—	—	—	—
Accounts receivable (net of reserve).......................	890	742	451	228	2
Inventories	3,556	4,050	2,801	2,234	2,1
Prepaid expenses and other current accounts	16	—	—	31	
Other assets..........................	59	1	3	4	
Fixed assets (net)	2,656	2,173	1,598	1,357	1,2
Total assets	7,654	7,314	5,095	4,126	3,6
Current liability totals	3,754	4,122	2,455	1,120	1,7
Notes payable to banks	1,500	2,000	—	30	8
Trade accounts payable.............	1,179	1,082	777	576	6
Federal and state income taxes	350	331	442	309	
Other current liabilities	725	709	1,236	205	1
Long-term debt	550	643	826	1,790	1,3
Deferred credits	35	—	—	—	
Total liabilities	4,339	4,765	3,281	2,910	3,0
Shareowners' equity	3,315	2,549	1,814	1,216	5
Stores and people:					
Number of stores	14	12	10	9	
Number of employees.................	266	235	188	139	1
Number of employees eligible for profit sharing	176	143	113	79	

* Based on average shares outstanding after giving retroactive effect to the merger of Wolohan Realty C and the 3-for-1 stock split in 1971.

EXHIBIT 2

THE WOLOHAN LUMBER COMPANY
Statement of Changes in Financial Position
Years Ended December 31, 1974, and 1973

	1974	1973
Sources of funds:		
From operations:		
Net income	$1,007,859	$1,200,329
Add expenses not requiring outlay of working capital:		
Provision for depreciation	740,559	518,160
Provision for deferred income taxes	100,000	150,000
Total from operations	$1,848,418	$1,868,489
Long-term borrowing	2,500,000	3,562,016
Other..	33,300	11,949
	$4,381,718	$5,442,454
Uses of funds:		
Business purchased in 1973, less net current assets acquired of $1,334,829:		
Properties	—0—	1,556,576
Long-term debt assumed (deduct)	—0—	(385,320)
	$ —0—	$1,171,256
Other additions to properties	1,473,076	2,251,275
Current maturities of long-term debt	526,181	520,637
Cash dividends paid	204,000	102,000
	$2,203,257	$4,045,168
Increase in working capital.........................	$2,178,461	$1,397,286
Working capital at beginning of year.................	7,012,855	5,615,569
Working capital at end of year......................	$9,191,316	$7,012,855

Case 15–4

Northwest Brokerage Company

In March 1975, Richard Wood, financial analyst for Northwest Brokerage Co., received financial statements on the Big Four automobile companies (General Motors, Ford, Chrysler, and American Motors). Wood's job involved advising clients on the relative merits of each of these companies. Wood took the financial data and compiled standard statements using his own account classifications. In this way he was able to compare the performance of these companies.

The combination of higher gasoline prices and the recession resulted in 1974 being a very difficult year for the automobile industry. Passenger car sales for the year were down 2.5 million from the record 10 million unit sales in 1973.

Many of Wood's clients were anxiously awaiting his assessment of the companies.

Required:

1. Using Wood's statements (Exhibits 1 through 4C), which company appears to be the strongest?
2. Do any of the companies appear to be in any particular trouble?
3. What was the impact of the recession in 1974 on each of the companies?
4. Why did each of the companies pay dividends in 1974? (three of the four paid record dividends despite lower earnings.)
5. Does the 1970–74 financial data provide clues to the financial difficulties experienced by certain automakers in the late 1970s?
6. As Wood, which company's stock would you advise the following people to purchase: (a) a retired couple interested in dividends, (b) a speculator looking for capital gains, and (c) an investor looking for a total return of both yield and capital appreciation.
7. Comment on the capital structure of each of the companies.

EXHIBIT 1

Domestic Auto Sales of the Big Four: 1970–1974 (000s)

Year	General Motors	Ford	Chrysler	American Motors	Total
1974	3,592 (48%)	2,359 (31%)	1,186 (16%)	385 (5%)	7,522
1973	5,251 (53%)	2,707 (27%)	1,572 (16%)	380 (4%)	9,910
1972	4,778 (53%)	2,639 (29%)	1,294 (14%)	312 (4%)	9,023
1971	4,857 (55%)	2,390 (27%)	1,320 (15%)	257 (3%)	8,824
1970	2,977 (44%)	2,266 (33%)	1,287 (19%)	254 (4%)	6,784

EXHIBIT 2

Income Statements for the Big Four: 1970–1974 (000,000)

	General Motors				
	1974	1973	1972	1971	1970
Net sales	$31,549	$35,798	$30,435	$28,263	$18,752
Cost of goods sold	26,918	28,114	23,336	21,620	15,595
Gross profit	$ 4,631	$ 7,684	$ 7,099	$ 6,643	$ 3,157
Operating expenses:					
Selling and administrative	1,364	1,328	1,163	1,107	1,006
Depreciation and amortization	1,704	1,983	1,787	1,790	1,498
Interest	194	257	184	225	58
Operating profit	$ 1,369	$ 4,116	$ 3,965	$ 3,521	$ 595
Other income	309	398	258	200	185
Net income	$ 1,678	$ 4,514	$ 4,223	$ 3,721	$ 780
Taxes	726	2,114	2,059	1,782	168
Net income	$ 952	$ 2,400	$ 2,164	$ 1,939	$ 612
Dividends	985	1,513	1,285	985	984
Addition (deduction) to retained earnings	($ 33)	$ 887	$ 879	$ 954	($ 372)

	Ford				
	1974	1973	1972	1971	1970
Net sales	$23,621	$23,015	$20,194	$16,433	$14,980
Cost of goods sold	20,668	19,069	16,280	13,190	12,453
Gross profit	$ 2,953	$ 3,946	$ 3,914	$ 3,243	$ 2,527
Operating expenses:					
Selling and administrative	1,417	1,444	1,383	1,152	1,098
Depreciation and amortization	923	948	913	824	414
Interest	281	174	134	114	90
Operating profit	$ 332	$ 1,380	$ 1,484	$ 1,153	$ 925
Other income	257	244	178	139	81
Net income	$ 589	$ 1,624	$ 1,662	$ 1,292	$ 1,006
Taxes	228	717	792	635	490
Net income	$ 361	$ 907	$ 870	$ 657	$ 516
Dividends	492	458	467	582	271
Addition (deduction) to retained earnings	($ 131)	$ 449	$ 403	$ 75	$ 245

EXHIBIT 2 (continued)

Chrysler Corporation

	1974	1973	1972	1971	197(
Net sales	$10,971	$11,774	$ 9,759	$ 7,999	$ 7,0(
Cost of goods sold	9,853	10,145	8,182	6,708	5,8(
Gross profit	$ 1,118	$ 1,629	$ 1,577	$ 1,291	$ 1,1
Operating expenses:					
Selling and administrative	759	701	709	693	6(
Depreciation and amortization	324	372	369	369	3
Interest	177	112	97	96	1(
Operating profit	($ 142)	$ 444	$ 402	$ 133	($
Other income	6	11	5	9	
Net income	($ 136)	$ 454	$ 407	$ 142	($
Taxes	86	193	187	58	
Net income	($ 50)	$ 262	$ 220	$ 84	($
Dividends	79	69	47	30	
Addition (deduction) to					
retained earnings..................	($ 129)	$ 193	$ 173	$ 54	($

American Motors

	1974	1973	1972	1971	197(
Net sales	$ 2,000	$ 1,739	$ 1,404	$ 1,233	$ 1,0(
Cost of goods sold	1,736	1,455	1,183	1,039	9(
Gross profit	$ 264	$ 284	$ 221	$ 194	$ 1
Operating expenses:					
Selling and administrative	198	186	155	144	1
Depreciation and amortization	40	34	38	35	
Interest	7	7	6	6	
Operating profit	$ 19	$ 57	$ 22	$ 9	($
Other income	23	18	9	3	
Net income	$ 42	$ 75	$ 31	$ 12	($
Taxes	14	31	15	7	—
Tax carryforward	—	42	14	4	—
Net income	$ 28	$ 86	$ 30	$ 9	($
Dividends	6	—	—	—	—
Addition (deduction) to					
retained earnings..................	$ 22	$ 86	$ 30	$ 9	($

EXHIBIT 3

Balance Sheet: 1970–1974 (000,000)

	General Motors				
	1974	1973	1972	1971	1970
Assets					
Cash	$ 1,338	$ 3,046	$ 2,947	$ 3,317	$ 394
Accounts receivable	3,001	3,083	2,806	2,724	1,726
Inventory	6,405	5,177	4,200	3,992	4,115
Prepaid assets	901	861	585	478	—
Total current assets	$11,645	$12,167	$10,538	$10,511	$ 6,235
Net equipment	6,215	5,671	5,478	5,507	5,413
Unamortized items	850	619	765	747	1,039
Other assets	1,757	1,841	1,492	1,475	1,486
Total assets	$20,467	$20,298	$18,273	$18,240	$14,173
Equities					
Accounts payable	$ 3,600	$ 3,276	$ 2,470	$ 2,206	$ 1,659
Accrued liabilities	2,503	2,673	2,504	3,775	1,564
Total current liabilities	$ 6,103	$ 5,949	$ 4,974	$ 5,981	$ 3,223
Deferred taxes	957	1,026	825	838	853
Long-term debt	876	756	791	616	287
Common stock	763	763	763	763	1,006
Paid-in surplus	767	767	767	766	325
Retained earnings	11,001	11,037	10,153	9,276	8,479
Total equities	$20,467	$20,298	$18,273	$18,240	$14,173

	Ford				
	1974	1973	1972	1971	1970
Assets					
Cash	$ 606	$ 1,082	$ 1,469	$ 1,084	$ 829
Accounts receivable	1,457	1,079	847	740	653
Inventory	4,253	3,593	2,781	2,540	2,487
Prepaid assets	525	436	448	404	390
Total current assets	$ 6,841	$ 6,190	$ 5,545	$ 4,768	$ 4,359
Net equipment	4,642	4,377	4,053	3,829	4,325
Unamortized items	1,042	816	684	680	—
Other assets	1,648	1,562	1,351	1,233	1,221
Total assets	$14,173	$12,945	$11,633	$10,510	$ 9,905

EXHIBIT 3 (*continued*)

	Ford				
	1974	*1973*	*1972*	*1971*	*1970*
Equities					
Accounts payable	$ 3,932	$ 3,537	$ 3,118	$ 2,606	$ 2,3
Accrued liabilities	1,409	992	742	814	9
Total current liabilities	$ 5,341	$ 4,529	$ 3,860	$ 3,420	$ 3,2
Deferred taxes	1,115	1,033	817	741	7
Long-term debt	1,476	977	994	802	4
Common stock	234	248	254	261	2
Paid-in surplus	362	381	280	361	3
Retained earnings	5,645	5,777	5,328	4,925	4,8
Total equities	$14,173	$12,945	$11,633	$10,510	$ 9,9

	Chrysler Corporation				
	1974	*1973*	*1972*	*1971*	*1970*
Assets					
Cash	$ 268	$ 562	$ 465	$ 278	$ 1
Accounts receivable	707	680	682	659	6
Inventory	2,453	1,803	1,575	1,409	1,2
Prepaid assets	269	191	174	165	1
Total current assets	$ 3,697	$ 3,236	$ 2,896	$ 2,411	$ 2,1
Net equipment	1,479	1,444	1,279	1,320	1,3
Unamortized items	583	482	401	409	4
Other assets	973	940	921	860	8
Total assets	$ 6,732	$ 6,102	$ 5,497	$ 5,000	$ 4,8
Equities					
Accounts payable	$ 1,282	$ 1,253	$ 1,190	$ 998	$ 9
Accrued liabilities	1,427	841	751	650	5
Total current liabilities	$ 2,709	$ 2,094	$ 1,941	$ 1,648	$ 1,5
Deferred taxes	368	325	277	265	4
Long-term debt	995	956	790	818	7
Common stock	370	340	340	324	3
Paid-in surplus	645	611	566	535	4
Retained earnings	1,645	1,776	1,583	1,410	1,3
Total equities	$ 6,732	$ 6,102	$ 5,497	$ 5,000	$ 4,8

EXHIBIT 3 (concluded)

	American Motors				
	1974	1973	1972	1971	1970
Assets					
Cash....................................	$ 76	$ 109	$ 101	$ 19	$ 23
Accounts receivable	105	108	105	124	107
Inventory...............................	299	201	167	172	203
Prepaid assets..........................	34	27	7	11	5
Total current assets...............	$ 514	$ 445	$ 380	$ 326	$ 338
Net equipment..........................	246	188	153	159	168
Unamortized items......................	—	—	—	—	—
Other assets............................	105	74	45	43	43
Total assets	$ 865	$ 707	$ 578	$ 528	$ 548
Equities					
Accounts payable.......................	$ 278	$ 184	$ 150	$ 154	$ 169
Accrued liabilities	78	81	86	80	90
Total current liabilities	$ 356	$ 265	$ 236	$ 234	$ 259
Deferred taxes.........................	47	34	30	35	59
Long-term debt	79	64	68	44	46
Common stock.........................	49	45	44	44	40
Paid-in surplus	128	115	102	102	105
Retained earnings	206	184	98	69	59
Total Equities	$ 865	$ 707	$ 578	$ 528	$ 548

EXHIBIT 4A

Comparison Ratios: Current Position

	1974	1973	1972	1971	1970
Current ratio (current assets to current liabilities)					
American Motors	1.44	1.68	1.61	1.39	1.31
Chrysler Corporation	1.36	1.55	1.49	1.46	1.40
Ford	1.28	1.37	1.44	1.39	1.33
General Motors	1.91	2.05	2.12	1.76	1.93
Acid test (quick assets to current liabilities)					
American Motors	.51	.82	.87	.61	.50
Chrysler Corporation	.36	.59	.59	.57	.52
Ford	.39	.48	.60	.53	.45
General Motors	.71	1.03	1.16	1.01	.66
Receivable turnover (sales over accounts receivable)					
American Motors	19.0	16.1	13.3	9.9	10.2
Chrysler Corporation	15.5	17.3	14.3	12.1	11.0
Ford	16.2	21.3	23.8	22.2	22.9
General Motors	10.5	11.6	10.8	10.4	10.9
Collection period (receivable expressed in average number of days sales)					
American Motors	18.9	22.4	26.9	36.2	35.1
Chrysler Corporation	23.2	20.8	25.2	29.7	32.8
Ford	22.2	16.9	15.1	16.2	15.7
General Motors	34.2	31.0	33.2	34.7	33.1
Inventory turnover (cost of goods sold to inventories)					
American Motors	5.8	7.2	7.1	6.0	4.7
Chrysler Corporation	4.0	5.6	5.2	4.8	4.8
Ford	4.9	5.3	5.9	5.5	5.0
General Motors	4.2	5.4	5.6	5.4	3.8

EXHIBIT 4B

Comparison Ratios: Profitability Indexes

	1974	1973	1972	1971	1970
Return on investment					
(net income to total assets)					
American Motors	3.2%	12.2%	5.2%	1.7%	(10.4%)
Chrysler Corporation	(0.7)	4.3	4.0	1.7	(0.2)
Ford	2.5	7.0	7.5	6.3	5.2
General Motors	4.7	11.8	11.8	10.6	4.3
Return on investment					
(net income to owner's equity)					
American Motors	7.3%	25.0%	12.3%	4.2%	(27.9%)
Chrysler Corporation	(1.9)	9.6	8.8	3.7	(0.4)
Ford	5.8	14.2	14.6	11.8	9.4
General Motors	7.6	19.1	18.5	17.9	6.2
Profit margin					
(net income to net sales)					
American Motors	1.4%	4.9%	2.1%	.1%	(5.1%)
Chrysler Corporation	(0.5)	2.2	2.3	1.1	(0.1)
Ford	1.5	3.9	4.3	4.0	3.4
General Motors	3.0	6.7	7.1	6.9	3.3
Sales to net worth					
(sales over average net worth)					
American Motors	5.49	5.92	6.10	5.87	5.38
Chrysler Corporation	4.12	4.51	4.10	3.62	3.25
Ford	3.73	3.72	3.51	2.98	2.74
General Motors	2.51	2.95	2.71	2.74	1.91

EXHIBIT 4C

Comparison Ratios: Equity Positions

	1974	1973	1972	1971	1970
Debt/asset ratio					
(total debts to total assets)					
American Motors	.56	.51	.58	.59	.66
Chrysler Corporation	.60	.55	.55	.55	.57
Ford	.56	.51	.49	.47	.45
General Motors	.39	.38	.36	.41	.31
Debt/equity ratio					
(long-term debt over long-term debt					
plus stockholders' equity)					
American Motors	17.1%	15.7%	21.7%	17.0%	18.4%
Chrysler Corporation	27.2	26.0	24.1	26.5	26.8
Ford	19.1	13.2	14.3	12.6	7.7
General Motors	6.5	5.7	6.3	5.4	2.8

Case 15–5

Peerless Manufacturing Company

On January 30, 1976, Thomas Bartell heard an interesting speech at the monthly meeting of the New York Society of Security Analysts. Bartell was a staff member of a large New York investment house, and he often attended these speeches to aid him in his work. This particular speech was given by Donald A. Sillers, President of Peerless Manufacturing Company of Dallas, Texas. Sillers discussed the investment opportunities which Peerless offered and described its particular business advantages. Bartell was interested enough to talk with Sillers after the speech, and asked the president to send him various reports.

At work the following week, Bartell asked his supervisor if he could initiate an in-depth study of Peerless. The investment firm had a thumbnail sketch of each company traded in the over-the-counter market, but Bartell felt that the detail was insufficient. Customers, he argued, were always looking for a small growth company like Peerless. His superior agreed but reminded Bartell that a serious study had to be objective. Too often, a young staff member hits upon a favorite company and tends to overlook possible hazards. His superior wanted both the negative as well as the positive features of this company. Bartell agreed and spent the next few days eagerly studying Peerless Manufacturing Company.

HISTORY

Peerless was founded in 1933 by Donald Sillers, Sr., father of the current president of the company. The initial business involved designing, producing, and marketing products for cleaning liquid and solid contaminants from gases. The company incorporated in 1946 and went public in 1970. Its stock has been traded over the counter since that time.

The company presently manufactures in three product areas:

1. Odorizers. An odorizer is a "device for injecting a malodorant liquid into a natural gas stream to give the gas a characteristic smell so that a leak can be detected." Peerless is the industry leader in this field, but the field is small with only about 10 percent of Peerless' sales coming from this product line.

2. Dampeners. Designed to smooth out the flow of gas in the pipelines, dampeners account for 8 percent of sales and the prospects for future growth are better than with the odorizers. According to Sillers, "We are the leaders in this field in the sense that designing of this equipment by our methods results in the most efficient and

reliable solution to the problems associated with reciprocating compressors that is available anywhere." However, Peerless faces much competition in this field.

3. Separators. Designed to separate various foreign elements from the pure transfer of natural gas at every step of production, separators have been the most important product line, with sales of separators usually comprising between 70 and 80 percent of total sales. Sillers rates the growth potential of this area as excellent and feels that Peerless is the technological leader in the area.

The concept of technological leadership in an industry is the hub of the company's long-term profit-making strategy. As Sillers said in his speech, "The payoff and point of this course is that technological leadership gains a reputation for product acceptance and then product preference on the part of the customers which then leads to high profitability and growth."

The majority of the company's sales are to big name oil and chemical companies like Exxon, Mobil, Texaco, DuPont, and Union Carbide. However, in the past five years, Peerless has managed to increase its sales overseas so that by June 1975, a full 25 percent of total sales revenues came from foreign firms. Sillers expects the foreign market to increase as OPEC countries begin to use technologically more advanced methods of oil separation.

RECENT DEVELOPMENTS

The OPEC embargo in 1973 had a mixed impact on the oil and related industries in the United States. On one hand, oil companies redoubled their exploration efforts and instituted technologically complex systems to maximize use efficiencies. On the other hand, Congress moved to take away some of the special advantages of the industry. The oil depletion allowance was removed in 1975. Moreover, the "ongoing confusion as to regulatory matters as well as bills in Congress to control the prices of oil and gas at the low levels that now exist are adding to the uncertainty of our customers' plans for capital equipment." (1975 Annual Report)

Notwithstanding Sillers' comment above, 1975 was an exceptional year for Peerless. Sales increased from $7,569,998 to $12,064,792 with a similar increase in profits. Peerless continued to maintain a steady backlog of future orders. Growth itself caused some problems, and Peerless had to borrow funds during 1975 to finance the increased level of activity. (See Exhibits 1 through 4.)

The first half of fiscal 1976 (from June 30, 1975, until December 31, 1975) had also been a good one for Peerless. Sales and profits continued at record paces and allowed Peerless to pay off virtually all its long-term and short-term debt. (See Exhibit 5.)

Required:

1. Using the data and description contained in the exhibits and the text, undertake Bartell's task and evaluate Peerless. Remember to include all positive and negative features, including:
   a. Industry outlook and possible trends.
   b. Present financial condition and operating performance of Peerless.
   c. Relative size of Peerless in continuing their long-term strategy.
   d. Possible future events which may affect Peerless.
2. Would you recommend that Bartell's company invest in Peerless? Why or why not?

EXHIBIT 1

PEERLESS MANUFACTURING COMPANY
Balance Sheet
As of June 30, 1975, and 1974
($000)

	1975		1974	
Assets				
Cash....................................		$ 325		$ 683
Accounts receivable		3,599		1,490
Inventories		2,423		1,415
Prepaid expenses......................		13		15
Total current assets..............		$6,360		$3,603
Property, plant, equipment, net		1,541		1,066
Other		157		123
Total assets		$8,058		$4,792
Liabilities and Shareholders' Equity				
Current liabilities:				
Notes payable to bank		$ 875		$ —
Current portion LTD		116		38
Accounts payable......................		933		485
Federal income tax		472		588
Accrued expenses		586		576
Customer advance payments............		963		34
Total current liabilities		$3,945		$1,721
Long-term debt		179		122
Other liabilities		131		81
Shareholders' equity:				
Common stock.........................	$ 829		$ 550	
Paid-in surplus	890		999	
Retained earnings	2,084	3,803	1,319	2,868
Total equities		$8,058		$4,792

EXHIBIT 2

PEERLESS MANUFACTURING COMPANY
Income Statement
For Fiscal Years 1975 and 1974
($000)

	1975		1974	
Net sales............................		$12,065		$7,570
Cost of goods sold		8,048		4,850
Gross profit		$ 4,017		$2,720
Operating expenses:				
General, administrative, and marketing	$2,025		$1,531	
Interest	78	2,103	22	1,553
Operating profit		$ 1,914		$1,167
Other income........................		345		261
Net income before tax..................		$ 2,259		$1,428
Federal income tax		1,021		629
Net income after tax		$ 1,238		$ 799
Extraordinary gain.....................		91		—
Net income		$ 1,329		$ 799

EXHIBIT 3

PEERLESS MANUFACTURING COMPANY
Five-Year Operating Summary
($000)

	1975	1974	1973	1972	1971
Sales	$12,065	$7,570	$5,612	$7,157	$6,030
Interest expense	78	22	35	35	44
Net earnings before extraordinary item	1,238	799	(13)	427	42
Extraordinary item	91	—	(550)	(353)	(647)
Net earnings	1,329	799	(563)	74	(605)
Earnings per share (before extraordinary item)...........	1.43	.90	(.02)	.48	.05
Earnings per share (after extraordinary item)...........	1.53	.90	(.63)	.08	(.68)

EXHIBIT 4 _____

PEERLESS MANUFACTURING COMPANY
Funds Statement
1975
($000)

Sources of working capital:

Net income	$1,329
Charges not using working capital	
Depreciation	204
Amortization	3
Deferred income tax	(2)
Amortization of deferred credit	(53)
Loss on sale	6
Working capital provided from operations	$1,487
Proceeds from additions to LTD	193
Proceeds from warrants	63
Increase in other liabilities	106
Total sources	$1,849

Applications of working capital:

Additions to property	$ 691
Payments on LTD.............................	58
Cash dividends paid	282
Increase in current maturities	
of long-term debt...........................	78
Purchase of treasury stock	170
Other.......................................	37
Total uses	$1,316
Increase in working capital	$ 533

EXHIBIT 5 _____

PEERLESS MANUFACTURING COMPANY
Balance Sheet—Unaudited
As of December 31, 1975
($000)

Assets

Cash..	$ 157
Receivables	3,337
Inventories	2,778
Prepaid expenses.................................	53
Total current assets.......................	$6,325
Fixed assets (net)	1,593
Other	56
Total assets	$7,974

Equities

Short-term debt..................................	$ 250
Accounts payable...............................	448
Customer advances.............................	1,076
Income tax payable.............................	605
Accruals	611
Total current liabilities	$2,990
LTD	—
Deferred taxes...................................	88
Shareholders' equity	4,896
Total equities	$7,974

Case 15–6 _____

Bulldog University

Early in 1977, Ann Nelson had become an assistant to the manager of the Bulldog University pension fund. Her first assignment from her superior was to identify a company in the ethical drug industry in which the fund might invest. After much research, Ann had narrowed the field to two candidates, Eli Lilly & Co., and Pfizer, Inc. As she prepared to make her choice, she reviewed Lilly's and Pfizer's comparative performance for the past decade. (See Exhibits 1–3.)

LILLY

During the 1967–76 period, U.S. ethical drug industry sales increased from $5.3 billion to $11.8 billion. Lilly sales for the same

EXHIBIT 1

Statistical Data on Earning Power and Financial Position

Year	Aftertax Return on Shareholders' Equity		Operating Profit Margin		Asset Turnover		Total Assets to Common Equity		Pretax Interest Coverage		Acid Test Ratio	
	Lilly	Pfizer	Lilly	Pfizer	Lilly	Pfizer	Lilly	Pfizer	Lilly	Pfizer	Lilly	Pfizer
1976.....	18.7%	15.6%	26.0%	14.1%	.85×	.87×	1.47×	2.13×	18.0×	4.9×	1.53×	1.44×
1975.....	19.2	15.2	25.0	14.4	.86	.83	1.49	2.18	17.5	5.2	1.45	1.28
1974.....	21.1	15.9	26.0	15.6	.88	.92	1.49	1.98	20.2	7.6	1.42	1.13
1973.....	21.3	15.9	25.8	17.4	.95	.91	1.40	1.86	34.5	8.4	.92	1.22
1972.....	20.4	15.0	24.0	17.8	.94	.86	1.40	1.84	32.7	11.7	1.51	1.55
1971.....	18.7	15.1	20.9	18.4	.92	.92	1.53	1.73	19.8	15.6	1.18	1.12
1970.....	20.7	15.0	24.4	19.1	.88	.96	1.49	1.68	32.0	17.3	1.13	1.26
1969.....	21.1	14.6	25.9	18.7	1.00	1.02	1.36	1.60	107.0	18.4	1.67	1.41
1968.....	21.1	13.9	26.0	18.4	1.05	.99	1.36	1.58	114.0	17.6	1.77	1.22
1967.....	19.2	13.9	23.3	17.2	1.09	.97	1.33	1.57	119.0	12.7	1.56	1.06

EXHIBIT 2

Growth in Sales, Earnings, and Dividends

Year	Earnings per Share		Dividends per Share	
	Lilly	Pfizer	Lilly	Pfizer
1976	$2.90	$2.28	$1.25	$.86
1975	2.66	2.00	1.10	.81
1974	2.59	1.93	.97	.79
1973	2.26	1.74	.79	.70
1972	1.85	1.50	.73	.67
1971	1.48	1.36	.70	.65
1970	1.40	1.28	.65	.63
1969	1.25	1.14	.52	.57
1968	1.08	1.03	.45	.50
1967	.83	.95	.40	.48
Growth rates				
1967–76	14.9%	10.3%	15.6%	7.7%
1972–76	9.4	10.3	15.1	6.7
1967–71	15.2	9.8	16.0	8.7

EXHIBIT 3

Market Valuations and Other Common Stock Data

	Range of Price-Earnings Ratios	
	Lilly	Pfizer
Year		
1976	21–15×	14–11×
1975	30–19	18–11
1974	32–22	23–11
1973	41–31	30–22
1972	43–30	31–24
1971	43–33	32–25
1970	39–27	30–21
1969	41–27	31–20
1968	41–22	25–18
1967	36–26	32–24
Averages		
1967–76	31.0×	22.5×
1972–76	28.5	19.2
1967–71	33.5	25.8
April 4, 1977		
1976–77 price range	60–40	31–25
Current price (April 1977)	43	28
1977 estimated earnings	$3.25	$2.60
Indicated annual dividend	$1.42	$ .88

period went from $408 million to $1.3 billion. Adjusted for inflation, real GNP rose 26 percent during this time, while drug industry sales were up 66 percent. Lilly's real growth was a phenomenal 145 percent. Moreover, this growth had occurred at a time when the Wholesale Price Index of all industrial commodities rose more than twice as fast as the WPI for pharmaceuticals.

Lilly sales were diversified among health care products (57 percent), agricultural products (29 percent), industrial chemicals (3 percent), and consumer products (10 percent); the remaining 1 percent coming from other unclassified areas. Thirty-nine percent of sales were international. Research and development expenditures in recent years had averaged about 8 percent of sales.

PFIZER

Pfizer sales in this period increased from $634 million to $1.89 billion. Real sales growth was 121 percent. Earnings per share were lower than for Lilly, but growth had been more consistent.

Pfizer's revenues were achieved in the same areas as Lilly's: health care (49 percent), agricultural (15 percent), industrial chemicals (16 percent), consumer products (12 percent), and 8 percent unclassified. International sales were 54 percent of the total. Research and development were 4 percent of sales.

Required:

Which company should Ann recommend? Back up your recommendation by citing each company's strengths and weaknesses and the factors supporting your conclusion.

Case 15–7

SmithKline Corp. versus Squibb Corp.

You are asked by your parents to help them determine whether they should make an investment in SmithKline or Squibb. The only information you have are the attached data sheets on the two companies. Your parents' investment objective is capital appreciation.

SmithKline Corp. 2050

NYSE Symbol SKL

Price	Range	P-E Ratio	Dividend	Yield	S&P Ranking
Dec. 17'79	1979				
61¾	63-38½	17	1.44	2.3%	A

Summary

Earnings of this established drug firm have shown renewed growth in recent years, aided by strong demand for diuretic drugs and the addition of new health care products. The recent improved earnings growth pattern has been extended during 1979, with longer-range prospects enhanced by planned expansion in overseas markets and expected better returns from the research effort. SKL has agreed in principle to acquire Allergan Pharmaceuticals for some $250 million in common stock.

Current Outlook

Share earnings for 1980 are projected at $4.60, versus the $3.85 estimated for 1979.

Dividends should continue at $0.36 quarterly.

For the company as currently constituted, sales for 1980 should rise 15%-20% as Tagamet continues its market penetration and Selacryn is made available in an increasing number of areas. Sales of Contac and other cough and cold related products should benefit if a resurgence in the incidence of upper respiratory maladies in the winter months materializes. The higher profitability of newer pharmaceutical compounds is expected to bolster margins.

Sales (Million $)

Quarter:	1979	1978	1977	1976
Mar.	308	245	169	153
Jun.	317	268	174	163
Sep.	354	285	204	171
Dec.		314	233	187
		1,112	780	674

Sales for the nine months ended September 30, 1979 rose 23%, year to year. Pretax income increased 36%. After taxes at 32.1%, versus 37.4%, net income advanced 47%. Share earnings rose to $2.84, from $1.95, as adjusted for the recent 2-for-1 stock split.

Common Share Earnings ($)

Quarter:	1979	1978	1977	1976
Mar.	0.86	0.57	0.30	0.27
Jun.	0.89	0.60	0.31	0.28
Sep.	1.09	0.77	0.39	0.32
Dec.		0.78	0.50	0.35
		2.73	1.50	1.22

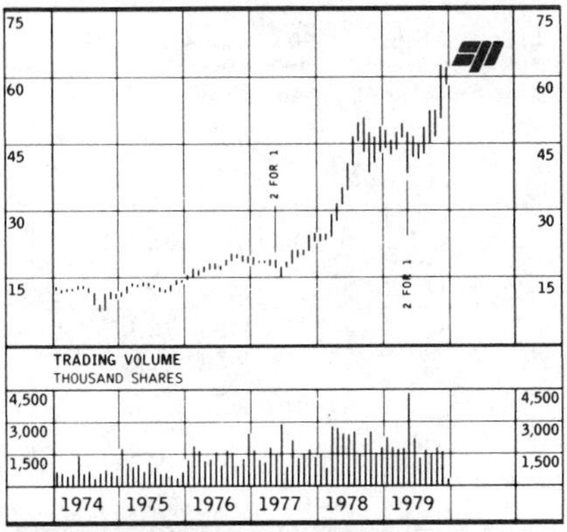

Important Developments

Dec. 10'79—An agreement in principle was announced for the acquisition by SKL of Allergan Pharmaceuticals for some 4 million SKL common shares. Allergan earned $9.4 million on sales of $62.4 million in 1978.

May 31'79—An FDA advisory panel recommended that SKL's Tagamet (cimetidine) be given approval for long-term maintenance therapy of certain high risk ulcer patients; at present, the maximum allowable treatment period is eight weeks. In reaching its recommendation, the panel concluded that the drug's benefits outweighed risks that have been the subject of recent studies finding evidence of sperm count reductions and possible nitrosamine formation.

Next earnings report due in mid-February.

Per Share Data ($)

Yr. End Dec. 31	1978	1977	1976	1975	[1] 1974	1973	[1] 1972	1971	[1] 1970	1969
Book Value	**8.34**	6.28	5.28	4.53	4.18	3.80	3.42	3.08	2.86	2.70
Earnings	**2.73**	1.49	1.21	1.07	0.98	0.89	0.82	0.77	0.75	0.70
Dividends	**0.78**	0.53⅞	0.50	0.50	0.50	0.50	0.50	0.50	0.50	0.50
Payout Ratio	**29%**	36%	41%	47%	51%	56%	61%	65%	67%	71%
Prices—High	**51¼**	25¼	20⅝	14⅞	13¾	15½	16⅝	14⅞	13⅞	13⅜
Low	**23⅛**	15½	14⅝	10⅞	7⅝	11¾	13⅛	11⅞	9⅜	9
P/E Ratio—	**19-8**	17-10	17-12	14-10	14-8	17-13	20-16	19-15	18-12	19-13

Data as orig. reptd. Adj. for stk. div(s). of 100% Jun. 1979, 100% Jun. 1977. **1.** Reflects merger or acquisition.

Standard NYSE Stock Reports
Vol. 46/No. 248/Sec. 25

December 26, 1979

Standard & Poor's Corp.
25 Broadway, NY, NY 10004

2050

Income Data (Million $)

Year Ended Dec. 31	Revs.	Oper. Inc.	% Oper. Inc. of Revs.	Cap. Exp.	Depr.	Int. Exp.	Net Bef. Taxes	Eff. Tax Rate	Net Inc.	% Net Inc. of Revs.
1978	1,112	281	25.2%	74.6	20.7	17.8	263	36.9%	164	14.8%
1977	780	152	19.4%	45.5	16.8	19.0	²134	33.5%	89	11.4%
1976	674	126	18.7%	37.9	15.0	16.3	²107	32.8%	72	10.7%
1975	589	108	18.3%	24.4	13.3	14.2	² 94	32.5%	64	10.8%
¹1974	518	95	18.4%	24.8	11.1	12.4	² 86	32.1%	58	11.2%
1973	444	84	18.8%	16.1	10.3	6.0	² 78	32.2%	53	11.9%
¹1972	402	78	19.4%	16.4	8.6	2.6	74	33.5%	49	12.2%
1971	357	75	21.0%	17.1	7.6	1.8	68	34.0%	45	12.6%
¹1970	347	85	24.5%	18.1	7.9	1.2	78	44.2%	44	12.6%
1969	315	90	28.4%	22.3	5.9	1.0	86	53.0%	41	12.8%

Balance Sheet Data (Million $)

Dec. 31	Cash	Current Assets	Current Liab.	Ratio	Total Assets	Ret. on Assets	Long Term Debt	Common Equity	Total Cap.	% LT Debt of Cap.	Ret. on Equity
1978	210	619	252	2.5	939	19.4%	112	548	664	16.9%	33.7%
1977	199	490	201	2.4	748	12.6%	105	422	527	20.0%	22.7%
1976	210	455	182	2.5	667	11.5%	105	361	466	22.5%	21.2%
1975	170	388	149	2.6	580	11.6%	101	316	417	24.2%	21.3%
¹1974	135	345	113	3.1	511	12.6%	102	282	384	26.6%	21.7%
1973	96	269	134	2.0	411	13.8%	14	253	267	5.2%	21.8%
¹1972	63	213	99	2.2	354	14.8%	14	234	248	5.7%	21.9%
1971	38	169	73	2.3	297	16.0%	16	208	224	7.0%	22.4%
¹1970	24	149	72	2.1	264	17.2%	Nil	192	192	Nil	23.6%
1969	48	144	67	2.2	242	17.5%	Nil	176	176	Nil	23.5%

Data as orig. reptd. **1.** Reflects merger or acquisition. **2.** Incl. equity in earns. of nonconsol. subs.

Business Summary

SmithKline Corp.'s sales and profit contributions in 1978 were:

	Sales	Profits
Human & Animal Health Care	79%	94%
Industrial & Medical Instr.	13%	5%
Food, Clinical Laboratories & Cosmetics	8%	1%

The contributions from foreign operations were 42% and 51%, respectively.

In ethical drugs (60% of sales), the most important products are gastrointestinal compounds including Tagamet and Combid. Also produced are Dyazide diuretic, Eskatrol, Dexedrine and Dexamyl amphetamines, and Ancef and Anspor antibiotics, and Selacryn antihypertensive.

Proprietary drug products (11%) include Contac, the world's largest selling over-the-counter cold product. Other items are Contac Nasal Mist, Sine-Off Sinus Spray and A.R.M. allergy relief medicine.

Animal health products (8%) are heavily dependent upon virginiamycin antibiotic feed additive. More than 30 vaccines and 100 veterinary pharmaceuticals are produced.

Instruments for industrial (9%) and medical (4%) applications largely utilize ultrasonic technology. Uses in the former area are nondestructive testing, and in the latter a variety of diagnostic procedures.

Remaining operations are a chain of clinical laboratories in the U.S. and Canada, Love cosmetics, Sea & Ski sun care preparations and Lip Savers lip balms.

Dividend Data

Dividends have been paid since 1923. A dividend reinvestment plan is available.

Amt. of Divd. $	Date Decl.	Ex-divd. Date	Stock of Record	Payment Date
0.60	Jan. 24	Feb. 1	Feb. 7	Mar. 19'79
0.60	Apr. 25	May 1	May 7	Jun. 14'79
2-for-1	---	Jun. 1	May 7	May 31'79
0.36	Jul. 25	Aug. 2	Aug. 8	Sep. 14'79
0.36	Oct. 24	Oct. 31	Nov. 7	Dec. 19'79

Next dividend meeting: late Jan. '80.

Capitalization

Long Term Debt: $111,868,000.

Common Stock: 60,800,432 shs. ($0.25 par). Institutions hold about 47%. Shareholders: 16,719.

Office— 1500 Spring Garden St. (P.O. Box 7929), Philadelphia, Pa. 19101. **Tel**—(215) 854-4000. **Chrmn & CEO**—R. F. Dee. **Pres**—W. Wendt. **VP-Secy**—R. V. Holmes. **Treas**—J. E. Hamblen. **Dirs**—S. H. Ballam, Jr., C. A. Berry, C. L. Burgess, R. F. Dee, W. R. Grant, L. E. Harris, M. T. Kimpton, S. P. Martin, T. M. Rauch, W. T. Rennie, J. M. Stewart, D. van Roden, H. Wendt. **Transfer Agents & Registrars**—Philadelphia National Bank; Morgan Guaranty Trust Co., NYC. **Incorporated** in Pa. in 1929.

Squibb Corp. 2096K

NYSE Symbol SQB   Options on CBOE

Price	Range	P-E Ratio	Dividend	Yield	S&P Ranking
Mar. 24'80 29⅝	1980 39¼–29¼	12	1.14	3.8%	A+

Summary

Although pharmaceuticals still account for a large portion of earnings, operations have been diversified into confectionery items, cosmetics, and surgical instruments. Earnings have been sluggish in recent periods, but longer term prospects are brightened by new pharmaceutical compounds under development which include Capoten, a potential breakthrough in antihypertension therapy now in the latter stages of testing.

Current Outlook

Share earnings for 1980 are projected at $2.75, up from the $2.52 from continuing operations of 1979.

Dividends should continue at $0.28½ quarterly.

Sales growth on the order of 15% is anticipated for 1980, bolstered by new pharmaceutical introductions, especially in overseas markets. Continued strength is looked for in the cosmetics area, highlighted by the Charles of the Ritz Group. The disposal of Dobbs should benefit margins, but stepped up expenditures for capital improvements and high interest costs may prove restrictive.

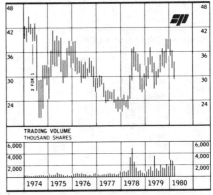

TRADING VOLUME
THOUSAND SHARES

Net Sales (Million $)

Quarter:	1979	1978	1977	1976
Mar.	378	327	294	276
Jun.	432	360	323	291
Sep.	³231	407	363	323
Dec.	412	423	363	324
	1,453	1,516	1,343	1,214

Sales from continuing operations for 1979 (preliminary) rose 17% from the prior-year level. Pretax income was virtually unchanged. After taxes at 23.3%, versus 27.1%, income was up 4.8%, to $2.52 a share from $2.44.

Common Share Earnings ($)

Quarter:	1979	1978	1977	1976
Mar.	0.36	0.43	0.44	0.43
Jun.	0.63	0.58	0.56	0.60
Sep.	³0.71	0.78	0.71	0.76
Dec.	0.82	0.81	0.79	0.61
	2.52	2.60	2.50	2.40

Important Developments

Feb. '80—SQB acquired Advanced Technology Laboratories, a maker of diagnostic ultrasound equipment, for some 1,242,700 shares. In the six months ended October 31, 1979 ATL earned $928,749 on sales of $11,144,425. Also, Squibb agreed in principle to acquire Spacelabs Inc. for some $34.4 million in stock.

Dec. '79—The FDA gave marketing approval to Squibb's Corgard (generically called nadolol) for the treatment of hypertension and angina pectoris. Approval is pending for the new antihypertensive Capoten (captopril) for which a New Drug Application was filed in January, 1980.

Next earnings report due in late April.

Per Share Data ($)

Yr. End Dec. 31	1979	1978	1977	1976	1975	1974	1973	1972	¹1971	1970
Book Value	NA	17.77	16.15	14.58	12.99	11.60	10.48	9.40	8.42	5.59
Earnings²	2.52	2.60	2.50	2.40	2.18	1.98	1.80	1.56	1.44	³1.32
Dividends	1.09½	1.03½	0.97½	0.91½	0.85½	0.83¼	0.78¾	0.75¾	0.75	0.75
Payout Ratio	43%	39%	39%	38%	39%	42%	43%	48%	54%	57%
Prices—High	39¼	37⅜	30½	38⅞	41½	45	57	55	45	36⅛
Low	27	21⅜	21⅜	26¼	24⅝	20	39½	40¼	33¼	25⅜
P/E Ratio—	16–11	14–8	12–9	16–11	19–11	23–10	32–22	34–25	31–23	28–20

Data as orig. reptd. Adj. for stk. div(s). of 100% Jun. 1974. **1.** Reflects merger or acquisition. **2.** Bef. results of disc. opers. of +0.19 in 1979, +0.05 in 1972. **3.** Ful. dil.: 1.29 in 1970. **3.** Reflects yr. end reclassification for 9 mos. NA-Not Available.

March 31, 1980

Standard & Poor's Corp.
25 Broadway, NY, NY 10004

2096K

Squibb Corporation

Income Data (Million $)

Year Ended Dec. 31	Revs.	Oper. Inc.	% Oper. Inc. of Revs.	Cap. Exp.	Depr.	Int. Exp.	Net Bef. Taxes	Eff. Tax Rate	[4]Net Inc.	% Net Inc. of Revs.
1978	1,516	213	14.0%	108	31.3	37.8	[3]165	28.8%	117	7.7%
1977	1,342	202	15.0%	109	27.3	30.1	[3]164	31.4%	113	8.4%
1976	1,215	189	15.6%	59	25.4	27.1	[3]156	30.6%	108	8.9%
1975	1,111	174	15.6%	62	23.2	26.5	[3]142	30.5%	98	8.8%
1974	1,005	156	15.5%	58	22.5	25.3	[3]130	31.4%	89	8.9%
1973	881	140	15.9%	41	19.6	18.6	[3]119	31.9%	81	9.2%
[1]1972	769	122	15.9%	40	17.5	16.2	[3]105	33.5%	70	9.1%
[2]1971	830	120	14.4%	66	18.3	14.1	[3]102	38.0%	63	7.6%
1970	705	92	13.0%	55	15.6	12.3	[3] 79	38.3%	49	6.9%
1969	645	81	12.5%	35	13.9	7.7	[3] 74	42.1%	43	6.6%

Balance Sheet Data (Million $)

Dec. 31	Cash	Current Assets	Current Liab.	Ratio	Total Assets	Ret. on Assets	Long Term Debt	Common Equity	Total Cap.	% LT Debt of Cap.	Ret. on Equity
1978	58	793	343	2.3	1,593	7.7%	335	846	1,223	27.4%	14.5%
1977	51	688	298	2.3	1,446	8.3%	316	774	1,125	28.1%	15.2%
1976	61	600	230	2.6	1,255	8.9%	270	706	1,004	26.8%	16.1%
1975	131	637	213	3.0	1,169	8.7%	273	636	936	29.1%	16.2%
1974	137	616	233	2.6	1,075	8.7%	225	574	823	27.3%	16.2%
1973	122	516	199	2.6	964	8.8%	199	524	749	26.6%	16.2%
[1]1972	60	430	194	2.2	867	8.5%	162	471	659	24.6%	15.5%
[2]1971	48	371	169	2.2	781	8.0%	154	431	600	25.7%	16.7%
1970	45	303	145	2.1	632	8.1%	120	242	477	25.1%	19.8%
1969	54	289	136	2.1	560	8.3%	86	214	415	20.6%	19.0%

Data as orig. reptd. **1.** Excludes discontinued operations. **2.** Reflects merger or acquisition. **3.** Incl. equity in earns. of nonconsol. subs. **4.** Bef. results of disc. opers. in 1972.

Business Summary

Squibb's business contributions in 1978:

	Sales	Profits
Health Care	48%	54%
Confections	25%	28%
Food Services	15%	8%
Fragrances/Cosmetics	12%	10%

International operations contributed 34% of sales and 27% of profits in 1978.

Health care products, largely pharmaceuticals, include a wide range of anti-inflammatories (Kenalog, Kenacort), hormonal compounds (Delestrogen, Delalutin), cardiovasculars (Pronestyl, Raudixin), antidepressants (Motival, Motipress) and antibiotics (Velosef, Principen, Sumycin). Other products include Theragran vitamins and Spec-T cold remedies.

Life Savers, Inc. produces hard roll candies, chewing gum, bubble gum, cough drops and lollipops under the Life Savers, Beech-Nut, Beechies, Fruit Stripe, Care*Free, Pine Bros. and Bubble Yum tradenames.

Dobbs House, currently treated as a discontinued operation, runs restaurants, provides catering services at domestic and foreign airports.

Charles of the Ritz Group Ltd. produces the Yves Saint Laurent and Jean Nate fragrance lines, and Charles of the Ritz, Revenescence and Alexandra de Markoff cosmetics lines.

Dividend Data

Dividends have been paid since 1902. A dividend reinvestment plan is available.

Amt. of Divd. $	Date Decl.	Ex-divd. Date	Stock of Record	Payment Date
0.27	May 8	May 14	May 18	Jun. 11'79
0.27	Jul. 25	Aug. 13	Aug. 17	Sep. 10'79
0.28½	Oct. 31	Nov. 9	Nov. 16	Dec. 10'79
0.28½	Jan. 30	Feb. 8	Feb. 15	Mar. 10'80

Next dividend meeting: early May '80.

Capitalization

Long Term Debt: $409,041,000, incl. $37,555,000 4¼% debs. due 1987, conv. into com. at $57 a sh.

Common Stock: 46,848,574 shs. ($1 par). Institutions hold about 35%. Shareholders: 59,900.

Office—40 W. 57th St., NYC. 10019. **Tel**—(212) 489-2000. **Chrmn & CEO**—R. M. Furlaud. **Pres**—D. C. Fill. **VP-Secy**—R. Reid. **VP-Treas**—E. F. Wiedenski. **Investor Contact**—D. A. Cuoco. **Dirs**—A. B. Chapman, R. H. Ebert, D. C. Fill, R. M. Furlaud, J. W. Hanes, Jr., G. B. Kuenster, M. L. Mace, G. P. Maginness, L. Marks, J. J. McCloy, W. F. O'Connell, G. M. Perry, H. M. Ranney, R. Reid, R. Salomon, M. H. Schmidt, L. Thomas, E. F. Williams, Jr. **Transfer Agents**—Manufacturers Hanover Trust Co., NYC; State Street Bank & Trust Co., Boston; St. Louis Union Trust Co. **Registrars**—Manufacturers Hanover Trust Co., NYC; First National Bank of Boston; St. Louis Union Trust Co. **Inc.** in Del. in 1968.

Case 15–8

Philip Morris Inc. versus R. J. Reynolds Industries

Standard and Poor's data sheets for Philip Morris and R. J. Reynolds Industries follow.

Why do you think Philip Morris traded at a higher price-earnings multiple than R. J. Reynolds?

In June 1978, Philip Morris completed the acquisition of Seven-Up Company for about $520 million. Seven-Up, a major soft drink producer, earned $25.8 million in 1977 on sales of $251 million.[1] Why would Philip Morris pay approximately 20 times earnings for Seven-Up?

[1] Standard and Poor's report of August 4, 1978

Philip Morris

1822

NYSE Symbol MO   Options on ASE

Price	Range	P-E Ratio	Dividend	Yield	S&P Ranking
Mar. 6'80	1980				
31⅜	36-31⅛	8	1.60	5.1%	A+

Summary

This well-managed company has achieved an outstanding earnings record over the past decade through the successful marketing of its major cigarette brands, particularly Marlboro, and beer through Miller Brewing, now the second largest U.S. brewer. Prospects are brightened by a high level of capital expenditures, much of which is for the expansion of capacity at Miller.

Current Outlook

Earnings for 1980 are expected to approximate $4.80 a share, up from the $4.08 of 1979.

The quarterly dividend has been raised 28%, to $0.40 from $0.31¼, with the April, 1980 payment.

Further gains in domestic cigarette market share, representation in foreign markets, cigarette price increases and recent additions to capacity at Miller should lead to a 15%-20% gain in revenues in 1980. Margins should be well maintained and implementation of FASB 34 could mitigate effects of rising interest rates.

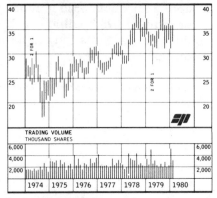

TRADING VOLUME
THOUSAND SHARES

²Sales (Million $)

Quarter:	1979	1978	1977	1976
Mar.	1,902	1,391	1,143	943
Jun.	2,115	1,672	1,329	1,070
Sep.	2,130	1,818	1,376	1,123
Dec.	2,157	1,752	1,354	1,158
	8,304	6,633	5,202	4,294

Revenues for 1979 (preliminary) rose 25%, year to year. Pretax income advanced 21%. After taxes at 43.9%, versus 45.2%, net income was up 24%. Share earnings were $4.08, against $3.38 (adjusted).

Common Share Earnings ($)

Quarter:	1979	1978	1977	1976
Mar.	0.88	0.73	0.60	0.48
Jun.	1.05	0.87	0.71	0.57
Sep.	1.16	0.95	0.79	0.63
Dec.	0.99	0.84	0.71	0.57
	4.08	3.39	2.81	2.25

Important Developments

Feb. '80—Capital expenditures for 1980-84 were projected at $3.5 billion, including $850 million for 1980. Outlays totaled $632 million in 1979.

Jan. '80—Production began at MO's new five million barrel brewery in Irwindale, Cal. A 10 million barrel facility in Albany, Ga. also recently opened.

Dec. '79—MO increased the domestic wholesale price of its cigarettes by $0.75 a thousand or about 5%. Prices were last increased in July, 1979, by $0.55 per thousand.

Jun. 5'79—The company sold $250 million of 9.55% notes due 1986.

Next earnings report due in late April.

Per Share Data ($)
Yr. End Dec. 31

	1979	1978	1977	1976	1975	1974	1973	1972	1971	1970
Book Value	NA	11.75	12.23	10.22	8.58	6.73	5.49	4.42	3.75	2.72
Earnings	4.08	3.39	2.80	2.24	1.81	¹1.58	¹1.36	¹1.17	¹1.01	¹0.84
Dividends	1.25	1.02½	0.78⅛	0.57½	0.46⅜	0.38⅞	0.33¾	0.31⅝	0.30⅜	0.26⅜
Payout Ratio	31%	31%	28%	26%	26%	25%	25%	28%	31%	33%
Prices—High	38⅝	38⅜	32½	31⅝	29⅝	30¾	34¼	29⅝	17⅞	12⅝
Low	31⅛	27⅞	25⅞	24⅞	20½	17⅛	24½	16⅞	11¾	7
P/E Ratio—	9-8	11-8	12-9	14-11	16-11	19-11	25-18	25-15	18-12	15-8

Data as orig. reptd. Adj. for stk. div(s). of 100% Jun. 1979, 100% Jun. 1974. 1. Ful. dil.: 1.54 in 1974, 1.30 in 1973, 1.09 in 1972, 0.91 in 1971, 0.71 in 1970. 2. Incl. excise taxes. NA-Not Available.

Standard NYSE Stock Reports
Vol. 47/No. 51/Sec. 19

March 13, 1980

Standard & Poor's Corp.
25 Broadway, NY, NY 10004

1822

Philip Morris Incorporated

Income Data (Million $)

Year Ended Dec. 31	Revs.	Oper. Inc.	% Oper. Inc. of Revs.	Cap. Exp.	Depr.	Int. Exp.	Net Bef. Taxes	Eff. Tax Rate	Net Inc.	% Net Inc. of Revs.
²1978	4,969	1,024	20.6%	601	113	163	¹745	45.2%	409	8.2%
1977	3,849	812	21.1%	303	80	109	¹626	46.5%	335	8.7%
1976	3,135	651	20.8%	220	66	109	¹472	43.7%	266	8.5%
1975	2,564	490	19.1%	244	50	107	¹361	41.3%	212	8.3%
1974	2,042	392	19.2%	216	38	92	¹298	41.0%	176	8.6%
1973	1,709	319	18.7%	175	31	60	¹256	41.9%	149	8.7%
1972	1,408	283	20.1%	132	27	38	¹230	45.8%	124	8.8%
1971	1,210	234	19.4%	69	22	35	¹190	46.5%	102	8.4%
1970	990	196	19.8%	164	18	35	¹150	48.3%	78	7.8%
1969	769	150	19.5%	24	14	29	¹116	49.5%	58	7.6%

Balance Sheet Data (Million $)

Dec. 31	Cash	Current Assets	Current Liab.	Ratio	Total Assets	Ret. on Assets	Long Term Debt	Common Equity	Total Cap.	% LT Debt of Cap.	Ret. on Equity
1978	72.9	2,757	1,172	2.4	5,608	8.3%	2,147	2,112	4,412	48.7%	21.2%
1977	72.2	2,221	805	2.8	4,048	8.7%	1,427	1,687	3,221	44.3%	21.4%
1976	64.4	2,006	804	2.5	3,582	7.9%	1,248	1,427	2,755	45.3%	20.0%
1975	79.3	1,788	897	2.0	3,134	7.2%	918	1,225	2,217	41.4%	19.0%
1974	61.9	1,558	833	1.9	2,653	7.3%	768	972	1,810	42.4%	19.4%
1973	56.1	1,246	731	1.7	2,108	7.7%	500	812	1,361	36.7%	19.7%
1972	54.5	990	465	2.1	1,701	7.9%	480	683	1,211	39.6%	19.5%
1971	48.3	826	409	2.0	1,392	7.4%	352	561	962	36.6%	19.6%
1970	52.0	729	381	1.9	1,239	6.8%	370	432	843	43.9%	19.4%
1969	41.9	575	262	2.2	976	6.6%	332	334	709	46.8%	18.3%

Data as orig. reptd. **1.** Incl. equity in earns. of nonconsol. subs. **2.** Reflects merger or acquisition.

Business Summary

Philip Morris is the second largest domestic cigarette company with an estimated 29% of the market. Including excise taxes, contributions in 1978 were:

	Revs.	Profits
Philip Morris U.S.A.	33%	59%
Philip Morris Int'l.	31%	22%
Miller Brewing.......................	27%	15%
Seven-Up..............................	4%	1%
Philip Morris Industrial...........	3%	1%
Mission Viejo........................	2%	2%

Domestic cigarette market share has increased steadily in recent years. Leading brands include Marlboro (17% of the U.S. market), Benson Hedges (5%) and Merit (4%).

In foreign markets, MO's cigarette volume was up 12% in 1979, giving it a 6% share of that market. The company sells over 160 brands in more than 170 countries.

Miller Brewing is the second largest brewer in the U.S., with roughly 21% of the market. Volume rose 14% in 1979 to 35.8 million barrels; important brands include Miller High Life, Lite and Lowenbrau.

The Seven-Up Company is the third-largest producer of soft drinks in the world. Products include 7UP and Diet 7UP.

Philip Morris Industrial consists of several companies that produce coatings and packagings.

Mission Viejo is a community development company with its main project in southern Calif.

Dividend Data

Dividends have been paid since 1928. A dividend reinvestment plan is available.

Amt. of Divd. $	Date Decl.	Ex-divd. Date	Stock of Record	Payment Date
0.31¼	May 23	Jun. 11	Jun. 15	Jul. 10'79
0.31¼	Aug. 29	Sep. 11	Sep. 17	Oct. 10'79
0.31¼	Nov. 28	Dec. 10	Dec. 14	Jan. 10'80
0.40	Feb. 27	Mar. 6	Mar. 12	Apr. 10'80

Next dividend meeting: late May '80.

Capitalization

Long Term Debt: $2,447,761,000.

Common Stock: 124,544,090 shs. ($1 par).
Institutions hold about 38%.
Shareholders: About 30,000.

Office—100 Park Ave., NYC 10017. **Tel**—(212) 679-1800. **Chrmn & CEO**—G. Weissman. **Pres**—C. H. Goldsmith. **Secy**—E. J. T. Flanagan. **VP-Treas**—F. H. Poole. **Dirs**—T. F. Ahrensfeld, J. Apodaca, J. C. Bowling, A. Brittain III, G. V. Comfort, J. A. Cordido-Freytes, H. Cullman, J. F. Cullman 3rd, W. H. Donaldson, C. H. Goldsmith, R. E. R. Huntley, J. T. Landry, E. Lasker, J. G. Maisonrouge, H. R. Marschalk, H. Maxwell, R. R. Millhiser, T. J. Moore, Jr., J. A. Murphy, S. P. Pollack, J. S. Reed, J. C. Sawhill, G. Weissman, M. B. Young. **Transfer Agents**—Morgan Guaranty Trust Co., NYC; United Virginia Bank, Richmond, Va. **Incorporated** in Virginia in 1919.

Reynolds (R. J.) Industries   1924

NYSE Symbol RJR   Options on CBOE

Price	Range	P-E Ratio	Dividend	Yield	S&P Ranking
Mar. 7'80	1980				
30¼	36⅝–30¼	6	2.10	6.9%	A+

Summary

This company is the largest U.S. producer of cigarettes, with some 32% of the market, and has been expanding its international tobacco business. Diversification moves, primarily into foods, containerized shipping and oil operations, have been taking on increased importance. Although nontobacco operations will tend to be volatile, overall prospects are favorable. The shares were recently split 2-for-1.

Current Outlook

Primary share earnings for 1980 are projected at about $5.75, up from the $5.23 of 1979.

Dividends at the current $0.52½ quarterly rate are the minimum expectation.

Revenue growth of perhaps 10% should materialize in 1980. As the domestic cigarette market gradually contracts, RJR's business will benefit largely from anticipated price hikes; international tobacco should be bolstered by continued unit volume expansion. Of the remaining areas, energy should be the fastest growing.

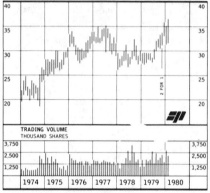

TRADING VOLUME
THOUSAND SHARES

⁴Sales & Oper. Revs. (Million $)

Quarter:	1979	1978	1977	1976
Mar.	1,970	1,565	1,551	1,306
Jun.	2,248	1,696	1,667	1,364
Sep.	2,229	1,652	1,623	1,497
Dec.	2,488	1,708	1,521	1,587
	8,935	6,621	6,362	5,754

Sales for 1979 (preliminary) rose 33%, year to year. Net income advanced 25%. Share earnings equaled $5.23, versus $4.51, as adjusted for the December, 1979 2-for-1 stock split.

Common Share Earnings ($)

Quarter:	1979	1978	1977	1976
Mar.	1.29	0.97	0.92	0.80
Jun.	1.31	1.14	1.03	1.02
Sep.	1.39	1.16	1.06	0.97
Dec.	1.26	1.24	1.36	0.95
	5.25	4.51	4.37	3.74

Important Developments

Dec. '79—RJR increased the wholesale price of its domestic cigarette brands by $0.75 per thousand. Prices were previously increased in mid-1979 by $0.55 per thousand.

Feb. 2'79—RJR acquired Del Monte Corp., a major producer of canned fruits and vegetables, for $276,934,600 in cash and 7,052,894 shares of a $4.10 series A cumulative preferred stock. Del Monte earned $51.4 million on sales of $1.58 billion in fiscal 1978.

Jan. 2'79—RJR sold an aluminum casting and rolling plant in Huntingdon, Tenn. for some $40 million, realizing a net profit of $10.8 million, or $0.11 a share (adjusted).

Next earnings report due in early May.

Per Share Data ($)

Yr. End Dec. 31	1979	1978	¹1977	²1976	²1975	²1974	1973	¹1972	1971	1970
Book Value	NA	25.36	22.77	20.46	18.45	17.09	15.13	13.65	12.36	11.13
Earnings	³5.23	³4.51	³4.36	³3.74	³3.70	³3.50	³2.95	³2.66	³2.55	³2.28
Dividends	1.95	1.78⅞	1.66⅞	1.56½	1.46½	1.36½	1.31⅞	1.24⅞	1.20	1.20
Payout Ratio	37%	40%	39%	42%	41%	39%	45%	47%	47%	53%
Prices—High	36	32½	35⅜	34⅛	30⅞	26¾	27⅞	39	34⅞	27¾
Low	27¼	26⅛	29	27½	24⅞	18⅝	18⅜	23⅞	25⅛	17¼
P/E Ratio—	7–5	7–6	8–7	9–7	8–7	8–5	9–6	15–9	14–10	12–8

Data as orig. reptd. Adj. for stk. div(s). of 100% Dec. 1979. **1.** Reflects accounting change. **2.** Reflects merger or acquisition. **3.** Ful. dil.: 5.05 in 1979, 4.29 in 1978, 4.10 in 1977, 3.45 in 1976, 3.36 in 1975, 3.12 in 1974, 2.67 in 1973, 2.37 in 1972, 2.27 in 1971, 2.05 in 1970. **4.** Incl. excise taxes. NA-Not Available.

Standard NYSE Stock Reports
Vol. 47/No. 52/Sec. 21

March 14, 1980
Copyright © 1980 Standard & Poor's Corp. All Rights Reserved

Standard & Poor's Corp.
25 Broadway, NY, NY 10004

1924

Reynolds (R. J.) Industries, Inc.

Income Data (Million $)

Year Ended Dec. 31	Revs.	Oper. Inc.	% Oper. Inc. of Revs.	Cap. Exp.	Depr.	Int. Exp.	Net Bef. Taxes	Eff. Tax Rate	Net Inc.	% Net Inc. of Revs.
1978	4,952	1,133	22.9%	383	226	71.4	854	48.3%	442	8.9%
¹1977	4,816	1,023	21.2%	285	209	83.5	790	46.4%	424	8.8%
²1976	4,291	943	22.0%	834	164	68.6	691	48.8%	354	8.2%
²1975	3,529	956	27.1%	190	114	54.5	817	58.6%	339	9.6%
²1974	3,300	925	28.0%	126	101	57.5	779	60.1%	311	9.4%
1973	2,330	608	26.1%	340	83	48.6	495	46.8%	264	11.3%
¹1972	2,072	567	27.3%	253	66	29.6	478	50.3%	237	11.5%
1971	1,816	531	29.2%	151	58	29.3	³485	53.4%	226	12.4%
1970	1,788	495	27.7%	165	57	30.9	³416	51.4%	202	11.3%
²1969	1,575	434	27.5%	198	46	23.1	³364	52.6%	172	10.9%

Balance Sheet Data (Million $)

Dec. 31	Cash	Current Assets	Current Liab.	Ratio	Total Assets	Ret. on Assets	Long Term Debt	Common Equity	Total Cap.	% LT Debt of Cap.	Ret. on Equity
1978	114	2,141	803	2.7	4,616	9.8%	740	2,630	3,706	20.0%	17.4%
1977	94	2,021	841	2.4	4,334	9.6%	761	2,360	3,404	22.3%	18.5%
1976	105	2,009	978	2.1	4,277	9.3%	646	2,068	2,953	21.9%	17.4%
1975	35	1,697	714	2.4	3,294	10.2%	435	1,848	2,529	17.2%	18.2%
1974	43	1,559	731	2.1	3,126	10.8%	455	1,624	2,317	19.7%	19.2%
1973	40	1,146	426	2.7	2,612	10.6%	479	1,437	2,133	22.5%	18.0%
1972	76	1,166	481	2.4	2,366	10.9%	364	1,307	1,839	19.8%	17.7%
1971	112	974	247	3.9	1,973	11.7%	390	1,173	1,705	22.9%	18.3%
1970	55	902	331	2.7	1,858	11.4%	296	1,082	1,510	19.6%	17.7%
1969	47	921	299	3.1	1,693	11.9%	274	993	1,382	19.8%	16.1%

Data as orig. reptd. **1.** Reflects accounting change. **2.** Reflects merger or acquisition. **3.** Incl. equity in earns. of nonconsol. subs.

Business Summary

R. J. Reynolds Industries derived sales and profits as follows in 1979:

	Sales	Profits
Domestic tobacco	35%	64%
International tobacco	20%	13%
Food and beverages	22%	11%
Transportation	14%	5%
Energy	7%	6%
Packaging products	2%	1%

RJR reported a slight gain in domestic cigarette volume in 1979. Key brands include Winston (13% of the U.S. market), Salem (9%), Camel (4%) and Vantage (3%). Volume abroad (brands are sold in over 140 countries) was ahead 7.3% in 1979.

Del Monte Corp. (acquired in February, 1979) is a major producer of canned foods. RJR Foods produces Hawaiian Punch beverages, Chun King foods and MY-T-FINE puddings.

Sea-Land Service is one of the world's largest containerized shipping companies, serving 136 ports in some 50 countries.

Aminoil USA, RJR's domestic energy subsidiary, produced daily in 1978 38,167 net barrels of oil and condensate, 113 million net cubic feet of natural gas and 7,353 barrels of natural gas liquids. Internationally, American Independent Oil Co. produced 35,016 net barrels of crude oil per day in 1978 (30,334 attributable to Iran).

RJR Archer manufactures packaging materials, including aluminum and vinyl film.

Dividend Data

Dividends have been paid since 1900. A dividend reinvestment plan is available.

Amt. of Div. $	Date Decl.	Ex-divd. Date	Stock of Record	Payment Date
0.95	Apr. 25	May 4	May 10	Jun. 5'79
0.95	Jul. 19	Aug. 6	Aug. 10	Sep. 5'79
1.05	Oct. 18	Nov. 2	Nov. 9	Dec. 5'79
2-for-1	---	Dec. 11	Nov. 14	Dec. 10'79
0.52½	Jan. 17	Feb. 4	Feb. 8	Mar. 5'80

Capitalization

Long Term Debt: $939,000,000.

$2.25 Cum. Conv. Pfd. Stk.: 1,318,588 shs. (no par); conv. into 3 com. with payment of $22.

$4.10 Ser. A Cum. Pfd. Stk.: 7,052,894 shs. (no par).

Common Stk.: 101,148,658 shs. ($5 par). Institutions hold about 28%.

Office—Reynolds Blvd., Winston-Salem, N.C. 27102. **Tel**—(919) 748-4000. **Chrmn & CEO**—J. P. Sticht. **Pres**—J. T. Wilson. **VP-Secy**—H. C. Roemer. **VP-Treas**—J. W. Dowdle. **Dirs**—J. F. Abely, Jr., W. S. Anderson, A. L. Butler, Jr., H. H. Cudd, G. Gray, R. H. Grierson, W. D. Hobbs, J. W. Hull, V. E. Jordan, Jr., J. M. Kreps, R. G. Landis, J. D. Macomber, C. F. Myers, Jr., J. R. Peterson, H. C. Roemer, J. P. Sticht, C. S. Stokes, J. T. Wilson, M. S. Wilson. **Transfer Agents & Registrars**—Manufacturers Hanover Trust Co., NYC; First Jersey National Bank, Jersey City, N.J. **Incorporated** in New York in 1899; reincorporated in Delaware in 1970.

Information has been obtained from sources believed to be reliable, but its accuracy and completeness are not guaranteed.

Case 15–9 _____

The Seagram Company versus Hiram Walker

Anne Dobbs was about to graduate from a well-known Eastern business school. She had decided to pursue a career as a financial analyst. During one employment interview, the interviewer had determined to test Anne's expertise with an investment decision problem.

"Anne," said Bruce Farrell, "I want you to advise us on which of two common stocks we should purchase. The companies are Seagram Company, Ltd., and Hiram Walker-Gooderham & Worts, Ltd. They are two of the four largest distillers in North America. Both companies have established whiskey product lines supported by substantial promotional budgets.

"Here is some operating data on the two firms. Please take an hour or so to work on this. When you return, please tell me which common stock should be purchased and why."

EXHIBIT 1
Earnings and Financial Position

Year	Operating Profit Margin*		Acid-Test Ratio		Total Interest-Bearing Debt to Total Assets		Asset Turnover		Pretax Interest Coverage		Aftertax Return on Shareholder's Equity	
	Seagram	Walker	Seagram	Walker	Seagram	Walker	Seagram	Walker	Seagram	Walker	Seagram	Walker
1977	17.8%	21.5%	1.19×	1.20×	30%	14%	.59×	.59×	3×	10×	8.8%	10.1%
1976	17.0	23.0	1.17	1.04	36	16	.53	.60	3	8	8.6	9.8
1975	18.5	22.8	.92	.60	38	21	.52	.57	3	6	8.3	9.5
1974	19.4	27.2	.84	.55	33	20	.53	.64	4	10	9.7	13.1
1973	18.7	27.8	.99	.72	32	12	.52	.68	5	17	9.2	13.6
1972	18.1	27.4	1.28	.69	28	16	.53	.60	6	14	8.8	13.1
1971	18.8	29.9	.97	.64	28	20	.54	.58	5	14	8.5	12.6
1970	19.7	30.8	.84	.68	28	13	.53	.62	5	18	8.5	12.8
1969	19.1	31.4	.89	.83	29	9	.53	.66	6	33	8.5	13.7
1968	19.6	31.2	1.08	1.00	25	6	.52	.67	8	55	8.5	13.6
Averages												
1968–77	18.7	27.3	1.02	0.80	31	15	.53	.62	5	18	8.7	12.2

* Income before interest and taxes.

EXHIBIT 2 ─────────────────────────────────────

Per Share Earnings and Dividends*

	Earnings per Share		Dividends per Share	
	Seagram	Walker	Seagram	Walker
Year				
1977	$2.48	$3.47	$.85	$1.50
1976	2.30	3.21	.80	1.50
1975	2.11	2.94	.80	1.65
1974	2.33	3.84	.78	1.65
1973	2.07	3.67	.70	1.50
1972	1.87	3.27	.68	1.45
1971	1.72	2.96	.60	1.45
1970	1.62	2.82	.60	1.45
1969	1.52	2.78	.58	1.45
1968	1.45	2.57	.50	1.30
Compound annual growth				
1968–77	2.7%	3.4%	6.1%	1.6%
1973–77	4.6	(1.4)	5.0	0.0
1968–73	7.4	7.4	7.0	2.9

* Shares outstanding essentially unchanged for each company for years 1968–77.

EXHIBIT 3 ─────────────────────────────────────

Market Valuations and Other Common Stock Data*

	Range of Price-Earnings Ratios	
Year	Seagram (VO)	Walker (HIR)
1977	10–8×	8–7×
1976	14–8	11–9
1975	18–12	15–9
1974	20–11	15–9
1973	24–18	16–14
1972	26–18	16–13
1971	20–14	15–12
1970	20–16	18–12
1969	19–15	18–13
1968	17–12	16–11
Averages		
1973–77	14.0	11.5
1968–77	16.0	13.0
1977–78 price range	24–19	29–23
Current price (April 1978)	21	27
1978 estimated earnings	$2.60	$3.75
Indicated annual dividend	$ .92	$1.50

* Industry shipments of all alcoholic beverages grew 9.0 percent annually from 1968–76 and were forecast to increase 8.5 percent through 1985.

INDEX

A

Absorption costing, use of, in manufacturing costing, 149–55 fa

Accelerated depreciation methods, 184, 187

Accountants, role of, 33

Accounting
mechanics of, 17–33
need for special treatment of unusual events, 241

Accounting changes
and interim reporting, 473
as requiring special disclosures in income statements, 248–49

Accounting cycle, 33

Accounting estimates, changes in, as requiring special disclosures in income statements, 250

Accounting income, as different from economic income, 75 n

Accounting principles, 71–77, 497; see also principles by name

Accounting Principles Board (APB) of the American Institute of Certified Public Accountants (AICPA), 71
APB Opinion No. 2, 333
APB Opinion No. 6, 334
APB Opinion No. 8, 479
APB Opinion No. 10, 334
APB Opinion No. 11, 247, 256 n, 334
APB Opinion No. 15, 93, 502 n
APB Opinion No. 16, 301–2, 305–6, 308, 332–61
APB Opinion No. 17, 189
APB Opinion No. 19, 373 n, 376
APB Opinion No. 21, 199–201, 209, 215
APB Opinion No. 28, 472
APB Opinion No. 30, 250
APB Opinion No. 31, 244 n

Accounting Research Bulletins
ARB No. 5, 333, 336
ARB No. 10, 333, 336
ARB No. 40, 335

Accounting Research Bulletins—Cont.
ARB No. 43, 111, 125, 334
ARB No. 51, 333–34

Accounting Series Releases (ASR), 71
ASR 173, 83
ASR 190, 404 n, 422 n

Accounts
chart of, 17 n
definition of, 17
major grouping of, 18
numbering of, 17

Accounts payable, 5–6

Accrual method of accounting, and revenue realization, 74

Accrued interest payable, 7

Accumulated depreciation, 7

Acid-test ratio, 503

Adjusting journal entries, 31, 39

Aggregate portfolio basis, 284

Alcolac, Inc., 80–82

Ale Company, 248–49

All resources concept, of statement of changes in financial position, 376–77

Allegheny Ludlum, 258–59

Allis Chalmers Corporation, 471

Allowance for uncollectible accounts, 50–51

American Greeting Corporation, 247–48

American Institute of Certified Public Accountants (AICPA), 71
Accounting Principles Board: see Accounting Principles Board
Committee on Accounting Procedures, 111 n

American Iron and Steel Institute, 424

American Motors, 515

American Red Cross, 172–74

APB; see Accounting Principles Board

ARB; see Accounting Research Bulletins

Asarco Incorporated and Consolidated Subsidiaries, 133–40, 396–97

Asset depreciation ranges, 179

Assets
as category of balance sheet, 1

This book has been set VIP in 10 and 9 point Memphis Medium, leaded 2 points. Chapter numbers and titles are 36 and 24 point Memphis Bold. The size of the type page is 27 by 45½ picas.